Ethics and Media Culture

Practices and Representations

Edited by
David Berry

Focal Press

OXFORD   AUCKLAND   BOSTON   JOHANNESBURG   MELBOURNE   NEW DELHI

Focal Press
An imprint of Butterworth-Heinemann
Linacre House, Jordan Hill, Oxford OX2 8DP
225 Wildwood Avenue, Woburn, MA 01801-2041
A division of Reed Educational and Professional Publishing Ltd

 A member of the Reed Elsevier plc group

First published 2000

© Reed Educational and Professional Publishing Ltd 2000
© of individual chapters retained by the contributors

British Library Cataloguing in Publication Data
A catalogue record for this book is available from the British Library

Library of Congress Cataloguing in Publication Data
A catalogue record for this book is available from the Library of Congress

ISBN 0 240 51603 6

Composition by Genesis Typesetting, Rochester, Kent
Printed and bound in Great Britain by
Biddles Ltd, www.Biddles.co.uk

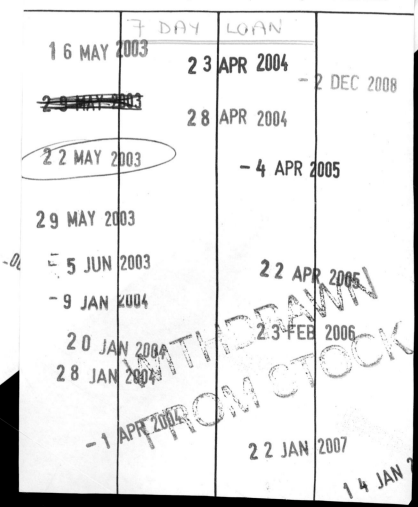

Dedication

For Jane

Contents

Contents

Contents

Contents

Preface

We are living in an age where the sheer scale of information is seen as a central feature of western societies. The power of the media to penetrate the lives of individuals is immense and whilst production and consumption are vitally important for areas of debate, ethics adds an interesting inflection to current debates, and to a large degree, represents a crucial departure for disciplines such as cultural studies, and the sociology of culture and communications that is inclusive of a discourse on ethics in the media, the consolidation of which would lead to a new paradigm for future media analysis. In this context, *Ethics and Media Culture: Practices and Representations*, is an interdisciplinary approach to ethical discourse in the media, thus broadening out the conceptual framework currently referred to as *Media Ethics*. This in part is reflected in the broad range of issues and discipline backgrounds that is inclusive of practitioners. Situating ethics as the common bond between the subject matters discussed in the articles opens a new focal point for media analysis.

This present collection of essays addresses many of the key issues that concern ethical debates in the media. Contributors present articles on responsibilities, duties, consequences, language and culture, trust, technology (rethinking media ethics), moral obligations, representing the *other*, manufacturing news, popular journalism, electoral representations, commercial representations of art, *shock*, cyber-ethics, secrecy, production and consumption of magazines, media violence, 'bad' journalism, statutory regulation, codes of conduct, and war correspondence.

Contributors: Stuart Allan, Jason Barker, Miranda Basner, David Berry, Michael Bromley, Cynthia Carter, Carol Davis, Philip Dring, Andrew Edgar, Stephen Hayward, Annette Hill, Mike Jempson, Joost van Loon, Sanda Miller, Bill Norris, Tom O'Malley, Nick Rayner, John Theobald, Paul Walton and Anna Gough-Yates

Editor: David Berry is Lecturer in Journalism at Southampton Institute. He is currently working on a PhD entitled: Cultural Representations and Identity in the Press and is co-authoring a book with Eugen Gergely of the University of Sibiu, Romania, entitled: *The Romanian Mass Media and Cultural Development* (Ashgate, 2001).

Notes on contributors

Stuart Allan is Senior Lecturer in Cultural and Media Studies at the University of the West of England, Bristol. He has written widely on the media, and currently has a special interest in news coverage of science and risk. His books include *News Culture* (Open University Press, 1999) and the co-edited collections *Theorizing Culture* (UCL Press/NYU Press, 1995), *News, Gender and Power* (Routledge, 1998) and *Environmental Risks and the Media* (UCL Press/Garland Press, 2000).

Jason Barker is Lecturer in Journalism at Southampton Institute. He published a paper entitled: 'New Applications in Linguistics: Introducing the "Pragmatics" of Gilles Deleuze', in the *Journal of Media and Communications Theory*, no.6 (1995). He is currently working on a PhD in philosophy on 'Marxism and Scientific Method in Althusser and Beyond' at the University of Cardiff, Wales.

South African-born **Miranda Basner** is Lecturer in the School of Journalism, Media and Cultural Studies at the University of Cardiff, Wales. Before joining the university, she worked variously as a reporter, features writer and sub-editor on newspapers in the Midlands, Wales and Bristol.

David Berry is Lecturer in Journalism at Southampton Institute. He is currently researching a PhD on 'Cultural Representations and Identity in the Press' and a co-authored book with Eugen Gergely of the University of Sibiu entitled: *The Romanian Mass Media and Cultural Development*, to be published by Ashgate (December, 2001).

Michael Bromley is Lecturer in Journalism Studies at the University of Cardiff, Wales. He has researched and published in the areas of the national newspaper industry, the press in Northern Ireland and the practices of journalism. He is the author of *An Introduction to Journalism* (1995) and co-editor of *A Journalism Reader* (1997) and *Sex, Lies and Democracy: The Press and the Public* (1998). He is contributor to the Institute of Contemporary British History 'Britain' series. He is currently researching the local press in Wales.

Cynthia Carter is Lecturer in the School of Journalism, Media and Cultural Studies at Cardiff University, Wales. She is a co-editor of *News, Gender and Power* (Routledge, 1998) and *Environmental Risks and the Media* (UCL Press/Garland Press, 2000). She is joint editor (with Lisa McLaughlin) of the forthcoming journal *Feminist Media Studies* (Routledge), and is currently writing a book with C. Kay Weaver on violence and the media (Open University Press).

Carol Davis is Lecturer in Sociology and Social Anthropology at the University of Southampton New College. She has written a number of articles on the Minangkabau, in particular on gender and kinship, and social and economic discourse.

Philip Dring is Head of Academic Operations in the Media Arts Faculty at Southampton Institute. He has worked in media related activities in the UK, USA, Europe and the Far East. He is a member of the Institute of Public Relations.

Andrew Edgar is Lecturer in the Department of Philosophy at the University of Cardiff, Wales. He has worked on a number of EC funded projects on health care and resource allocation. A book related to this work was published in 1998, by Euromed Communications, entitled: *The Ethical QALY*. He has published articles on health care in Bioethics in *The Journal of Medicine and Philosophy*, and in *Health Care Analysis*. He is currently working on a book (co-authored with Peter Sedgwick) entitled: *Concepts in Cultural Theory* (Routledge), and articles on Adorno forthcoming in *New Formations* and the *Journal of Aesthetics and Art Criticism*.

Anna Gough-Yates is Senior Lecturer in Media and Cultural Studies at the University of East London and an MA Associate Lecturer in Humanities (by distance learning) at the Open University. She is currently researching a PhD in 'Women's Magazines and Readerships in Contemporary Britain'. She has written a number of articles on feminism, femininity and popular culture and is currently working on a book entitled: *Understanding Women's Magazines* (Routledge, 2000).

Until recently **Stephen Hayward** was Lecturer in Cultural History at the University of Teeside and Southampton Institute. He is currently writing a book entitled: *National Myths and Home Truths.*

Annette Hill is Senior Lecturer in Mass Media at the University of Westminster, and Research Fellow at the British Film Institute. She is the author of *Shocking Entertainment: Viewer Response to Violent Movies*, forthcoming book, *Natural Born Killer: Risk and Media Violence*, co-author of *Living Media: Television, Culture and Everyday Life* (Routledge, 1999), as well as several articles on media audiences. She is also the editor of *Framework: The Journal of Cinema and Media.*

Mike Jempson has been a journalist for over twenty years working for local, national papers, TV and PR. He has also taught journalism and is a regular broadcaster and lecturer. He runs media training courses and is the author of several non-fiction books. After working with Clive Soley MP on his unsuccessful Freedom and Responsibility of the Press Bill, he helped to set up PressWise becoming its Executive Director. He also represents the NUJ on the National Council of the Campaign for Press and Broadcasting Freedom. In 1997 he was appointed to the EC Information Society Forum, and became Media Child Rights co-ordinator for the International Federation of Journalists.

Joost van Loon is Lecturer in Social and Cultural Theory at the Nottingham Trent University and is affiliated with the Theory Culture and Society Centre. He has published extensively on cultural theory, media technologies and risk. He is co-editor of the journal, *Space and Culture* with Barbara Adam, and with Ulrich Beck of *Repositioning Risk: Critical Issues for Social Theory* (Sage, forthcoming).

Sanda Miller is Senior Lecturer at the Southampton Institute. She is the author of a book on the sculptor Constantin Brancusi and Paris at the beginning of the 20th century entitled: *Constantin Brancusi: A Survey of His Work*, published by Oxford University Press (1995). She is currently working on *La vida es sueno: the art of Ana Maria*

Pacheco, in collaboration with photographer John Hedgecoe, to be published by Ashgate (Spring, 2000). An author of articles, book and exhibition reviews for specialised art magazines both from Great Britain and overseas, as well as the national press. She is a researcher and compiler of documentaries (mostly 45 minutes) for BBC Radio 3, since 1982. Currently, she is preparing a documentary on the work of Ana Maria Pacheco, artist in residence at the National Gallery, London to be broadcast in September 1999, on the occasion of the opening of her exhibition at the National Gallery.

William Norris has been working in journalism for 49 years. He left school at 16 to become a 'cub' reporter on the *Worthing Herald*. At the age of 26 he was appointed Parliamentary Correspondent of *The Times*. In 1967 he became Africa Correspondent of *The Times*, subsequently moving into television as Political Correspondent for Independent Television News (ITN). He worked as a freelance in the United States for 13 years, and is an Emeritus member of the Academy of Senior Professionals at Florida's Eckerd College. He is currently Associate Director of PressWise, the media ethics watchdog.

Tom O'Malley is Lecturer in Media Studies at the University of Glamorgan. His publications include, *Closedown: The BBC and Government Broadcasting Policy 1979–1992* (Pluto Press, 1994), and as co-editor with Michael Bromley, *A Journalism Reader* (Routledge, 1997). He is a founder editor of *Media History*, writes on press and broadcasting history and policy and is a member of the Campaign For Press and Broadcasting Freedom.

Nick Rayner is a Doctoral Research Student in the Social Science Faculty of Southampton Institute. He also lectures in Classical and Modern Social Theory and is currently researching ethnic cultural migration into an English South-coast tourist resort.

John Theobald is Associate Professor in Modern Languages at the Southampton Institute. He is the author of the book *The Paper Ghetto, Karl Kraus and Anti-Semitism* (1996) and is co-editor with Patrick Stevenson of *Relocating Germaness: Disunited Discourses in Unified Germany* (Macmillan, forthcoming). He has published on stereotypes and stereotype formation in relation to East Germany and unified Germany, and on media influence in historical processes. He is currently working on contrasting linguistic constructions of contemporary Germany using comparative critical media discourse analysis.

Paul Walton is a sociologist, criminologist and media and communications analyst. He was a founding member of the Glasgow University Media Group which included the publication *Bad News* (1976) and *More Bad News* (1980). His work in criminology includes *The New Criminology* (1973) and more recently *The New Criminology Revisited* (Macmillan, 1997). His latest work is co-edited with Elizabeth Mossop and is entitled: *City Spaces* (Craftsman Press forthcoming). He is currently co-authoring a book with Richard Adams entitled: *Digital Dilemmas* due to be published by Macmillan in 1999. He is currently researching digital, cultural and communication issues.

Acknowledgements

Let me just say thank you to all the contributors who responded positively to my editorial requests. Also, thank you to Colorific for their permission to reproduce the image of *The Smiling Iraqi* and to Mike Richards at the Media Arts Research Centre, Southampton Institute for his support in providing financial assistance for purchasing the above named photograph. Also thanks to Paul Walton who first suggested this project one afternoon in a pub in Cardiff, without which this project may have never began. Jennifer Welham at Focal Press for her patience and enthusiasm for the project. Also, thanks to Ken Burtenshaw for his time and imagination in designing the front cover of the book, and to Stephen Hayward for his very interesting thoughts on post-cultural studies.

Introduction

The debate concerning the discourse on media ethics has intensified in the UK in recent times due mainly to a perception that there has been a qualitative drop in standards in journalist and media practices. The role of practitioners has taken centre-stage as concerns grow over what constitutes ethical and socially acceptable practice and behaviour, by the public, practitioners and intellectuals. The discursive relationship between the production and consumption of information is central to the debate regarding moral conduct particularly in light of the commercialisation of the media. Considering that media institutions operate in a climate of intense competition the 'value' of information and its corresponding quality have begun to be critically assessed in terms of ethical understanding.

Undoubtedly, moral philosophy is empowering in gaining *some* understanding of the complexities involved in attempting to resolve the issues raised. However, a normative approach can only work effectively within an *interdisciplinary* framework and analysis. Therefore, juxtaposing normative methods with sociological analysis, critical cultural studies, psychoanalytical perspectives, and importantly, historical analysis, to mention a few, enables us not only to comment and deliberate upon ethics but equally *further* empowers us to comprehend the complexities involved in the motives of media organisations and the types of *structural imperatives* that routinise the daily productivity of media workers that produce unethical conduct in the first instance. To a certain degree the nuances involved in practices and their corresponding structures can be conceptualised as underlying themes which a moral philosophical approach cannot resolve in isolation. The result is a holistic capturing of social relations.

This present collection of essays is concerned with journalistic/media *practices* and *representations*. Therefore, questions of *power* and *ideology* emerge and the reader should perceive them as central features to the following discussions. That equally applies to the various ethical perspectives concerning the media such as *duties, responsibilities, deception, truth, objectivity* and so on. However, at times they are implicit rather than explicit and therefore it is incumbent upon the reader to respond accordingly. As a consequence, media ethics as described here, has a large degree of *open-endedness* and therefore readers determine their own resolutions. Within this framework it is important to point out that whilst ethics is equally about *feelings* and *emotions*, any deliberation in the context of media ethics, however, is non-descriptive and therefore is prescriptive.

In this context there is a focus upon the commodification of information for commercial purposes by the media, which is a result of capitalist development and its corresponding social relations. The consequence is a shift in types of journalism and media practices that correspond to the new forms of information increasingly based on entertainment and trivia. The *effects* on media practices has a corresponding *effect* on public reception and forms of mediation as a formal process is therefore scrutinised as concerns for social and cultural development emerge.

It is in this light that the Press Complaints Commission (PCC) and the National Union of Journalists (NUJ), with their separate codes, should be considered in redressing the imbalance in terms of *organisational power* that increasingly heightens pressures for media practitioners to be productive even though this may 'de-value' standards, quality and performance. Both the NUJ and the PCC are, regardless of their power or lack of it, perceived as *protective agencies* to safeguard ethical practice.

Considering the impact the media has in society, its role/function raises key epistemological questions in terms of the value and quality of the knowledge that it produces. The performance of media practitioners are brought to the fore and measured qualitatively in terms of the media's role in aiding the socio-political, economic and cultural development of a society. The requirement of society in part is the development of a democratic citizenship who are constantly informed of key political matters and a public interest and rights to information are asserted accordingly. Equally, and this is the rub, ethical decision making should be made in collaboration with, and participation of the citizenship, and therefore questions of media *duties* and *responsibilities* ensue.

We begin in chapter one with John Theobald's contribution on the works of the Austrian satirist Karl Kraus and his criticism of the emerging mass media from 1899 to 1934. Krausian observations have a poignancy for the practice of journalism today and the role it plays in terms of its relationship with the both the public and the establishment. Theobald argues that a full account of radical mass media criticism has yet to be documented, therefore, this article is additional material and strengthens current debates in this field. The chapter discusses the relationship between the press and the public as information in terms of the *cliché* as it asserts an influence of linguistic styles upon the reader. Kraus was concerned with the danger and threat to language from the rising commercial project. The relationship and role of journalism in culture is addressed by Theobald's assessment. The chapter draws on some interesting comparisons with contemporary figures such as the British journalist John Pilger, and comments on Chomsky and the French thinker Pierre Bourdieu in terms of an intellectual continuity of media criticism.

Concerns over the development of culture are continued in Chapter 2. I begin with a discussion on the crisis that has emerged within the media in relation to the number of *faked* programmes in circulation in the public domain and consequently the impact upon truth in journalistic practice and trust between the public and the media to produce reliable information. Documentary film making in particular has come under sustained attack for the high levels of fakes, deceptive media practices and distortions, and I argue that 'truth', as a value in terms of media practices and the public, is constantly under seige from the commercialisation of the media industry. The chapter also considers George Simmel's thoughts of 'cultural development' in terms of the quality of knowledge and argues that the media have a moral duty to nurture public consciousness.

Joost van Loon addresses the question of 'media ethics' and our understanding of the complexities involved in the production and responses to ethical discourse produced in media communication. The article begins by questioning claims that normative approaches to media ethics is the only method for a greater understanding of ethical issues in the media. Therefore, van Loon proposes a new way of rethinking media ethics that considers a phenomelogical perspective that contextualises the media as a 'technology'. The article considers Heidegger's argument that technologies 'reveal' and van Loon links this to McLuhan's notion that the media is an extension of humans that 'enframe' social life. The chapter further discusses technology as a form of mediation through which ethical sense-making is produced. Finally, the chapter considers the work of Jacques Derrida and his claim that technologies engender their own normativity.

Andrew Edgar's article deliberates on the question of 'moral responsibilities' that the 'fourth estate' should have in relation to the community. Whilst Edgar is critical of the liberal theory of news production and interpretation, he argues, nevertheless, that the media has a specific role to play in culture in that the media both 'promote' and 'deepen' a political consciousness so that the community, posed in terms of a political entity, become empowered to articulate and interpret news as competent readers. Edgar further argues, that perceived in this way the 'overriding moral responsibility' is to develop a 'public debate' and to encourage 'public involvement'.

In Chapter 5 Carol Davies and Nick Rayner discuss representations of Indonesia and how the western media limit perceptions of the other. They argue that institutionalised journalistic practices select events exclusively which subsequently misrepresent and whilst it may not be deliberate lying it nevertheless reduces our understanding of Indonesia. They argue that as a result, journalistic misrepresentations occur and are posed in terms of deceptions and omissions of other relevant factors which would enable the audience to understand the complexities of Indonesia. By using Bourdieu's concept of *habitus* they provide an understanding of the discursive relationship between production of text/image and consumption. They further argue that we should consider other discourses and practices indigenous to Indonesia for a more comprehensive understanding of the complex reality.

The role of journalism is taken up in Chapter 6 where Michael Bromley posits the notion that journalists need to develop an independence or autonomy from market and commercial logic.

Bromley argues that in doing so, it breaks the bonds of subservience where news is increasingly perceived in commercial terms with its emphasis on productivity akin to other consumer durables, and provides what is seen as the essence of good journalistic practice, a public service based on sound ethical principles. It is this tension between market forces with its principal objective, profit, and journalism as a public service which Bromley attempts to resolve. Bromley considers the threats and dangers from the material project and considers an ideal type of journalism and its essential ethical practice based on social responsibility.

Stuart Allan's and Cynthia Carter's article is a discussion of the current state of popular journalism. It considers the narrowing gap between news and entertainment and the consequences of this trend in terms of the development of 'infotainment' and the impact that 'tabloidisation' has upon truth and content in the media. They go on to consider the tensions between commercialism and ethical practice and develop a number of ethical perspectives in relation to 'market-driven' journalism and its impact upon good journalistic practice. They consider whether journalism is a profession, and therefore, whether 'statutory regulation' or 'self-policing' is the most realistic option for determining a code of ethics.

Stephen Hayward's article is on political and electoral representations in the media. Hayward argues that broadsheet media debates of the 1997 election heralded a crisis in representation in terms of the relationship between the media and politics. He argues that tabloids were seen to be creating their own agendas and therefore the crisis is measured in ethical terms over good journalistic practice and responsibilities to the electorate. He begins the discussion with a comparative analysis between the Labour Party's 1964 election campaign and New Labour's campaign in 1997 and argues that although there are striking linguistic and structural similarities between media presentation of the two campaigns, there were, however, crucial differences. Hayward maintains that *The Daily Telegraph* and *The Guardian's* presentation of the 1997 campaign signified a battle for cultural hegemony and distinction and in doing so news discourse acquires a 'cultural authority' in the public space that helps explain the emergence of 'New Labour's' image. Ethics comes to the fore in terms of journalistic practice and content in terms of a shift in political media communications from a public service model to one based on 'consumer citizenship', the consequences of which, in part, has led to a dumbing down of political discourse.

In Chapter 9 representations are discussed in Sanda Miller's article which is based on works of art and how they are appropriated by the commercial world of advertising. Miller uses two case studies to highlight the complex issues surrounding the 'borrowing' of ideas in art form to their representations in commercial forms such as advertising. The first case study used is the work of the 1960s artist Bridgit Riley, whilst the second example is based on the work of photographer/artist Gillian Wearing. In both cases they claimed that *their* work turned up in a series of advertisements. Miller argues that in both cases this is tantamount to purloining and the article raises important issues for the future, such as ownership/control and value of the image.

In Chapter 10 Jason Barker discusses matters related to photojournalism, particularly the notion that certain images can 'shock' the viewer. Barker uses a specific image of a dead Iraqi soldier on the road to Basra, *The Smiling Iraqi* photographed by Ken Jarecke and argues that representations produce moral concerns between groups with various claims as to whether such images should be published in the public domain. Barker argues that distinguishing between 'viewers rights' and 'media responsibilities' is problematic and provides a critique of media effects in mediating experience in either 'positive' or 'negative' terms.

In Chapter 11 Paul Walton discusses some of the contemporary issues concerning the information superhighway and the Internet. As this technological space expands questions of regulation begin to emerge from large corporate businesses and threats to free speech ensue. Walton argues that there is a tension between corporate and community interests over access and control and that this constitutes the central issue of a cyber-ethical debate. Part of the 'crisis' is that citizens are increasingly using encryption methods to protect both their *privacy* and *rights* to communicate from external interference.

Anna Gough-Yates's contribution is on the question of female representation and sexual content in magazine culture and its impact upon the development of a sexual identity for women which challenge gender norms. It is particularly poignant for media ethics in that Gough discusses the production of femininities for a young readership.

The commercial growth of both 'Teen' magazines and other mainstream magazines that reach an older audience has led to a debate regarding the questions of taste, morality and responsibilities to others in terms of the harm that may be caused as a consequence of the type of images and text produced. Equally, the question of censorship and freedom of speech are implicit to the argument in terms of the moral dilemmas practitioners confront when addressing their audience.

In Chapter 13, Annette Hill addresses the issue of violence in the media and the controversies that emerge. Hill specifically focuses upon the role of anti-violence campaign groups in the UK and contextualises the debate on media violence in terms of moral risks and environmental hazards to the public. Hill argues that various groups with a Christian perspective call for the adoption of public ethical standards and decency. These groups are particularly concerned with the protection of children from harmful images and narrative. The article considers Ingmar Palmund's theory of social drama in understanding how risks are produced and incorporated into public discourse and the influence that campaign groups have in determining legislation and control over the media and the challenges for us all when considering whether violence is responsible for individual violent actions.

In Chapter 14, Miranda Basner discusses the moral requirement of journalists to penetrate the 'culture of secrecy' that pervades British society. Basner considers the weaknesses in the Press Complaint Commission's code of conduct in not fully addressing public requirements for receiving news and that concealment of information is posed in terms of consequences and seen as harmful to citizens. Basner argues that there are shortcomings in both the quantity and quality of news production and therefore conceptualises the argument in terms of deprivation to public needs. The role of the journalist is addressed to provide a reliable service, one in which news corresponds to the needs of the political citizen.

In Chapter 15 Mike Jempson considers the consequences of unethical journalism and its effect upon people who become victims of unscrupulous methods and practice. The chapter begins with an outline of the work of PressWise who provide advice to individuals at the receiving end of unethical or 'bad' journalism. Jempson cites a number of case studies which provide harrowing reading and argues that self-regulation has failed to curb the excesses of some newspapers and that an independent body should be set up to adjudicate on serious matters concerning press conduct. The UK law, he argues, is correct to incorporate the European Convention of Human Rights, something which PressWise has campaigned on for a long time.

Tom O'Malley's contribution in Chapter 16 is a historical account of press reform and the levels of uncertainty that have accompanied the debates surrounding the issue of press regulation. O'Malley argues that the three Royal Commissions (1949, 1962, 1977), the Younger Report (1972) and the Calcutt Reports (1990, 1993) have all tried to grapple with balancing between the liberal notion of press freedom and its maintenance and statutory regulation by state intervention. Considering the ethical concerns in terms of press standards and conduct the debate raises important issues in terms of the types of legal restraints government regulatory bodies should consider for the future.

In Chapter 17, Phil Dring begins his article with a discussion of the tensions between academics and journalists over the issue of ethics in the media and the adoption of codes in relation to specific cultures. Whatever the disagreements, Dring argues that as European states increasingly draw closer in terms of integration, discussions of a European code of conduct emerge. Dring presents an analysis of the Swedish media model as an example of good practice, but argues that different European cultural and historical backgrounds, in terms of press and media development, are stumbling blocks to any future discussion. However, he argues that a framework is in place to build upon for future debate.

The issue of consequences for practising journalists are taken up in Bill Norris's article which is based on his long experience as a war correspondent in the Nigerian civil war in 1967 and then later in the early 1970s when he investigated issues surrounding the Hudson Report. Norris considers individual responsibilities for their actions and argues that codes of conduct play little if any role in a journalist's behaviour and that the stark choice between getting the story and ethical conduct is not something a book of codes can resolve that easily. It's a personal story of the conflicts and tensions that exist between commercial interests and personal survival, the need to publish, and avoiding undue harm to innocent people in the process.

Although there are many issues and perspectives addressed in this book, *Ethics and Media Culture: Practices and Representations*, is in part an attempt to broaden out the debates particularly in relation to Journalism Studies, Cultural Studies, Sociology of Culture and Communications, Philosophy and History. Many of the issues raised here and the context therein signify a turn to ethics as a centrifugal force that raises the possibility of the further development of a new paradigm that signifies a *post-cultural studies perspective* within the framework of media ethics. To date, moral philosophy has played an important role for producing an *identity* for media ethics and applying normative approaches to a critical cultural studies opens up new horizons. Media ethics, as a specific discourse, is beginning to incorporate a wide number of disciplines, or to put it another way, a media ethics which subsumes key analytical elements of other disciplines enables it to become interdisciplinary, critical and contextual.

In this framework we may consider the *value of ethics* in relation to both ownership and power as a starting point for discussion. Equally a post-cultural studies perspective, articulated now as media ethics that considers, whatever the faults, a *rights-oriented perspective*. I say faults because Marxists, for example, would argue that *rights* are in part, linked to property *rights* and are therefore neither natural nor legitimate but an extension of ownership/control and exploitation, but at least a discussion within this framework opens up a critical debate. In many ways this vision should be perceived in terms of settling accounts over the appropriation of the media for commercial purposes and what media content has for cultural development and a discussion on *rights*, engaged critically, at least allows us to discuss the contradictions and any impending crisis. Of course it would be foolhardy for me to expect that other contributors share this perspective which of course is one of the great difficulties of editing a book. That I hope is a matter for future debate.

1 Radical mass media criticism: elements of a history from Kraus to Bourdieu

'In the beginning was the press, and then the world appeared' **Karl Kraus, 1923**

John Theobald

A full historical survey of radical mass media criticism has yet to be published. When it is, its early sections covering the late nineteenth and early twentieth centuries will surely be dominated by the seminal work of Karl Kraus. Despite being 'shamelessly ignored' (Jameson 1990, p. 63), Kraus stands out as a major figure, many of whose ideas have been, often unknowingly, rediscovered by present-day writers on the media. His work is still a mine of challenging thought, taking its ethical–satirical critique of media discourse and practice further than many present-day analysts will find comfortable. It is the aim here to start to provide a proper acknowledgement as well as a critique of Kraus's ideas and writings, to give a flavour of the moral passion and black humour which characterises them, and to make comparisons with some writers – Pilger, Chomsky and Herman, Bourdieu – who stepped into his shoes at the end of the twentieth century.

The contemporary comparisons, and the ease with which one can show links between current formulations and ideas first expressed by Kraus, demonstrate the relevance of the Krausian legacy for today's debates on media power and media ethics. His controversial writings during earlier crises, particularly in the prologues of the twentieth century's two world wars, serve both to strengthen and inspire, and to add credibility and urgency to the work of contemporary writers and activists. His views surrounding the role of mass media oligarchies in the creation of public acceptance of barbarism, and in the willing public renunciation of civic and human rights, and of democratic ideals and practices – the most fundamental of twentieth century ethical issues – are startlingly relevant in today's era of market forces leading to increasing concentration of ownership of globalised media corporations.

Radical mass media criticism is habitually but inaccurately adjudged to have started with the Frankfurt School, although tangential reference is also made to Gramsci's ideas on discursive hegemony, and to Walter Lippmann's *Public Opinion*, published in 1921. By the early 1920s, however, Kraus had already produced over 500 numbers of his critical–satirical journal *Die Fackel (The Torch)* and written his massive condemnation of the role of the press in the First World War – *The Last Days of Humanity*. Taking Kraus's work into account, a more appropriate date for the start of radical mass media criticism may be set in 1899, the year in which his main body of writing commenced. In support of this, Walter Benjamin makes explicit the debt of the Frankfurt Critical Theorists to Kraus. In his essay on Kraus, he acknowledged him as the one who first posited that 'journalism is the prime expression of the changed function of language in the capitalist world', and that 'the cliché is the trademark which turns the thought into a commodity'. In the same passage, Benjamin also recognises Kraus's insight that:

The newspaper is an instrument of power. It can derive its value only from the nature of the power which it serves. It is the expression of that power not only with regard to what *it represents, but with regard to* how *it expresses it* (Benjamin 1969, p. 106. Translation: JT).

Karl Kraus spent his working life in Vienna, where he wrote, almost single-handedly, the 922 numbers of *Die Fackel* between 1899 and 1934. While he was acclaimed, loved, hated, and criticised there for his devastating satirical polemics against individual *bêtes noires* in the press and on the cultural scene, his more threatening underlying radical critique of media structures, motivation, and discourse, which takes the writings beyond ephemeral satire and into radical cultural criticism, beyond early twentieth century Vienna into global contemporary relevance, has not always been well understood. Yet Vienna, as in so many other cultural fields, was in this field also a fertile seed bed for major innovative ways of seeing – and this is Kraus's achievement in relation to language and the media.

The context for Kraus's particular development was Austria's industrial revolution, belated relative to Britain and France, which transformed much of Central Europe in the second half of the nineteenth century, bringing with it the mechanisation of transport and communication, paper manufacture and printing, providing the technological and economic pre-requisites for the rapid collection, production and distribution of newspapers and thence 'news' to a mass public. Between the 1860s and the 1880s the first artefacts which could be described as 'mass media' were produced in Vienna, a city whose population doubled to reach about three million between 1850 and 1900, becoming an industrial metropolis while remaining one of Europe's main centres of imperial power. Born in 1874, and arriving in Vienna three years later, Karl Kraus thus grew up through the founding years and rise to prominence of the German language mass media. Journalism in this context was a transformed profession engendering new genres, new styles of writing subject to new pressures, new uses of language, new kinds of discourse, and a new influential elite of editors and writers with potentially greater influence on a mass public than had ever been possible before. Kraus was part of the first generation to be socialised in a society in which the first mass medium – the press – was an established fact of life, but an as yet unanalysed cultural presence. The job of journalist on one of the major papers was a glamorous and much sought after career, bringing fame and fortune to its successful practitioners, but whose ethical implications and socio-cultural significance had not yet been properly considered or debated.

Kraus's early writings and development looked to be leading him towards a successful career in journalism, but when the opportunity came in his mid-twenties to join the staff of Vienna's leading newspaper – the *Neue Freie Presse* – he rejected it. Early insights into the cliqueishness and corruption of the milieu, and growing confidence in his own satirical talent, led him to decide to found his own journal. *Die Fackel*, which announced itself as an anti-press, anti-corruptionist, anti-journalist magazine, appeared on the Viennese news-stands at the beginning of April 1899, achieving an immediate *succés de scandale*. As he wrote in the fifth issue, it was not he who was ripe for the *Neue Freie Presse*, but the *Neue Freie Presse* which was ripe for him.

This paper was to remain the pivot of his criticism throughout his career, with Moriz Benedikt, its owner/editor, his most frequent target. While others from the range of 'serious' and 'popular' journals, and individuals who owned or worked on them did not go unscathed, it was this prestigious agenda-setter of the Viennese press scene, with its pretensions to quality, accuracy, and rectitude, the most respectable and respected pillar of the liberal, right-thinking establishment, which Kraus used as his prime example of financial and linguistic corruption, terminal cultural decay, and the dulling of readers' minds to the extent that they became willing accomplices to the direst inhumanity.

Kraus's writing covers a period which includes both the sordid conflagration of the First World War, and the rise of fascism in Germany and Austria with Hitler's take-over of power. The linking of the possibility of these barbaric events with his view of the destructive socio-cultural role played by the mass media is central to Kraus's position – built not so much on theory as on the massive accumulation of evidence – which rests on the conviction that journalism had risen to become the real power in the land, subjugating all other influences. In 1905, he wrote:

Someone – was it Burke? – called journalism the fourth *estate. In his time, that was doubtless true. But in our time, it is actually the* only *estate. It has gobbled up the other three. The lay nobility says nothing, the bishops have nothing to say, and the House of Commons has nothing to say, and says it. Journalism rules us* (Kraus 1899–1934, no. 167, p. 12. All Kraus translations: JT).

Kraus witnessed on the streets of Vienna in 1914, the popular acclaim for a supposedly glorious struggle whose actual bloody slaughter had had to be pushed beyond the bounds of the addled imaginations of the news-consuming public for it to be able to happen. In the following decades, he witnessed the undermining and destruction of the first Austrian Republic, and the neighbouring Weimar Republic, which prefaced the enthusiastic public welcome of Hitler on the balcony of Vienna's *Hofburg*, and the majority acceptance of the *Anschluß* in 1938. This too he saw to be only possible following a media-induced state of collective asthenia. Characteristic of both of these horrifying failures of a supposedly enlightened culture to resist the worst conceivable barbarism was dominant public compliance. To imagine the opposite – active majority *dis*approval and *non*-acceptance of these developments, is to imagine an alternative fictional history. In Krausian terms, it was the particular interaction over time between press and public which brought about this repeated consent to barbarism, and thus determined the actual course of historical development.

We are not here, it should be added, dealing with an early advocate of the 'hypodermic syringe' theory of media effects, wherein it is assumed that the media can inject a passive public mind with attitudes or ideas; rather, we are looking at a more stealthy process of gradual confusion and erosion of faculties by the press's substitution of the pure water of information with the seductive perfume of the cliché. Once the cliché, or resonant phrase takes over, argued Kraus, then a gap has opened up between language and the communication of unadulterated news; the link between the event and its understanding by the public has been broken. Once this has happened, the lie or the distortion can be presented and accepted as truth, a whole structure of misinformation can be presented and believed, comment, propaganda and titillation can be subtly mixed with fact, values and priorities can be surreptitiously intermingled with description such that, over a period, readers' perceptions are able to be moulded, their views of the past, present and future shaped, through the linguistic hegemony of those maintaining control of the dominant medium. Kraus is clearly not positing here an *a priori* passive audience, he is asking us to observe the long-term, continuous process of distraction and '*passivication*' of an audience which could otherwise be active. Kraus's view of the power and motivation of the press and its corruption of language developed between 1899 and 1914. His clearest pre-1914 formulations came in polemic essays which use the pretexts of attacks on the Berlin satirist Maximilian Harden, and on the nineteenth century poet Heinrich Heine, to elaborate his position. The essays are more interesting for what they reveal about Kraus than for what they tell us about Harden and Heine, defining his position in the pre-war decade.

They portray a struggle between embattled positive influences and overwhelming negative influences on German language and culture. Underlying this cultural struggle is the belief that use of language is at the root both of cultural – and hence political and social – self-destruction, and, conversely, of the dwindling possibility of regeneration. Language is conceived by Kraus as a determining force,

15

for better or worse, in historical development. The flow of his polemic consistently locates the battlefield in the linguistic sphere before ever a shot is fired in physical war, and demonstrates that the subordination of language to material or commercial interests, the capture of discursive hegemony in struggles for political power or imperialist expansion, are both cultural pre-requisites, and prophetic indicators, of catastrophic descents into war and barbarism.

These are controversial assertions of a sort which we can locate today on the radical–critical wing of media and discourse analytical studies. On the contemporary scene there is substantial contestation of such positions as well as support. It is thus worth looking more closely at the Krausian position, as set out in the *first* decade of the twentieth century, to compare his arguments and evidence with the state of perceptions of these issues in the *last*. Kraus's main observations concern the structural, commercial, and power-related motivations and values of the press as they interact with the superstructural linguistic and discursive techniques and processes it employs to achieve its ends.

In the early years of *Die Fackel* – 1899–1903 – Kraus, influenced by socialist perspectives, viewed the rival newspapers on the Viennese scene as competing capitalist enterprises, whose prime motivation was not to inform the public but to make profits for their owners and their fellow entrepreneurs. He accused the press of hypocrisy – in its pretence that its aim was to bring news and information to its readers – and corruption – in that it used its columns to print stories that would sell copies or serve the interests of its advertisers and financial backers. From 1907 onwards, in the period when he wrote the Harden and Heine essays, his anti-liberal/capitalist position remained, but was couched in the rhetoric of cultural conservatism as he polemicised against materialist values – desire for possessions, lust for power, and the pervasiveness of what he called 'the language of the world', meaning language subjugated to the motive of, and itself creating, material gain. Kraus's panacea at this stage (itself aberrant) was aristocratic, *pre*-liberal cultural nostalgia, expressed in idealisation of a formerly elite, but now moribund nobility, and of a purer, non-commercialised usage of the German language with which he associated it.

Typifying this, and his method of taking ephemeral events and using them as symptoms of cosmic cultural struggle, he put the events of the

Moltke versus Harden trial at the centre of his polemic against Maximilian Harden (1908). Harden, independent journalist and producer of the Berlin-based magazine *Die Zukunft* (The Future) had, as part of a campaign to undermine the monarchy, made assertions of homosexuality among the Emperor's friends and advisors, Prince Eulenberg and Count Kuno Moltke. Moltke sued, and this led to a courtroom confrontation between the laconic land-owning aristocrat and military officer, and the brilliantly eloquent entrepreneurial journalist, who was gaining huge celebrity from the case, and increasing sales of his journal through publishing his version of the trial there in his florid, sensationalising prose style. For Kraus, this had all the elements he needed to build up the two figures as icons of the cultural struggle he perceived to be raging. He wrote:

Never has the nobility been looked upon with such arrogance as in this heyday of the journalistic spirit . . . A real count and former town commander (is) chained to the pillory of journalistic information and delivered up to the merciless pity of the press in attendance . . . The reporters *win hands down, the generals flee from the public gaze. No pardon is given. The Harden–Moltke trial is a victory of* information over *culture. To come out on top in such battles, humanity must learn to inform itself about journalism'* (Kraus 1899–1934, no. 234, p. 34).

Thus Kraus sees a separation of honest, undecorated self-expression, equated with culture, from elaborate eloquence and linguistic manipulation in the service of power and profit. The journalist dazzles and distracts from the real issues with his resonant phrases, prostituting language to the paying public, while the representative of culture is mocked, humiliated, isolated and silenced. The decorated, seductive assertion is believed; the unadulterated minimal expression of genuine feeling is rejected.

The essay *Heine and the Consequences* (1911) takes the issue further. Kraus turns Heine into the instigator of linguistic decoration and manipulation of fact, the stifler of the reader's imagination since he is not prepared to provide just bare information, he has to colour it in his own way such that the readers have no effort of imagination or critical judgement to make, since these are already insinuated into the text. Through this technique, unsuspecting readers are deliberately reduced to passive consumers, while retaining the illusion that they are just being informed, remaining free to form independent judgements. Kraus re-interprets Heine in the form he requires – that of the role model for modern journalism. He wrote:

Heine was a Moses who struck the rock of the German language with his staff. But conjuring is not magic, the water did not flow out of the rock, but he turned it on by sleight of hand; and it was Eau de Cologne. Heine turned the wonder of linguistic creativity into a conjuring trick. He provided the highest that one can manufacture out of *language; higher than that is what can be* created through *language* (Kraus 1899–1934, no. 329–3, p. 22).

What Kraus made of the specific object of his polemic is less important than what he was saying about language, journalistic discourse, and his view of the press as a distorting mirror rather than a direct channel between event and reader. He made this explicit when he wrote of journalism as:

A dangerous intermediary between art and life, surviving as a parasite on both; singing where it should merely be reporting, but reporting where it ought to be singing; casting a functional eye when confronted with a feast of colour, but forgetting the functional out of delight in the picturesque; reducing literature to a utility, but breathing spirit into utilitarian verbiage . . . (Kraus 1899–34, no. 329–30, p. 7).

This may sound like marginal aesthetic debate until Kraus's model of the role of the press is applied to life and death situations. The Balkan wars of 1912 provided the first such situation, and were a theme in Kraus's intense apocalyptic essay *End of the World through Black Magic* – the black magic being printer's ink. Here, the possibility of war and its acceptance by the public, brought about by its description by journalists in poetic or romanticised form, is seen by Kraus as clear evidence of the lethality of journalistic manipulation of language and destruction of imagination. His earlier appeals to the public to inform itself about journalism had not been heard; the progressive '*passivication*' process of the public had proceeded to the extent that now the terror, misery, and slaughter of the battle front were no longer conceivable, replaced in the readers' minds by reporters, at a safe distance from the fighting, evoking landscapes and sunsets, interviewing officers and prisoners, and speculating on the significance of distant gunfire. The war is mediated to the public as the reporter's adventure. The barbaric is rendered acceptable by the distracting nature of the report.

Kraus built this into final evidence of the total severance of humanity, culture and imagination from public discourse and journalistic use of language. Language was now so subjugated to techno-capitalist materialistic ends (words he used in his great drama of the 1914–18 war, *The Last Days of Humanity*), and the public so evidently not making the imaginative leap out of the parameters of mediated reality, that this signified for Kraus 'the end of the world'. The consequence of the divorce between culture and language was barbarism. His 1912 analysis told him that Austria was on the point of self-destruction. The public mind had been induced into readiness for destruction by journalistic manipulation of discourse and consequent deadening of the reader's imagination.

At this point, the Habsburg Empire was indeed not many months from sliding into the war which destroyed it; one might thus add the cliché 'and the rest is history', confirming the accuracy of Kraus's analysis. Yet what is being posited here by Kraus is the assertion: But *this* is history; the linguistic struggles and processes in media discourse leading up to catastrophic or crucial events are key active ingredients in determining the form those events take. We may wish to unpick the hyperbolic and nostalgic elements of Kraus's claims, but fundamentally he makes a case, while Gramsci was still a schoolboy, about the power of linguistic hegemony in the historical process. It is, importantly, not a determinist account. His own obsessive output is a testament to his belief in the value of struggle against the odds.

Little needed to be added to Kraus's model of the cultural-linguistic determinants of the 1914–18 war when he had to confront the discursive antecedents of the subsequent wave of barbarism that was the destruction of the Weimar and Austrian republics and the rise of Fascism.

'Journalism', he wrote in 1933, 'created National Socialism' (Kraus 1952, p. 280). As in the previous period, he was not thereby portraying a simplistic process of propaganda – in this case Nazi propaganda – being soaked up by a spongiform public mind. Indeed, he saw the cultural harm to have been done well before most perceived Nazism as a major threat, with the decisive moment occuring in Austria as early as 1927.

With the end of the 1914–18 war, and the establishment of the Weimar and Austrian republics, Kraus had briefly hoped that social democracy would prove to be strong enough to thwart the return of the materialist–capitalist elites which had been thrown into disarray by the military defeat. The story of the early and mid-1920s became for Kraus, however, that of the progressive advance of the ghosts of the previous era in a republican disguise. Thus, when in July 1927, the point came when the police could gun down ninety demonstrators on the streets of Vienna, and be supported in its action by the Christian Social government and the entire bourgeois press, Kraus saw the end of the democratic republic and its final delivery back into the hands of the old enemies of culture, the 'unconquerables' who had already led Austria into the catastrophe of the 1914 war. For Kraus, even though Austria continued in the shell of republican structures for a few more years, it was morally and culturally delivered up to renewed barbarism. Kraus saw press corruption of language to be at the centre of this second debacle of culture and humanity; even shortly before the 1927 massacre, he wrote:

That the bourgeois press had the power to unleash the (1914) war was something we had to experience. But that it could also emerge from it unscathed, and more insolent than ever, raise its head on which the cross of corruptibility is drawn; that the revolution not only failed to cut off even one of the heads of the Hydra which has the body of the people in its clutches, but also that these heads are multiplying and causing offence in even greater numbers – this is the terrifying experience of these seven lean years . . .' (Kraus 1899–1934, no. 712–716, p. 2).

When, following the massacre, police chief Schober, known to have links with right wing paramilitary groups was presented by the bourgeois press, and accepted by its readership as the 'protector of the republic', Kraus was convinced that the press's ability to deaden the imagination, turning an evident truth and humane reactions on their heads, was again controlling Austrian culture and society. The way was clearly open for a further descent into barbarism, and broad acceptance of the 'troglodytes', as he called the Nazis and their sympathisers.

From this point, Kraus became a progressively more embattled voice, waging a desperate literary campaign against what he in June 1928 called, 'the unconquerable powers of the Austrian bourgeoisie, ranging from the swastika to the stock-exchange' (Kraus 1899–1934, no. 781–786, p. 21), but always identifying the press as the prime enemy, and placing *Sprachlehre* – linguistic teaching – at the centre of his polemic. His subsequent, deeply pessimistic exposures of Nazi abuse of language, written in 1933 and 1934, give further evidence for the causal link he draws between linguistic corruption in the media, and public approval or acceptance of barbarism.

Today, a mass of recent writing witnesses to continuing controversy, now extended to the electronic media, over precisely the questions about language, mass media, and power that Kraus was the first to raise. One may expect that his particular answers will be problematised, but his big questions will not go away, although the debates they have generated have taken on their own momentum.

The appropriation of Krausian perspectives at the end of the twentieth century rarely takes the form of direct influence. The genealogy has rather to be established via the clear affinities which can be noted between Kraus's writings and those of critics and analysts several generations later. Here, three indicative examples will be given.

John Pilger, working in Britain, describes his recent book *Hidden Agendas* (1998) as 'something of a '*J'accuse*' directed at a journalism claiming to be free, and as 'a tribute to those journalists who, by not consorting with power, begin the process of demystifying and disarming it' (Pilger 1998, p.15). He does not cite Kraus, but a more cogent summary of the Krausian mission would be hard to find. Like Kraus, Pilger believes perceptions of reality to be to a great extent controlled by the media. He states: 'In fact, we live in a media age, in which the available information is repetitive, "safe", and limited by invisible boundaries' (ibid., p. 4). Furthermore, he adopts the perspective, first formulated by Kraus in relation to the media in free market economies, that language and meaning in the service of economic and political power and market forces are bound to be corrupted, and, in the case of news, to create a barrier of manipulation and 'infotainment' or 'newszack' between event and reader:

In the day-to-day media, much of this (information) is the propaganda of Western power, whose narcissism, dissembling language and omissions often prevent us from understanding the meaning of contemporary events (ibid.).

He also quotes Bob Franklin, who, echoing Kraus's critiques of Harden and Heine, condemns the transformation of news into entertainment, and the corresponding decline of news in favour of marketable stories. Pilger also follows Kraus in his pursuit of an individual *bête noire*. Kraus's Moriz Benedikt and *Neue Freie Presse* become in the 1990s Rupert Murdoch and News Corp. Kraus's 'end of the world through black magic' becomes for Pilger a 'cultural Chernobyl', his adopted epithet for Wapping, 'spewing its poison across the whole journalistic landscape' (ibid., p. 452).

At the end of his First World War drama *The Last Days of Humanity*, Kraus presents Benedikt as a diabolic anti-Christ, who now rules the world through his seizure of power over the public via control of language, as the editor-in-charge of the war. Pilger perceives Murdoch's rise to power in comparable terms, giving examples of his influence over governments, and quoting the alarming conclusions of Australian journalist David Bowman:

The danger is that the media of the future, the channels of mass communication, will be dominated locally and world-wide by the values – social, cultural, and political – of a few individuals and their huge corporations. Democrats ought to fight to the last ditch against what Murdoch and the other media giants represent (ibid., p.482/Bowman, *Adelaide Express*, Feb. 1996).

Noam Chomsky and Ed Herman in *Manufacturing Consent* (1988) also, without citing Kraus, reflect his perspectives with remarkable closeness, although their work concentrates on the American scene in the 1980s. Certainly, both analyses stress the socio-cultural role of dominant media and their creation through discourse of actual majority public passivity and conformity to media agendas in the face of the most horrific events.

Chomsky and Herman reiterate and elaborate on Kraus's portrayal of the integration of the media into capitalist structures, and the resulting thought control. Comparisons with Kraus's ideas are evident:

Perhaps this is an obvious point, but the democratic postulate is that the media are independent and committed to discovering and reporting the truth, and that they do not merely reflect the world as powerful groups wish it to be perceived. Leaders of the mass media claim that their news choices rest on unbiased, professional and objective criteria ... If, however, the powerful are able to fix the premises of discourse, to decide what the general populace is allowed to see, hear, and think about, and to 'manage' public opinion by regular propaganda campaigns, the standard view of how the system works is at serious odds with reality (ibid., p. xii).

They go on:

The dominant media firms are quite large businesses; they are controlled by very wealthy people or by managers who are subject to sharp constraints by owners and other market-profit-oriented forces; and they are closely interlocked, and have important common interests, with other major corporations, banks and governments. This is the first powerful filter that will affect news choices (ibid., p. 14).

On this basis, Chomsky and Herman elaborate on their 'propaganda model' of the political–economic role of the media, which sees their function not as delivering information to the public, but as delivering a consenting, consuming public to the power elites. Clearly, this 'propaganda model' is close to that which emerges from Kraus's earlier writings, and underlies his whole *oeuvre*.

Congruent too with Kraus's views on the manipulation of language are these formulations:

That the media provide some *facts about an issue, however, proves absolutely nothing about the adequacy or accuracy of that coverage. The mass media do, in fact, literally suppress a great deal ... But even more important in this context is the question of the attention given to a fact – its placement, tone, and repetitions, the framework of analysis within which it is presented, and the related facts that accompany it and give it meaning (or preclude understanding)* (ibid., p. xv).

Fom here, Chomsky and Herman go on to elucidate 'the observable pattern of ... shading and emphasis, and of selection of content, premises and general agenda, as being 'highly functional for established power' (ibid.), demonstrating this with a range of case studies from the recent US past. As with Kraus, the emphasis of the writing is not on theory, but on actual cases and the accumulation of concrete evidence.

Chomsky and Herman are conscious of the voluminous intervening debates on media effects, yet they choose to re-assert, from a radical left-libertarian perspective, thoughts similar to those of Kraus, a self-styled conservative.

The final example here of late twentieth century appropriation of the Krausian legacy is the French sociologist Pierre Bourdieu's 1996 essay *On Television and Journalism*. While Bourdieu does refer to Kraus, he does not admit that his key analytical points – transposed into France in the television age – are well known to anyone who is familiar with Krausian ideas.

Essential to Bourdieu's account is not just the fundamental framework of market structures and forces controlling media output, but analysis of *how* this control takes place, how 'the relentless competition for an ever larger audience share' (Bourdieu 1998, p. 10.) leads to production of a discourse which is there to distract and entertain rather than inform: 'Sensationalism attracts notice, and it also diverts it, like magicians, whose basic operating principle is to direct attention to something other than what they are doing' (ibid., pp. 17–18). We recall Kraus's reference to newsprint as 'black magic', and his reference to Heine as a magician who turned the pure water of information into the *Eau de Cologne* of journalism.

Bourdieu echoes Kraus in his view of the power of the media over the public mind. He asserts that 'television enjoys a *de facto* monopoly on what goes into the heads of a significant part of the population and what they think' (ibid., p. 18), and argues that television:

Can hide things by showing something other than what would be shown if television did what it's supposed to do, provide information. Or by showing what has to be shown, but in such a way that it isn't really shown, or is turned into something insignificant; or by constructing it in such a way that it takes on a meaning that has nothing at all to do with reality (ibid., p. 19).

Thus, Bourdieu states later, 'with their permanent access to public visibility . . . journalists can impose on the whole of society their vision of the world, their conception of problems, and their point of view'. They operate, he goes on, with a common set of assumptions and mental categories which 'reside in a characteristic relationship to language'. Through manipulation of discourse, they not only distort news, but also 'help create the event' (ibid., p. 47), and thus create history. Bourdieu uses as an example the French media's disproportionate attention to National Front leader Le Pen, playing into the hands of his publicity seeking campaigns and inflating his political importance and success. Kraus made exactly the same point about press treatment of the Dreyfus Case – that it exploited a marketable story which sold newspapers, but fanned and lent credibility to racism while protesting against it.

A further reflection of Krausian ideas in Bourdieu's formulations is the centrality of language – words – to the process of control and manipulation. Bourdieu writes:

Sometimes I want to go back over every word the television newspeople use, often without thinking and with no idea of the difficulty and the seriousness of the subjects they are talking about or the responsibilities they assume by talking about them in front of the thousands of people who watch the news without understanding what they see and without understanding that they don't understand. Because these words do things, they make things – they create phantasms, fears, and phobias, or simply false representations' (ibid., p. 20).

The central thrust of 922 numbers of Kraus's *Die Fackel* was to perform precisely such a task of going back over the formulations of journalists to reveal what they were making words *do*.

A final comparison may be made between Kraus's and Bourdieu's views on media effects. Both see journalism as a barrier to information about events and positive reactions to those events by a potentially active audience. The public *'passivication'* that Kraus saw the press to be inducing is paralleled in Bourdieu's essay by the view that reporting leads to public withdrawal from the political arena in the face of a barrage of facts which appear threatening, but unchangeable. Giving the example of French reporting of Africa, he states:

The journalistic evocation of the world does not serve to mobilise or politicise; on the contrary, it only increases xenophobic fears . . . The world shown by television is one that lies beyond the grasp of ordinary individuals . . . Especially among those who are basically apolitical, this worldview fosters fatalism and disengagement, which obviously favours the status quo (ibid., p. 8).

Kraus would doubtless have agreed. These words of his, written during the First World War, deliver a strikingly similar message:

We were turned into invalids by the rotary presses before *there were any sacrifices to the cannons. Had not all realms of the imagination been evacuated by the time of that written declaration of war on the earth's population? . . . It is not that the press set in motion the machinery of death, but that it hollowed out our heart, so that we could no longer imagine how it would be; that is its war guilt* (Kraus 1964 pp. 228–30).

Comparisons made between Kraus and later writers in no way represent any attempt to discredit the latter. On the contrary, they wish to strengthen the tradition in which they are working and provide historical underpinning for views which are still controversial and often dismissed without cogent argument by those who feel targeted by them. Pilger, Chomsky and Herman, and Bourdieu are, in their varied contexts both advancing the debate, and making it relevant to the globalised, multi-media context of the late twentieth century. From to-day's perspective, Kraus's writing serves as both a mine of ideas, an example, and a warning. There is still immense scope for applying his ideas to present-day media discourse analysis and criticism; his whole *oeuvre* demonstrates the size, complexity and salience of the issues he raises; and his ultimate failure as an individual critic and campaigner in his historical context must provoke his present-day counterparts, and those to whom they communicate their ideas, to redouble their efforts and find ways to convert critical cultural analysis into broad public recognition, awareness and social action.

REFERENCES

Adorno, T.W. (1965) *Noten zur Literatur III*, Frankfurt: M. Suhrkamp.
Barsky, R.F. (1997) *Noam Chomsky. A Life of Dissent*, Massachussetts: MIT Press.
Benjamin, W. (1969) *Über Literatur*, Frankfurt: M. Suhrkamp.

Bourdieu, P. (1997) *Sur la Télévision*, Paris: Liber-Raisons d'Agir. Translated (1998) as *On Television and Journalism*, London: Pluto Press.

Bowman, D. (1988) *The Captive Press*, Sydney: Penguin

Chomsky, N. and Herman, E. (1988) *Manufacturing Consent*, London: Vintage.

Franklin, B. (1997) *Newszack and the News Media*, London: Arnold.

Kraus, K. (1899–1934) *Die Fackel*, Vienna: Verlag Die Fackel.

Kraus, K. (1952) *Die Dritte Walpurgisnacht*, Munich: Kösel.

Kraus, K. (1964) *Die Letzten Tage der Menschheit*, Munich: DTV.

Jameson, F. (1990) *Late Marxism*, London: Verso.

Marlière, P. (1998) The Rules of the Journalistic Field. Pierre Bourdieu's Contribution to the Sociology of the Media, *European Journal of Communication*, **13**/2, 219–234.

McChesney, R.W. (1997) *Corporate Media and the Threat to Democracy*, New York: Seven Stories Press.

Pilger, J. (1998) *Hidden Agendas*, London: Vintage.

Theobald, J. (1996) *The Paper Ghetto. Karl Kraus and Anti-Semitism*, Frankfurt: M. Lang.

2 Trust in media practices: towards cultural development

David Berry

Modern media forms of communication are extremely complex and their relationship with the community is discursive, not simply in terms of a dialectical relationship between the production and consumption of information, but equally discursive in terms of developing trust relations. That is trust in the knowledge that content has been based on the premise of truth which is seen to be a central feature of journalistic practice that forms but one part of an ideal-type of journalism.

The role of the media is broad but one very important function is the idea that it is seen to bridge a gap between events and audiences, and therefore to mediate experience. I think it's fair to say that accordingly the public afford a great deal of trust in the media for reliable information to enable the public to make informed decisions. Equally, sections of society may invest trust in the media, particularly in its investigative journalistic manifestation, to confront powerful elites in society, including media owners, rather than consort with them by associating practices towards an ideology which is largely based on crude commercial logic which essentially elevates commodity production over ethical discourse fit for public consumption.

Therefore, theories of what constitutes a 'public interest' can be developed, particularly in the light of revelations over the number of faked television programmes in circulation mainly through the form of documentary film making. Journalistic practices frame the content in that documentary seeks to mediate factual/truthful material to the audience.

This chapter is concerned with *deceptive media practices* and further examines the consequences of unethical journalism within current patterns of media ownership and power. It is in this context that I critically evaluate the role of truth and trust in media practices.

1998 was, to put it mildly, an interesting year for the media in the UK in terms of the revelations that exposed parts of the industry for producing fake television programmes. That discussion spilled over into 1999 with further discoveries of both serious documentaries and talk-show programmes falling foul to deceptive practices. Considering this, I want to examine the consequences that lying may have for the trust between society and the institutions which we rely upon for genuine forms of information.

In terms of documentary film making it seems to me that it has distinct types of practices that set it aside from social realism, for example, as a form of film making: it is fair to say that the audience of social realism understand that it is a representation and a constructed text and image. Furthermore, the audience may infer a sense of reality from it in terms of relating to life outside of the film. Documentary on the other hand has more in common with journalistic practices because it attempts to capture social life and present them as factual accounts. Of course films such as *Yol, Battle of Algiers* or even *Prêt à Porter* is a fusion of styles and forms which incorporates documentary techniques and the boundaries are blurred as a consequence.

Nevertheless, the audience engagement and negotiation with documentary is fundamentally different from social realism because documentary situates truth as a reflection of reality and equally as a central tenet of its form in productive terms without the spin of a director's interpretation, or at least that is the theory. The reality may be significantly different. Whatever the complexities on the production side, we can assume that the audience trust in documentary as a true account is similar to the types of trust invested in news accounts.

Historically, trust between individuals and between individuals and institutions has been perceived as central for maintaining social order (Parsons 1991). Trust, it has been argued, involves integration which actively promotes solidarity and collectiveness amongst individuals similar to Durkheim's concept of solidarity which relies upon moral consensus and conformity. Locke's emphasis on the *promise*, for example, as a duty to oneself and others would result in embedding trust for cementing order in civil society. In this way, trust is perceived not in terms of democratic ownership of the media, but rather upon a tacit agreement of the status quo. Whatever the faults of this perception we cannot, it seems, depart from the notion that trust is central to any social system, and it is not only indicative of a capitalist society. For example, levels of trust differ or have differed in western societies and the former communist states where levels of trust in the latter were extremely low and that was extended to media practices where it was perceived as a tool of propaganda.

In contemporary western terms, individuals display a degree of trust in the media to impart knowledge and provide truthful information. This is essentially based upon an audience perception that journalists have a commitment to pursue the truth. In essence what we have here is a reflection of the Hobbsian insistence that society is held together through trust in powerful institutions and, in contemporary life, trust in the media industry and by definition in media practices. What is interesting is that any form of trust in reliable information invariably constitutes a trust in the type and structure – if only unwittingly – of media industries and those who control it.

Whatever the structure type, it appears that trust in journalistic practices and the broadcast media is increasingly under threat because of the level of fakes, lies and distortions that are taking place within the industry. If the public choose to ignore unethical practices whether they are misrepresenting or faking information there remains the possibility that a *culture of indifference* develops as a level of social consciousness in certain sections of the community. Currently, there is evidence of indifference to lies and image manipulation. Why else would people in the UK buy the *Sun, Mirror, Star* or *Sport*?

Considering this, what future the truth? What future trust? What future knowledge? The epistemological question lies at the very heart of this debate. We need to consider carefully the effect, in terms of the quality of knowledge, on the social and cultural environment, i.e. individual and consequently, social group development. I want, therefore, to conceptualise or foreground this discussion in terms of George Simmel's theory of the discursive and dialectical relationship between subjective culture (individual development) and objective culture.

Allow me, for the sake of this debate, to use media communication industries as a major component of objective culture. In this way I seek to argue that what constitutes a 'public interest' is a system based on 'trust' but accountable to the public, and secondly that a 'public interest' is one in which situates 'cultural development', in terms of the quality and status of knowledge and language, as *the* privileged site in the democratic process which empowers cultural and social interests, rather than debasing them.

Simmel wrote in *Crisis in Modern Culture* (1998) that the separation of the 'objective' from the 'subjective' would render difficult the creative development of the individual. Simmel's notion of 'life' and 'forms' provide some understanding of the discursive relationship which would benefit the development of a subjective culture. However, what Simmel had recognised was that 'life' creates 'forms' that increasingly lose their meaning for the human subject.

Autonomous cultural development within the objective cultural sphere threatened the synthesis between objective and subjective cultural development. This, according to Simmel in *Culture and Crisis* (1998) would constitute a form of cultural production which would detach itself from subjective cultural meaning and would in turn form a 'fateful autonomy' along the lines of an 'immanent developmental logic'. This is where – and here I shall use modern media industries as an example – these industries construct events according to *their* defined logic and laws.

This, I will argue, forms a separation between media forms and society and constitutes a contradiction, and therefore becomes a crisis which can be measured dialectically. The contradiction between the transcendence of society (measured here in terms of attaining greater knowledge) and the dominance of media control over objectives (measured in terms of ownership and self-valorisation of capital, and at times an indifferent audience). The struggle therefore, is a vision of what exactly is the objective of modern media forms in terms of the dissemination of information and what practical/theoretical 'use-value' it has for society and cultural development.

I begin by providing a number of case studies of unethical practices which is necessary for us to grasp the seriousness of the problem.[1] Then I pose the first question, what is the value of truth in journalistic/media practices? Secondly, what is the effect on public trust in forms of information that are deliberately manipulated from source to consumption? Finally, what is the effect upon subjective cultural development considering the levels of deception?

FAKING

1998 was certainly the year for concern over journalistic practices. Besides *The Guardian's* revelations that in May Carlton TV had faked two documentaries, the Huw Wheldon lecture in October of that same year saw Andy Hamilton (script writer of *Drop the Dead Donkey*) address the nation on some of the dubious practices that seem to be institutionalised within the industry. Then in November David Arronovitch presented a three-part series called, *'On Air: The truth about TV'* on similar issues. For practitioners at least, 'The Connection' became the catalyst for ethical concerns over standards.

But what does it mean to deliberately relay false information for public consumption? It can take many forms, and to lie is, as Bok (1980) argues, but one component in the art of deception, which for Black, Steele and Barney (1995) can equally incorporate 'misleading or misrepresenting, or merely being less than forthright' (ibid., p.119). Harris (1992) raises the point that the deliberate act of lying requires a 'greater moral condemnation' (ibid., p.69) than the failure to accommodate all aspects of an event through the normal routines of journalistic activity.

Ethics is about standards and conduct, as well as feelings and emotions, but also it is about the right and wrongs of both statements and actions. Journalistic practices are governed by codes of conduct[2] which serve only as loose guidelines and therefore they serve as an ideal type in terms of rules. Wrongdoing, or the deliberate process of lying to benefit commercially and for status in the profession has to be justified and if it fails to do so action should be taken against the perpetrators because the public lose trust in media practitioners who lie. In Germany, for example, the German film director Michael Born, served two years in prison for *faking* sixteen documentaries. Why then do media practitioners set out to construct false stories, to deliberately mislead the public and others in the profession? Certainly the most influential cases, for Britain at least, was *The Guardian's* claim that two of Carlton's TV programmes 'The Connection' and 'Inside Castro's Cuba' were fake. On Wednesday 6 May 1998, *The Guardian's* headline read: 'Exposed: the TV drug fake', it began by stating on its front page that:

An award-winning documentary by Carlton TV which purported to penetrate Colombia's Cali drugs cartel and track a new heroin smuggling route to London is today exposed by the Guardian as fake. The documentary, called The Connection, was broadcast on ITV's flagship Network First series and later sold to 14 countries. It won eight international awards and was praised world-wide for 'risk-taking investigative reporting' and its educational content. The Royal Television Society described it as 'an exceptional journey into the world of drug-trafficking.

The terms 'investigative reporting' and 'educational content' is really what is at issue here. What type of knowledge can the public construct based on false 'educational content'? And what 'value' has investigative reporting based on deceit and the deliberate objective to profit financially in the marketplace?

'The Connection' was first broadcast on Carlton's *Network First* series in 1996. The significance lies in the fact that *Network First* is seen to be a source of reliable information which the 3.7 million viewers – figures for this programme – trust. Why else would they watch it?

What we need to consider is that there are social and economic pressures that bear down upon practitioners – seen to be productive – and that they conflict with the ideal-type of journalistic practices; that is the pursuit of truth and sound ethical standards. Journalists operate in a hostile environment that values commodity 'production' over principle and disregards an individual's claim to moral sanctity. There should not be any ethical dilemma between economic considerations and the pursuit of truth once a journalist posits the truth as fundamental to journalistic practices. It is the *organisational imperatives* that restrict such principles.

What is so disturbing about this case study is the fact that the documentary won numerous international awards, and was sold to fourteen networks worldwide including the CBS flagship programme *60 Minutes* with an estimated audience of 17 million, which is on top of the 3.7 million ITV viewers who were duped in the process.

At the time of writing the governing body, the Independent Television Commission (ITC)[3] investigating the accusations, fined Carlton £2 million in December 1998. It has a legally binding code that insists upon truth, fairness and respect for privacy. Besides the ITC there is the Broadcasting Standards Commission which has a code of its own which includes the question of taste.

On Tuesday 9 June 1998 *The Guardian* accused a second documentary programme by Carlton called 'Inside Castro's Cuba' of faking. It won two international awards and was hailed as a major broadcasting breakthrough based on a one-to-one interview with Fidel Castro. However, *The Guardian* claimed that:

Clips in the film of President Castro talking to the camera were in reality unlabelled archive footage provided in good faith by the Cuban government. Those were passed off as a one-to-one interview with Marc de Beaufort' (de Beaufort was the producer responsible for both of the examples presented here).

This is an act of self-interest and therefore contravenes journalistic obligations towards *duties* to the truth. This second example is equally as troubling, although its coverage was less extensive. *The Guardian* claimed on page 5:

It is the interview which every major television broadcaster covets – a one-on-one question and answer session with the world's longest-serving revolutionary leader, Fidel Castro, president of Cuba.

Concerning other fakes, *The Sunday Times* media correspondent, Nicholas Hellen claimed that: 'The disclosures, by a leading archivist, threaten to undermine the credibility of one of the most popular and critically acclaimed programme genres' (Sunday 20 June 1998). The reference was to Jerome Kuehl associate producer of *The World at War* and advisor on footage to the BBC's *Cold War*, that images were *faked*.

Other offending programmes were Channel 4's *Secret History* which screened faked images regarding *HMS Glorious* and another Channel 4 programme called, *D-Day Disaster* which claimed to have filmed a German E-boat attack at night in Devon in 1944. However, it appears that specialised camera use of high-speed photography only came into use in the 1980s. The BBC2's account of the Arab–Israeli conflict used images of an Israeli occupation of a Palestinian village. Footage which, according to Hellen, does not exist. Hellen further claimed that the producer of the aforementioned programme could not prove that the footage was of the event and that Alex Hayling from Channel 4's *Secret History* stated that the public:

Don't want everything to have the word reconstruction flashed across the screen. I don't believe that they are easily misled.

Considering, that in general terms, the 'dumbing down' of media content through the narrowing of the gap between news and entertainment (infotainment), the need to rely and trust documentary and investigation to provide high quality and truthful news accounts becomes imperative. As a consequence, the historical documentaries are probably more shocking because of the high use-value for the audience and these revelations begin to disrupt whatever trust we may have in their ability to transmit accurate accounts of key historical events.

But it's not only documentary that distorts the truth. There were the cases of the American columnist, Patricia Smith of the highly respected *Boston Globe* and Stephen Glass, associate editor and reporter of the *New Republic*. Smith made up her characters and Glass fabricated events and both, therefore, deliberately misled the public and betrayed the trust that they invest in news. It is a complete denial of their responsibilities for personal gain.

The Independent on Sunday 5 July 1998, revealed that CNN and *Time* Magazine's joint venture *NewsStand* claimed that sarin nerve gas was used by American troops in Vietnam in 'Operation Tailwind' on defectors. It was all a pack of unsubstantiated claims[4] and was subsequently dismissed. CNN went to some considerable lengths to dispel the claims.

What we have here is a fight for the soul and meaning of journalism. What we witness is the *outing* of wrongdoing committed by journalists and media practitioners *by* journalists in the struggle for respectability and the re-investment of trust as a guideline for ethical practices. There are countless other examples too numerous to mention here which is an indication of the problems we need to confront.

THE PURSUIT OF TRUTH

The worst professional offence a journalist can commit is knowingly and deliberately to publish fiction as fact. That is what happened to Carlton Television's programme, The Connection, and that is the reason why the story should be read carefully by everyone working in

*British television today. Journalism should be a process of searching for the truth. Once that process is poisoned the bond of trust between programme-maker and viewer is broken (*Guardian *Leader Comment, Friday, 8 May 1998).*

Certainly, we perceive the pursuit of the truth in general terms to be a fundamental objective towards the maintenance of democratic rights and principles. What happens to a society that abandons truth as a central organising principle? What are the consequences for a society when we become *indifferent* to forms of deception and lying because they are perceived as parts of a human nature? When can we condone the deliberate manipulation of information as a morally justifiable and defensible act?

The consequence of deception according to Adorno (1990) is that culture becomes ruptured in terms of a systematic attack upon the 'authentic'. We can trace the same type of rupture through mass communication networks and its negative effect. The result is the opposite to the Cartesian vision of a subject who is capable of aesthetic and moral will and judgement to distinguish between truth and lies. This situates the subject in a contradictory position with statements that produce a neurotic condition, a type of *unknowing*.

Distinguishing the *authentic* from its opposite becomes a process of attack upon subjective and rational autonomy to make sound judgements based on the evidence available. The neurosis lies, therefore, in the idea that we begin to doubt the validity of statements. A condition which at times may be unwarranted.

The human interest in truth stems from the notion then of effects upon the individual and thus society. The *culture of indifference* emanates from the belief that morality is temporarily suspended because of the widespread acceptances – in this case – of dubious news practices by sections of the reading and viewing public.

Considering the constraints capitalist relations place upon the journalistic environment, what we are left with is a fascination with the manner in which practitioners conduct themselves and the standards executed as a part of various journalistic codes of conduct. But what actually accounts for the truth in journalistic practices? Incorporating every minute detail is impossible but at least *striving* towards it by gathering evidence is good, ethical practice.

In contemporary terms, the audience has expanded into a global context and the concept of truth remains a central feature considering the globalising effects of both *time* and *space*. New concerns have now emerged particularly over the monopoly ownership of the media in broad terms and the control of information which becomes more valuable in the productive sense than commitments to truth in journalism.

THE VALUE OF TRUTH

It is useful for our purposes to consider a number of thinkers in relation to truth. The list is exhaustive and here I condense it accordingly to the size of this chapter, beginning with Mill (1989) in relation to a public space. The commitment to free expression was, for Mill, essential for the active production of the truth. Mill had argued that the truth could only be realised if the suppression of opinion or 'silencing the expression of an opinion' (ibid., p.20) was negated from discourse. In other words the truth could be achieved by means of a variety of speakers actively producing differing ranges of opinions free from restraint. Accordingly, truth emerges through rational and reasonable means of evaluating each statement. Thus, one should not suppress wrong or deceitful statements because these exposed, truth shall triumph.

The controversies over Mill's argument is that in reality (as opposed to a construction of an ideal-type wrapped in liberal consciousness) large sections of the population were effectively (and indeed currently remain) isolated from democratic discourse based on equality of access. Opinion-formers were the elite of their day. Equally, opinion was based on the amount of knowledge an individual had and in a class society then, as it is today, knowledge is unequally distributed and controlled. This *economy of knowledge* is what Bourdieu (1980) refers to as 'cultural capital'. That is in class-divided societies, particularly through the promotion of public or comprehensive schooling, the result in general terms is a disparity of acquired knowledge.

However, Mill was correct to point out the difference between 'their' certainty, those who seek to impose the truth onto the public, and 'absolute' certainty, which would be the result of free opinion formation. This is what Habermas (1989) hypothesised as the 'discursive-will formation'. This is a democratic dialogue central to the functioning of a public sphere.

In contemporary communication both the press and broadcast media play an ever increasing role in the development of knowledge and opinion formation. This relationship between text/television and reader is what Pecheux (1982) referred to as 'discursive formations'. This is a process of subjectification and in communication terms this process is seen to be based on an unequal power relationship. It is also a denial that according to idealist philosophy the subject (self) is the primary (and therefore actively productive) site of consciousness and rather that subjectivity is the result of complex and interconnected social relations in which the media are one, and here the text/image engages with the discursive subject, and the state is another whereby the process of subjectification is the political citizen. We can add 'family, class, nation, ethnicity' (Hartley 1983), but the point is subjectivity is a result of a power struggle. In an individual's passive manifestation the media can dominate and in its resistive form the self confronts rather than consorts with power.

Foucault's (1981) 'The order of Discourse' is a discussion of truth but in conjunction with power, knowledge and discourse. The discussion is of exclusions, and in the first instance 'prohibitions' placed on subjects. This signifies discrepancies or inequalities in social life and restrictions on certain members of a community to have the preconceived knowledge to speak on equal terms with others, say from a privileged background, or one that is defined by class and power distinctions. The *economy of knowledge* reflects the source of information and its dependence upon it for knowledge. Quite evidently, relying solely on the media for information/knowledge has distinct disadvantages considering the amount of lies, distortions and selectivity in circulation, and thus effects the development of subjective culture. Just think of cartoon characters such as *Beavis and Butthead* and you get the picture. People do construct their view of the world through televisual imagery and text so the consequences for development of consciousness and knowledge are enormous.

Michèle Barrett (1991) provides an interesting account of the concept of truth, and discusses Foucault's third principle of the exclusions which are the 'will to know' and the 'will to truth'. As Barrett claimed:

It involved a shift from seeing truth as a given property of the discourse of those in power to seeing truth as a property of the referent of discourse (ibid., p. 142).

As Foucault asserts, discourse asks a specific question: 'how is it that one particular statement appeared rather than another' (ibid., p. 126). And what is said or acted upon may, as Said (1988) claimed, be bound by rules. Journalists, for example, work within ever changing parameters whereby determinant factors influence their daily productive activity. One glance at a number of British tabloids will indicate a desire to satisfy the commercial rules for market survival more based on the rules of deception and sensationalism than the truth. In this way news as a discourse is determined more by internal organisational logic than the pursuit of truth.

Teun A. van Dijk (1998) commenting in his book *Ideology a Multidisciplinary Approach* argues that although discourse is 'highly complex and ambiguous'(ibid., p. 195), nevertheless its 'primary meaning' (ibid., p. 193) is that in infers a 'specific communicative event'(ibid., p. 194). I do not intend to discuss in any great detail here the complexities of this argument suffice to say that in terms of deceptive methods used by the media in the dissemination of language and ideas it can only form *non-essential* information in the public realm and creates uncertainty, when uncovered as lies, about the validity of mass communication. News discourse is largely based upon the assumption that what is being communicated is honest and truthful. Discourse in this way is perceived in terms of trust and taken-for-granted assumptions in the message and it is difficult to see through it because of the imbalance in terms of power relations between text/image and reader. These are its social contexts and the act of communicating is not always based on the premise that this news account is lying to me.

The interest in truth, as Foucault notes in Kritzman (1988), was raised by Nietzche who deliberated on the status of truth in western systems and the 'value' it has to them. In journalistic terms the war correspondent William Howard Russell understood that even in special conditions, truth should be striven for. The Crimean War of 1854–56 resulted in Russell writing some damning accounts of the political and military leadership. Russell wrote to John Delane, the editor of *The*

Times, requesting advice of news gathering and reporting. Delane replied, 'Continue as you have done, tell the truth, and as much of it as you can' (in John Pilger, *Heroes*, 1989, p. 574).

Gordon *et al.* (1996) has posed truth-telling as a 'first principle'. This is where truth has primacy over all subsequent concepts in journalistic practices. Although Gordon does not pose truth as an ideal-type the inference is exactly that. The ideal-type becomes a standard or model to which we measure qualitatively. I suspect that the ideal-type is closely related to the 'correspondence theory' or 'common sense' theory of truth which would state that a statement is seen to be true if it directly and unequivocally corresponds to the facts. Thus conformity to the facts and agreement with reality. Whatever its weakness, this latter formulation would have strong resonances for news practices in terms of maintaining standards.

When Derrida's statement on truth includes 'rules of competence, criteria of discussion and of consensus, good faith, rigour, lucidity, criticism and pedagogy' (Norris 1991, p. 156) we can infer that 'rules of competence' for journalists promote quality of performance and good standards, 'rigour' is to strive *towards* objective reporting, and 'good faith' in rules promotes a certain degree of trust by the public towards news practices. For our purposes, the reason that some practitioners choose to fake and distort is a reflection of a corporate ideology that centres journalistic practices within the framework of commercialisation.

TRUST OR DEMOCRATIC ACCOUNTABILITY?

So far, we have discussed truth and the ethical consequences when we abandon it. The manipulation of information raises the issues of journalistic duties towards standards and ethical conduct. Maintaining whatever modicum of trust there may be in the public towards the media to deliver information depends on the pursuit of truth and not its systematic distortion for commercial and self-interested reasons to achieve status and symbolic power.

Learning to trust and investing in it begins at a very early age. Indeed, Erikson (1950) argued that it is during childhood that we begin this process of socialisation which is an investment in rules and trust in them and in those who determine them. The concept of trust is a heuristic device that can be applied to evaluate human relationships in most social settings. In part, learning to trust and indeed distrust become survival strategies throughout life.

The ideas expressed by Emile Durkheim concerning solidarity between individuals is one based on the notion of consensus of moral beliefs and social integration. The development of humanity depends on the development of trust relations. We can unite this with Simmel's idea of cultural development of humanity based on worthy knowledge, particularly if we consider Durkheim's thoughts on the conceptual distinction/opposition between 'ideology' and 'scientific knowledge'. In terms of media forms based on deception they are articulated as ideological because they prioritise the production of material (self-valorised) over facts. Identifying false statements is difficult and scientific knowledge requires 'Us' to have control over 'certainties'.

The essential point is that lies, in this context, are *negative ideologies* or *pejorative constructs* in that they distort information but somehow remain legitimate sources of information (as undetected forms) which are embedded as natural within social relations, that systematically corrupt a 'public interest' to be self-reflective and develop accordingly, plus the exclusion of true information from media discourse and the mystification of real relations.

The distortions in communications, the dubious practices that inhabit practitioners' daily productive activity help towards the construction of a polluted social environment. A contamination based on the production of deception and lies. The effect is that interpretation becomes problematic because the process of mediation is based upon the assumption or trust in truthful statements in which audiences premise information.

Luhmann's (1988) account of the modern world is that it is presented as an 'unmanageable complexity'. The media, by presenting and sorting-out (selection) vast amounts of information provides a sense of security. That realises itself in the construction of identities which is the result of the discursive and dialectical relationship with the media and *trust* in sense making. This making-sense of the complex world is disrupted when newspapers such as *The Guardian* reveal unethical practices in other forms of informational presentation but by the very same token is reconstituted by the very revelation. So revealing bad practices has dualistic and contradictory consequences. The whole process is a complex vacillation between trust and distrust. Identity, and here we recall Simmel's concern for the development of a subjective culture, is continually being reformulated and reconstituted.

Losing confidence in the media to provide reliable information results in an increase of uncertainty. It threatens the routine taken-for-granted norms – switching the TV on or reading newspapers without critically engaging with – which is a comforting and secure act. One may seek out alternative accounts of information. By doing so trust shifts and subsequently the *parameters of objectivity in reception* change. This relocation of trust in media practices constitutes a manoeuvrability within the self that extends *habitus* (see Bourdieu 1977, for a discussion on his concept of habitus).

Although Simmel and Bourdieu were writing in very different historical circumstances and this is partly reflected in a slightly different analysis. For Simmel, human creativity would be threatened with little or no room for escape, whereas for Bourdieu an individual's life disposition re-energises or redirects itself. The latter, therefore, does allow a degree of autonomy for subjective manouvrability, albeit, within dominant objective structures. My point is, however, that distrust in media practices may reveal itself as a form of resistance even though the 'immanent law of the structure' Bourdieu (1992) – curiously close to Simmel's 'immanent developmental logic' (stated earlier) internalises itself in the form of *habitus*.

Whatever the complexities over this argument, we return to the point of identity and cultural development and therefore the relationship with trust and its effects upon self-identity. We are then concerned with the quantitative shifts in amount and forms of distribution and qualitative changes or the validity of received knowledge and shifts in the standards of information that are being produced and consumed. As Giddens (1993) argued in terms of modernity as opposed to pre-modern, individuals construct their identities 'self-reflexively' because modern life lacks the guidance of traditional authorities (I argued earlier that even this process is under threat).

We can see that the media construct an environment which socially determine risks – here I consider risks to *essential knowledge* – and dangers that intensify the types of contamination indicative of modern culture in that 'we' tend to rely on autonomous organisations for truth statements.

Conversely, understanding the motives of practitioners to distort, misrepresent, deceive or fake is equally important. Bourdieu's (1977) theory of *habitus* goes someway to explain why individuals aspire towards certain goals according to their social circumstances. Different *habitus* inhabit different 'fields' of social life which are competitive systems for survival in the marketplace. The ultimate goal is dominance which in turn lends a degree of authority and legitimacy within working environments such as journalism/documentary film-making. How one strives for this does not necessarily depend upon ethical behaviour and duty to the truth but its desire, in socio-economic terms, seem greater than ethical considerations which ultimately result in corruptive forms of practices. For individuals to be successful they need to build up 'symbolic-capital' necessary for the dominance in their particular 'field' of work. Bourdieu conceptualises the above in terms of power, its attainment and its legitimate place in a dominant social order.

Undoubtedly, individual drive to compete successfully is part of a broad capitalist ideology for socially defining news practices? But so too is the production of trust relations with the type of information being relayed to its audience. If there is widespread manipulation of events, then supporters of this system may have to consider that not to manipulate is the negation of success in an intensely competitive field. Balancing the two poses something of an ethical dilemma for liberal perceptions of the media based on its concept of freedom to organise without external constraints.

State and legislative intervention in the freedom of the media and press is a position which, according to liberal thought, is contradictory. Preserving trust in the public's perception of the media ultimately leads us to the protection of certain rights, one of which is the right to receive information uncontaminated by commercial and corrupt practices. Consequently, the ethical dilemma for liberal theory is balancing between the two without state intervention.

In terms of public trust in the media, I argue that it is not simply a matter of trust in the media to deliver truthful statements, but equally a matter of trust in ethics as a pre-condition to professional work practices. In a society where power relations are structured, differentiated and hierarchically coupled with the notion of a ubiquitous media framing social life through modes of addressing, the reliance on trust in media practices (signifying discrepancies in terms of ownership and social status) or even the abandonment of it (signifying a partial re-empowerment expressed in forms of resistance), ethics, discussed here in terms of media standards, are both liberating and obstacles to the wider democratic ownership of the means of communications because it is assumed that trust in ethics by media practitioners in faithfully disseminating information obscures the real relations in which ownership and power (which incidentally sees information as a commodity for news organisations) are socially and unequally organised.

In terms of trusting and mistrusting we may inhabit contradictory subjective positions whereby their juxtaposing cause forms of anxiety. This type of social contradiction is eloquently illuminated by Bauman (1996) in his comparative and diametrically opposed discussion of Løgstrup who maintains that it is 'characteristic of human life that we mutually trust each other' and Shestov who holds that each of us is to be mistrusted and that only law can restrain the 'evil-minded' (ibid., p. 115).

Trust may work in a dialectical and symbiotic fashion between the producer of information and the consumer. The development of trust relations between the above goes some way to explaining the media's legitimisation and naturalisation within the consciousness of beings. But in terms of the examples that I have used quite evidently it is not enough simply to trust journalistic practices because they are subsumed within the commercial realm to pursue profit at any cost which dominates ethical conduct.

Trust (as well as truth) is also seen to have considerable 'value' in terms of western societies (Mitszal 1996) and as Bok (1980, pp. 26–27) argued that in general terms, 'When it (trust) is damaged the community as a whole suffers; and when it is destroyed, societies falter and collapse'. Luhmann (1979) perceived distrust as a 'destructive force' and both, therefore, alert us to the dangers and threat to the cohesion of society when trust is undermined. In general terms when we consider the collapse of the 'communist' states in the former USSR and central/eastern Europe, in part it was due to a complete lack of trust. Although here, I am concerned with a micro-analysis in terms of the media, nevertheless we can conceptualise it within the wider scene and a dialectic in terms of contradictions (antagonisms between different interests) and the new forms that emerge. The autonomy of the media (perceived as having its own logic) – in Simmel's language this would constitute a 'hostile autonomy' as opposed to unity or harmony – is however a part of a contradictory unity (Bonefeld *et al.* 1992), in terms of a need for cultural development as socially useful/necessary and a media institutions inherent drive for maximising profit. Both are 'extreme poles of a dialectical continuum' (Bonefeld 1992). The struggle for change results as a consequence of the opposition measured in terms of *difference* (see Negt and Kluge 1993 for a discussion on a proletarian public sphere).

The example that I have used are but one part of a social system. Indeed, Giddens (1976, 1979) 'Theory of Structuration' is an attempt to understand the relationship between structures and social activity. The 'Duality of Structure' perceived the object/subject relationship not in opposing terms but rather one which conditioned each other. In essence trust in media practices becomes a part of western ideological practices for maintaining an unequal relationship between owners/producers of information and consumers who invest in trust.

It seems to me that the problem with trust alone is that it invariably depends upon a high degree of respect and subjugation to authority which determines allegiances to the dominant norms and values of a social system which, during the process of socialisation, become naturalised within the self as common practice. Trust in media institutions and their contemporary practices may only produce uncritical beings in large sections of modern society. The type which Michel Foucault referred to as a 'docile body' subject to a greater 'disciplinary power' (1977).

In terms of Marxist political thought there is a *distrust* of the concept of trust based on social order, cohesion, integration. It is dismissed because Marx's concept of class is formulated in terms of antagonism between classes and high levels of exploitation.

Undoubtedly, in terms of media ownership and power, information becomes a commodity which has exchange-value in commercial terms which benefits the producers and does nothing for building trust which is, in my opinion, a method for legitimising the present functions of capital and, therefore, a mythologising process for sustaining inequalities in the ownership of the means of communication and therefore, to paraphrase Raymond Williams, the means of production.

Democratic accountability, in my opinion, is preferable to trust alone, based on what now appears to be false promises.

The technological means of promoting falsehoods are institutionalised within the self (practitioner) to the extent that they become unrecognisable. This familiarity of technology breeds an *indifference* to content, the consequences of which obliterate any meaning outside of itself. It quite literally becomes self-referential and self-perpetuating.

ON THE QUESTION OF CULTURAL DEVELOPMENT

We began this discussion with an account of Simmel's idea of the relationship between subjective culture and objective culture. The deliberate misleading or lying to the public has detrimental consequences not just for trust but for the development of a political community. In this view trust is perceived as a *cultural value*.

To this I ask (with Simmel in mind) what constitutes human goals? What are the requirements of democracy if not to provide information allowing that community to mature and so make informed decisions of the world around them. This is based on development of the mind in terms of a 'cultural approachment to objective forms' and therefore the necessary 'synthesis' *in* and *of* culture. In Simmel's (1998) essay 'The Crisis of Culture', he states that culture is:

the improvement of the soul which the latter attains from within . . . but indirectly, by way of intellectual achievement of the societies, the products of its history: knowledge, lifestyles. . . experience of life – these constitute the path of culture by which subjective spirit returns to itself in a higher, improved state (ibid., p. 91).

For Simmel the 'acquisition of culture', the self-improvement of individuals was under sustained attack by industries or for our purposes media organisations as they impose *their* content onto the rest of us:

they follow an immanent logic which is by no means always appropriate to the process of individual development and self-realisation, which is the whole point of all the products of culture as such (ibid).

Accordingly, we can use these insights to argue that the media 'are like kingdoms according to their own laws, but they demand that we should make them the content and norms of our own individual lives' (ibid., pp. 91–92). Simmel contests the idea that 'technological progress is unquestionably equated with cultural progress' (ibid., p. 92). But somehow we *trust* that it is, not only in terms of technology but in the safety of its content. Criticising the media for its failure to inform correctly and serve the interests for its maturation is nothing new. As far back as 1949 a report by The British Royal Commission on the Press argued that in general terms the press failed to inform the public of the necessary 'materials for sound judgement' (paragraph 572).

Any discourse of media ethics must recognise the shortcomings of trying to resolve the dilemmas between commercial interests and the public interest based on an informed political community mature enough to enter into a sphere of public debate, within the framework of monopoly capitalism, that neither considers the contextual framework nor is critical of those structures. It's all very well arguing that the way to re-ignite trust in the public towards the media is based on *them* telling the truth. As long as business and advertisers perceive the public as units of capital then that ideology will remain for the foreseeable future as the dominant pre-requisite to news as discourse. Schramm's theory on the press in western systems is partly built on the idea that, 'Our press tries to contribute to the search for the truth' (Siebert *et al.*, 1963, pp. 5–6), seems to be rather misguided, and note the emphasis on 'our' in the statement as if there were some sort of democratic ownership. This is, in part, what Simmel referred to as the 'Tragedy of Culture' and deceptive practices and consequences thereof, lack any valid contribution to cultural development in that knowledge promotes the 'cultivation of humanity'.

CONCLUSION

The real tragedy is that individuals lose the freedom of autonomy through rational choice because liars plus the media used for propaganda purposes, effectively dupe the consumer by disseminating either false or distorted/selected information. Faked programmes are but one small part of the larger scene where information has no objective other than the *perpetuity of the message* for its own sake. An ethics that situates 'cultural development' as central to a 'public interest' which does not debase culture, demands a set of responsibilities both of the object and subject. This is a refutation of Foucault's *ethics of the self*, a self-referential moral identity that does not consider exogenous factors that define the boundaries of self-survival in an otherwise hostile social and political environment.

Media ethics, constructed dialectically, requires an understanding of the relationship of 'power' and 'practices' that is differentiated and complex, that connects the media with its audience and constructs ethical identity. The media viewed this way is distinct from scientific notions of rationalisation, which for Habermas brings 'freedom', whereas for Foucault, individuals are subsumed within disciplinary regimes. Oddly, there is some truth in either of these positions, and those whose lives may be bound and defined by their intense relationship with the media (measured in degrees of trust and truth in the media and its practices) are restricted in terms of freedom, an *imprisoned-self* with restricted subjective moral development. Once a totality or unity of objects/subject is accepted it becomes a collective duty to address the unequal distribution of knowledge to determine a more equitable subjective awareness which is the realisation of cultural development. A media ethics is not solely regulation of the object then, but equally a self-realisation or the *awakening* of a subjective regulation and adjustment, and one that recognises external power and control.

Unethical journalistic practice is a by-product of current social conditions, and the 'public interest', measured here in terms of trust and cultural development, is marginalised in terms of importance. In many ways Pilger's (1998) 'vigilant journalism' is a dual process of reawakening journalistic duties to the truth and consequently, public perception.

In a society that lacks an 'oral culture',[5] unlike Spain or Portugal for example, the UK, with approximately 40 per cent of the population reading newspapers and around 98 per cent television owners, relies heavily upon the press and broadcast media for information, and therefore the moral responsibilities in terms of duties performed by the media to the public are greater. Both the 'use-value' and 'exchange-value' vary accordingly.

The media, in part, are perceived by the public as a transcending force of reality from source to consumption – and indeed perception is intrinsic to the logic of the media and internalised accordingly as a regulatory force. These qualities are erased and challenged when it emerges that manipulation either from source or in the editing/cutting room, occurs. The value therefore of mediation becomes a negative rather than a positive one and technology is the means and extension of human deception. Such *cyborg-type* constructs – integration of human and machine in its negative deceptive form – is one in which the meaning or value of truth and/or the concept of a socially useful technology as a means to greater knowledge evaporates into thin air.

This is its 'disjunctive' state between viewer and viewed, a separation of the objective (vision in terms of capital) and subjective culture (expansion of language and knowledge). After all, if culture is to mean anything it is the nurturing, growth and expansion of ideas in social life for humanity, and the public may have to review the amount of trust and time spent in consuming media for subjective and collective cultural development. If it is true that the maintenance of trust is dependent on, and/or subordinate to media practices then the prospect for enlightenment is bleak.

Furthermore, 'autonomous disciplines', such as journalism or documentary as distinctive fields of operation and practices, become synonymous with providing truthful accounts, but I have argued that it's not possible because of the *separation* between object and subject. What I have argued is for a unity between object and subject, and as Lukács (1971), had argued, that society was fragmented into specialised regions and commodities pervade every aspect of capitalist life, whose autonomy threatens cultural development and dehumanises it in the process. I have argued, using Simmel, that the media industries practice according to their own logic and news is a commodity, which provides us with some understanding why programmes are faked because of the logic of the free market and competition.

Indeed, we may argue that 'documentaries' which choose to fake events are not documentaries at all in the strict sense of the word, but are rather crude and contrived forms. If the distinction that separates documentary from other forms or genres is broken then we may infer that there is no such form as documentary in practical terms, but only as an ideal-type with no relationship to the real world it claims to capture.

POSTSCRIPT

At the time of writing the *Daily Mirror* (12 February 1999) revealed the 'Scandal of the fake chat shows' which cited the *Vanessa Show* using deceptive methods. All this and the faked Channel 4's *Daddy's Girl, Rogue Males* and ITV's *Tale of the Tides* where it was discovered that tame rather than wild animals were used.

Also, Channel 4 had screened a faked documentary called *Too Much Too Young: Chickens*, whereby members of the production team posed as clients to expose a scandal involving rent boys. Marine Devine, the programme producer, has been banned from working for the channel, and their director of programmes made this statement:

Our procedures are robust, but no procedures are proof against deliberate and organised deception (The Independent, Friday 5 February 1999).

According to *The Independent*, Channel 4 'is planning a series of seminars for producers and directors in which it will remind them of their ethical and regulatory responsibilities', and finally in *The Guardian*, Tuesday 23 March 1999, nearly a year from the revelations regarding Carlton's 'Connection', a headline announced: 'Channel 4 in new documentary fake row' and led by stating:

A Channel 4 documentary (Guns On The Street, March 1996) that purported to investigate how Manchester's gangsters got hold of illegal guns and which resulted in the imprisonment of a man for seven years was faked in key parts . . . .

ENDNOTES

1. Considering that levels of faked programmes plus deceptive practices in the press which complaints to both PressWise and the Press Complaints Commission seem to indicate, we then become concerned about the *effects* on culture and human development.
2. The National Union of Journalists Code. It was founded in 1936. Clause 1 states 'A journalist has a duty to maintain the highest professional ethical standards'. A duty presumes a moral obligation

beyond the self-interest of a practitioner. Self-interest may involve lying or other forms of deception. The Press Complaints Commission is seen as the industry regulator. The creation of the PCC was one of the recommendations of the Calcutt Report in June 1990. Its weakness lies in the fact that it is controlled by members of the industry which are the people it seeks to regulate.

3. The minimum punishment the ITC could administer is to insist on an apology and a correction to the faked programme or it could impose a fine or even reduce the licence period. The issue we need to ask is whether it should be free to go further and stop those responsible from further practice? In doing so it would in effect produce a blacklist based on unethical practice.

4. *The Guardian*, Tuesday 7 July 1998, revealed that the *Daily Mail* was responsible for deceiving the public when it offered a 'Dream Cottage Beside The Sea' in a competition primarily to boost circulation, when in fact the cottage was perilously close to the sea and had experienced flooding on a number of occasions.

5. See Raymond Williams (1961) *The Long Revolution*, London: Chatto and Windus, for a discussion of an active oral culture in Britain during the early to mid-20th century. Its subsequent breakdown was due in part to the dominance of a mass media.

REFERENCES

Adorno, T. and Horkheimer, M. (1990) *Dialectics of Enlightenment*, London: Verso.

Barrett, M. (1991) *The Politics of Truth: from Marx to Foucault*, Cambridge: Polity Press.

Bauman, Z. (1996) *Postmodern Ethics*, Oxford: Blackwell.

Black, J., Steele, B. and Barney, R. (1995) *Doing Ethics in Journalism – a Handbook with Case Studies*, 2nd edn. Needham Heights, MA: Allyn & Bacon.

Bok, S. (1980) *Lying: Moral Choice in Public and Private Life*, London: Quartet.

Bonefeld, W., Gunn, R., and Kosmas Psychopedis (1992) *Open Marxism: Volume 1, 'Dialectics and History'*, London: Pluto Press.

Bourdieu, P. (1977) *Outline of a Theory of Practice*, trans. R. Nice), Cambridge: Cambridge University Press.

Bourdieu, P. (1980) 'The Aristocracy of Culture', *Media, Culture and Society*, **2**, 225–54.

Bourdieu, P. (1992) *Language and Symbolic Power*, edited by J.B. Thompson, trans. G. Raymond and M. Adamson, Cambridge: Polity Press.

Dijk, Teun A. van (1998) *Ideology, a Multidisciplinary Approach*, London: Sage.

Erikson, E. (1950) *Childhood and Society*, New York: Norton.

Foucault, M. (1977) *Discipline and Punish: The Birth of the Prison*, trans. of *Surveiller at punir* (1975) by A. M. Sheridan-Smith, Harmondsworth: Penguin.

Foucault, M. (1981) 'The Order of Discourse', trans. I. McLeod, in *Untying the Text*, R. Young, ed., London: Routledge.

Giddens, A. (1976) *New Rules of Sociological Analysis: A Positive Critique of Interpretative Sociologies*, London: Hutchinson.

Giddens, A. (1979) *Central Problems in Social Theory: Action, Structure, and Contradiction in Social Analysis*, London: Macmillan.

Giddens, A. (1993) *Modernity And Self-Identity: Self and Society in Late Modern Age*, Oxford: Blackwell.

Gordon, A.D., Kittross, J.M., Reuss, C. and Merrill, J.C. (1996) *Controversies in Media Ethics*, New York: Longman.

Habermas, J. (1989) *The Structural Transformation of the Public Sphere*, Cambridge: Polity Press.

Hartley, J. (1983) 'Television and the Power of Dirt', in *Australian Journal of Cultural Studies*, **1**(2), 62–82.

Harris, Nigel G.E. (1992) 'Codes of conduct for journalists', in *Ethical Issues in Journalism and the Media*, A. Belsey and R. Chadwick eds, London: Routledge.

Kritzman, L. (1988) *Michel Foucault: Politics, Philosophy, Culture*, London: Routledge.

Luhmann, N. (1979) *Trust and Power*, Chichester: Wiley.

Luhmann, N. (1988) 'Familiarity, confidence, trust: problems and alternatives', in *Trust: Making and Breaking Cooperative Relations*, D. Ganbetta ed., Oxford: Basil Blackwell.

Lukács, G. (1971) *History and Class Consciousness: Studies in Marxist Dialectics*, trans. R. Livingstone, MA: MIT Press.

McNay, L. (1994) *Foucault: A Critical Introduction*, Cambridge: Polity Press.

Mill, J.S. (1989) *On Liberty and other writings*, S. Collini ed., Cambridge University Press.

Mitszal, B.A. (1996) *Trust in Modern Societies*, Polity Press: Cambridge.

Negt, O. and Kluge, A. (1993) *Public Sphere and Experience: Toward an Analysis of the Bourgeois and Proletarian Public Sphere*, trans. P. Labanyi, J.O. Daniel and A. Oksiloff. University of Minnesota Press.

Norris, C. (1991) *Deconstruction: Theory and Practice*, 2nd edn, London: Routledge.

Parsons, T. (1991) *The Social System*, new edn, London: Routledge.

Pecheux, M. (1982) 'Les Verites de la Palice', in *Language, Semantics and Ideology: Stating the Obvious*, trans. II. Nagpul, London: Macmillan.

Pilger, J. (1989) *Heroes*, London: Pan.

Pilger, J. (1998) *Hidden Agendas*, London: Vintage.

Royal Commission on the Press 1947–1949 Report (1949) Cmnd 7700. London. HMSO.

Said, E. (1988) 'Michel Foucault, 1926–1984', in *After Foucault*, J. Arac ed., New Brunswick: Rutgers University Press.

Simmel, G. (1998) 'Tragedy of Culture', in *Simmel on Culture: Selected Writings*, D. Frisby and M. Featherstone, eds, London: Sage.

Simmel, G. (1998) 'Crisis and Culture', in *Simmel on Culture: Selected Writings*, D. Frisby and M. Featherstone, eds, London: Sage.

Simmel, G. (1998) 'Crisis and Modern Culture', in *Simmel on Culture: Selected Writings*, D. Frisby, and M. Featherstone, eds, London: Sage.

The Daily Mirror, 12 February 1999.

The Guardian, Wednesday 6 May 1998.

The Guardian, Friday 8 May 1998.

The Guardian, Tuesday 9 June 1998.

The Guardian, Tuesday 23 March 1999.

The Independent on Sunday, 5 July 1998.

The Independent, Friday 5 February 1999.

The Sunday Times, 20 June 1998.

3 Enframing/revealing: on the question of ethics and difference in technologies of mediation

Joost van Loon

Only when man, in the disclosing coming-to-pass of the insight by which he himself is beheld, renounces human self-will and projects himself toward that insight, away from himself, does he correspond in this essence to the claim of that insight. In thus corresponding man is gathered into his own, that he, within that safeguarded element of the world, may, as the mortal, look out toward the divine (Heidegger 1977, p. 47).

In the introduction to the edited collection *Media Ethics*, Matthew Kieran (1998) declares that only philosophy is able to reveal an understanding of the ethical and moral issues of media-practices. In good Kantian fashion, he claims that social consensus about moral issues cannot provide us with a definitive judgement on the rights and wrongs of particular acts, as 'people's preferences and moral judgements can be mistaken' (1998, p. xi). In doing this, he places his philosophy on a different, indeed higher, level of knowledge than common sense. Philosophy provides a basis for judgement that is not corrupted by the despotism of the collective will. It provides a different type of 'grounding' of judgements, Kieran implies, one that is more fundamental. In other words, whilst seeking a higher plane of knowledge, moral philosophy finds itself in the metaphorical 'dirt' of fundamental 'ground work'.

Clearly, in the face of 'tabloid journalism' and a more general tendency of broadcasting media to mix information with entertainment, to a degree that very recently a documentary and two talk-shows in the UK have been 'exposed' as having planted 'actors', there is cause for concern over the ethical implications of all media-practices. How such a concern should be 'addressed', however, is a more difficult issue. The question whether 'ethics' are a matter of democratic debate or involve a more fundamental and even universal set of principles is one that is as old as philosophy itself. Of course, there is nothing inherently ethical in any collective will that asserts itself simply as the force of the greater number. Indeed, there is nothing inherently ethical about consensus either. However, to turn this around and claim that ethics can therefore only be grounded in logic or rule-bound normativity over which the philosopher-king presides, is likewise suspect. Such moral philosophy sets itself up as the Law, from which universal rules can be deduced. The application of these rules, however, remains to be enforced. This enforcement can only entail violence, and hence, a violation of the Law, for there is no rule that engages in determining the rule of its own application. Out of logical necessity, this rule of application remains exterior to it. Hence, the imperatives that journalists *should* be objective, impartial, strive towards balanced accounts as well as 'uncovering' the truth and serve the public interest, are all assertions of a moral philosophy that transforms a specific set of rules, media ethics, into universal Law which only becomes effective when reinforced via discipline and punishment.

When the question of the legitimacy of such reinforcement is raised, it becomes obvious that we cannot avoid 'the state'. It is the state which is granted the responsibility of enforcing media-ethics in modern western societies. The state is that strange hybrid of paternalistic care and collective will; both are gathered under the banner of the public interest. Paternalistic care functions as a safeguard of the public interest against the public's own myopic self-destructive tendencies. As Gramsci (1971) noted, the state takes care of the longer-term well-being of society, and in particular the ruling classes who are often blinded by short-term interests.

Needless to say, the moral philosophy that Kieran advocates is on the side of these long-term interests. It also speaks on behalf of a sovereign Law against the collective will. However, as a consequence, it speaks on behalf of the existing order. In other words, although suspicious of common-sense as the expression of a collective will, Kieran's moral philosophy does speak on behalf of another 'common sense' namely that of a paternalistic elite who are granted the moral responsibility of defending the long-term stability of the state itself.

Consequently, what Kieran seeks to avoid, a media-ethics derived from common-sense, is exactly reproduced by moral philosophy; the only difference being that the collective sense that underscores the 'common' is limited to that of an elite – philosophers. Indeed, most contributions to the aforementioned volume on media-ethics argue that moral philosophy is often indiscernible from an ongoing declaration of opinions. What is striking is that such opinions, for example that good journalism is that which serves the public interest, remain rather implicit. Indeed, this type of moral philosophy appeals to a particular common-sense in order to justify its opinions as being derived from a universal moral perspective. It shows that at the 'bottom line' of any moral–philosophical argument, every expression of universal Law is actually an expression of a *particular* collective will (Lyotard 1988).

It is no surprise that moral philosophy and common-sense find themselves in discussions over media-ethics on modern, western, society. Western philosophy has been marked for almost two centuries now by the philosophies of Kant and Hegel who both attempted to integrate 'morality' and 'collective will' within a secular philosophical framework. The binding force of this framework was to be provided by 'reason' as opposed to 'rhetoric, prejudice and emotional responses'. Indeed, the subsequent history of modern thought after Kant and Hegel shows that it has proved to be a difficult task to find an ethics without God. However, whenever the philosophers thought they found a universal rule, they ended up having asserted a particular value (Vattimo 1988). It is therefore not surprising that an increasing number of thinkers, inside and outside philosophy, have begun to question the viability of a universal ethics based on (human/secular) reason. Phenomenology, hermeneutics and later poststructuralism, postmodernism and feminism all provided powerful philosophical antidotes against rational moral philosophy. All these approaches are characterised by a desire to steer clear of the pitfalls of asserting universal ethics under the terror of the republic and engaging in the rule of the lynch-mob under democratic despotism. Neither the Law nor the collectivised will are adequate engagements of ethical issues because they both seek to suspend thinking and assert their imperatives as being beyond doubt.

In this chapter, I shall address one possible way of rethinking ethics, and more specifically media-ethics. The aim is to radically engage the issue of ethics in relation to a more phenomenological understanding of media that foregrounds it as a 'technology'. From the philosophy of Martin Heidegger (1977) we can learn that modern technology is a challenging-revealing that turns 'Nature' into a standing reserve. For Heidegger, the essence of technology is revealing. If we link this to Marshall McLuhan's (1964) famous aphorism that media are extensions of human faculties, we can develop a sense of technology as mediation. Technologies of mediation reveal and enframe the world. To put it more specifically, they engender particular modalities of understanding our being-in-the-world.

This seems an obvious if not superfluous point to make. Perhaps so obvious that it generally passes unnoticed in contemporary media-studies. As, for example, debates over media-violence have shown, students of media are often more concerned with assessing the degrees in which enframing and revealing are 'fixed' by media, which are simultaneously and all too quickly posed as negative correlates to the degrees of autonomy of interpretation, consumption and reception of messages by audiences (Abercrombie *et al.* 1990).

However, when the issue of media-ethics is raised, the dichotomy between fixation and autonomy seems unintelligible without a thorough understanding of the mediation-process itself. For what are these 'ethics' to be about if not about enframing and revealing? Even the most ardent defender of autonomous (or 'active') audiences cannot assume that media do not enframe and reveal. Even when we would consider an ethics of reception, or interpretation, and call this 'hermeneutics', we would still have to return to the question of mediation, since we would still have to engage with that which is being interpreted. A quick glance at the practices and routines (Cottle 1993; Hall *et al.* 1978; K. Thompson 1998) of news-production reveals that media-ethics is essentially concerned with everyday processes of mediation. Mediation involves a series of 'negotiations' and 'selections' – of what is being gathered, who is to be contacted, what angles and spins are to be produced, what texts, sound and image-bytes are to be part of the 'item' and in what order they are to be presented. The logic of the institution, which is based on the production and dissemination of news, is operationalized in a complex set of criteria and 'rules of thumb'. These involve financial as well as political considerations which place large constraints on ethical and aesthetic ones (J.B. Thompson, 1995). Such constraints are an essential part of the dynamics of enframing/revealing.

After all, media-ethics is concerned with the way in which 'sense' is being 'made'. This sense-making is organised and structured by what one, following Latour (1987), may call 'actor networks', which include 'human beings', 'technologies' and 'spirits'. In media-studies, one would be more inclined to refer to media-corporations, organisations and professions, but also to technologies as well as discourses. However, rather than adjudicating between 'good' and 'bad' sense, which is something that dominated critical media-studies for decades but has become less fashionable recently, I want to direct the issue of ethics to good versus bad sense-*making*. More precisely, the issue of ethics is about cultivating sensibilities in technologies of mediation which allow for modes of revealing and enframing that enhance our ability to be responsive. In other words, the imperative of mediation is the ability to affect and be affected. Although this does not *necessarily* contravene with the logic of the media-institution to (a) make profits (commercial media) and (b) socialise 'the nation' (public media), *affect* entails a rather different type of responsiveness than *effect*. Whereas affect entails a process of transformation through interaction; effect merely suggests an instrumental and quantifiable result. Given the economic and political constraints that make up the mediation-process, we should not be surprised that far from enhancing our ability to be responsive, the media have predominantly worked towards increasing the *effect* of advertising, marketing, spinning and manipulating. Infotainment, the mixture of information and entertainment, is a particular form of enframing that reveals particular knowledge in a closed and self-evident manner. There is no responsiveness required to such mediation apart from 'consuming or not consuming'.

In this chapter I want to address the question of how to cultivate an ethical sensibility in technologies of mediation. This ethical sensibility is of course embedded in working practices, organisational processes, relations of ownership and control, and the manipulation, regulation and management of flows of information and finance (Dahlgren 1995; J.B. Thompson 1995). However, the starting point is the technology itself for without an understanding of the way in which technologies imply their own normativity, our engagement with media-ethics remains trapped between the humanist-legislative ethos of universal law and the democratic ethos of *sensis communis*. I argue therefore that enframing/revealing is the essence of technologies of mediation. After discussing Heidegger's and McLuhan's concepts of technology, I will invoke some ideas offered by Jacques Derrida on différance as a particularly effective way of understanding mediation. Finally, I introduce the notion of 'ethics' into the discussion by engaging with Derrida's work *Given Time*. This will show that for Derrida, the question of ethics is fundamentally engaged with a deconstruction of the opposition between the substantial and the procedural, and hence between the communitarian privileging of the *sensus communis* (e.g. the dictatorship of a proletariat, democratic despotism – or the rule of the lynch mob) and the universalist ethics of procedural rationality and communicative action (the terror of the sublime). Derrida, like Lyotard (1988) and Deleuze and Guattari (1988), produces a rather different model of ethics, one that is neither particularist nor generalist, but one that is responsive to difference – heteronomy.

UNDERSTANDING MEDIA TECHNOLOGIES

What has the essence of technology to do with revealing? The answer: everything. For every bringing-forth is grounded in revealing (. . .). The possibility of all productive manufacturing lies in revealing. Technology is therefore no mere means. Technology is a way of revealing (Heidegger 1977, p. 12).

For Heidegger, technology is not a tool, or a piece of equipment, but a way of presencing, or enpresenting. This enpresenting is first of all, a form of 'showing' or 'making visible'. Heidegger uses the term *Entbergen* (revealing) to argue that the essence of technology is a bringing-forth (*poiesis*) of that which is hidden; that is, technology brings concealment forth into unconcealment. Technology is derived from two Greek words: *Techne* and *Logos*. In ancient Greece, the word *Techne* was used in two ways: (1) as designating the activities and skills of craftsmen and artisans (here techne is linked to *poiesis* (creation); (2) as linked with the word *episteme*, referring to 'knowing' in the widest sense. It was Aristotle who enforced a distinction between *techne* and *episteme*. *Techne* is that which brings forth anything that cannot bring forth itself. *Episteme*, instead, is used in a way far closer to *logos*, as forms of abstract knowledge, ideas that are ruled by logic, language and law, that stem from the world of abstract ideas, that is, pure knowledge.

59

Heidegger argues that in modernity, technology has intensified its essence of revealing to a degree that its instrumentality has reversed its relationship with natural resources so that it the revealing becomes as challenging (*Herausfordern* – also extracting or provoking). Nature thereby becomes a standing-reserve for technology. For example, whereas agriculture used to be taking place in a relationship of care/concern with the soil (cultivation as concern), it is now a mechanised food industry. Technology as expedition has thus become an unlocking and an exposure. Nature is predisposed – ready to hand – at our command.

Unlocking, transforming, storing, distributing and switching about are ways of revealing. But the revealing never simply comes to an end. Neither does it run off into the indeterminate. The revealing reveals to itself its own manifold interlocking paths, through regulating their course. This regulating itself is, for its part, everywhere secured. Regulating and securing become the chief characteristics of the challenging revealing (Heidegger 1977, p. 16).

In other words, modern technology shows that revealing is also a way of ordering. By setting upon an object, technology places it within its own course of action. In other words, technology 'enframes' the world. It does so not by simply placing it within a framework (that is, similar to putting a frame around a painting), but by assembling, calling forth, ordering for use. 'Enframing means that the way of revealing which holds sway in the essence of technology and which is itself nothing technological' (Heidegger 1977, p. 20). In order to avoid the all-too-seductive association between enframing and an imposed structure, it is important to always connect it with revealing. In a way, the double sense in which the verb 'to order' could refer to either 'to put in place' and 'to command' may work as a reminder that every form of enframing, or indeed of 'fixing' (including fixations), are more than an instrumental activity that man imposes upon his world. Whereas we are initiated first by the instrumentality of technology, its toolness, it is the essence of technology (enframing/revealing) which is concealed to the last. In this way, Heidegger speaks about enframing as a form of destining. What is being revealed therefore is an engagement of the future into the present. The future, the unknown, is destined by enframing/revealing as the danger – that which must be revealed. The danger of enframing is that in the unconcealment of that which it brings-forth, it conceals revealing itself (ibid., p. 27).

The Italian philosopher, Gianni Vattimo (1992), has taken up this notion of technology as unconcealment with reference to the newly emerging information and communication. Vattimo argues that the new ICTs have intensified the challenging-revealing of modern technology in terms of a rendering-visible. However, far from bringing greater insight into the order of things, such technologies have had the paradoxical effect of engendering the erosion of the principle of reality (hyperreality). They imply the reduction of the world to images. Essential to the image, however, is, as Barthes (1977) noted, its reduction of history to the level of simultaneity. This has profoundly disturbing effects on the very epistemic formation of modern thought, which is, as we know, based on the principle of causality. It has led to 'a kind of entropy linked to the very proliferation of the centres of history, that is, of the places where information is gathered, unified and transmitted' (Vattimo 1992, p. 22). The singularity of perspective, which was enframed by modern technology and constitutive of the humanist ideal of self-transparency, is shattered by the visual cultures of the new ICTs.

Instead of moving towards self-transparency, the society of the human sciences and generalized communication has moved towards what could, in general, be called the 'fabling of the world'. The images of the world we receive from the media and the human sciences, albeit on different levels, are not simply different interpretations of a 'reality' that is 'given' regardless, but rather constitute the very objectivity of the world (ibid, pp. 24–25).

If we turn to Marshall McLuhan we can see that, albeit in a completely different ethos, the notion of enframing/revealing returns in a highly prophetic visionary account of media-technologies. Vattimo's observation that new information and communication technologies have engendered a more radical relativism, or perhaps more accurately, an entropy of perspectives, are indeed rather close to McLuhan's famous assertion that 'the medium is the message'. Perhaps it is only after the arrival of the Internet that McLuhan's prophecy has become a matter of fact rather than futurist speculation.

However, it is not the newness of digital information-processing or telecommunications as such that has produced such radical challenges to existing social forms. Instead it is their rapidly accelerating degrees of inter-connectedness, or assemblage. Assemblage is a term coined by Deleuze and Guattari (1988) to refer to the specific ways in which forces are being combined, and which have as an effect the transformation of matter into particular (energy-) flows. Media-technologies constitute an assemblage because they are 'extensions of human functions'; these human – embodied – functions are the connecting interface between media and social forms. Media are indeed '*extensions of "man"*' (the subtitle of McLuhan's (1964) famously acclaimed *Understanding Media*). Although he did not use the notion of cyborg, McLuhan's concept of what could be called 'agency' was certainly 'prosthetic', as for him, there was no fundamental ontological difference between human and non-human forms of being-in-the-world.

Assemblage refers to a coming together of technologies, of particular forces and their effects, that have no reference outside themselves. This self-referentiality simply means that whatever the forms of content that these media entail; they have no 'purport' outside the forms in which they are being cast. For example, in the videotaped beating of Rodney King it is quite clear that what the case was actually about was not the beating as such but its meaning in the light of the videotape which allegedly captured it. Without the tape, there would never have been a case to begin with (Butler 1993; Fiske 1994; Thompson, 1995; Van Loon 1999).

Characteristic of the media-assemblage is that its horizons of meaning are always already informed by media. The idea of media referring to other media, however, does not mean that this 'dealing' is always literal or explicit; say for example a television programme about television. Instead it means that there is no ontological difference between the making of a television programme and that to which it refers. With his famous statement 'the medium is the message', McLuhan envisaged a world in which the content of a medium was always another medium, hence obliterating the notions of 'pure' form and 'pure' content.[1]

[T]he personal and social consequences of every medium – that is of the extension of ourselves – result from the new scale that is introduced into our affairs by each extension of ourselves, or by any new technology (McLuhan 1964, p. 23).

Whenever the alliance between medium and mediator is complete, the difference ceases to be noticed, and the medium seems to become void of any content. In this sense, mediators (human beings for example) become 'numb' to the technology that extends a particular function. This numbness, caused by the self-referentiality of the medium, engendered a particular form of narcosis for which McLuhan (ibid, pp. 51–56) used the term 'narcissistic' – embroiled in love of and for a self that is mistaken for another.[2] It is the mistaking of the self for another that causes the numbing trap of self-referentiality. Hence not a case of auto-eroticism but of auto-amputation; one is no longer capable of recognising the self as self.

Prosthetic numbness is a common feeling for those whose bodies have been supplemented by prostheses; we forget that we wear glasses (spectacles) or contact lenses perhaps as easily as we can be drawn into a movie on a big screen. When driving a car, it is necessary to become one with the machine, for most responses require embodied reflexivity, that is, instantaneous reaction without mediation by cognition, a know-how-without-knowing ('know' how to brake, change gear, use indicators, use mirrors).[3]

It would be mistaken, however, to suggest that we can simply extend this notion of prosthetic numbness to the relationship between mediator and media-technology on an institutional level. Mediators are working in complex environments which are riddled with conflicts and tensions and struggles over scarce resources and discursive positions. Most journalists and editors are fully aware of institutional power and how it structures the logic of news broadcasting. The prosthetic numbness, however, operates on a different level: not that of political consciousness but of practical routines. It is a necessary process of incorporation of some rules, be it the professional rules of telling the truth (see for example, John Pilger's *Distant Voices*) or simply the corporate rules of 'entertaining the audience'. Prosthetic numbness is required for 'doing the job well', that is, being able to work effectively and efficiently within the tight temporal, financial, legal and political-discursive frameworks of media-institutions.

DANGERS AND SAVING POWERS

From the notion of media-assemblage one might get the impression that the connectivities are always smooth and operationally functional, for example, the case with the telephone–computers–cable-television assemblage. However, such smoothness is not immanent to media as their compatibility is never to be taken for granted. For example, hot and cold media might balance each other, but they might also constitute a far more explosive mix, or media-hybrid.

Various authors have written about the beating of Rodney King and its consequences and argued that the sudden eruption of the 1992 Los Angeles riots after the verdict was not as 'surprising' as was often suggested. The specific usage of the video recording in court, which was subsequently transformed into a series of photographic still frames for the purpose of legal deliberation, generated a violently explosive hybrid form, which could already be anticipated well before the trial came to its tragic conclusion, as Black communities in South Central were expecting the not-guilty outcome. After all, as Gooding-Williams (1993) and others have shown, an outcome such as this is fairly regular. What made this case specific, however, was the presence of the video recording, which functioned as an anomaly in the media-ensemble of police brutality (. . . + cars + weapons + bodies + training + rules and procedures + helicopter + spotlights + . . .) that was displayed during the beating itself (Van Loon 1999; Fiske 1994; Thompson 1995).

This resonates Marshall McLuhan's enormously insightful comment that media-hybridisation is a release of energy in new forms:

The hybrid of the meeting of two media is a moment of truth and revelation from which new form is born. For the parallel between two media holds us on the frontiers between forms that snap us out of the Narcissus-narcosis. The moment of the meeting of media is a moment of freedom and release from the ordinary trance and numbness imposed by them on our senses (McLuhan 1964, p. 63).

This release of energy took the form of violence in the 1992 Los Angeles 'riots', but also in the subsequent actions taken by civil rights organisations, political movements, justice departments, governmental agencies and even the police force itself. Moreover, these effects were not limited to the United States but had a global impact, as the LA 'riots' became a world-widely used icon for race-relations in the western world, as well as for the explosiveness of social injustice as a threat simmering below the smooth surface of global capitalism. In any case, such global impact would have been unthinkable without instantaneous news coverage through satellite television.

In other words, new media, and in particular new media-hybrids, allow us to 'open up' to our being-in-the-world a revelation via shock-therapy, as it were. However, and in contrast to some commentators who saw in McLuhan an ardent optimist and technological determinist, he did put forward some reservations about human being's capacity to take on the revealing challenges of new, hybrid, media technologies:

As long as we adopt the Narcissus attitude of regarding the extensions of our own bodies as really out there *and really independent of us, we will meet all technological challenges with the same sort of banana-skin pirouette and collapse* (ibid., p. 73).

In other words, the assemblage of media-technologies may be seen as an opening up of an event, a possibility for intervention, a revealing whose course may be enframed as 'destined' towards a particular unfolding, but such destining is only 'determined' if accompanied by a narcissus narcosis of prosthetic numbness. This understanding of media-technologies accomplishes two important interventions into modern thought and its rather suspect dualistic politics of philosophical fundamentalism. First, the enframing/revealing model radically evacuates the implicit anthropocentric understanding of being-in-the-world and its historical unfolding. Secondly, it breaks with the tradition that reason is destined towards the *necessary* attunement of truth and justice. 'Progress' has marked not the increased autonomy of the human, but instead has been the unfolding of an increased self-enclosure of technology, turning everything into a standing reserve, including itself. This seems to resonate a particular anti-technological romanticism which appropriates the same technological determinism as the technocrats it despises. Certainly, Heidegger's pessimistic writings in particular are often seen as leaning towards technological determinism and an almost mystical romanticism. However, this is not a necessary ethos in which enframing/revealing needs to be cast. McLuhan's notion of hybrid energy also reveals a sensibility towards possibilities for radical intervention – a turning against the narcissus narcosis. And indeed, Heidegger himself wrote '[a]nd yet – in all the disguising belong to Enframing, the bright-open space of the world lights up, the truth of Being flashes. And the instant, that is, when Enframing lights up, in its coming to presence, as the danger, i.e., as the saving power' (1977, p. 47).

The question now becomes how to 'seize' the moment of this flash of light, this opening up, this release of hybrid energy; this, for me, is the essential question of media-ethics. It is the way in which we may encounter the enframing/revealing of media-technologies in a turning of its destining. One crucial problem with this question is that neither McLuhan nor Heidegger have been effective in providing a philosophy of ethics. For Heidegger's inherently pessimistic ontic philosophy, the most 'ethical' engagement of the philosopher would be an anticipation of an epochal shift, as only the gods could save us. His later works do have a more religious than phenomenological ambience but fail to articulate what enables such anticipation except 'reading well', that is, 'understanding Being'. McLuhan was even less concerned with ethics. Although in many ways one can detect resonances of modernist emancipatory tendencies, these were certainly not humanist. His orientation towards 'Being' was inherently overcoded by a futurism in promises of a better life and were still not corrupted by the technological tendency towards enclosure.

Hence, in order to turn towards the question of media-ethics, we must look elsewhere. It is in the work of Jacques Derrida that an ethical moment can be traced that is compatible with the understanding of media-technologies as enframing/revealing and which does not resort to either the democratic despotism of the lynch-mob or the terror of the sublime of the benign sovereign.

DIFFÉRANCE AND MEDIATION

One of the key concerns in Derrida's earlier works has been what he refers to as 'the metaphysics of presence'. The metaphysics of presence refers to the conflation of 'truth' to that which takes place in 'the present' through transcendental 'knowing'. It appears in many forms, for example, in the realist fallacy of a correspondence between reason and necessary cause, or in the constructionist fallacy of a correspondence between reality and representation; and it underscores a range of 'mentalist' notions such as 'cognition', 'consciousness' and 'intentionality'. A metaphysics of presence is a form of 'forgetting' the difference between Being and Presence. For our understanding of media-technologies this may be translated into the forgetting that every revealing is an enframing, that every act of 'disclosure' (one may think here of the example of 'investigative journalism') is necessarily also an act of obscuration (hence the frequent use of 'hidden' cameras).

One particularly effective way of undoing a metaphysics of presence has been developed by Derrida through that which he has named 'différance'. *Différance* highlights the *movement* of the signifier which is bound to the movement of the event 'in/with/as time'. If '*différance*' is (and I also cross out the 'is') what makes possible the presentation of the being-present, it is never presented as such' (1972/1982, p. 6). In other words, the time-of-the-event remains in excess of the event itself. This existential temporality reserves itself 'without dissimulating itself as something'. For Derrida (1972/1982, p. 8):

Différer in this sense is to temporize, to take recourse, consciously or unconsciously, in the temporal and temporizing mediation of a detour that suspends the accomplishment or fulfilment of 'desire' or 'will' and equally effects this suspension in a mode that annuls or tempers its own effect.

The event of temporizing is temporalizing because it brings to bear the displacement of the time of the event as a becoming. *Différance* is used to compensate the loss of meaning that comes with this temporalized displacement. The deferred presence of the sign puts into question the authority of presence *and* of its symmetrical opposite absence or *lack* as 'the limit of Being' and thus opens up an *excess*. In Derrida's (1972/1982, p. 13) words:

It is because of différance *that the movement of signification is possible only if each so-called 'present' element, each element appearing on the scene of presence, is related to something other than itself, thereby keeping within itself the mark of the past element, and already letting itself be vitiated by the mark of its relation to the future element, this trace being related no less to what is called the future than to what is called the past and constituting what is called the present by means of this very relation to what it is not: what it absolutely is not, not even a past or future as a modified present.*

Whereas for Heidegger, the truth of Being can only be revealed in an unmediated insight, that flash of light that opens itself up in the enframing/revealing of technology, Derrida transforms the very notion of a truth of Being as that which is endlessly deferred. Hence, for Derrida and in contrast to Heidegger, mediation is no longer that which stands in the way of understanding the truth of Being, but that to which we are inevitably and necessarily bound. The 'turning' then, arrives in a dissolution of the metaphysics of presence and a radical turning towards difference, not as the opposite of identity (the truth of Being), but as *différance*. It is no longer the opposition between the disclosed and the concealed, but the infinity of disclosure/concealment and enclosure/unconcealment. With this insight, Derrida engages with an 'opening up' of an ethical moment that is disclosed in its mediation; mediation is infinity; it is always in excess of that which can be enpresented.

In *Given Time*, Derrida (1992) presents a crucial turning in his critique of the metaphysics of presence, which is no longer primarily engaged with its ontological fallacy, but with its a-moral indifference towards Being. A metaphysics of presence interpellates infinity in terms of a concrete and material 'now'; and demands it to surrender to its will. It is like a child praying to God for a new toy. Instead, the gift shows that what is given is not the gift, but the giving, indeed, mediation. Gifts are never exclusively measured out in terms of exchange, their valorization also operates on use-value and sign-value (symbolic exchange). Mauss (1990, p. 11) made a similar point when addressing the Maorian *hau*, the spirit of things, that is given with the giving, but never simply exchangeable (it only comes into effect after the intervention of a third person). Mauss only addresses the *hau* as far as it relates to things, as far as it is part and parcel of the present. What he does not speak about, however, is the *hau* of giving, the giving that enables one to accept something from someone in the first place. For the Maori, retaining the *hau* from its origin ('by accepting something from somebody is to accept part of his spiritual essence, of his soul' – ibid: p. 12) is like placing oneself under the spell of the spirit of the giver. The gift in this sense is like the Socratic *pharmakon* – both a cure and a poison (in German as well as Dutch '*(Ver)gift*' is also used to designate poison as well as gift). In other words, gifts are not only valorizing, they are infectious, they incubate you with the soul of the giver, and thus with the giving.

In other words, if we are able to refuse gift-exchange entrapment of the metaphysics of presence, which is equally a refutation of foundationalist philosophy, we may arrive at a possibility for engaging a media-ethics that is rather contagious. Once infected with the spirit of the gift, one is inspired to actualize the event, to engage in friendship or community. Such a media-ethics delivers itself not in the form of suspicion that there is always an obscurity with every revelation, or in the paranoia that we may actually have been seduced by evil, which informs most of the conspiracy-theories that dominate media-sociology, but in the form of an engendering of a turning-away from the human-centred reason of modern philosophy. Instead, it heightens a sensibility that every technology implies its own forms of normativity. Indeed, it discloses an ethics of mediation.

CONCLUSION

More concretely this means that changing the political commitments of journalism, for example by providing a public service that works on a critical understanding of the world we live in, rather than one manipulated by spin-doctors for the benefit of audience ratings will not in itself enhance the ethical sensibilities of enframing/revealing. What is required, instead, is an understanding of mediation as a giving. The ability to give, and to receive, enables one to be 'affected'. Learning to be affected is not just something that journalists, editors and producers have to engage in, audiences too are not to be excluded from the normativity of technology. They too are engaged (or not) in the actualisation of media-ethics. Hence, the normativity of technologies of mediation is not closure, for example, 'telling the truth' without constraints, but a revealing of its enframing.

This may not be the most preferable option for either commercial or public service media; nor may it appeal to politically committed journalists who believe that a truth out there needs to be disclosed in spite of all the distortions of mediation. Disclosure and distortion are part of the same process of enframing/revealing. The question is not to distort or to distort, but which distortions disable and which enable our attunement to being in the world. In the first case, distortions merely mirror the cynicism of exploitation and subjugation, in the second distortion we can sense a trace of the spirit of the gift, a transformation of sense, a mode of affect.

For journalists it means becoming more reflexive and engaging with the audience, not merely in the representation-product, but also in the representation-process. For editors it means allowing the editing to reveal its distortions, for spin-doctors it means giving away the spin, and for audiences it means learning to be affected. It also becomes obvious that there is very little a state, legislator or governing body can actually do to enforce media-ethics apart from managing and preventing the excessive forms of abuse and manipulation. Ethics are embedded in social forms, in human relationships and their spiritual engagement. This means that our understanding of media-ethics is better served within frameworks of analyses that emphasise the everyday social, cultural, economic and political embedding of technological processes. Ethics are not abstractions, but practically engaged normativities of sense-making that are situational and local. They are neither universal procedures nor absolute moral codes, but lived sensibilities of human beings, technologies and spirits concerned with cultivating a being-in-the-world on the basis of affect.

ENDNOTES

1. It is along these lines that we could interpret Deleuze and Guattari's (1988) forceful claim that books do not signify; a book is not 'about' anything but itself. On a more general point it helps us to remember that 'content' analysis of media should not be absorbed with for example, textual analysis, but also include, not even depart from, an analysis of 'form' – that is, the purport (matter) of the medium-technology that it brings forth.
2. Actually, Narcissus is derived from the Greek word 'narcosis', which means 'numbness' (McLuhan 1964, p. 51).
3. Note that this notion of reflexivity is very different from the one used by Giddens (1991, 1993) and Lash (1993).

REFERENCES

Abercrombie, N. (1990) 'Popular culture and ideological effects', in Abercrombie, N., Hill, S. and Turner, B. eds, *Dominant Ideologies*, London: Unwin Hyman, pp. 199–228.

Barthes, R. (1977) *Image Music Text* (trans. S. Heath), London: Fontana Press.

Butler, J. (1993) 'Endangered/Endangering: Schematic Racism and White Paranoia', in Gooding-Williams, R. ed., *Reading Rodney King. Reading Urban Uprising*. London: Routledge, pp. 15–22.

Cottle, S. (1993) *TV News, Urban Conflict and the Inner City*, Leicester: Leceister University Press.

Dahlgren, P. (1995) *Television and the Public Sphere. Citizenship, Democracy and the Media*, London: Sage.

Deleuze, G. and Guattari, F. (1988) *A Thousand Plateaux. Capitalism and Schizophrenia*, Minneapolis: University of Minnesota Press.

Derrida, J. (1967/1978) *Writing and Difference* (trans. A. Bass), Chicago: University of Chicago Press.

Derrida, J. (1972/1982) *Margins of Philosophy* (trans. A. Bass), Hemel Hempstead: Harvester Wheatsheaf.

Derrida, J. (1992) *Given Time I: Counterfeit Money*, Chicago: Chicago University Press.

Fiske, J. (1994) *Media Matters, Everyday Culture and Political Change*, Minneapolis, University of Minnesota Press.

Giddens, A. (1991) *Modernity and Self-Identity*, Cambridge: Polity Press.

Giddens, A. (1993) 'Living in a Post-Traditional Society' in Beck, U., Giddens, A. and Lash, S. *Reflexive Modernization. Politics, Tradition and Aesthetics in the Modern Social Order*, Cambridge: Polity Press.

Gooding-Williams, R. ed. (1993) *Reading Rodney King, Reading Urban Uprising*, London: Routledge.

Gramsci, A. (1971) *Selections from the Prison Notebooks*, New York: International Publishers.

Hall, S., Critcher, C., Jefferson, T., Clark, J., and Roberts, B. (1978) *Policing the Crisis, Mugging, the State and Law and Order*, London: Macmillan Press.

Heidegger, M. (1927/1986) *Sein und Zeit* (16th edition), Tübingen: Max Niemeyer Verlag.

Heidegger, M. (1977) *The Question Concerning Technology and Other Essays*, New York: Harper & Row.

Kieran, M. ed. (1998) *Media Ethics*, London: Routledge.

Lash, S. (1993) 'Reflexivity and its Doubles: Structure, Aesthetics, Community', in Beck, U., Giddens, A. and Lash, S. *Reflexive Modernization. Politics, Tradition and Aesthetics in the Modern Social Order*, Cambridge: Polity Press.

Latour, B. (1987) *Science in Action. How to Follow Scientists and Engineers through Society*, Milton Keynes: Open University Press.

Lyotard, J.F. (1983/1988) *The Differend: Phrases in Dispute*, Manchester: Manchester University Press.

Mauss, M. (1990) *The Gift: The Form and Reason for Exchange in Archaic Societies*, London: Routledge.

McLuhan, M. (1964) *Understanding Media. The Extensions of Man*, Harmondsworth: Penguin Books.

Pilger, J. (1992) *Distant Voices*, London: Vintage.

Thompson, J.B. (1995) *The Media and Modernity. A Social Theory of the Media*, Cambridge: Polity Press.

Thompson, K. (1998) *Moral Panics*, London: Routledge.

Van Loon, J. (1999) 'Whiter Shades of Pale: Media-Hybridities of Rodney King', in Brah, A., Hickman, M. and Mac an Ghail, M. eds. *Thinking Identities: Ethnicity, Racism and Culture*, London: Macmillan.

Vattimo, G. (1988) *The End of Modernity. Nihilism and Hermeneutics in Post-Modern Culture*, Cambridge: Polity Press.

Vattimo, G. (1992) *The Transparent Society*, Cambridge: Polity Press.

4 The 'fourth estate' and moral responsibilities

Andrew Edgar

INTRODUCTION

The notion of the press as a fourth estate, that provides a check on the abuse of government power, is a cornerstone of liberal accounts of the press. In a society that is increasingly self-conscious of its pluralism, the promotion of this traditional conception of the fourth estate becomes ever more urgent. Hence, the thesis to be presented in this chapter is that the overriding moral responsibility of the 'fourth estate', by which is understood both print and electronic news media, is precisely a responsibility to the maintenance and development of vital public debate, and thus to public involvement in politics (in the current argot, the 'public sphere') (Habermas 1989). The argument of the chapter will follow a somewhat familiar trajectory, by beginning with a presentation and criticism of liberal accounts of the relationship between the fourth estate, the free market and democracy, and concluding with a defence of something akin to 'radical public service' (Curran and Seaton 1997, pp. 345–9).

It will be argued that despite the centrality of the notion of a fourth estate to liberalism, (and more specifically liberal social contract theory), it does not provide an adequate account of the way in which news is constructed and interpreted. This absence inhibits any integral liberal defence of the fourth estate. More precisely, it will be suggested that its focus on the individual agent prevents liberalism from developing an adequate hermeneutics. Liberal theory is repaired and surpassed, not merely through the provision of an adequate account of the embedding of the journalist and news audience in what might be termed communities of readers, and thus the provision of a hermeneutics, but in recognising that hermeneutics is coterminous with an account of the necessary embedding of individual agents within political communities. It will be argued that it is only as members of a political community that agents become competent interpreters of the news. The role of the fourth estate is therefore to promote and deepen this embedding of the individual within a community.

THE INDIVIDUAL AND THE SOCIAL CONTRACT

Classical liberalism, rooted in the social contract theory of the seventeenth century political philosopher John Locke, strives to articulate a political system that will serve to defend individual freedom (Boucher and Kelly 1994). Individuals, it is argued, are uniquely able to judge whatever may be in their own best interests and that will satisfy their preferences and desires. No one, including the state, can legitimately interfere in the individual's choice of goals. The advantage of the liberal political system therefore lies in its supposed ability to maximise the citizen's freedom to pursue these preferences in the way in which he or she considers best, and without hindrance from others. This is because the liberal state is understood as the guarantor of a series of minimal entitlements (or rights) that are the preconditions of individual freedom and prosperity. Essentially, this framework of rights is something to which any rational person would subscribe (Rawls 1973, pp. 17–22). The individual citizen is understood (in a more or less metaphorical manner) to be in a contract with the state, where the individual relinquishes certain freedoms (for example to seek revenge for perceived injustices), in return for the long-term security that the state (with a police and judiciary) can provide.

Agents within a market-based fourth estate are therefore constrained only by the legal framework that constrains all action within the society, which itself ideally reflects the basic freedoms (or rights) to which all individuals are entitled. The media organisations may themselves be understood as associations of individuals (including proprietors and shareholders, editors and journalists, as well as an array of managers, secretaries, accountants, cleaners, printers and other support staff) who have been brought together, again exercising their freedom to seek employment where they so choose, to achieve the goals of the organisation. The role of the fourth estate therefore rests upon a series of contractual relationships, from the fleeting and repeated economic contracts that occur when news, as a commodity, is sold to members of the public, through the employment contracts that define the roles of the media personnel, to the social contract of society as a whole.

While the state plays a necessary role in enforcing the legal framework within which individuals act, liberals remain traditionally suspicious of the power that is invested in the state. The very notion of the fourth estate entails that the principal role of the press within a liberal democracy is to check state power. The state itself can no more be allowed to infringe the freedoms of its citizens than can one individual be allowed to infringe the freedoms of another. While the press must itself stay within the law (and thus cannot act to undermine the freedom of others, for example through unjustified intrusions upon their privacy), it checks and oversees the state by being free to publicise abuses of power. Such abuse may occur either through the state exceeding the legitimate limits of its own power (exemplified, for example, by the case of Sarah Tisdall, who was gaoled in 1984 for leaking British government plans concerning public relations over the installation of Cruise missiles); or through its failure to pursue and prosecute wrongdoing within society (as, for example, in the case of Stephen Lawrence, where seemingly entrenched attitudes and mishandled procedures within the metropolitan police led to the failure effectively to investigate the murder of a black teenager). The political role of the fourth estate thus lies in its ability to publicise the failures of government, and thus to inform the electorate and to articulate public opinion in the demand for a change of policy or law.

This explicitly political role of the press may be seen to be complemented by a more subtle defence of individual freedom. It may be argued that individuals can freely choose and pursue goals only if they have appropriate information upon which to act. Ignorance is a key inhibition to autonomous action. The press is therefore an important, although by no means exclusive, source of information and opinion. It is through an open press that the public can become aware, not merely of facts about how the world is, but also about the range of available opinion on how it should be.

Given that the liberal is suspicious of state power, and thus of state interference in the media, the free market is therefore promoted as the source of the strength and flourishing of the fourth estate. In principle, anybody is free to enter the media market as the proprietor of a newspaper, magazine or other news outlet.[1] Such outlets will flourish, providing a multiplicity of opinions and perspectives from which citizens can choose. If the opinions expressed, or indeed the depth or nature of news coverage offered, are judged to be distasteful or otherwise unsatisfactory, then the outlet will not have an audience, and will disappear from the market. Any claims as to the worth or quality of news coverage and opinion independently of this market test is, for the liberal, largely spurious. If an opinion or news item is dull, however worthy it may be, free individuals will not waste precious time and money in consuming it. (Thus has Rupert Murdoch explicitly identified quality with 'satisfaction of market values' (1989).) As the Peacock report on the financing of the BBC affirmed: viewers and listeners are 'the best judges of their own interests' (Peacock 1986, p. 128).

In summary, the liberal model assumes that a free and open market will allow individuals to formulate and express their political opinions by freely exercising what are essentially property rights (either in the production and dissemination of news and comment upon the news, or in consumption). The 1949 Royal Commission on the Press exemplified this view, claiming that free enterprise was a prerequisite of a free press. Subsequent Commissions, in 1962 and 1977, echoed this sentiment (Curran and Seaton 1997, pp. 288 and 322).

THE INDETERMINACY OF JOURNALISM

In questioning the coherence and relevance of liberalism to the analysis of the moral status of the news media, it is precisely this contractual model that will be the focus of attention. The notion of the contract allows an initial account of what moral responsibilities might be within the context of the fourth estate. A contractual model directs moral reflection along certain channels, by making specific presuppositions about the way in which human beings relate to each other within society. Bluntly, as has already been suggested and as is coherent with liberalism in general, it assumes that society as a whole, as well as particular institutions within society, are composed through autonomous individuals coming together, to mutual benefit, to achieve some specific purpose. Thus, John Rawls understands society in terms of the mutually beneficial co-operation of its members (1973, p. 126). It will be argued that a liberal contract model is problematic (and ultimately demonstrates a grave insensitivity to what is specific about journalism as a social practice), because it reduces moral judgement to conscience (that is itself grounded in an intuition of the social contract); it fails to substantiate the link between commercial media organisations and democratic politics; and it offers an unacceptably superficial account of the activities of the media audience.

Journalists are bound to their news organisation by an employment contract. The journalist is essentially agreeing to deploy his or her professional skills, in co-operation with others, to realise the immediate goal of the news organisation. In return, the news organisation agrees to pay the journalist. The specific contract serves to define the freedoms and responsibilities of the journalist and his or her employer. Just as it is assumed that all parties were free to enter the contract, so (within certain agreed limitations, such as a period of notice) all parties are free to leave the contract, should it no longer be in their interests to stay. If agents are free to enter and leave contracts, then journalistic morality would appear to be clear cut. The journalist is obliged to do whatever he or she has freely contracted to do.

This model may be problematic, insofar as it apparently reduces morality to the pursuit of mutual self-interest. Consider the problem of privacy. On this account, there would appear to be nothing to prevent the photo-journalist and newspaper editor from freely contracting to trade compromising or intrusive photographs of a celebrity, particularly if there is an audience willing to buy the newspaper. One response to this is to assert that certain actions may appear to run contrary to the journalist's conscience. It is thus that a number of liberal commentators, including the 1990 Calcutt Committee on privacy, articulate moral restraint. However, conscience is not easily theorised, and suggests, at this point, little more than a subjective intuition.

The problem of self-interest may be pursued further by recognising the disciplinary role of an over-arching social contract, and thus of society's legal framework. Certain activities infringe the freedom of others. In an ideal liberal society, the moral responsibilities of the individual might be taken to overlap with the legal framework of rights (so that actual law would realise the social contract). Thus, for example, given a right to freedom from physical and mental harm, then no journalist can act in such a way as to incite violence against an individual, or directly cause harm, for example through exercising undue pressure in the pursuit of a story. The particular contract, in which anyone is in principle free to contract to do anything, is thus constrained by the morally prior social contract. This, and this alone, curtails the pursuit of self-interest.

An argument of this form is not obviously deficient. It effectively suggests that the projection of some social contract, to which all rational persons would agree, provides a benchmark according to which the actions of individuals can be judged. What is crucial here is the manner in which the social contract is derived, and the relationship of the social contract to the moral intuitions (and thus conscience) of the individual agent. A great deal of liberal argument, from Locke through to Rawls, has tended to assume that the contract can be deduced by any suitably rational individual.[2] Knowledge of the social contract (and thus of the moral limits to action) is available to any suitably reflective, rational individual. Such an approach is weak, precisely because it appears to side-line the importance of actual debate over moral and legal frameworks. Such debate would encompass the existence or nature of a right to privacy (Calcutt 1990) and issues of freedom of information, and the scope and validity of an Official Secrets Act or even Blasphemy laws (Curran and Seaton 1997, p. 351). The prick of liberal conscience therefore appears to have little force outside a strongly defended legal framework.

It may also be noted that the appeal to conscience says nothing specifically about journalism. The journalist's contract must not infringe the social contract, but as such is no different to any other contract. This would suggest that there is no such thing as media ethics, for there is just ethics. It may therefore be important to turn back to what has previously been left somewhat imprecise, and thus look at the specific goals of news organisations (for it is these goals that structure the specific contracts within media organisations).

The objectives of a news organisation are not clear cut, as disputes between proprietors and editors indicate (see Hanlin 1992). The obvious assertion that news organisations exist to collect and report news (and comment upon the news) is undermined as soon as the organisation is recognised as a commercial enterprise (as the liberal link between a free press and the market insists that it is). A news organisation exists to make a profit (or, more specifically for many national newspapers or broadcasters, to contribute to the profits of a more diversified parent organisation). It cannot even simply be assumed that a news organisation makes profits by reporting news (so that reporting could at least be salvaged as an important intermediary goal), for profits are typically made through advertising. The news organisation therefore makes a profit by selling audiences to advertisers. There is again a series of contractual relationships involved, between proprietor and shareholders, and between proprietor and advertisers, as well as those between the proprietor and the editor and other employees. If the proprietor fails to deliver satisfactory profits or ratings, the newspaper or broadcaster will be forced from the market. Again, contractual analysis appears to indicate nothing that is specific to journalism, in contradistinction to any other commercial activity.

If a news organisation exists primarily to make profit, then it would be unreasonable to expect it to publish specific items of news or comment that might compromise its commercial viability. Thus, a newspaper need no more be expected to carry a report that would offend a specific section of its audience than a car manufacturer would be expected to continue producing a model that was unattractive to its buyers. On this argument, Rupert Murdoch's only offence, in 1997, in refusing to publish the memoirs of Chris Patten (the last governor of Hong Kong), having realised that this act would offend the potentially lucrative Chinese market, was ever to have become contracted to Patten in the first place. Similarly, if Murdoch perceives a unified European currency to be against his long-term commercial interests, then he may exercise his property rights and use his newspapers to present the argument against that policy.[3] Such actions need not worry the liberal, if he or she can be assured that there will be a plurality of opinions published. (Thus, Murdoch's attitude towards Patten was criticised elsewhere in the press, and Patten has a new publisher.) However, by reducing news organisations down to their commercial goals, there is no guarantee that journalism demonstrates any necessary commitment to democracy. If democracy is not in the commercial interests of the proprietors of the news media, then there is no reason why they should promote democratic ideals. As such, the liberal defence of the fourth estate, as a check upon government, no longer appears coherent, precisely because still nothing has been said specifically about journalism.

If the liberal contractual model is indifferent to the specific aims of journalism at the level of the individual journalist and of the news organisation, it is similarly indifferent at the level of readership. The reader of a newspaper is reduced to a mere consumer, and as such what matters is not the meaning that the audience derives from the news (or indeed the hermeneutic process by which a report is interpreted), but rather the apparent satisfaction of preferences that reading realises. If so, news is indeed merely entertainment (O'Neill 1992, p. 19). Interpretation is therefore either ignored, or assumed to be an unproblematic recovery of a given message. Readership figures, market share and ratings alone indicate the success or failure of the news outlet. Even if the consumption of news and opinion is taken seriously as an attempt by the reader to become politically informed, the model still assumes that the reader exists, prior to any consumption, as a rational but politically uncommitted being, scanning the range of opinions available for the one that most appeals. News reports are therefore seen to be consumed like any other good, with information and opinions alike coming to be seen not simply as possessions, but as goods that satisfy pre-existing subjective preferences.

At the core of this view there appears to be a simple paradox. It was noted above that the fourth estate has an obligation to inform the public, and it might be further argued that it is important for information and opinion to be clearly separated. Reporting, that strives to 'tell it as it is', is to be kept clear from leader columns and other expressions of opinion (Glasser and Craft 1998, pp. 203–4). However, if the consumer is freely exercising his or her property rights in buying a newspaper, one might ask whether or not he or she is free to buy misinformation? If the consumer wants a prejudiced, xenophobic or otherwise biased report and expression of opinion (not least for the satisfaction he or she gets from having a personal view of the world confirmed), why can he or she not have it? The paradox is that the consumer of a newspaper appears to have the freedom to throw away that very autonomy by buying misinformation.

Again, the liberal contract model has failed to substantiate the moral role of the fourth estate, precisely because it has little to say that is specific to journalistic practice. On the one hand, the individual is reduced to an already autonomous (and morally conscientious) being, that exists prior to any social act or cultural possession. On the other hand, relationships between individuals tend to be reduced to contracts. The negotiation of contracts is little more than the free defence of perceived self-interest, with the over-arching social contract providing an unambiguous and given framework. The process of negotiation is therefore taken to be unproblematic, and this overlaps with the assumption that the negotiation of meaning is unproblematic. (Contracts and newspapers are equally transparent.) While overtly defending the role of the fourth estate, the liberal account has therefore in fact trivialised both journalism and politics, for it has reduced both to the accumulation of consumer preferences.

CULTURAL POLITICS

It has been suggested that liberalism seeks to defend the fourth estate as a source of factual information, and that this was justified as facilitating individual autonomy, but that the paradox of autonomy serves to throw this defence into question. This may be pursued further, by noting that the facilitation of autonomy presupposes the possibility of a fact/value distinction, by appealing to a traditional journalistic virtue of separating opinion and reporting. If this distinction is questioned, then the paradox of autonomy itself may dissolve, allowing an enriched account of journalistic practice, albeit at the cost of the liberal account of individual agency.

A fact/value distinction suggests that it is possible to report the news objectively, with objectivity being initially understood as a correspondence between the content of the news report and the events that are reported. The complexity of any newsworthy event, however, entails that its reporting requires some degree of selectivity and organisation on the part of the reporter. First, it may be suggested that the true nature or meaning of an event may typically be contested by those directly involved. Thus there is rarely, if ever, a definitive account of events that the reporter can reproduce. In practice, objectivity may then be understood as impartiality, where no single viewpoint is allowed to dominate, and no relevant viewpoint is excluded. However, to shift from 'objectivity' to 'impartiality' already entails abandoning a commitment to 'facts' in favour of some balance of values or perspectives. Secondly, it may be argued that without selection and structuring, a report will make no more sense to the reader than would the original event (with the news report being akin to a map that is the same size as the territory mapped).[4] This is, effectively, to suggest that newsworthy events are not just there, and thus that they are not 'facts' that can be unproblematically recovered and reported. Rather, it is to recognise that news is the reporting of social actions, and that social actions are such that meaning must be ascribed to them, and that meaning can be contested. The journalist is a participant in the interpretation of the social actions (Edgar 1992).

In terms of the paradox of autonomy, the rejection of the possibility of objective fact, at least in the context of journalism, suggests that the fourth estate has no obligation to maintain the autonomy of its readers. If they are autonomous, it is not on the grounds of basing their actions on good information, and therefore the consumption of misinformation cannot be condemned. However, the above argument has already suggested a shift away from the model of news consumption. The news report is as much a social act as the event that it reports. It is therefore itself something that can be interpreted and reinterpreted. While it may be accepted that the reader gains satisfaction from having his or her opinions reinforced by the news he or she reads, this still leaves the issue of interpretation untouched. That is, it does not allow for an account of how the reader makes the sense that he or she does of the news report. To present this process of interpretation as a purely subjective act of recovery, akin to that of consumption, is implausible, for it opens up a semantic chaos, where each individual divines whatever meaning he or she likes within a text. Accepting this, one may then enquire into the conditions that make a news report meaningful, which is to say, make it an act of communication, for its audience.

It may be suggested that the task of a reporter is to offer an account of events that makes sense in terms of the cultural references and priorities that the audience already possesses. There is, therefore, no assumption that the audience has autonomy in the sense indicated by liberal theory. A news report is directed to a particular readership (and not to readers in general). In practice, audiences are embedded within specific communities and traditions, and these provide the cultural resources necessary to the interpretation of social actions (Taylor 1985). The culture provides what may be understood as the 'hermeneutic horizon' of interpretation (Gadamer 1975, pp. 269–274). Hermeneutics works from the assumption that a text cannot be interpreted without a prior estimation of what that text contains. Interpretation begins by directing appropriate questions at the text. This anticipation of content will be revised and enriched as it is challenged by the particular details of the text. The hermeneutic horizon is, therefore, the basic competence that readers have to approach a text. It structures that approach but is also vulnerable to change in the light of experience. The reporter therefore assumes that the reader will come to his or her report with certain expectations (and not least, expectations of exactly what news is). If those expectations are radically disappointed the report will be meaningless, for the reader will be incapable of interpreting it. In effect, this is to refigure the liberal's recognition that people will only consume news if it satisfies some subjective preference, in order to suggest that unsatisfying news is simply meaningless or irrelevant news.

The autonomous liberal individual has therefore been abandoned. The argument is not simply that individuals are embedded within communities and within hermeneutic horizons, but that they are significantly constituted by those horizons. Individual identity is understood in terms of the horizon, for, if the horizon structures the possibility that the individual has for making sense of the ambient social world, then the individual's very scope for action, including self-understanding and the ability to express preferences, will be mediated by that horizon.

The danger inherent in the hermeneutic argument is that it appears to collapse into relativism. The certainties of the liberal social contract, with its enshrined respect for certain freedoms, have been abandoned. The subjective choice of the liberal individual is seemingly replaced by the mere assertion of cultural values, as the individual appears to be wholly identified with the culture. However, such criticisms hold only if the communal horizons are assumed to be fixed, unambiguous and impermeable. It has been noted that hermeneutics presupposes that the horizon is dynamic. The general understanding that one has of the world will change, as one responds to new experiences. This may be reformulated. While it may be accepted that the individual is constituted by the horizon, it may also be noted that the individual is the source of particular experiences that challenge the horizon. More precisely, if the horizon is not to be reified, as an entity that exists independently of real human beings, then it exists only in the imaginations and actions of those human beings, and each individual will imagine and enact that horizon slightly differently. Bluntly put, the horizon is not simply the determinant of the individual's self-identity; it is rather the focus of the expression and, most importantly, the contesting of that identity. To borrow a phrase from the political philosophy of Michael Oakeshott, the hermeneutic horizons are 'languages of self-disclosure and self-enactment' (Oakeshott 1975, p. 120). It is through the horizon that we recognise people like us.

This argument entails the abandonment of the liberal conception of politics, and thus to a degree, of the liberal suspicion of state power. Politics shifts from a narrow concern with elections and an informed electorate, to a cultural politics in which communities struggle, at diverse levels, to define and redefine themselves. It may then be suggested that the role of the press, as a fourth estate, is not simply to check the state, but rather to maintain the vitality of this debate over cultural identity. The conception of the news audience therefore changes, from a predominantly passive consumer, to an active interpreter. In reading a newspaper or in watching a newscast, one actively engages in interpreting it, and through that interpretation one will reflect, perhaps implicitly but always through the medium of the hermeneutic horizon, on one's own understanding of one's cultural identity. To actively discuss that interpretation with others, and in particular to discuss differences in interpretation, is to negotiate that identity. To do so on a 'phone-in' is an embarrassment of riches.

CONCLUSION

In conclusion, the hermeneutic model, so briefly sketched, may be given further substance by considering two criticisms. First, the suspicion of relativism has not been dispelled. This may be articulated by noting that communities will have undue influence in determining what is newsworthy, so that news coverage is likely to include significant distortions. O'Neill gives the example of the way in which Greenpeace's capacity for publicity distorts public perception of environmental issues (1992, p. 23). Second, in a pluralistic society, there will not be a single community, but a multiplicity. Given sufficient economic resources, there is no reason why each community should not have its own fourth estate. However, as Gitlin has noted, that may still leave dialogue between communities (which in a pluralistic society is most pressing) conspicuously absent (Gitlin 1998, p. 173).

Media coverage of events is readily criticised in terms of its sensationalism or superficiality. To represent audience interest in a news story in terms of its coherence with an existing hermeneutic horizon, rather than in terms of satisfaction of consumer desire, does little obviously to dispel the fear that news coverage is becoming more superficial. A person may respond to superficial and sensational news coverage precisely because his or her view of the world is superficial and sensational. That may be the only form of news that makes sense. Similarly, he or she may not have the cultural resources to deal with cultural challenges, and may therefore retreat into the mere reaffirmation of an existing horizon. However, if the news media is to take itself seriously as a fourth estate, then it has been argued that it has a moral responsibility to promote, not simply the reaffirmation of cultural identity, but rather its renewal. The moral responsibility of the press is to expand, not ossify, the hermeneutic horizon.

Superficial, fearful and prejudiced audiences cannot be eliminated (for some people no doubt do want to surrender their autonomy), and to a significant degree, it may be beyond the scope of any media to tackle the causes of such retreats. Yet the typical member of the media audience does not encounter a single media outlet, but rather a plurality. This plurality of outlets opens up a fragile but valuable possibility for vitalising public debate. It may be suggested that the fourth estate can respond to the demands of both sensationalism and pluralism by actively recognising the diversity of audience experience as a basis for engaging in its own cultural politics. That is to say, that a responsible fourth estate is itself both diverse and self-critical. At the core of this model may therefore be found, not the disciplines of the market or even state regulation and subsidy,[5] but rather radio and television reviews in newspapers, and television and radio programmes devoted to the media (such as UK Channel 4's 'What the Papers Say', and BBC Radio 4's 'The Message'). Such columns and programmes bring to the audience's attention a plurality of viewpoints, and thus at least the semblance of a public debate that is at once over the nature of news coverage, and of how different individuals and communities within the wider society understand and respond to that news coverage. Such debate[6] effectively poses the question of whether or not we have a press that is representative of a community (or communities) like ours. (It is here, for example, that issues of press privacy and freedom of information are publicly discussed.)

The issue upon which the liberal free-market model had little or nothing to say about the nature of journalism, is thereby brought into the centre of the hermeneutic model, not as a something already determined, but as something under constant negotiation. This in turn revitalises the issue of journalistic conscience, for conscience need no longer be seen as a subjective intuition of wrongdoing, but rather as a concern over the nature and meaning of journalism. While the liberal model presented the journalist as an autonomous self that possesses journalistic skills that could be freely traded, the hermeneutic model suggests that journalism is at least constitutive of the individual's self-identity. Thus, in a cultural politics of journalism, the journalist addresses his or her self-understanding as a journalist (and more precisely, as a journalist within this particular community). This self-understanding is cashed out in actual practice, and in debate over that practice, as core moral issues concerning the objectives of news organisations (such as profit making and delivery of an audience), are transformed into questions as to the way in which a journalist handles those objectives, while still able to publicly defend his or her actions as primarily actions of a journalist.

ENDNOTES

1. Much debate over the liberal model of the media market has focused on the degree to which there is actual freedom to enter the market as a proprietor. In practice, the expense of producing a new pubication, at least to a national audience, is prohibitive. This has lead to an overconcentration of media control in a few hands, as opposed to a genuinely open and competitive market. While this problem of market failure must be acknowledged, it is not the immediate concern of this chapter. The argument here is rather that the liberal model, even if free entry was possible, is based on a distorted understanding of journalism and the interpretation of news.

2. Following Habermas (1990, p. 66), it would be argued that Rawls's appeal to debate within the 'original position' is actually illusory, and the conditions of the veil of ignorance make all disputants alike, thus predetermining consensus position.
3. In June 1998, the Murdoch-owned *Sun* condemned Tony Blair as the most dangerous man in Britain, due to his qualified support for a single currency.
4. Euronews's daily 'No Comment' news sequence, that consists of news footage without any commentary, provides a test case. While even this footage will be structured to some degree (if by nothing else, than by the decision to point the camera here rather than there), it may be suggested that the viewer will only make sense of this footage by bringing to it prior expectations, derived from previously seen reports (MacGregor 1997, p. 23).
5. While the hermeneutic model is critical of free-market accounts, it has little to say about media ownership and control. To stimulate diversity (and crucially, this will be a diversity of voices within a cultural politics) a co-existence of state sponsorship and the free market may be advocated.
6. It may be argued that the objection that media coverage distorts issues can only be made by presupposing a position of objective knowledge, or at least of assuming that it is possible to determine, prior to any debate, which voices should be allowed a say. Something of this is found in Habermasian discussions of the public sphere and the ideal speech situation, as Habermas appears to set quite daunting criteria of communicative competence as the conditions for entry to the debate. In order to avoid predetermining the debate the metaphor of conversation, borrowed from Oakeshott (1991), may be preferred. Conversations are more open-ended and unpredictable than debates. Anyone can join, and the rules of engagement are negotiated as one goes along. While they are vulnerable to breakdown, and as Oakeshott himself notes, to being dominated by a single voice, the imposition of strict rules before the conversation begins may only serve to institutionalise that single voice.

REFERENCES

Boucher, D. and Kelly, P. eds (1994) *The Social Contract from Hobbes to Rawls*, London: Routledge.

Calcutt (1990) *Report of the Committee on Privacy and Related Matters*, London: HMSO.

Curran, J. and Seaton, J. (1997) *Power Without Responsibility: The Press and Broadcasting in Britain*, 5th edition, London: Routledge.

Edgar, A. (1992) 'Objectivity, Bias and Truth', in Andrew Belsey and Ruth Chadwick, eds., *Ethical Issues in Journalism and the Media*, London: Routledge.

Gadamar, Hans-Georg. (1975) *Truth and Method*, London: Sheed and Ward.

Gitlin, T. (1998) 'Public Sphere or Public Sphericules?', in Tamar Liebes and James Curran, eds., *Media, Ritual and Identity*, London: Routledge.

Glasser, T.L. and Craft, S. (1998) 'Public Journalism and the Search for Democratic Ideas' in Tamar Liebes and James Curran, eds., *Media, Ritual and Identity*, London: Routledge.

Habermas, J. (1989) *The Structual Transformation of the Public Sphere: An Inquiry into a Category of Bourgeois Society*, Cambridge: Polity Press.

Habermas, J. (1990) *Moral Consciousness and Communicative Action*, Cambridge: Polity Press.

Hanlin, B. (1992) 'Owners, Editors and Journalists', in Andrew Belsey and Ruth Chadwick, eds., *Ethical Issues in Journalism and the Media*, London: Routledge.

MacGregor, B. (1997) *Live, Direct and Biased? Making Television News in the Satellite Age*, London: Arnold.

Murdoch, R. (1989) 'Freedom in Broadcasting', *MacTaggart Lecture 1989*, London: News International.

Oakeshott, M. (1975) *On Human Conduct*, Oxford: Clarendon Press.

Oakeshott, M. (1991) 'The Voice of Poetry in the Conversation of Mankind', in his *Rationalism in Politics and Other Essays*, 2nd edition, Indianapolis: Liberty Press.

O'Neill, J. (1992) 'Journalism in the Market Place', in Andrew Belsey and Ruth Chadwick, eds., *Ethical Issues in Journalism and the Media*, London: Routledge.

Peacock (1986) *Report of the Committee on Financing the BBC*. London: HMSO.

Rawls, J. (1973) *A Theory of Justice*, Oxford: Oxford University Press.

Taylor, C. (1985) 'What is Human Agency?', in his *Human Agency and Language: Philosophical Papers I*, Cambridge: Cambridge University Press.

5 Reproducing consciousness: what *is* Indonesia?

Carol Davis and Nick Rayner

The blue frog slips through the textual undergrowth, a no less impassioned and resonant object when we recognize its origins in mis-recognition and mis-translation. Its affective charge is not diminished under the knowing gaze of rational inquiry. Like the 'marvels and wonders' sought by early explorers and travellers, it speaks to an impossible search for discovery and completion conducted with all the baggage of the place from which we have come (Robertson *et al.* 1994, p. 6).

One of the predominant features of the late twentieth century has been the growth in global communications. We can switch on our television sets or pick up any newspaper and receive news about events in the world about us, even as they are unfolding in real-time. It would seem that we depend on the mass media 'for our images of non-local peoples, places and events, and the further the "event" from our own direct experience, the more we depend on media images for the totality of our knowledge' (Morley and Robins 1995, p. 133). However, can we be sure that the representations made by the Western media about these non-local 'Others' have any accuracy?

Taking Indonesia as our example, we can identify three recent media 'stories': the 'invasion' of East Timor by Indonesian troops, the environmental crisis, and the 1998 change in political leadership. What kind of image of Indonesia has been generated by this coverage in the collective minds of British people? Has this image been allocated the status of 'truth' in our minds? Do we ever question this 'truth' and, if so, on what basis? How many of us in our everyday lives consciously attempt to gather knowledge beyond mass media representations?

This chapter considers, first, how British media reports, often based upon selective and dramatic cores of information, represent non-Western Others and impose Western-derived ideas upon the Other's political and cultural worlds. Do such representations reproduce a collective consciousness about what Indonesia *is*? Secondly, can we, the audience, make accurate social comment about Indonesia and Indonesians based upon what we believe to know about them? Would our perceptions change significantly if we were exposed to alternative sources of information?

Perhaps the mis-representation of a local story is a less deliberate act than telling lies or tales of deception. There may be more subtle, underlying, processes at work that complicate the harsher realities of reliance upon mass media establishments and news organisational imperatives. Being on the horns of a two-fold ethical dilemma between the constraints of a political economy of news production and the autonomy of accurate representation of a local act is only one dimension of the representation issue. This chapter considers whether the routinised norms through which journalists frame news accounts are based upon their culturally acquired bases of perception, assessment and classification – what Bourdieu calls *habitus* (Bourdieu 1990b, pp. 52–65).

We begin by examining the processes that potentially structure our perceptions of Indonesia. Then we consider whether media representations would have any meaning to 'an Indonesian'. On one level, if we take account of state ideology, then certain parallels may become apparent. However, if we look below this surface into the contested nature of state discourses through an examination of local practices and customs, then we may begin to appreciate that 'Indonesia' is rather more complex than British media reports suggest.

In modern Britain we constantly search for solidity of meaning and truth in order to make some sense of what we do not, and probably cannot, ever fully know (Bauman 1995; Giddens 1991). With some degree of success, and with some degree of error, such patterns can be comparatively cast out into the wider global world. Such a search witnesses the constant grasping of information that appears legitimate by its own apparent solidity. If we are ever able to grasp such information and compare this with our own lived experiences of what it purports to report, we are always in a reflective position to watch that solidity melt into air (Berman 1988). We may, after all, be able to directly challenge the apparent solidity of what we are told (Touraine 1977). The process of experiencing life is akin to grasping straws that sometimes hold and sometimes tear out of their roots. All information may become, with either conscious deliberation or habitual unintentional reproductive consequence, symbolically codified, to transmit a certain constructed message (Bourdieu 1990a).

Certain institutionally embedded capital-based elite social groups have personal interests in ensuring a flexible exercise of power through which a symbolic exchange between their own interests and a given audience always rests on a foundation of shared belief (Bourdieu 1991). Consensus-building exercises are always being practised, despite the ability of an audience to either absorb or reason with its codified signals. In times of crises a potential exists for dominant nationalistic rhetorics to combine along the lines of constructing a visionary hold on the future construction of a putative homogeneity and its institutionalisation within civil society (Williams 1989). If we are honest to ourselves we can probably accept, with dubious personal reservations, that in the desperate search for rooted solidity we are quite able (no matter how 'intelligent' we like to think that we are) to passively absorb information whilst also being, within other conditional circumstances, quite able to actively reason with information. No person is an island, able to be cognitively free to separate their own individual vision of the world from the influence of another's construction (Lyotard 1984). Social persons cannot be fully able to break themselves reflexively from the social processes that delicately combine to make them what they are today (Bourdieu 1984).

As journalistic licence allows the transmitted word and image to invade an ever growing number of private spaces, there appears to be a greater need to focus sociological attention upon these new invasions. The technological pulling together of time and space has to be monitored by an accustomed eye that is somewhat less incorporated into the political and economic body than the vision of the journalist/reporter tends to be. But can sociologists stand back from the action and study the complex world of a professional at work and offer something to the professional? This may appear somewhat arrogant. If one were to reject this need for criticism, then one would have to consider one's own degree of arrogance. Professional elites never relish the external investigation of their own practices but, in the case of the journalist who sits monkey-like upon the shoulders of social action, they must expect other monkeys to be found chattering away upon their own invasive shoulders.

Recently, mass media reception studies have argued that the receiver of news information is capable of reasoning with what is relayed via institutionalised communication systems (television, radio, newspapers, etc.). However, we ask how can one reason with information if one is not exposed to differing sources about a particular event, or series of events? Where does one receive the knowledge to exercise any ability to 'reason' with information if the same kind of story is told over and over again by the journalist? Do similar tellings of similar stories become so embedded within the expectations and regurgitations of a receiving audience, that they combine to form the practical logic of durable judgemental classifications within what Bourdieu calls *habitus*? Bourdieu argues that the internal structure of the habitus functions as a cognitive set of durable dispositions that categorise and classify the world. The habitus underlies and structures out human practice which, in turn, structures out social space in terms of sets of categorical assumptions via the process of making social judgements based upon distinctions between those who have different sets of habitus, practice, etc. In some ways, people cut the cloth of their vision in relation to the social clothing that they already wear (Bourdieu 1990b). *Habitus* is the already known historically structured individual 'sorting frame' into which we structure out incoming informational letters from the outside world. However, our individual sorting frames are themselves structured by certain objective conditions of shared existence mediated through subjective experiences. The *habitus* should be seen as being structured more through connections of objective *similarity* than through hypersubjective *differences* (Bourdieu 1990a). Bourdieu argues that shared sets of economic and political conditions in society structure similar dispositional qualities in people. People from similar backgrounds appear to share similar visions of the world. By virtue of necessity, they share the same *habitus*, the same styles of life, the same way of interpreting what and who they experience along their life trajectories (Bourdieu 1984).

Consider the political economy of journalism; the constraints that limit and often sidetrack the autonomy of the individual. They may become the operational, or practical, stakes to which all working people, not only journalists, find themselves tied with ropes of varying length, strength and elasticity. Despite our hypersubjective thoughts and desires – our own creative imaginations, if you like – political and economic constraints ensure a certain reproductive stasis that forces analytical consideration. The production of news is a business and in the cold light of everyday practice it becomes embedded within habitual ethical minefields of money, time, and competition which combine with the inherent *power* contained within the process of representation. Maybe journalism, as with any form of purposive institutionalised intellectual practice, should not be constrained by such habitual ethics – *but it is*.

For Herman and Chomsky (1988) and Chomsky (1989), the potential for divergent stories becomes filtered through the machinery of political and economic systems which have a constant interest in squeezing out a singular story. Their US-based 'propaganda model' attempts to identify the routes by which economic capital and power filter out newsworthy news, marginalise dissent, and allow the government and other dominant private interests to get their messages across to the public:

1 Those who actively control capitalist power have an interest in reproducing a consensus of mass opinion that maintains the status quo via influence within institutions of the mass media;
2 Private media forms rely upon pro-capitalist advertising to keep their operational costs in line with other comparable media forms. A private media form cannot afford to voice opinions that may upset their sponsors;
3 Mass media forms need to produce regular news. It is more cost effective to rely upon institutionalised news sources (controlled by the interest groups mentioned in 1, above) than it is to send reporters into the field to gather information at grass roots level;
4 Those who wish to defend the interests of the status quo will be prepared to invoke a violent ideological language, presenting alternatives as dangerous, evil, negative or deviant.

British media forms arguably enjoy greater autonomy than their US counterparts. It is unlikely that the propaganda model exists in such a tight manner. It may be more accurate to consider whether its filters operate as structures which wax and wane, rather than as existing in such a permanent and deterministic manner. Hallin (1986) argues that media forms are never as closed and collectively homogeneous as the propaganda model suggests. There cannot be any singular, dominant power at work that is able effectively to produce a dominant mode of perception within the minds of an audience. Hallin's hegemonic model argues that media forms do extend processes into what is reported but these are marked by periods of alternative and overlapping shifts between (a) an openness of diverse counter-hegemonic voices and (b) a closure around a regulating and dominant voice. However, at times of national or global crises it is debatable whether Hallin would argue against the potential predominance of the propaganda model's focus upon a prevailing dominant voice.

It is our contention that Bourdieu's theoretical perspective provides both an insight into the individual person (the journalist, etc.) *within* the institution, and the processes that connect the journalist as story-teller with their audience. The predominant contemporary assertion – that an audience receives such a wide range of journalistic stories that the story pieced together in the active minds of a given population can never be coherently solidified into a dominant, or singular story – is an attractive one. However, one must be wary of being totally seduced by its appeal. First, can it be accepted that people are free to actively reason beyond what they already know? This may combine with either a deliberate reluctance to go beyond what is known, or certain less deliberate – even unconscious – processes embedded within Bourdieu's *habitus*. It cannot be simply accepted that people are free to choose, free to reason, in some pure sense. We all, on an everyday basis, produce our own ability to reason out of the necessities of daily existence (Coombes 1994). How often are we free, in some subjective sense, to break from the constraints of such necessities? Second, one has to consider whether people have the time and inclination to expose themselves to a wide range of available reported news during the routines of their everyday lives. How much variance do people engage with even within temporary discursive communities at work, in the pub, or at home with friends or family? Moreover, how many people in Britain are genuinely concerned with what happens in places as geographically distant as Indonesia?

REPRESENTATION

Representation: that which simultaneously speaks for and stands in for something else (Chambers 1994, p. 22).

The public gets what the public wants . . . the public wants what the public gets (Paul Weller *Going Underground* 1980).

For Chambers (1994), there can be no neutral means of representation whilst there is also no privileged representation of a given reality. There can be no single dominant 'tongue or language' in which truth can be confidently asserted. No voice, no story that is told, can claim to represent the truth. This almost hypersubjective approach is problematic: it ignores the realism that certain representations are constructed by particular historical institutions that enjoy greater influence than others. Representation is, after all, a process soaked with intent, purpose and power.

A story told is always told with a given certainty. Such stories are constantly relayed within a linguistic style saturated with a claim to know the 'truth' and, by degree, is likely to be accepted as such by an audience. An audience *expects* to be given a certain certainty through a story presented by the story-telling mediator. Of course, there can be no real certainty and no beyond-any-doubt conclusions in reality – but this docs not stop an audience *wanting* what it cannot have. How many of us are receptive to stories honest enough *not* to present a coherent whole? The professional story-teller has a kind of audience-led desire to attain and report a systematic presentation of unequivocal and absolute knowledge *despite the fact that this never can be so.* Audiences like to be told what they expect to hear. If they hear what they expect to hear then they are more likely to accept it as 'truth'. There may be an ontological need for personal security in the narrative of the story. If an audience were to move beyond the ambit of their culture's narrative constructions they would no longer recognise the 'sites of expression' that locate what they know (Rapport and Dawson 1998). People would lose trust in their personal perceptions of themselves, and their historical place in the wider social world. Systems of signification, relayed on the part of the story-teller, construct habitual perceptions of reality which reinforce the already structured language-world of the audience.

The story-teller sits on the narrative fence with one eye on their audience and one eye on the original local act. To move beyond what is known by their audience threatens to take their story into the 'unknown' and potentially 'incoherent' side of the fence occupied by the Other, the 'Indonesian'. In some ways, the story-teller has a vested personal interest in avoiding telling their story from the perspective of the Other. Who, after all, would listen to a story-teller who tells incoherent stories? Furthermore, the story is based upon similarities between the *habitus* of the journalist and that of the audience. The process of mis-representation is probably less deliberate than injecting lies or deceptions into a story. The closer the fit between expectation and similarity of *habitus* then, maybe, the more accurate the story?

In Bourdieu's world, it appears that sets of interacting social relations are likely to ensure a reproductive status quo of social conditions through the active, but not always deliberate, exclusion of difference. We constantly collapse new experiences into what we already know without an active inquisitive search into the unknown world of otherness. This takes us back to the power inherent within the practice of representation. Reporters are likely to apply representational models of knowledge upon encounters with 'foreign' experience based upon the knowledge they accept as ontologically secure. They are less likely to use loose generative models that give primacy to the multiple meanings held by their actors. In this sense, the story that is told over and over again – despite vastly different cultural and social contexts – becomes that of the reporting story-teller and not that of the people that are reported. This knowledge has been accumulated over time through the West's long-standing colonial and post-colonial politico-economic relationship with the Other. Hence, the Other becomes an integral part of Western culture, its 'cultural contestant, and helps to define the West as its contrasting image, idea, personality, experience' (Said 1995, p. 1). We are presented with definitions of how we distinguish ourselves from 'them'. This one-way flow of information involves a power relationship in which meanings from 'alien contexts' are imposed upon peoples (Hobart 1987; Morley and Robins 1995). Stories are rarely constructed upon local categories and meanings but are often built upon the categories habitually internalised within the 'foreign' mediator. At best, the story that is eventually told to an audience becomes a kind of hybrid semblance of the original act – a paradoxical double discourse of mediated fact/fiction. France 1968,

Tiananmen Square 1989 and Jakarta 1998 all collapse into each other. Castro, Banda, Suharto all become potential 'dictatorial' bedfellows. Western Marxists see the patterns, Western capitalists see the patterns, Western audiences see the patterns, but are the patterns ever really *there*? The story told becomes indistinguishable from the world it tells about and therefore becomes 'real' in the vision of its audience beyond the popularising reporter (Bauman 1991). To assume that we can ever 'know' the other's lived reality is naive arrogance, but exploring the other's sources of knowledge allows us to question dominant Western media images and to present a different picture of reality.

Thus we can ask, what is Indonesia to its inhabitants? How do *they* formulate *their* perceptions of Indonesian culture and identity? As we discuss below, national culture was constructed initially in an attempt to achieve independence from colonial rule, and subsequently to fulfil the need to subsume over 300 ethnic groups under one nation-state. However, these groups each have their own interpretations of the world around them, their own habitus, reflected in *adat*. Succinctly, this refers to customary law but encompasses social, political and value systems, unique to each of these ethnic groups. A Western audience – and indeed an 'Indonesian' audience – cannot have a personal frame of reference upon which to compare the story that is told for they cannot walk in the same time-space shoes of the reporter and therefore cannot effectively critically investigate the accuracy of the story as it unfolds. Despite all of the technological apparatus at the disposal of the story-teller, their audience is never provided with a completely open picture of events until after the event is politically secure in some form of interest-based conclusion. Journalists often return to the scene – and to our living-room screens – when the 'dust has settled' to produce a retrospective post-conflict story. It is often here that they safely carve out much more critically open visions of the wider picture.

When a reporter thrusts a microphone in front of an Indonesian and asks why s/he is engaged in violent protest on the streets of *Jakarta* and the answer comes back, 'Suharto must go!', the reporter is left with little more than the cognitive assumption that forms the structure of a story that *all of Indonesia* thinks: 'Suharto's dictatorship must come to an end soon'. Maybe, after all, the desire for democracy was *the* reason why *all* of Indonesia was throwing metaphorical bricks at the symbol of Suharto? Generalisations haunt the practicalities of producing a tell-able story.

What *was* Indonesia within this constructed story? Was it a nation of subservient and downtrodden peoples who suddenly rebelled against Suharto's military domination (*The Independent* 22/01/98, p. 4)? Was this indicative of a qualitative shift towards a true revolution or was it merely a venting of years of frustration boiling over into the reactionary anarchy of mindless destruction and theft portrayed on numerous news programmes as British nationals fled a burning Jakarta?[1] Was Indonesia suffering from the reverberations of the 1997/98 'South East Asian financial crisis' (*The Guardian* 07/01/1998, p. 1 London)? Was it about internal historical ethnic divisions, re-opened as Suharto's legitimacy dissipated (*The Guardian* 25/01/98, p. 19 London) with 'Indonesian masses turning on minorities' (*The Daily Express* 15/05/98, p. 29)? Were these ethnic conflicts being led by 'Muslim mobs on the rampage . . . on an anti-Chinese pogrom' (*The Times* 12/05/98, p. 17)?

Could all of these perspectives be true? What was more apparent was that, in typical Western style, an individual scapegoat – or was it devil? – became collectively isolated as the embodied one-and-only cause of all of Indonesia's problems. The collective shout went up – '*Suharto must go!*' Significantly such stories represented Indonesia's problems as being *only* internal in nature and not linked into wider global events such as the widespread Western loss of faith and investment in Tiger, Chinese and even Japanese economies.[2]

Between all of these perspectives was a more unified story being told? As we attempted to reason with this information were we cognitively shifting from the divergent to the convergent? Were we shifting respectively from the denotative to the connotative (Barthes 1977)? Moreover, were we constructing, to a significant degree, a mythologised reality of Indonesia in our collective consciousness based upon the cultural codes and conventions of both putting stories together and receiving them (Barthes 1972)? Could all of the divergent stories being told at the time converge into a single narrative?

CONSTRUCTING INDONESIA

We have suggested that our perceptions of Indonesia are based on historically accumulated knowledge about the cultural Other, reinforced by Western media representations. But can we assume that our perceptions have any resonance with Indonesian perceptions of themselves? Dominant national discourses on Indonesia as a nation-state might appear to validate these Western perceptions. But, we argue, this is only one version of a far more complex reality. To appreciate the multiple meanings of Indonesia for its inhabitants, we must consider other discourses and local practices which contest this national ideology.

Indonesia as a nation-state is a twentieth century phenomenon. Prior to Dutch colonial rule, this territory comprised thousands of independent states (Geertz 1980). Rebellions against colonialism were localised and powerless against European military and technological might (Christie 1996). Then, in 1906, the Budi Utomo movement was established. Western ideas of nationalism were adopted as a means of striving for independence. Indonesia 'had to be created before it could be liberated' (Hubinger 1992, p. 15). Diverse local historiographies, heroes and customs were appropriated and reconstructed within a nationalist framework. After independence this 'invention of traditions' (Hobsbawn 1992) continues to reproduce national consciousness.

In 1945, two months before the Proclamation of Independence, *Pancasila* was constructed. This state ideology sets out five principles – belief in a supreme being, national unity, humanitarianism, democracy and social justice. *Pancasila* has retained its ideological hold, forming the foundation of all social, religious and political organisations. Those organisations which failed to conform were banned (Ramage 1995, p. 3).

With so many ethnic groups and languages *Bahasa Indonesia*, the national language, was important in promoting a national identity and culture. It furthered state control, promoted a particular perception of development and reinforced the ideological dominance of the national over the local (Heryanto [nd] cited in Foulcher 1990). *Bahasa Indonesia* is used in the bureaucracy, government, economy, broadcasting and schooling. At a local level it is less successful at developing a national identity as ethnic groups continue to speak their own languages in daily life with Jakarta as the only real exception (Anderson 1990).

In 1965, following years of weak government and regional dissent, Suharto took over leadership under the New Order regime. He sought to impose and legitimate a strong central government and to establish economic stability as a base for development (MacAndrews 1986, p. 10). This was realised through the *Repelita*, five-year development plans, which themselves were informed by *Pancasila*. Suharto proclaimed that to 'deviate from *Pancasila* is to undermine development efforts, national stability and the character of the Indonesian people' (Morfit 1986, p. 43).

Until recently, economic development (especially compared to the previous period) had been viewed as one of the successes of the New Order. Pragmatic economic policies, investment, labour productivity and oil revenues collectively had an impact on economic annual growth (7% from 1968–1981, 4.3% from 1981–1988, and 7% from 1989–1993). The focus on agricultural development in government planning meant that by 1984 Indonesia had moved from being the world's largest rice importer to self-sufficiency (Schwarz 1994). This is an achievement of the Suharto era frequently cited by Indonesians. Infrastructural, transport and communication networks have significantly improved since 1966. Education, literacy and health indicators reflect a better standard of living. The numbers of Indonesians living below the poverty line (at least until the recent crisis) had significantly decreased. Although statistical data varies, commentators agree that this had been one of the New Order achievements (Hill 1994; Schwarz 1994). Together, these economic and social improvements have, in the past, 'provided a hospitable context for ideological appeals for legitimacy' (Ramage 1995, p. 39).

Repelita VI (1993 to 1998) – covering economic development, defence and security, education, health and cultural issues – reinforces the relationship between economic development, stability, and national unity. *Pancasila's* influence is apparent. For example, the primary objective of the media during Repelita VI is to implement:

The values put forth in Pancasila . . . *to improve people's awareness, strengthen national resilience and maintain stability . . . promote active community participation in the development process and improve the distribution of information to reach a larger segment of society* (Department of Information 1997, pp. 22–23).

The Department of Information monitors state and commercial television and radio stations, which have been obliged to broadcast daily news bulletins on the official engagements of the President and other government ministers, state ceremonies and successful development projects. This facilitates the 'reinforce[ment of] the government's rhetorical commitment to its trilogy of development, equity and stability' (Hill and Mackie 1994, p. xxix). Newspapers overtly critical of the government, have been closed down (Mallarengeng and Liddle 1996). Films, books and newspapers are liable to censorship and prominent writers critical of government policy have been imprisoned and their works banned (Hatley 1994).

The maxim for TVRI, the national, state-run television station, broadcast intermittently, is *menjalin persatuan dan kesatuan* (promoting national unity and integrity) and is accompanied by visual images of Indonesia. The camera sweeps across mountains, rice fields, the sea, through 'local' dance performances, to agriculture and industry (fishing, oil refineries and freight transportation) and finally arrives at Jakarta's cityscape. By proceeding from rural to urban environments, images of both economic development and the incorporation of diverse regions, livelihoods and customs into a national culture are presented.

Local culture is appropriated by the state in the furtherance of national unity. Regional musical performances are broadcast daily on national television but their ethnic origins are not identified (Guinness 1994). Indonesian films 'almost exclusively' use the Indonesian language and 'depict generalized Indonesian behaviour patterns stripped of ethnic markers' (Heider 1991, p. 10). In the past, artistic forms have been employed by the state to disseminate and encourage acceptance of government policies. For example, the Javanese *Wayang kulit* (shadow plays) and their puppeteers have been used to promote *Repelita* objectives of agricultural development and family planning (Hatley 1994).

CONTESTING NATIONAL CONSTRUCTIONS

The dominant national discourse and government rhetoric, however, are contested in the media, the arts and in local discourses. The banned novels of one of Indonesia's most famous writers, Pramudya Ananta Tur, set at the turn of the century and dealing with nationalist associations, continue to be circulated 'underground'. They offer both a powerful insight into a rarely debated period of Indonesian history and a challenge to the official version of the establishment of the nation (Foulcher 1990; Hatley 1994).

The government prefers traditional apolitical theatrical performances. Instead, modern Javanese theatre groups use traditional settings and myths, but satirise kings and courtiers while depicting villagers as resourceful and strong. These subversive performances, parallelling the contemporary state hierarchy, make social and political comment about the government (Hatley 1994, p. 250).

News items, features and editorials (about 95 per cent of newsprint) in Jakartan newspapers are written in Indonesian, conform to censorship rules and use words – such as development and progress – favoured by the government. The remaining 5 per cent of newsprint comprise *pojok* (corner-columns). Written in Bahasa Jakarta (a lower class language developed by Balinese, Sundanese, Buginese, Javanese and Chinese settlers) they make indirect political comment about events which, if explicitly stated, could lead to the newspaper's closure (Anderson 1990, p. 142).

The art of pojok writing is one of allusion, innuendo, sarcasm, and mock surprise. For example, a pojok may quote a senior minister or army officer making an uplifting speech in Indonesian about the need to live simply, work hard, and avoid corruption. On a separate line comes the rejoinder Bener deh! *(Absolutely!) Evidently a simple agreement with what the great man has said. But the metropolitan reader immediately notes that the pojok writer has used not the Indonesian* benar *but the Jakartan* bener *which has strong 'come off it' connotations, and has added the untranslatable but salty Jakartan particle* deh *(something like 'indeed'), which pithily expresses ridicule and disbelief. In just two words, then, the pojok formally praises the minister or officer while at the same time implying that he is hypocritical, lazy, corrupt, and pompous* (Anderson 1990, p. 143).

On a recent visit to West Sumatra, the site of earlier fieldwork (Davis 1994), the opportunity arose to observe friends and adoptive family watching television and to discuss some of the issues raised. One news item 'celebrated' the 21st anniversary of East Timor's 'integration into Indonesia' (TVRI news broadcast 17.7.97). The reconstruction of history was presented thus: in the post-colonial world, there had been five political parties in East Timor; four had wanted to integrate with Indonesia, the fifth had not; civil war had ensued. Since 'integration' there had been 'a great deal of development' especially more hospitals and roads. The report acknowledged many countries did not recognise East Timor as part of Indonesia, but concluded that Indonesia was indeed 'one family'. Comments from those watching this news item suggested they accepted the 'truth' of the report.

Yet, we should not assume that 'Indonesians' simply absorb and accept unquestioningly the national ideology. There are other regional conflicts such as the ongoing Acehnese rebellion (North Sumatra) but these are rarely reported in the West. Without alternative sources of knowledge, it may be difficult for them to discern ideological intentions (just as we in the West might simply accept what we hear about Indonesia from news items and choose to ignore or fail to recognise hegemonic processes at work). In other areas, they challenge these ideas. In 1993, students in Jakarta demonstrated against poor government performance and ineptitude (Schwarz 1994). At a 1990 concert given in Java by the popular singer/songwriter Iwan Fals, reports suggested that the entire audience joined him in singing his hit *Bongkar* (Demolish): 'Oppression and abuses of power/are too numerous to mention . . . we're fed up with greed and uncertainty' (Hatley 1994, p. 262). Seemingly, Western media representations of Indonesians living under an authoritarian state, unable to express dissent until recent events, is not entirely the case.

Alternative sources of news to that provided by the media are sought, for example through personal communication between people inhabiting different parts of Indonesia. The Minangkabau have a long-established tradition of rural to urban migration. This practice is embedded in their culture, through proverbs and historiography (Taufik Abdullah 1972) and is perceived as enriching the Minangkabau world by providing new ideas and information from outside its boundaries (Pelly Usman 1983). Visits between migrants and their village relatives are commonplace and communication between a wide circle of people is assured (Davis 1994). During one such city encounter, migrants and visitors gathered together. Initial conversation was dominated by the comparative costs of city and village schooling which led to a discussion about national government policies. Their comments suggested that they do not simply accept government rhetoric on national unity and equity for all but make their own (critical) judgements based on other information sources.

It is also important to recognise that although 'local powers of self-definition become engulfed by national and international agendas about identity . . . these non-local agendas have interests at odds with regional, local and personal agendas' (Vass and Davis 1996, p. 132). Nelson (1998, p. 149) explores the significance of national and local politics in Rejang-Lebong, Sumatra. Inhabitants of her field location were relatively unconcerned with the somewhat 'straightforward' 1992 national election. The village head election was a different matter, described as 'hot' and therefore 'dangerous'. A heated and lengthy campaign resulted in divisive factions based on ethnic and kinship loyalties. Clearly, local politics received far more attention than national politics.

There seems little recognition in the British media that local concerns might influence the national political scene. Equally, ethnic constitution and the attendant diversity of beliefs and practices are rarely reported. Coverage of recent events was constructed around only two ethnic groups: the Indonesian 'masses' and the Chinese minority. 'Indonesians' effectively became forced together into one homogeneous group, almost invariably being mis-represented as Muslims who are both violent and irrational. Time and time again Islam is made to cover everything one most disapproves of from the standpoint of civilised 'Western' rationality (Said 1997, p. 8).

Adat

Local identity is founded on each ethnic group's *adat*. Minangkabau *adat* defines its geographical boundaries and provides the basis of its social organisation and value system. *Adat* orders everyday life, by prescribing marriage rules, social relationships, authority and ritual life. 'On the highest level of meaning [*adat*] suggests group cohesion and social identity pertaining to . . . notions of ethnic exclusiveness and unity' (Karim 1993, pp. 14–15). *Adat* is not static: although some *adat* rules (e.g. on descent and inheritance) are regarded as central to Minangkabau identity and thus unchanging, it is also recognised that in certain aspects of social life change is inevitable; *adat* allows for this adaptation in response to community discussions and consensus (Datuk Rajo Penghulu 1978; Nasroen 1957). These two principles provide the central tenet of Minangkabau social action. Dispute and decision-making processes are managed within a system of three strata of kinship groupings – the extended matrilineal family, the lineage and the clan. If a resolution cannot be agreed at the lower level, then it is referred to a wider body of kin. Although political manoeuvring is evident behind the scenes to facilitate a favourable outcome, once a decision has been reached, all parties must conform.

Adat is frequently used to make sense of national policies which impact at the local level. In most Minangkabau villages national government representation and the local *adat* council co-exist. The latter is not officially recognised in national law, but is indirectly acknowledged through taking its members on to the Village Council, a state institution (Benda-Beckmann 1979, p. 126). Changes to national inheritance law have been negotiated by Minangkabau *adat* authorities to ensure that whilst earned wealth could be inherited bilaterally (in accordance with changes to national policy), *adat* principles of matrilineal inheritance of ancestral property would remain intact (Ng 1987 cited in Guinness 1994).

At the local level then, *adat* is a significant foundation for social organisation, political and moral value systems, ideology and identity:

The tenacity of adat *derives from its pivotal role in social change, providing both a sense of continuity to temporal and geographical discontinuity, and an ideal cultural operator by which authorities have 'translated' radically new ideas and practices into ideologically familiar terms . . .* Adat *offers an opportunity to formulate a kind of counter identity at the local level which may redefine and reinterpret authority when and where state structures are weak* (Guinness 1994, p. 300).

Can we now question the appropriateness of Western media images and our reception of them? We have argued that these representations offer a picture of reality which excludes difference. They seem to be premised on Western derived interpretations of the political and cultural worlds of Indonesia without making allowance for local agency. Is it the case then that we construct images of otherness in our imaginations which relate knowledge only in terms comprehensible to us (Watson 1992)?

Our intention has been to show that this is a somewhat myopic vision of the other. By taking account of *adat* we are able to make two important points. First, that counter-hegemonic systems of thought, embodied in *adat*, facilitate a challenge to the ideology of the nation state from Indonesians' perspectives. Second, an appreciation of what *adat* entails enables us to question our own Western perceptions of Indonesia by acknowledging the diversity of peoples within its geographical boundaries and by recognising their different approaches to and interpretations of the world around them.

CONCLUSION

Whether we report what we see with our own vision, or whether we are in concert with the vision of another's report, yesterday's person, as incorporated culturally constructed *habitus*, always haunts our present practices (Bourdieu 1990b). We may not always be conscious of the influential presence of such cultural ghosts.

Our vision is always ideologically shaped. Whatever we see we cut out and turn over in our *habitus* before serving it out on our own plate of practice (de Certeau 1984). What the journalist witnesses becomes immediately removed from the productive activity of its own actors to become packaged through the habitual constructions of the story-teller. The reported ethnographic present is one constructed out of the *habitus* of the reporter, not the practices of those people the reporter observes. This process becomes even more distant from original acts if the reporter attempts to produce a recipe fit for the taste of a particular editor, institution, or audience.

This process structures out local productive activity in terms of what is already known, rather than through the inclusive provision of local categories of perception, assessment and classification. The quality of relayed knowledge, transmitted via the act of representation, constantly takes real-life experiences to the gallows of mis-representation. It was this process that provided a regular course of representation that denied audiences a holistic understanding of what Indonesia really was during the events of 1998. Undoubtedly, such styles of representation will continue to deny audiences a more accurate vision of what Indonesia *is*.

ENDNOTES

1. During this period widespread media representations portrayed two distinct and highly generalised groups responsible for spearheading anti-government events in Jakarta. The first group – identified as 'the students' – were represented as the intellectual and rational leaders of directed political action. The second group – labelled 'the urban masses' or 'the workers' – were associated with a lack of political direction coupled with ongoing acts of criminal behaviour and violence. Can one accurately segregate such distinct practices and dispositions into distinct groupings of people in such situations?

2. Existing Western interests had to be first cut away before being re-injected in the form of structural adjustments within Indonesia. There was no option but to adopt US-style free markets and Western-style models of liberal democratic political reform within an over-arching attempt to bring the Asian 'them' in line with the rest of 'us'. The critical voices against such analytical conclusions were few and far between (e.g. John Gray *The Guardian* 17/12/1997, p. 17 London). It was almost as if all 'Orientals' were represented as somehow unfit to share star billing alongside the legitimate stars on the global stage unless they were reading from the same economic and political scripts as ourselves.

REFERENCES

Anderson, B. (1990) *Language and Power: Exploring Political Cultures in Indonesia*, Ithaca: Cornell University Press.

Barthes, R. (1972) *Mythologies*, London: Jonathan Cape.

Barthes, R. (1977) *Image, Music, Text* (selected and translated by Stephen Heath), London: Fontana.

Bauman, Z. (1991) *Modernity and Ambivalence*, Cambridge: Polity Press.

Bauman, Z. (1995) 'Searching for a centre that holds', in M. Featherstone, S. Lash and R. Robertson, eds, *Global Modernities*, London: Sage.

Benda-Beckmann, F. von. (1979) *Property in Social Continuity. Continuity and Change in the Maintenance of Property Relationships through Time in Minangkabau, West Sumatra*, The Hague: Martinus Nijhoff.

Berman, M. (1988) *All That is Solid Melts Into Air*, New York: Penguin.

Bourdieu, P. (1984) *Distinction: A social critique of the judgement of taste*, London/Harvard College: Routledge and Kegan Paul.

Bourdieu, P. (1990a) *In Other Words: Essays towards a reflexive sociology*, Cambridge: Polity Press.

Bourdieu, P. (1990b) *The Logic of Practice*, Cambridge: Polity Press.

Bourdieu, P. (1991) *Language and Symbolic Power*, Cambridge: Polity Press.

Certeau, M, de (1984) *The Practice of Everyday Life*, Berkeley: The University of California Press.

Chambers, I. (1994) *Migrancy, Culture, Identity*, London: Routledge.

Chomsky, N. (1989) *Necessary Illusions: Thought control in democratic societies*, London: Pluto Press.

Christie, C. (1996) *A Modern History of Southeast Asia. Decolonization, Nationalism and Separatism*, London: Tauris Academic Studies.

Coombes, A.E. (1994) '*The distance between two points: Global culture and the liberal dilemma*' in G. Robertson, *et al.*, eds, *Travellers' Tales: Narratives of home and displacement*, London: Routledge.

Datuk Rajo Penghulu (1978) *Pokok-pokok Pengetahuan Adat Alat Minangkabau*, Bandung: Remaja Rosdakarya.

Davis, C. (1994) *Gender Relations and Networks in a West Sumatran Minangkabau Village*, PhD Thesis, University of Hull.

Department of Information, Republic of Indonesia (1997) *Repelita VI (1993–1998)*. www.indonesianet.com/indotoda/chapter4.htm.

Foulcher, K. (1990) 'The Construction of an Indonesian National Culture: Patterns of Hegemony and Resistance', in A. Budiman, ed., *State and Civil Society in Indonesia*, Monash Papers in Southeast Asia no 22.

Geertz, C. (1980) *Negara: The Theatre State in Nineteenth Century Bali*, Princeton: Princeton University Press.

Giddens, A. (1991) *Modernity and Self-identity: Self and society in the late modern age*, Cambridge: Polity Press.

Guinness, P. (1994) 'Local Society and Culture' in H. Hill, ed., *Indonesia's New Order: The Dynamics of Socio-economic Transformation*. Honolulu: University of Hawaii Press.

Hallin, D.C. (1986) *The 'Uncensored' War: The media and Vietnam*, New York: Oxford University Press.

Hatley, B. (1994) 'Cultural Expression' in H. Hill, ed., *Indonesia's New Order: The Dynamics of Socio-economic Transformation*, Honolulu: University of Hawaii Press.

Heider, K. (1991) *Indonesian Cinema: National Culture on Screen*, Honolulu: University of Hawaii Press.

Herman, E. and Chomsky, N. (1988) *Manufacturing Consent*, Toronto: Panthean.

Hill, H. (1994) 'The Economy' in H. Hill, ed., *Indonesia's New Order: The Dynamics of Socio-economic Transformation*, Honolulu: University of Hawaii Press.

Hill, H. and Mackie, J. (1994) 'Introduction' in H. Hill, ed., *Indonesia's New Order: The Dynamics of Socio-economic Transformation*, Honolulu: University of Hawaii Press.

Hobart, M. (1987) 'Introduction: Context, Meaning and Power' in M. Hobart and R. Taylor, eds, *Context, Meaning and Power in Southeast Asia*, Ithaca: Cornell Southeast Asian Program.

Hobsbawm, E. (1992) 'Inventing Traditions', in E. Hobsbawm and T. Ranger, eds., *The Invention of Traditions*, Cambridge: Cambridge University Press.

Hubinger, V. (1992) 'The Creation of Indonesian National Identity', *Prague Occasional Papers in Ethnology*, pp. 1–35.

Karim, W.J. (1993) *Women and Culture: Between Malay Adat and Islam*, Boulder: Westview Press.

Lyotard, J-F. (1984) *The Postmodern Condition: A report on knowledge*, Manchester: Manchester University Press.

MacAndrews, C. (1986) 'Central Government and Local Development in Indonesia: An Overview', in C. MacAndrews, ed., *Central Government and Local Development in Indonesia*, Singapore: Oxford University Press.

Mallarangeng R. and Liddle, R.W. (1996) 'Indonesia in 1995: The Struggle for Power and Policy', *Asian Survey*, **36**(2), pp. 109–116.

Morfit, M. (1986) 'Pancasila Orthodoxy', in C. MacAndrews, ed., *Central Government and Local Development in Indonesia*, Singapore: Oxford University Press.

Morley, D. and Robins, K. (1995) *Spaces of Identity: Global Media, Electronic Landscapes and Cultural Boundaries*, London: Routledge.

Nasroen, M. (1957) *Dasar Falsafah Adat Minangkabau*, Jakarta: Pasaman.

Nelson, E. (1998) 'Women's Empty Talk: Gender and Local Politics in a Rejang Village', in I-B. Trankell and L. Summers, eds., *Facets of*

Power and its Limitations. Political Culture in Southeast Asia, Uppsala Studies in Cultural Anthropology 24.

Pelly Usman (1983) *Urban Migrants and Adaptation in Indonesia: A Case Study of Minangkabau and Mandailing Batak Migrants in Medan, North Sumatra*, PhD Thesis, University of Illinois.

Ramage, D. (1995) *Politics in Indonesia: Democracy, Islam and the Ideology of Tolerance*, London: Routledge.

Rapport, N. and Dawson, A. (1998) 'Opening a debate' and 'Home and movement: A polemic', in N. Rapport and A. Dawson, eds., *Migrants of Identity: Perceptions of home in a world of movement*, Oxford: Berg.

Robertson, G., Mash, M., Tickner, L., Bird, J., Curtis., B. and Putnam, T., eds. (1994) *Travellers' Tales: Narratives of home and displacement*, London: Routledge.

Said, E. (1995) *Orientalism: Western Conceptions of the Orient*, Handsworth: Penguin.

Said, E. (1997) *Covering Islam: How the media and the experts determine how we see the rest of the world*, London: Vintage.

Schwarz, A. (1994) *A Nation in Waiting: Indonesia in the 1990s*, St Leonards: Allen and Unwin.

Taufik Abdullah (1972) 'Modernisation in the Minangkabau World: West Sumatra in the Early Decades of the Twentieth Century', in C. Holt, ed., *Culture and Politics in Indonesia*, Ithaca: Cornell University Press.

Touraine, A. (1977) *Self Production of Society*, Chicago/London: University of Chicago Press.

Vass, J. and Davis, C. (1996) 'International, National and Local Constructions of Social and Economic Worlds', *Children's Social and Economics Education*, **1**(2), pp. 131–145.

Watson, C. (1992) 'Autobiography, Anthropology and the Experience of Indonesia' in J. Okely and H. Callaway, eds, *Anthropology and Autobiography*, London: Routledge.

Williams, B. (1989) 'A class act: Anthropology and the race to nation across ethnic terrain', *Annual Review of Anthropology*, **18**, pp. 401–444.

6 The manufacture of news – fast moving consumer goods production, or public service?

Michael Bromley

We do not have a duty to inform: we have a duty to supply information to our customers – information they are willing to pay for, Mark Wood, editor-in-chief, Reuters Ltd, Reporting Africa: Return to the Agenda, Cardiff *(23 November 1998).*

The 1980s were characterised by the ascendancy of what C.P. Scott (1921; 1997, p. 108) called the 'material' existence of the press. The dominant libertarian view was that all other freedoms, including those of speech and expression, were dependent on the prior establishment of the freedom of the market (see Schudson 1978, pp. 57–60). The media were progressively deregulated, and sections were themselves mobilised in support of the wider agenda of economic liberalisation. This seemed to be epitomised by the dispersion of the national newspaper industry from Fleet Street; the introduction of so-called new technology; the proliferation of television channels, led by the largely unregulated development of satellite TV; the auctioning of terrestrial television franchises; the expansion of cross-media conglomerates, promoted via aggressive marketing, and attacks on the supposed corporatist privileges of the public service media, particularly the BBC (Elstein 1998; Stephenson 1998, pp. 21–3). Yet the decade 1987–1997 was also one of recurrent crisis in the media and especially the press, beginning with national newspapers 'drinking in the last-chance saloon', and culminating in the public responses to the death of Diana, Princess of Wales: relative commercial vigour was accompanied by a steep decline in public confidence in editorial propriety (see Wilson 1997).

This has been seen as a distortion of the 'Darwinian logic of capitalism' (*Daily Telegraph*, cited in Toynbee 1998b), in which 'honest reporting' has been understandably but unjustifiably sacrificed to 'business interests' (Toynbee 1998a). The over-arching need for a social responsibility dimension to the media, it has been argued, means that (in the words of the Liberal-Democrat leader Paddy Ashdown) the output of news cannot be treated 'like the production of a tin of baked beans' (BBC Radio 4 1998). Nevertheless, attempts to interpose mechanisms to regulate the balance between 'good journalism and the commercial imperatives of newspaper publishing' have largely met with failure (Soley 1992; see also Tulloch 1998).

The question asked here is whether journalists can play a specific role in asserting and defending an autonomy of calling to provide a public service – and resist the market imperatives of media corporations which, in the words of one newspaper editor, increasingly view news as a fast moving consumer good (Fowler 1994). It delineates the role of ethics in establishing journalism as a relatively autonomous practice. Journalists, as opposed to the commercialised media, have a longer recent history of, and have demonstrated greater diligence in, attempting to establish and protect editorial standards: the National Union of Journalists' (NUJ) code of conduct dates from 1936, while attempts by the Association of European Journalists to establish a charter for journalism continued into the 1990s (D'Arcy 1993; Soley 1993). At the core of this project has lain a desire to:

separate the function of journalism from the business of the media . . . [and] create a new and distinctive role in the debate for editors, allowing them to concentrate solely on the duty of journalists within a democracy to act as the accepted agents of the public right to know and communicate (D'Arcy 1993, p. 8).

Since the 1980s, the tendency in the UK has been in the opposite direction – for journalists to become increasingly enmeshed within the business of the media, emerging in some instances as 'entrepreneurial editors', and no more than 'pay[ing] lip service to the concepts of truth, light and the virtuous way' (Randall 1996, pp. 1–6; Tunstall 1993, pp. 15–16; Tunstall 1996, pp. 116–35). The idea which for many underpinned the formation of the Press Council in the 1950s, that all those involved in newspapers – 'proprietor, manager, editor and working journalists' – ought to come together in 'a single profession' (Levy 1967, pp. 418–19), has subsequently been turned on its head. What now appears to be threatened is the editor's traditional role as 'the custodian of a newspaper's reputation and values' (Griffith 1995). By the 1980s the Press Council was viewed as 'dominated by the representatives of the owners' and alongside them sat the editors.[1] Journalism is seen as having become purely 'market-driven', one result being the process of so-called dumbing-down in pursuit of market share and profitability (Bromley 1998). British media proprietors have never entered into the kind of voluntary agreement which, for example, protects the rights of editors in Norway. There an *Editor's Code*, to which both the Norwegian Editors' Association and the National Association of Norwegian Newspapers are signatories, entitles editors to:

free and independent leadership of the editorial department and editorial work and full freedom to shape the opinions of the paper even if they in single matters (sic) *are not shared by the publisher or the board . . . The editor must never allow himself/herself to be influenced to advocate opinions that are not in accord with the editor's own conviction.*

It charges that editors 'shall always keep in mind the ideal purpose of the press' (Norsk Presseforbund 1973). By comparison, the code of practice framed by the UK newspaper and periodical industry and applied by the Press Complaints Commission (PCC), as the major self-regulatory mechanism, eschews any such idealisation. This is in part itself a consequence of the 'untrammelled' commercialisation of the media which has led to the casualisation and routinisation of journalism (Bromley 1997, Tulloch 1998, p. 81). Simultaneously, the media's use of technology has affected journalism's function as a profession, or a craft, which can develop and maintain its own internal standards (MacGregor 1995; Rosenblum 1993). The results, it has been argued, are traceable in a further, decisive shift from news to 'newszack', the expansion of 'industrial' journalism, and the decline of high-value professional or craft practices, such as investigative reporting (Belsey 1998, pp. 3–7; Doig 1997; Franklin 1997). Moreover, the public right to know is construed as a fundamental but qualified human or civil right, as enshrined in the First Amendment to the US constitution, Article 19 of the Universal Declaration of Human

Rights and Article 10 of the European Convention on Human Rights (Burnet 1992, p. 49), and which continues to be recognised as such (for example in the Canadian Charter of Rights and Freedoms of 1982). Milton (1644; 1995, p. 19) called it 'the liberty to know', which together with the liberty 'to utter, and to argue freely' was constitutive of freedom of speech. The development of the commercialised media, structurally separating author from audience, has resulted in a conflict between individual and corporate proprietorial 'editorial rights' and this broader public right to know, in which the latter is dependent on journalism promoting 'the recognition and discovery of important truths and a willingness to report them' – a function sometimes categorised as 'editorial independence' (O'Neill, 1992, p. 17ff; see also Orwell 1946, 1957).

Thus, at its inception the *British Journalism Review* (1989) felt the need to raise the alarm over the menace of what it identified as a series of 'interlocking crises: a crisis of standards, a crisis of credibility, a crisis of freedom itself' within journalism in the 1980s. Such anxieties were closely associated with a supposed shift in the role of the press from 'watchdogs . . . [to] press barons' poodles' (Baistow cited in Snoddy 1993, p. 13). Of course, even if proven, this did not automatically equate to the unrestrained prostitution of journalism (O'Neill 1992, p. 28). Nor were such fears new, of course; but whereas the Conservative Prime Minister of the 1930s, Stanley Baldwin, was prepared to make some distinction between commercial enterprise and 'public interest', Thatcherism regarded 'profit-making . . . [as] the only real measure of socially worthwhile performance' (Stephenson 1998).

DEALING WITH 'THE CRISIS': PROFESSIONALS AND WORKERS

Most of the substantial attempts to develop new approaches to journalism in the 1980s and 1990s, unlike say the New Journalism and the 'gonzo' journalism of the 1960s, have come not from practitioners but media managements as marketing responses to perceptions of changes in the audiences for both the press and broadcasting (Bromley 1998, pp. 27–32). One notable development of the 1990s, which did originate chiefly among journalists and former practitioners in journalism schools in the United States of America, 'civic' or 'public' journalism, has had practically no impact in the UK.

The leaders in innovation in UK journalism (attempted or realised) have been provincial newspaper groups, commercial and especially cable television companies, News International and the BBC. The only significant mainstream project initiated by journalists was the short-lived attempt to return to traditional broadsheet journalism values through the establishment of *The Independent* in 1986 (Bertrand 1998, pp. 120–21; Rosen 1996; Stephenson 1998, pp. 20–21). Moreover, despite the injunction that 'discussion and information' are crucial to the development of internal professional or craft analysis (Black *et al.* 1995, p. 14), there remains 'a lack of a reflective and analytical culture' in British journalism (*BJR* 1989).

No journalism school in the UK publishes a regular review comparable to the *Columbia Journalism Review*, and the circulation of the *British Journalism Review* is small.[2] Academic journals, such as *Media, Culture and Society*, are not read by practitioners, and, in any event, a considerable tension continues to pervade relationships between journalists and theorists on a number of levels (see Leapman 1993; Phillips and Gaber 1996); while the main trade publications (*Press Gazette, Broadcast*) are no more than weekly papers. Since at least 1989, the NUJ has been on the defensive: membership has declined by about a third, and de-recognition has become commonplace (Gall 1997, p. 241). Although the union has not given up taking a critical stance,[3] its ethics council has been 'bogged down' since the early 1990s.[4] The UK has undoubtedly participated in a wider European rise in interest in media ethics in general (Bertrand 1998, p. 114; Heinonen 1993). Nevertheless, the number of books published in the UK on media ethics is small (Christians 1996).[5] Groups which are constituted to monitor the performance of journalists feel they run the risk of being marginalised as 'carping critics' (Townley n.d.). On the other hand, over the past two decades the media have themselves begun to report routinely on the practices of journalism, having abandoned the maxim that 'dog doesn't eat dog' – exemplified in 1998 by *The Guardian's* reporting of the supposed falsification of evidence in a Carlton Television documentary programme on drug dealing (Gibson *et al.* 1998), and a small number of individual journalists, mainly on the political left, also offer public criticisms of journalism practices (see Pilger 1998).

Recent experiences suggest that journalists who do question the performance of journalism run considerable risks by doing so, however. At the beginning of 1998, Jonathan Mirsky, the former East Asia editor of *The Times* who was subsequently retained as a special writer on China, criticised the roles of both the editor, Peter Stothard, and the proprietor, Rupert Murdoch, in shaping the paper's coverage of the PRC and Hong Kong. When Mirsky's comments were made public, they were disputed in an article written by Stothard and published in *The Times*. Stothard then refused to print unedited a letter of reply from Mirsky. At that point, Mirsky resigned. For about two weeks, the case was something of a *cause célèbre*, having being taken up particularly by the *Daily Telegraph, Guardian* and *Independent*, all of which were in direct competition with *The Times* and pursuing complaints against News International over the alleged predatory pricing of its paper. As a result, the former foreign correspondent got his '15 minutes of fame'. Even so, the case of the rather obscure journalist is unlikely to have produced even this amount of interest if it had not coincided with another, well publicised dispute which had arisen between Murdoch and the former Governor of Hong Kong, Chris Patten, over the cancellation of the agreement by one of Murdoch's publishing houses to publish Patten's memoirs (Mirsky 1998).

While Mirksy no doubt elicited the sympathy of many journalists, and the actual attacks on him were confined, at least in public, to those of his editor, when the BBC journalist Martin Bell suggested that the traditions of objectivity and impartiality in television journalism ought to be superseded by a more subjective 'journalism of attachment', the idea evoked a far more broadly-based hostility among the managerial cadre of the corporation's news and current affairs division (Bell 1998, pp. 15–18). Some years before, the journalist and news anchor Martyn Lewis had reportedly been warned by the head of the BBC's news and current affairs, Tony Hall, against launching the so-called 'good news' debate (Chittenden 1993). The problem, it seemed, was that 'he broke the cardinal rule of not appealing over the head of your boss' (*Observer* 1993). It was perhaps not surprising then that Lewis was careful to deny that 'he was criticising BBC news and current affairs bosses' (Culf 1993),[6] or that he attempted to demonstrate a convergence between his own views on 'good news' and the ways in which both Hall and the director-general of the corporation, John Birt, were re-thinking broadcast news as a whole (Lewis 1993a; White 1993). He even invoked the ethos of the corporation's public service remit in support of his call for a more 'responsible' and 'realistic' television news agenda (Lewis 1993b).

Although Lewis has blamed 'pressure from the top' for inculcating a tendency towards prioritising 'bad news', most of the debate around the 'good news' project has been conducted among senior BBC journalists like Peter Sissons, Jeremy Paxman, John Cole, John Humphrys and John Simpson, rather than embroiling editorial management. The issue has been projected as one concerned primarily with professional standards (Lewis 1998). In this way the manufacture of news is treated as a professional service performed within a larger corporate entity, and in which editorial management and workers at more or less all levels share a community of calling. To that extent, journalists are viewed as a relatively autonomous, self-managing group: matters of professional standards and values are interwoven with more material concerns, such as newsroom routines and resourcing (Goffee and Scase 1995, pp. 137–57; Lewis 1998, p. 6). This sense of vocation may be mobilised, too, not as an expression of a shared professionalism, but to articulate managerialist objectives. In the words of a former editor of the *Daily Mirror*, David Banks:

The relationship between the journalist and his (sic) *editor is a very personal one, and an important part of that relationship is the belief that it is the editor's right to control all aspects of editorial staffing and editorial content* (cited in Morgan 1992).

Such a proposition begs a response, which may result in a 'battle' between managements and journalists, and matters of industrial relations become entangled with journalistic concepts of exposure, scrutiny and explanation (Gall 1997, pp. 238–41; p. 246). The defence of journalistic standards and values thus becomes dependent on, rather than coterminous with, the material situation in which journalists work. The journalist Paul Foot, reflecting on the situation in the national newspaper sector in the summer of 1991, wrote:

Newspapers, like all other capitalist enterprises, are organised hierarchically. People don't look down to the ideas and talent in the rank and file. They look up and wonder how they can impress the Great Man at the top. The result is an atmosphere of abjectness, which is the most deadly poison for invigorating, challenging or entertaining journalism (Foot 1991, p. 8).

The enemy of good journalism, in Foot's view, was 'the fear and obsequiousness' which resulted from the collapse of collectivism among journalists in national newspapers in the 1980s, and better journalism would follow a 'revival of some sort of trade union spirit' (ibid., pp. 7–8). While Lewis chose to defy (if that is indeed what he did) BBC editorial managers by delivering a speech on news values to journalism students at the University of Colorado, Foot decided to publish his criticisms of Mirror Group Newspapers in the *Daily Mirror* itself, devoting his regular page to a 'Look in the *Mirror*!', charting 'mass sackings', windfall bonuses for directors, falling circulation, and cuts in resources (Foot 1993). Of course, the page was not carried by the *Mirror* and Foot left the paper the same day (Gall 1997, p. 237). His actions, however, help to map not only the distinctions which may be made between 'professional' debate and collectivist action by journalists, but also the extent to which 'professionals' may wish to distance themselves from expressions of collectivism which they regard as 'crusading and campaigning journalism . . . [whose] place is in political and polemical literature and not in the daily chronicling of the news' (Bell 1998, p. 16).

A SHARED IDEOLOGY AND SHARED ETHICS?

The idea that, while for some journalism is at times a rather glamorous profession, for others it is mundane and often poorly paid white collar work, is well established (Tunstall 1983, pp. 188–92). There is also a great deal of evidence to suggest that in the latter half of the twentieth century the existence of 'editorial sovereignty' (the journalistic freedom of editors) has been largely a myth (Tunstall 1977). In the 1970s, the NUJ's commitment to the closed shop led to many editors and others with editorial managerial responsibilities leaving the union, often at the behest of media corporations.[7] As a consequence, constraints on the sovereign power of editors since then have come far less from the collective strength of rank-and-file journalists than from managements who, particularly in the mid-1980s, began to view media production as primarily a 'competitive struggle . . . for market share' (Knight 1992, p. 70). Management domination, one Fleet Street veteran has argued, has fostered 'the cowardice of editors', which in turn encourages newsroom executives to ride 'Dissident reporters . . . [to] professional death' (Bevins 1990, p. 15).

Journalists as whole appear less persuaded that journalism has been so completely demeaned, however, and it has been suggested that the potential for professionalisation is greater in the 1990s than it has been at any previous time this century (Bromley 1998, pp. 34–5; Delano and Henningham 1996, pp. 20–22). Furthermore, other research has found that the movement towards a more reflective and responsible culture in journalism is beginning to pervade the training of journalists, raising the prospect that future journalists will claim greater autonomy (Thomass 1998). Similarly, while collectivism among UK journalists has clearly declined, a commitment to it as a form of organisation remains strong (Delano and Henningham 1996, pp. 9–10). This 'two-sided reality . . . in which the two sides contradict rather than complement each other' (Belsey 1998, p. 3) can be said to reflect a lack of a specific journalistic ideology which makes it difficult for journalists to lay claim to their own defensible, occupational space (equivalent to clinical practice in medicine), as they are unsure whether they are professionals, or more or less skilled workers (Elliott 1978, pp. 189–91). Indeed, it is not only journalists as trade unionists who are vulnerable to counter-attack by managements (see Foot 1993). 'Professionals' are put under pressure, too (Fiddick 1993), and may see a need to defend their position by pointing to the evidence provided by the marketing tool of audience research in support of their argument (Fletcher 1993; Lewis 1998), while other 'professionals' may invoke journalistic norms to condemn what they see as pandering to populism (Paxman 1993). The trade paper, *UK Press Gazette* (1989), argued 'it is not the job of newspapers to create a false, cosy glow . . . because that is what readers, and market researchers, would like to believe . . . one thing is non-negotiable, and it is that the news agenda is set by events . . .' Thus, what have been ostensibly debates about professional standards and values have been conducted largely on grounds delineated by media managerialism.

In trying to establish whether there may be purely journalistic determinants of practice (which some doubt – see Frost 1996), it is worth considering two quite recent judicial pronouncements. Judge Elisheva Barak, of the Jerusalem Regional Labour Court, asserted that a journalist is 'not an ordinary worker'; journalists and editors enjoy the right to 'journalistic freedom' which equates to the broader freedoms of expression and of the press in society at large. Any tension which may exist lies between the owner and publisher on the one hand, and the editor and journalists on the other, and not within the editorial function, between editors, as agents of proprietors, and journalists (Barak 1993, p. 23e). The latter, not the former, are the guardians of these wider freedoms. He who pays the piper does NOT call the tune 'unrestrictedly' (ibid., p. 26e). Moreover, the public's right to know is served by journalists being 'given maximum freedom of expression', and by owners not being allowed to turn their media properties into 'a mouthpiece' for their own ideas (ibid., p. 29e).

In a majority decision, the European Court of Human Rights addressed the issue of the ways in which journalists exercise their freedoms. It acknowledged the considerable variability which existed in journalistic methods, but granted that journalists ought to have discretion in choosing how to pursue and present stories. 'It is not for this court, nor for the national courts for that matter, to substitute their own views for those of the press as to what technique of reporting should be adopted by journalists'. Not only the substance of what journalists publish or broadcast, but the forms in which they are conveyed, it noted, are protected under the notion of freedom of expression (Jersild *v.* Denmark 1994, p. 20). Indeed, the validity of the way in which journalists do their job can compensate for the messages they transmit, for example:

news reporting based on interviews, whether edited or not, constitutes one of the most important means whereby the press is able to play its vital role of 'public watchdog' . . . The punishment of a journalist for assisting in the dissemination of statements made by another person in an interview would seriously hamper the contribution of the press to discussion of matters of public interest and should not be envisaged unless there are particularly strong reasons for doing so (ibid., p. 22).

These judgements amount to an argument for journalists (including editors) being primarily servants of the public interest and who, as such, are granted extensive rights to determine not only where that public interest lies, but also the ways in which it will be expressed, and how they will exercise their duties to serve it – even down to the journalistic techniques employed. The legitimation of the exercise of editorial control arises out of the 'independence' of journalism as a practice and not the ownership of the media (see O'Neill 1992, p. 16). In the UK the distinction is not always drawn between the ethics of journalism and the ethics of the media. Indeed, the latter predominate, with practice being regulated through a number of codes written and implemented by either industry or through statutory intervention.[8] The most recent book on media ethics does not mention the NUJ at all, even though its code of conduct has been in force for more than sixty years.[9] Ironically, a media magnate like Murdoch appears to distinguish quite precisely between his personal, business and editorial ethics (see Thomas Kiernan in Pilger 1997). Moreover, it is clear that, at least in the case of the PCC, the implementation of codified media ethics rarely satisfies public concerns or meets public expectations. This has led some to conjecture that in the press at least 'Proprietorial pressures [are] the real regulatory power' (Davy 1998; Franklin and Pilling 1998, pp. 112–15). The 'two-sided reality' of journalism manifests itself in the area of ethics, too, of course. In the 1980s those who saw membership of the NUJ as a sign of qualification as a 'professional' also often resented the concomitant disciplinary role of the ethics council.[10] Journalists, therefore, rarely form a consensus on praxis in any related area – for example, recently there have been deep divisions among editors and journalists over, *inter alia*, the introduction of privacy legislation, the incorporation of the European Convention on Human Rights into UK domestic law, and working definitions of the term 'in the public interest' (see *Guardian* 1997; Wakeham 1997; Morgan 1998). Even within the NUJ, where majorities have consistently supported the work of the ethics council since 1986, 'there are plenty of members who are happy to be a part of the "tabloid culture" '.[11]

CAUGHT IN THE MIDDLE

We media pundits need to pick our proprietor carefully for, like it or not, we always end up being economical with the truth about the media organisation that pays our monthly mortgage . . . Let's get real, no media company – certainly no plc – would pay anyone to [wash the company's dirty linen in public] (Brown 1998).

No national newspaper in the UK covers its own affairs really well and owners of even the quite recent past have used their papers to promote their own interests and attack those of their rivals . . . All that is needed is that simple facts are honestly told (Snoddy 1998).

121

In this general journalistic culture, all journalists, but perhaps especially journalists whose specialism is the coverage of the media themselves, are open to accusations that they lose their 'journalistic soul' as a result of the conditions attached to their employment. This may be exceptionally so if their employer is viewed as antithetical to 'professional' or craft standards, and as guilty of having 'stripped [his media property] of its intellectual integrity and . . . objectivity'. It only adds grist to the mill if the journalists in question also gain financially from such arrangements (Brown 1998). They 'can easily be caught in an uncomfortable crossfire'. The lack of a shared, precise understanding of the role of journalists and journalism has resulted in the media's own coverage of the media and journalism occurring 'almost by accident', largely dictated by a market competitiveness in which embarrassing one's rivals, and boosting one's own performance substitute for reporting and analysis because they are viewed as advantageous (Snoddy 1998). In these conditions, 'professional' or craft values, such as a reliance on 'simple facts . . . honestly told', are likely to be considered irrelevant, and market conviction leaves little room for the journalist 'who shares with the audience the processes, the doubts, the uncertainties, the excitements of the activity which leads to the ultimate choice of words and images put before the audience' (Tusa 1992, p. 9). Journalism, along with much of the media, it seems, has been privatised.

Even journalists who have established well-recognised prior credibility for their 'professionalism' may find their reputations threatened by the simple act of changing employer. This is what happened to Raymond Snoddy, who left the *Financial Times*, where he had been widely regarded as the best media correspondent working in the national daily press, to join *The Times* as media editor in 1997. Ten years previously, Snoddy had been vilified and even threatened by sections of the national press while presenting the television programme *Hard News*, which had adopted as its remit the calling to account of journalists and journalism (Snoddy and Woolwich 1990, p. 15). Then Snoddy had argued that it was essential that a journalist 'asks the sort of questions any intelligent journalist should be asking about his (*sic*) trade at a time when journalists are rated in public esteem behind politicians and estate agents and only just ahead of used car dealers' (ibid., p. 20). He implied incredulity that some newspapers exercised so much control over their journalists that they were able to forbid them even from appearing on the programme to defend their own practices (ibid., p. 16). This represented the corruption of the 'trade'. In 1988 it was Snoddy who stood accused, by 'join[ing] the payroll of a man who views his newspapers as nothing more than business products', of mobilising journalism in the service of the 'corporate affairs department' of News Corp, the ultimate owners of *The Times* (Brown 1998). Snoddy's answer was a vague prescription for media correspondents to 'push a little harder and be just that bit more determined' to fulfil their 'professional', or 'trade', obligations (Snoddy 1998).

The obligation to publish (or broadcast) 'simple facts . . . honestly told' is widely recognised, and is privileged in both the PCC and NUJ codes.[12] There is far less agreement, however, over the wider question of the purpose of such a stricture. The NUJ code (clause 3) acknowledges the possibility of falsification by distortion, selection and misrepresentation, and links the avoidance of distortion with the duty to oppose news suppression and censorship, and, more broadly, to the journalist's role in defending freedom of the press (clause 2). The code addresses itself to the individual journalist, and each member of the union is bound by its provisions. Thus, the 'fairness and accuracy' injunction may be regarded as a central tenet of 'professionalism' in, or the trade of, journalism (NUJ 1936). In the PCC code of practice,[13] which was originally drawn up by a committee of national newspaper editors and is now the responsibility of a board composed of newspaper and magazine industry representatives, insofar as any connection is made, the obligation to 'accuracy' (clause 1) is presented as part and parcel of a general regard for 'safeguarding the public's right to know', which is itself a constituent of 'professional and ethical standards' (preamble). There is, however, no definition of *what* the public has a right to know – whether it is everything, or just what the journalists want to reveal. The social ideal of freedom of expression is not mentioned. Furthermore, the code is unambiguous in stating that 'Editors are responsible for the actions of journalists employed by their publications' (Press Standards Board of Finance 1995). In this approach, 'fairness and accuracy' becomes a term of employment (as evidenced by attempts in the 1990s to have the code written into journalists' contracts).

CONCLUSION

Journalists in the UK routinely refer to their practice as *a profession, a trade, a craft*, or simply as *work:* the terms are often used interchangeably and more or less indiscriminately. This betokens a degree of confusion which is founded in the reality of that practice: even the codes to which journalists are enjoined to work do not concur on basic principles, such as the function of the 'fairness and accuracy' principle. What is most apparent is the distinction drawn between 'professionals', with some primary duty to the public as their clients, and media employees who are subject primarily to the terms and conditions of their employment. The concerns of employers impact on even 'professional' discourses, however, and in the 1980s and 1990s the market has been as much a feature of considerations over standards and values in journalism as has freedom of expression. To some extent, the PCC has enshrined the primacy of the media, and editorial managements (in the form of editors) in its code, and the duties of individual journalists are regarded chiefly as conditions of employment. On the other hand, for all its collectivism, the NUJ expresses an over-riding concern with the 'professionalism' of journalists, and has been at least ambivalent towards the conflicting requirements both to protect its members as employees, and to police them as 'professionals'. Furthermore, some journalists argue that such collectivism is itself the best guarantee of the general right to freedom of expression, and to underwrite journalism as a public service. Essentially, the codes of the PCC and NUJ are at odds each with the other.

The ascendancy of the PCC, following the systematic weakening of the NUJ in the 1980s, represented the emergence of a *force majeure* in keeping with the Thatcherite assault on corporatism. Statutory regulation continues in broadcasting, but has been weakened, and for long-standing and obvious reasons remains problematical for journalists (see Stephenson 1994). In any event, the Labour government elected in 1997 appears unlikely to extend statutory intervention: it prefers what it has called a Third Way between collectivism and the free market, which depends heavily on the concept of self-policing. Existing mechanisms of regulation, from the form of self-regulation implemented via the PCC to the 'lighter' touch of the broadcasting authorities, appear to have done little to mitigate the over-arching influence of market discourse. For its part, the NUJ has been unable to resolve the internal conflict between protecting and policing its members. Nevertheless, it is clear that journalists, whether they consider themselves 'professionals' or white-collar workers, retain a concern with standards and values. This suggests that there is a role for ethical guidelines. The status of the journalist, however, is articulated substantively in the codification of those standards and values.

At present, there are codes for editors and editorial employees, for members of the NUJ and for those working in the regulated broadcasting sector. Given the origins of these codes, journalists are categorised overwhelmingly as 'operatives within a system' (Morrison and Tumber 1988, p. x), with any public service role deriving principally from their employment (for example, in public service broadcasting). That is not to say that journalists working in such a public service environment are necessarily as restricted in raising issues of standards and values in journalism as were those Fleet Street journalist forbidden by their editors to appear on *Hard News*: the evidence suggests this is not so. Nevertheless, there is no code, as it were, for and by journalists, and, therefore, no articulation of the status of journalism *per se*. There is no conclusive proof that, if given the opportunity to devise a journalists' code of practice, UK journalists would necessarily mark out a purely public service role for themselves – but at least they would have the choice.

ENDNOTES

1. Jacob Ecclestone, deputy general-secretary of the NUJ, cited Tewary 1993, p. 255.
2. Around 450 in 1995.
3. For example, it organised a conference, *The Media We Deserve?*, on 16 April 1994 in London.
4. Information taken from an unpublished paper, 'The NUJ's ethics council', written by Jenny Vaughan in 1993. A copy is held by the author.
5. I am aware of only two books on media ethics having been published in the UK since Christians's article was written in June 1995.
6. The headline on Mirsky's article in the *Spectator* was '*Not* embarrassing Peter (or Rupert)' – emphasis added (21 March 1998), p. 22.

7. Author's own experience as a daily newspaper journalist in the 1970s.
8. The main instruments are the code of practice enforced by the PCC; the BBC's *Producer Guidelines* and internal Programme Complaints Unit, and the statutory codified regulation of the Independent Television Commission, the Radio Authority and the Broadcasting Standards Commission (see Peak and Fisher 1997: 272).
9. *Media Ethics*, ed. M. Kieran (London, Routledge, 1998).
10. See note 4 (above).
11. Ibid.
12. I am indebted to Jenny Vaughan for many of the ideas in this paragraph. In 1993 she supplied me with a written comparison of the codes of the NUJ, the PCC and the House of Commons Heritage Committee on which I have drawn extensively.
13. The fundamental distinction between a code of *conduct* and a code of *practice* needs elaboration, although none is attempted here.

REFERENCES

Barak, E. (1993) 'Is a journalist like any other employee?', *Quesher* **14** (November), 21e–34e.
BBC Radio 4 (1998), *Today* (2 April).
Bell, M. (1998) 'The journalism of attachment', in *Media Ethics*, M. Kieran, ed., London: Routledge, pp. 15–22.
Belsey, A. (1998) 'Journalism and ethics: can they co-exist?' in *Media Ethics*, M. Kieran, ed., London: Routledge, pp. 1–14.
Bertrand, C.-J. (1998) 'Media quality control in the USA and Europe' in *Sex, Lies and Democracy: The Press and the Public*, H. Stephenson and M. Bromley, eds., London: Longman, pp. 111–123.
Bevins, A. (1990) 'The crippling of the scribes', *British Journalism Review* **1**(2), pp. 13–17.
Black, J. Steele, B. and Barney, R. (1995) *Doing Ethics in Journalism: A Handbook With Case Studies,* Greencastle, Indiana: Society of Professional Journalists.
British Journalism Review (1989) 'Why we are here', *BJR* **1**(1), pp. 2–6.

Bromley, M. (1997) 'The end of journalism? changes in workplace practices in the press and broadcasting in the 1990s', in *A Journalism Reader*, M. Bromley and T. O'Malley, eds, London: Routledge, pp. 330–50.

Bromley, M. (1998) 'The "tabloiding" of Britain: quality newspapers in the 1990s', in *Sex, Lies and Democracy: The Press and the Public*, H. Stephenson and M. Bromley, eds, Harlow: Longman, pp. 25–38.

Brown, R. (1998) 'Poor old Ray Snoddy. I wouldn't be the Media Editor of the Murdochian *Times* for all the TVs in China', *The Independent Media+* (9 March): p. 2.

Burnet, D. (1992) 'Freedom of speech, the media and the law', in *Ethical Issues in Journalism and the Media*, A. Belsey and R. Chadwick, eds, London: Routledge, pp. 49–61.

Chittenden, M. (1993) 'BBC's Lewis defiant over "happy news"', *Sunday Times* (27 June), p. 15.

Christians, C.G. (1996) 'Current trends in media ethics', *European Journal of Communication* **10**(4), pp. 545–558.

Culf, A. (1993) ' "Good news junkie" renews push against negative values', *The Guardian* (16 November), p. 3.

D'Arcy, K. (1993), 'Eurocharter for journalists', *British Editor* (Spring), pp. 7–8.

Davy, R. (1998) 'Murdoch always backs a winner', *The Independent Media+* (9 March), p. 3.

Delano, A. and Henningham, J. (1996) *The News Breed: British Journalists in the 1990s*, London: London Institute.

Doig, A. (1997) 'The decline of investigatory journalism', in *A Journalism Reader*, M. Bromley and T. O'Malley, eds, London: Routledge, pp. 189–213.

Elliott, P. (1978) 'Professional ideology and organisational change: the journalist since 1800', in *Newspaper History: From the 17th Century to the Present Day*, G. Boyce, J. Curran and P. Wingate, eds, London: Constable, pp. 172–91.

Elstein, D. (1998) 'What are we getting for our money?', *The Guardian Media* (20 July), p. 6.

Fiddick, P. (1993) 'Research', *The Guardian Media* (5 July), p. 17

Fletcher, R. (1993) 'Why bright is right', *The Guardian Media* (22 November), p. 15.

Foot, P. (1991) 'Strenuous liberty . . . a nervous revival?', *British Journalism Review* **2**(4), pp. 5–8.

Foot, P. (1993) 'Look in the *Mirror!*', unpub. (April): photocopy held by author.

Fowler, N. (1994) 'What makes an award winning regional paper?' *Headlines* (April/May), p. 3.

Franklin, B. (1997) *News Media and Newszak*, London: Arnold.

Franklin, B. and Pilling, R. (1998) 'Taming the tabloids: market, moguls and media regulation', in *Media Ethics*, M. Kieran, ed., London: Routledge, pp. 111–22.

Frost, C. (1996) 'Approaches to media ethics', Module 7, unit 42, MA in Mass Communications, Centre of Mass Communications Research, Leicester: University of Leicester, pp. 250–93.

Gall, G. (1997) 'Looking in the *Mirror*: a case study of industrial relations in a national newspaper', in *A Journalism Reader*, M. Bromley and T. O'Malley, eds, London: Routledge, pp. 233–46.

Gibson, J., Gillard, M.S. and Flynn, L. (1998) 'Falsehood, deception and fakes: a Connection that never was', *The Guardian* (5 December), pp. 4–5.

Goffee, R. and Scase, R. (1995) *Corporate Realities: The Dynamics of Large and Small Organisations*, London: Routledge.

Griffith, J. (1995), 'The glorified brand manager', *UK Press Gazette* (16 October), p. 16.

Guardian, The (1997) 'A private sector' (6 December), p. 24.

Heinonen, A. (1993), 'Project ETHICNET: an international databank', *Media Ethics* **6**(1) p. 10.

Jersild v. Denmark (1994) Judgment of the European Court of Human Rights (23 September), 36/1993/431/510 (Strasbourg, Council of Europe).

Knight, A. (1992) 'Snoddy in *Sun*-land', *British Journalism Review* **3**(2), pp. 68–71.

Leapman, M. (1993) 'The misanthropic media gurus', *British Journalism Review* **4**(3), pp. 54–5.

Levy, H.P. (1967) *The Press Council: History, Procedure and Cases*, London: Macmillan.

Lewis, M. (1993a) 'Not my idea of good news', *The Independent* (26 April), p. 19.

Lewis, M. (1993b) 'Good/bad/real news', Royal Society of Arts Lecture (15 November), London.

Lewis, M. (1998) 'Is good news bad news?', in *Reporters and the Reported. Contemporary Issues in British Journalism*, the 1998 Vauxhall Lectures (Cardiff, Centre for Journalism Studies, Cardiff University), pp. 1–12.

MacGregor, B. (1995) 'Our wanton use of the technology: television news gathering in the age of the satellite', *Convergence* **1**, pp. 80–93.

Milton, J. (1644, 1995) *Areopagitica*, extract in *The Journalist's Moral Compass: Basic Principles*, eds. S.R. Knowlton and P.R. Parsons. London, Praeger, pp. 13–20.

Mirsky, J. (1998) ' "Spiked" and attacked by my editor: why I was forced to leave *The Times*', *Daily Telegraph* (19 March), p. 20.

Morgan, J. (1992) 'Don't slag us off, join us, say angry *Mirror* hacks', *UK Press Gazette* (21/28 December), p. 5.

Morgan, P. (1998) 'Innocents in a hell-hole', *The Guardian Media* (25 May), p. 9.

NUJ (1936) *Code of Conduct* (London, National Union of Journalists).

Morrison, D.E. and Tumber H. (1988) *Journalists at War: The Dynamics of News Reporting during the Falklands Conflict*, London: Sage.

Norsk Presseforbund (1973) *Rights and Duties of the Editor (The Editor's Code)*, originally signed 22 October 1953, Oslo: Norwegian Press Association.

Observer (1993) 'And now for the good news' (2 May), p. 19.

O'Neill, J. (1992) 'Journalism in the market place', in *Ethical Issues in Journalism and the Media*, eds. A. Belsey and R. Chadwick, London: Routledge, pp. 15–32.

Orwell, G. (1946, 1957) 'The prevention of literature', *Selected Essays*, Harmondsworth: Penguin Books, pp. 159–74.

Paxman, J. (1993) 'Here is the news: 56 million people alive and well . . .', *Evening Standard* (29 April), p. 9.

Peak, S. and Fisher, P., eds, (1997) *The 1998 Media Guide*, London: Fourth Estate.

Phillips, A. and Gaber, I. (1996) 'The case for media degrees', *British Journalism Review* **7**(3), pp. 62 5.

Pilger, J. (1997) 'Breaking the *Mirror*: the Murdoch effect', *Network First* (London, Carlton Television), dir: David Munro, Central/Carlton Television, 21 January.

Pilger, J. (1998) *Hidden Agendas*, London: Vintage.

Press Standards Board of Finance (1995) *Code of Practice*, London: PCC.

Randall, D. (1996) *The Universal Journalist*, London: Pluto Press.

Rosen, J. (1996) *Getting the Connections Right: Public Journalism and the Troubles in the Press*, New York: Twentieth Century Fund Press.

Rosenblum, M. (1993) *Who Stole the News?*, New York: John Wiley.

Schudson, M. (1978) *Discovering the News: A Social History of the American Press*, New York: Basic Books.

Scott, C.P. (1921, 1997) 'The *Manchester Guardian's* first hundred years', in *A Journalism Reader*, M. Bromley and T. O'Malley, eds, London: Routledge, pp. 108–09.

Snoddy, R. (1993) *The Good, the Bad and the Unacceptable: The Hard News about the British Press*, London: Faber and Faber.

Snoddy, R. (1998) 'It's our job to tell the truth about the Corp', *The Times* (6 March), p. 45.

Snoddy, R. and Woolwich, P. (1990) 'The poodle bites back', *British Journalism Review* **2**(2), pp. 15–21.

Soley, C. (1992) 'Is accuracy too high a price to pay?', *UK Press Gazette* (7 September), pp. 18–19.

Stephenson, H. (1994) *Media Freedom and Media Regulation*, London: Association of British Editors, Guild of Editors and International Press Institute.

Stephenson, H. (1998) 'Tickle the public: consumerism rules', in *Sex, Lies and Democracy: The Press and the Public*, H. Stephenson and M. Bromley, eds, Harlow: Longman, pp. 13–24.

Tewary, S.K. (1993) 'Self-regulation of the press: a study of the British and Indian experience[s]', PhD thesis, University of Wales.

Thomass, B. (1998) 'Teaching ethics to journalists in the United Kingdom', in *Sex, Lies and Democracy: The Press and the Public*, H. Stephenson and M. Bromley, eds,. Harlow: Longman, pp. 136–46.

Townley, L. (n.d.) Open letter (Chester, *Press*Wise): photocopy held by author.

Toynbee, P. (1998a) 'Will Blair dare?', *The Guardian* (2 February), p. 17.

Toynbee, P. (1998b) 'My Lords, stop this bully now', *The Guardian* (9 February), p. 15.

Tulloch, J. (1998) 'Managing the press in a medium-sized European power', in *Sex, Lies and Democracy: The Press and the Public*, H. Stephenson and M. Bromley, eds, Harlow: Longman, pp. 63–83.

Tunstall, J. (1977) ' "Editorial sovereignty" in the British press', *Studies on the Press*, London: HMSO, pp. 249–341.

Tunstall, J. (1983) *The Media in Britain*, London: Constable.

Tunstall, J. (1993) *Television Producers*, London: Routledge.

Tunstall, J. (1996) *Newspaper Power: The New National Press in Britain*, Oxford: Clarendon Press.

Tusa, J. (1992) 'A mission to be there', *British Journalism Review* **3**(4), pp. 5–9.

UK Press Gazette (1989) 'Our job to inform mustn't be neglected in our hurry to sell' (19 February), p. 2.

Wakeham, The Lord (1997) 'This back door privacy law is a threat to all our freedoms', *Mail on Sunday* (2 November), p. 32.

White, R. (1993) 'And finally . . .', *Sunday Times* (4 July), p. 9.

Wilson, J. (1997) 'Companies cashing in on trust', *The Guardian* (14 October), p. 11.

7 'If it bleeds, it leads': ethical questions about popular journalism

Cynthia Carter and Stuart Allan

Good journalism is popular culture, but popular culture that stretches and informs its consumers rather than that which appeals to the ever descending lowest common denominator. If, by popular culture, we mean expressions of thought or feeling that require no work of those who consume them, then decent popular journalism is finished. What is happening today, unfortunately, is that the lowest form of popular culture – lack of information, misinformation, disinformation, and a contempt for the truth or the reality of most people's lives – has overrun real journalism (Carl Bernstein, US journalist).

I believe that writing for a mass audience is not an intrinsically debased form of literature but, in theory, the highest and most noble form. But it has become debased. Over a hundred years much of British journalism turned into an institutionalised force for distortion and half-truth (Matthew Engel, British journalist).

INTRODUCTION

'If it bleeds', the old saying goes, 'it leads'. This succinct – and, it has to be said, rather vulgar – declaration of 'news values' has long been associated with certain disreputable practices held to be characteristic of the 'popular' press in Europe and North America. Today, though, growing numbers of critics – many of whom are journalists – are contending that the ceaseless quest for ever larger news audiences is intensifying to the point that journalism's ethical responsibilities are being all but abandoned across the mediasphere.

As will be apparent from the first of the two quotations above, one such intervention into debates about the ethics of journalistic practice has been initiated by one of the most famous reporters in the world, Carl Bernstein.[1] His name, along with that of his former colleague Bob Woodward, is for many people synonymous with the phrase 'investigative reporting'. These were the two reporters who broke the 'Watergate' story on the pages of the *Washington Post*, thereby sparking an investigation into one of the most significant political scandals in United States history. Together with their sources, one of the most important of which was identified only as 'deep throat', they exposed a range of illegal activities being conducted in the highest echelons of the US Government. Their news reports, produced under extremely difficult circumstances, set in motion a chain of events which eventually led to the resignation of a disgraced President Richard Nixon under threat of imminent impeachment on 9 August 1974. Bernstein and Woodward proceeded to write a book about their experiences, entitled *All The Presidents Men*, which was subsequently turned into a critically-acclaimed Hollywood film of the same title.

Almost two decades after these momentous events, Bernstein (1992) offered several reflections on post-Watergate journalism to the readers of *The New Republic* magazine in an essay entitled 'The Idiot Culture'. In sharp, incisive terms, he pinpoints a series of ongoing developments which together appear to be threatening the integrity of what he calls 'real journalism'. Where principled reporting typically relies on 'shoe leather', 'common sense' and a 'respect for the truth', he argues, what currently passes as journalism is regularly failing its audience in many crucial respects. In Bernstein's (1992, p. 22) words:

Increasingly the America rendered today in the American media is illusionary and delusionary – disfigured, unreal, disconnected from the true context of our lives. In covering actually existing American life, the media – weekly, daily, hourly – break new ground in getting it wrong. The coverage is distorted by celebrity and the worship of celebrity; by the reduction of news to gossip, which is the lowest form of news; by sensationalism, which is always a turning away from a society's real condition; and by a political and social discourse that we – the press, the media, the politicians, and the people – are turning into a sewer.

It is Bernstein's perception that there is an alarming degree of arrogance amongst journalism's practitioners, attributable in part to a persistent failure to engage in self-reflexive scrutiny where their social obligations are concerned. Particularly troubling are the ethical implications of what is a growing emphasis on 'speed and quantity' at the expense of 'thoroughness and quality', let alone 'accuracy and context'. 'The pressure to compete, the fear that somebody else will make the splash first', he observes, 'creates a frenzied environment in which a blizzard of information is presented and serious questions may not be raised' (ibid., p. 24). Even in those rare instances where such questions are posed, he argues, only seldomly do they engender the considered, thoughtful reporting they deserve.

Accordingly, as the types of reporting Bernstein holds to be indicative of 'real journalism' recede, a 'sleazoid info-tainment culture' is slowly becoming entrenched as the norm. The once clear division between the 'serious' and the 'popular' newspaper press, for example, is now increasingly being blurred. Such is also the case between talk show programmes, such as the *Oprah Winfrey Show, Donahue* or *Geraldo*, and news programmes, such as *60 Minutes* or *Nightline*, where differences in their news values are often virtually indistinguishable (see also Langer 1998; Lull and Hinerman 1997; Shattuc 1997; Sholle 1993). To the extent that it is possible to speak of news agendas when using a language of 'info-tainment', he suggests that there is a direct correlation between the rise of these 'Donahue–Geraldo–Oprah freak shows' and the more recently emergent forms of 'trash journalism'. As Bernstein (1992, pp. 24–25) declares:

In this new culture of journalistic titillation, we teach our readers and our viewers that the trivial is significant, that the lurid and the loopy are more important than real news. We do not serve our readers and viewers, we pander to them. And we condescend to them, giving them what we think they want and what we calculate will sell and boost ratings and readership. Many of them, sadly, seem to justify our condescension, and to kindle at the trash. Still, it is the role of journalists to challenge people, not merely to amuse them.

Hence the fear expressed by Bernstein that journalists are contributing to the formation of an 'idiot culture', one which is rendered distinct from popular culture by its obsession with 'the weird and the stupid and the coarse'. The US, it follows, is gradually being transformed into a 'talk-show nation', where 'public discourse is reduced to ranting and raving and posturing'. At a time when 'good journalism' is 'the exception and not the rule', he contends, searching questions need to asked about the ethical responsibilities of the news media *vis-à-vis* the public interest.

REPRESENTING THE PUBLIC INTEREST

Many of these points strike an equally powerful resonance in other national contexts. In France, for example, the highly influential sociologist Pierre Bourdieu recently found himself at the centre of a heated public controversy following two lectures he delivered concerning the current state of journalism via the television station of the Collège de France (chosen so as to bypass network control). The lectures were subsequently developed into a short book which became a surprise best-seller in France. Publicity for Bourdieu's intervention was provided, if not with that precise intention in mind, by several journalists furious with his characterisation of their profession and its alleged failings. There followed a series of (often acrimonious) exchanges between Bourdieu and his critics which appeared, amongst other places, on the pages of the monthly journal *Le Monde diplomatique* (see also Marlière 1998). Several interesting insights into the nature of the dispute are provided in the 'Prologue' to the English-language edition of the book, published as *On Television and Journalism*.

Over the course of these lectures, Bourdieu (1998, p. 2) sought to show how what he terms the 'journalistic field', for him a 'microcosm with its own laws', 'produces and imposes on the public a very particular vision of the political field, a vision that is grounded in the very structure of the journalistic field and in journalists' specific interests produced in and by that field'. Any form of serious political commentary, he argues, is consistently losing out to those forms of news discourse which give priority to simply entertaining the viewer, listener or reader. In-depth current affairs interviews on television, for example, are routinely being transformed into 'mindless talk show chatter' between 'approved' (that is to say, 'safe') speakers willing to participate in what are largely staged 'exchanges'. This relentless search for the sensational and the spectacular, he argues, ensures that an undue emphasis is placed on certain types of dramatic events which are simple to cover. As Bourdieu (ibid., pp. 3–4) elaborates:

To justify this policy of demagogic simplification (which is absolutely and utterly contrary to the democratic goal of informing or educating people by interesting them), journalists point to the public's expectations. But in fact they are projecting onto the public their own inclinations and their own views. Because they're so afraid of being boring, they opt for confrontations over debates, prefer polemics over rigorous argument, and in general, do whatever they can to promote conflict.

It follows that individuals seeking to secure access to what he terms 'public space', particularly politicians, have little choice but to adapt to the demands of the journalistic field. Journalists effectively control who can be recognised as a public figure, a process shaped by their perception of who or what is 'interesting', 'exceptional' or 'catchy' *for them*, that is, from the position they occupy in this space. 'In short', Bourdieu (ibid., p. 51) argues, 'the focus is on those things which are apt to arouse curiosity but require no analysis, especially in the political sphere'.

In suggesting that the journalistic field possesses a relative degree of autonomy from other fields of cultural production, such as the juridical, literary, artistic or scientific fields, Bourdieu is attempting to move beyond any explanation of its characteristics which points exclusively to economic factors. As important as these factors are in shaping what is reported and how, he is aiming to identify the social conditions underpinning journalism as a collective activity which 'smoothes over things, brings them into line, and depoliticizes them' to the 'level of anecdote and scandal'. If sensational news equals market success, then professional standards cannot help but be influenced by audience ratings in a detrimental way. 'Everybody knows the "law" that if a newspaper or other news vehicle wants to reach a broad public,' he writes, 'it has to dispense with sharp edges and anything that might divide or exclude readers'. In other words, he adds: 'It must attempt to be inoffensive, not to "offend anyone", and it must never bring up problems – or, if it does, problems that don't pose any problems' (ibid., p. 44). Hence despite the fierce relations of competition which exist between different news organisations, quest for exclusivity (or 'scoops') recurrently yields coverage which is as uniform as it is banal. Consequently, he argues, once the decisive impact of the journalistic field upon other fields is taken into consideration, the current extent of pubic disenchantment with politics is hardly surprising.

In Britain, it is similarly possible to map the growing prominence of these types of arguments across the public sphere, not least in the forums of debate created by journalists who are more often than not finding themselves on the defensive. One need not agree with every aspect of the arguments advanced above to recognise, as of course many journalists do, that the types of news values once associated with 'serious reporting' are being dramatically recast (Aldridge 1998; Bromley 1998; Bromley and O'Malley 1997; Engel 1996; MacGregor 1997; Petley 1997). In the words of a recent editorial leader in *The Economist* (4 July 1998, p. 13) magazine, the features of a 'modern paradox' are becoming evermore pronounced:

In this age of globalisation, news is much more parochial than in the days when communications from abroad ticked slowly across the world by telegraph. And here is another [paradox]: that in this information age, newspapers which used to be full of politics and economics are thick with stars and sport.

Recent trends in journalism, at least from the vantage point of *The Economist*, suggest that news is 'moving away from foreign affairs towards domestic concerns; away from politics towards human-interest stories; away from issues to people'. The principal explanation cited for these trends is the rapidly growing array of specialist information sources (as 'rolling' televisual newscasts such as BBC News 24 and Sky News proliferate, publishing costs drop, and the Internet expands) becoming available as competition between increasingly market-sensitive news organisations accelerates. It is significant, however, that the editorial leader goes on to reassure its readers that at the end of the day there is little cause for concern: 'People absorb what interests them: if news is too worthy, it goes in one ear and out the other'.

To declare that journalism is in a state of crisis, some commentators maintain, risks overstating the severity of these developments.

Frequently taking a broad historical perspective, they make the argument that these types of debates about reportorial integrity are as old as journalism itself. Even if it is true that the gap between 'news' and 'entertainment' is narrowing (which they dispute), it does not necessarily follow in their view that there is a corresponding 'dumbing-down' of news content. Rather, they insist, the criteria being used to judge standards of 'quality' are quickly becoming out of date. Where some critics hold journalists responsible for pandering to populist prejudices, a number of these commentators are of the view that news values are undergoing a process of democratisation. They believe that people want 'news you can use,' that is, news which speaks directly to their personal experiences of daily life, as opposed to news content driven by the interests of politicians and other 'talking heads'. The resultant 'tabloidisation' of international news coverage, they suggest, thus has as much to do with an enhanced concern with local issues as it does with ever sharper 'efficiency cuts' in the financial budgets of news organisations (see also Allan 1999).

Bob Franklin (1997) employs the term 'newszak' to characterise what he agrees is a contemporary trend in British journalism to retreat from investigative, 'hard' news reporting in favour of ever 'softer', 'lighter' stories. 'Newszak', he writes, 'understands news as a product designed and "processed" for a particular market and delivered in increasingly homogeneous "snippets" which make only modest demands on the audience. Newszak is news converted into entertainment' (ibid., pp. 4–5). In a similar vein, journalist Simon Hoggart refers to these 'lighter' stories as products of a 'Filet O'Facts' formula of news reporting – an 'undemanding means of filling you up'. In Hoggart's (1995: p. 20) words:

The Filet O'Facts approach is headed this way, fast. We haven't quite reached the standards of the worst tabloid TV 'news' shows in the US (I once watched a report on the Brazilian economy which consisted entirely of shots of young women on the beach), but the news is becoming increasingly a ready processed product, designed to make no call on understanding or imagination.[2]

Needless to say, Hoggart is in good company with many other reporters when expressing his concerns about the implications these trends have for journalistic ethics. So-called entertainment-led journalism is being subjected to ever closer scrutiny, a development not entirely unconnected with recent revelations about 'fakery' in televisual documentaries or that several 'talk-shows' allegedly hired actors from talent agencies to pose as guests. These kinds of incidents have prompted strong reactions from critics actively questioning the ethical standards of programmes that purport to offer audiences factual and reliable information on a range of important public issues. In light of developments such as these ones, then, both journalists and their audiences are struggling to come to terms with important ethical questions. It appears that in the current news environment, what counts as 'truth' is in real danger of becoming hopelessly blurred amid the drama and superficiality of tabloidised news formats obsessed with sex, crime and scandal (see Auletta 1997; Belsey and Chadwick 1992; Bok 1997; Carter *et al.* 1998; Graham 1998; Hoggart 1995). Some commentators vigorously contend that this apparent 'dumbing down' of the news will have profound consequences for the future of parliamentary democracy, not least because the number of reliable sources of information is shrinking (see Crispin Miller 1996; Williams 1995). Interestingly, a recent editorial leader in *The Independent* (6 March 1999, p. 3) maintains that, taken overall, the so-called 'dumbing down' of British culture is in fact a 'broadening out'. That is to say, an increased emphasis on popular culture, the editorial voice maintains, is actually making British cultural life more open and democratic. Nevertheless, news is identified as a crucial exception to this argument:

But there is one area where the drive towards the lowest common denominator should genuinely be worrying, and that is in journalism. The ending of News At Ten *and the convergence of tabloid and broadsheet newspapers on the middle ground of celebrity soap opera is a real threat, not to our cultural life but to our democratic citizenship.*

JOURNALISM ETHICS: CRITICAL ISSUES

To directly address several of the more pronounced ethical implications of these developments, we shall proceed to outline a series of questions revolving around a specific aspect of the changing nature of news culture. Our aim is to bring to the fore a range of ethical issues for further discussion and debate.

FREEDOM OF THE PRESS

What does 'freedom of the press' mean today? What impact are the changing dynamics of news media ownership (particularly with respect to the growing degree of concentration, conglomeration and globalisation) having on these same 'freedoms'? Is news slowly turning into a commodity like any other, its value to be measured primarily in terms of 'bottom-line' profitability?

'Can the watchdog be trusted,' ask US media researchers Philip Patterson and Lee Wilkins (1998, p. 192), 'when it is inexorably entwined with the institutions it is watching? As media corporations expand exponentially in the pursuit of profit, who will watch the watchdogs?' Such questions now preoccupy a growing number of newsworkers concerned about the pressures brought to bear by market-driven journalism. Winning a larger share of the broadcast news audience, or of the newspaper reading public, means that ever closer ties are being forged between the newsroom and the finance departments in many US news organisations. 'All around the country', explains former reporter Doug Underwood (1998, p. 1), 'at newspaper after newspaper, the walls between the newsroom and the business departments, once a sacred barrier, are being knocked down, and replaced by a commitment across all departments to the marketing mission of the newspaper – to sell ads, raise circulation, and promote itself'. Neil Hickey (1998b, p. 3), takes the argument even further, declaring that the 'blurring of editorial–advertising distinctions' has been developed in order to boost corporate profits at the expense of critical news reporting. Blurring these distinctions has, in his view, compromised news judgements 'resulting not so much in fawning pieces about major advertisers but rather in self-censorship, a reluctance by some editors to take the heat for doing stories critical of space-buyers'.

In Britain, media critic Granville Williams (1995, p. 11) observes that commercial television newscasts currently exhibit many of the features typically associated with their counterparts in the tabloid press. Commenting on changes in news selection and treatment at ITN, for example, he maintains that to boost ratings it has become more 'tabloid' in its orientation, 'emphasising crime and human-interest stories and carrying fewer foreign and political stories than the BBC'. Concurring with this stance, Hoggart (1995, p. 21) suggests that commercial pressures have prompted ITN to place a higher emphasis on reporting sports activities (on one day, for example, ITN led one of its bulletins with news of the death of a racing driver while, in contrast, the BBC Nine O'Clock News began with the first results in the South African elections). Increasingly, then, it appears that discourses of 'the market' and 'the bottom-line' are systematically shaping what is reported in the news, and how. With regard to media ethics, philosopher John O'Neill (1992, pp. 22–23) argues that such changes in emphasis have not necessarily resulted in the reporting of falsehoods, but rather 'the failure to report what is of significance and a simplified presentation of events'. More to the point, many commentators on both sides of the Atlantic seem to agree with US journalist Carol Marin who contends that: 'We're more and more uncomfortable with challenging power. We're afraid of being unpopular, we are afraid of shrinking markets. We have forgotten to say the words "public trust". And the worst corruption of all is the creeping commercialism' (cited in *CJR* Forum 1998, p. 3).

THE PUBLIC TRUST

Is the notion of the 'pubic trust' still viable and, if so, how can journalism best fulfil its social responsibilities to 'the people'? Are critics such as Jurgen Habermas (1989) correct to argue that the commercialisation of mass communication networks has virtually displaced 'rational-critical debate' into the realm of cultural consumption, thereby transforming active citizens into indifferent consumers?

It would be a rare media commentator indeed who would not agree that the news media play a vitally important role in keeping a democratic citizenry informed of the key political issues and debates of the day. How, then, to balance this role with that of a particular news organisation's owner's desire to make money? In a recent interview, US network newsreader Dan Rather commented on this dilemma:

News is a business. It has always been. Journalists understand and accept that. But journalism is something else too. Something more. It is a light on the horizon. A beacon that helps the citizens of a democracy find their way. News is an essential component of a free society. News is a business, but it is also a public trust (cited in Patterson and Wilkins 1998, p. 193).

The 'public trust' accorded to journalism to uphold such ideals becomes more difficult to sustain at a time when trends toward the concentration, conglomeration and globalisation of media ownership are becoming evermore pronounced. Media researchers Patterson and Wilkins maintain that what is most troubling about these types of ownership trends is that the news media are increasingly being operated by an élite few who 'control an important ingredient of democracy: news. And when the few who own the media view it only as a business, the problem gets worse'(ibid., p. 193).

Is news what is in the public interest or, alternatively, simply what the public happens to be interested in on a given day? Reuven Frank, former president of NBC News, responds to this question by declaring:

This business of giving people what they want is a dope pusher's argument. News is something people don't know they're interested in until they hear about it. The job of a journalist is to take what's important and make it interesting (cited in Hickey 1998b, p. 4).

Marin agrees with this viewpoint, adding that a journalist's role is to 'tell people the things they don't know. Our job is to tell people the things they can't ask for in a survey. Whoever would have asked for Watergate?' (*CJR* Forum 1998, p. 3).

British media observers often make similar arguments, suggesting that the ever-growing commercialisation of journalism is having a negative effect on British democracy. O'Neill (1992, p. 25) maintains that to address this problem 'we need to start from where we are, that is, a context in which market-driven media do not appear to respond to [critical] preferences'. Addressing the claim often made by the popular news media that they are merely giving the public what it wants, O'Neill responds by declaring that the media construct and reproduce certain audience preferences. One of the aims of a critical, ethical journalism which seeks to strengthen democracy by informing the public about public issues of great importance (their so-called 'public trust'), therefore, lies in 'developing a critical political citizenry with preference for the products of such media' (ibid.). The market, claims O'Neill, undermines the democratic principles of journalism.

Elaborating on this point, he asserts that there 'is a tension between the internal goals of journalism and the market contexts in which it operates; and the market inhibits the dissemination of information and diverse opinions required of a democratic society' (ibid., p. 15).

Interestingly, Colin Sparks (1992) suggests that like their counterparts in the popular press, members of the 'serious' press are now increasingly preoccupied with the 'immediate issues of daily life' rather than with issues which circulate in the 'public sphere'. The consequences of this are truly alarming, in Sparks's view, because:

The structure of 'the popular' in modern journalism is [. . .] one which is massively and systematically 'depoliticised' [. . .] a conception of politics which concentrates on the everyday at the expense of the historical is one which remains within the existing relations of exploitation and oppression (ibid., p. 39).

TRUTH, FACTS AND OBJECTIVITY

How does 'truth' relate to 'fact'? Do journalists, as some of them argue, have a fundamental ethical obligation to determining 'the truth' of any given situation? Or is it their task to secure the best available definition of the truth, thereby conceding that absolute truth does not exist? Then again, would it be advantageous for journalists to dispense with the notion of truth altogether in favour of concentrating strictly on matters of fact?

US journalist Tom Rosenstiel insists that 'serious' journalism is now experiencing a 'crisis of conviction', that is, or a 'philosophical collapse in the belief in the purpose of journalism and the meaning of news' (*CJR* Forum 1998, p. 3). Most importantly, he observes: 'When supposedly responsible news organisations stop pursuit of the best obtainable version of the truth and reproduce rumour and gossip, they are shedding long-standing principles'. Rosenstiel cites intense commercial pressures on 'serious' news media as being responsible for adversely affecting reporters' ability to seek out the 'truth' of various events (see also Gordon and Kittross 1998). Elaborating on this line of argument, Carol Reuss (1999) recently remarked that she is now increasingly troubled by the fact that:

Infotainment media too often stretch the truth and give false perceptions of reality. To entice audiences and to fit the constraints of media time and space, they rely heavily on stereotypes, exaggeration, half-truths, and innuendo that impressionable audiences accept as reality (ibid., p. 232).

Still, to concentrate critical attention on the ethical standards of the infotainment and tabloid news media, claims former supermarket tabloid journalist Neil Hogshire (1997), is unjust (see also Bird 1992). In Hogshire's (1997, p. 17) view: 'The blurring between fact and fiction is essential in both mainstream and tabloid press. The only difference is the tabloids don't claim to be the Final Truth on anything'. However, Hogshire also concedes that these tabloid newspapers frequently run completely 'fake' stories. What worries him most about the tabloids is that the line between fiction and fact has become 'so thin and arbitrary, even the writers of the fake stories [. . .] could not always distinguish between stories they had invented and ones that were real and simply culled from obscure newspapers'(ibid., pp. 88–89).

'To tickle the public', claims Matthew Engel (1996, p. 272), 'you tickle up the facts. So it goes. It's the game'. This has long been the case with regard to the British tabloid press, according to Engel's broad historical survey. This issue of 'tickling' presumes, of course, that the public wants to be tickled – but is this always the case? Some might say that members of the audience expect from journalists an unvarnished presentation of the facts, a truthful reflection of reality. Then again, it is philosopher Andrew Belsey's (1998) contention that:

If people are told that the essence of journalism is truth-telling, they will react with some scepticism or derision. If they are told the practice of journalism is founded on ethical principles they will either laugh or, if they are prepared to take the matter seriously, point out that the typical tabloid story is trivial, scurrilous or invented' (ibid., p. 1).

Indeed, media critic Teresa Stratford (1992, p. 132) asserts that although the tabloid press is replete with gossip and anecdote about celebrities, they 'include just enough news to avoid being dismissed as total fiction, but only just, and [a tabloid like] the *Sport* has abandoned all claims to news reportage; its sales are based on the popularity of items which no one relies on as true' (see also Livesey 1998).

If 'serious' reporting is now being fundamentally changed by its adoption of tabloid formats, it is interesting to consider former BBC foreign correspondent Martin Bell's (1998) claim that the BBC's institutional status as a public service broadcaster has tended to protect it from some of the worst pressures of commercialisation. In his words: 'I am fortunate in having worked for a news organisation, the BBC, in which – despite all its trials and travails – a culture of truthfulness still prevails, and which is not driven by the commercial imperative of maximising profits' (ibid., p. 17). Nevertheless, in his efforts to engage in more ethical forms of war reporting, he has become an impassioned advocate of the need to replace 'dispassionate' journalistic practices with what he calls a 'journalism of attachment'. By this phrase Bell (ibid., p. 16) means 'a journalism that cares as well as knows; that is aware of its responsibilities; that will not stand neutrally between good and evil, right and wrong, the victim and the oppressor'. As he endeavours to make it clear, however, he is not calling for journalists to champion one view or group against another. Instead, Bell is challenging the notion of 'objectivity' because he believes that 'we in the press, and especially in television, which is its most powerful division, do not stand apart from the world. We are part of it. We exercise a certain influence, and we have to know that. The influence may be for better or for worse, and we have to know that too' (ibid., see also Hoyt 1995; Kieran 1998).

INFOTAINMENT

While some journalists and critics are charging that the division between 'news' and 'entertainment' is becoming dangerously blurred ('infotainment'), what form should a truly popular journalism take? In the words of Neal Gabler:

When everything is looked at for its entertainment value, when the news is examined for its entertainment value, when politics is essentially analysed for its entertainment value, when religion is examined for its entertainment value, and when entertainment, frankly, is the pre-eminent value in American life, everything tends to get trivialised. Serious issues that don't conform themselves to entertainment will not get addressed (cited in Kelley 1997, p. 178).

Television news, in the eyes of many critics, is becoming less 'serious' by the day in its search for ever greater audience ratings. Veteran PBS journalist, Robert MacNeil, insists that the news is now much less sober in tone and presentation than it was in his early career. In his view, such changes have had an adverse effect on reporting the news:

I don't think it's new that American journalism has found ways to follow the crowd and to find the cheaper end of the carnival side-show with the two-headed woman and the calf that gives birth to a pop singer. That's always been there. What's interesting is that serious journalists are beginning to follow that now' (MacNeil cited in Hickey 1995, p. 4).

That is to say, this general trend 'downward' leads journalists 'to report from fewer places and report more obsessively and hysterically about those things we know will capture the largest audience' (cited in Hickey 1995, p. 3). As Hickey (1998b, p. 1) asserts: 'The temptation is great in every news medium to sweeten the product for easier consumption' (see also Fuller 1996; Johnson 1997; Jones 1998).

In his examination of how these pressures are shaping the 'news values' indicative of 'serious' journalism, Hoggart (1995) offers a useful outline of the stages events go through as they are processed by news organisations and turned into bite sized morsels which can be easily consumed by audiences. In the first stage, he suggests, news is turned into human interest stories. So, for example, public issues like gun control are explored 'through the eyes of an innocent victim or, if your agenda is different, someone who saved her own life by keeping a gun at home' (ibid., p. 21). In the second stage, stories which cannot be turned into human interest are 'bit by bit, junked from the schedules'. Finally, if a given story has a wider general significance this aspect is typically ignored. For instance, Hoggart maintains that the O.J. Simpson trial was actually about race relations, yet the news media tended to acknowledge this point 'only in a tangential and highly embarrassed fashion'. What particularly troubles Hoggart about the move toward entertainment-led news is not only that it is being turned into the equivalent of fast food, but more importantly the 'real, slippery, hard-to-handle news will soon be forgotten' (ibid.) in the process.

Nevertheless, certain critics propose that there is nothing necessarily wrong with the media presenting the news in more entertaining ways.

Indeed, some media observers contend that infotainment programmes can be very useful sources of information on a range of important public issues. Carol Reuss (1999, p. 231), for example, notes that:

The infotainment media often appeal to audiences that give little, if any, attention to more serious media. In that respect, those that contain even minimal amounts of information can *help these people make decisions – they can help make democracy work.*

That said, of course, she also acknowledges that 'infotainment media tend to overemphasise entertainment, to oversimplify, trivialise, and titillate, too often they confuse their audiences about important issues' (ibid.). Similarly, media critic A. David Gordon (1999) contends that infotainment journalism may be reaching audiences who would not be otherwise aware of certain issues: 'Even the supermarket tabloids', he argues, 'occasionally provide information that helps the democratic decision-making process' (ibid., p. 224). Nevertheless, Gordon also warns that the sensationalism associated with these information outlets tends to elicit personal and emotional responses to issues rather than reasoned responses. Such forms of sensational material, in his view, 'limits experience as a source of knowledge in favour of emotional or sensory stimulation'; 'too much of it', he adds, 'could be a barrier to disseminating useful information to the public through these infotainment channels' (ibid., p. 225).

PROFESSIONALISM

Is journalism a profession and, if so, does it need a formal code of ethics? Might professional status unduly restrict or even control how journalists go about their work, or would it enhance their relative autonomy from managerial influence within a news organisation?

Debates which began hundreds of years ago continue to rage over whether or not journalism is a profession, a vocation or a craft. Some commentators argue that not only is it not a profession, but that this lack of professional status is one of its principal strengths. As media critic John Merrill (1996) suggests, if journalism were to become a profession it would become increasingly organised around its own interests, including that of 'self-protection' and therefore less inclined to live up to its social responsibility to keep the public informed. On the other hand, Everette Dennis (1996) insists that journalism already is a profession since it demands that its practitioners acquire a specialised knowledge through intensive training in the provision of a 'public service.'

Somewhere in between these two positions is Tom Rosensteil, who remains uncertain whether journalism may be considered a profession (*CJR* Forum 1998). He claims that one of the most important revelations during this period of rapid commercialisation of the news media has been that there is no clear set of ethical standards and responsibilities upon which journalism is based. In his opinion, journalists have been 'traumatised' by recent commercial pressures because 'we were never really very clear about what we were doing in the first place' (ibid., p. 4). This situation is most troubling, in his opinion, because in the past journalists have tended to be rather proud of the fact that they paid little critical attention to an examination of ethical practices and social responsibilities. 'We talked about journalism in mystical terms, instinctive terms. A good story was something we could smell or sense, and we insisted on being left alone to pursue it (ibid.). Rosenstiel claims that greater self-criticism would be healthy for journalism as it would demonstrate to the public that journalists are willing to examine their own practices as well as those of others. 'The public often will be there to support us when we do the right thing', he argues: 'They will support us as we attempt to reform and renew our profession' (ibid., p. 7).

Even so, as Richard Keeble (1998) asserts, newsworkers tend to be rather sceptical about the value of ethical debate for its own sake. In his view, such scepticism arises amongst journalists because 'the dominant attitude prioritises "getting the story" and the demands of the deadline above all else. Ethical and political concerns are secondary, if they are ever considered at all' (ibid., p. 23). Any worries newsworkers might have about the ethics of their own practices also tend to be dismissed because there is a widespread feeling that individual journalists have little power to improve standards of reporting. According to Keeble (ibid., p. 24), cynicism around ethical issues and standards is:

In part, a consequence of the ethical contradictions within the newspaper industry. Its central position as a largely monopolistic industry in a profit-oriented economic system means business and entertainment priorities dominate. News becomes, above all, a commodity to be sold. Yet journalists' rhetoric [. . .] promotes notions of the public interest, the right to know, the free press, which are often in conflict with the priorities of the market-place.

Returning to Merrill's (1999) stance above, he similarly insists that a commitment to exploring questions of ethics does not come naturally to most journalists. Instead, he maintains, a 'sense of right conduct [. . .] must be developed, thought about, reasoned through, cared deeply about. In short, it must be nurtured' (ibid., p. 2; see also Merrill 1998).

How, then, to encourage and sustain this 'nurturing' process? Some commentators have called for statutory regulation of the news media, while others have appealed for greater self-policing by journalists themselves. Responding to these types of issues, Franklin (1997, p. 66) argues that, in his view, most British journalists are already 'motivated by the highest professional commitment despite the rather routine nature of much of the daily practice of journalism'. Accordingly, it follows in his view that if 'declining standards are merely symptomatic of a more profound malaise, effective regulation must try to effect a cure on the root cause rather than the symptoms' (ibid., p. 231; see also Franklin and Pilling 1998). Unless the regulation of the news media is fundamentally rethought, he maintains, market driven journalism will 'continue to offend individual privacy as well as standards of journalistic quality into the next millennium. Newszak will flourish without restraint' (1997, p. 231).

To conclude, it is our hope that this chapter's brief sketch of several particularly salient ethical issues associated with popular journalism will prove to be useful. Specifically, it is hoped that it will help to establish several possible points of departure for critical efforts to contribute to this process of rethinking the ethical implications of market-driven journalism.

ENDNOTES

1. Small portions of this chapter have appeared previously in S. Allan (1999) *News Culture*, Buckingham and Philadelphia: Open University Press.

2. This 'Filet O'Facts' approach is also significantly affecting journalists' understanding of the role the press in democratic society and the importance of the news media in the lives of news audiences. For example, a 1995 newspaper Guild of Editors survey found that British journalists are now 'placing a much greater emphasis on journalism as a provider of entertainment with the great majority accepting that the provision of entertainment and relaxation is a very (47 per cent) or fairly (44 per cent) important function of media' (Franklin 1997, p. 66).

REFERENCES

Aldridge, M. (1998) 'The tentative hell-raisers: identity and mythology in contemporary UK press journalism', *Media, Culture & Society* **20**(1), pp. 109–127.

Allan, S. (1999) *News Culture*, Buckingham and Philadelphia: Open University Press.

Auletta, K. (1997) 'Peering over the edge', in E.E. Dennis and R.W. Snyder, eds, *Media & Public Life*, New Brunswick, NJ and London: Transaction Publishers.

Bell, M. (1998) 'The journalism of attachment', in M. Kieran, ed., *Media Ethics*, London: Routledge.

Belsey, A. (1998) 'Journalism and ethics: can they co-exist?', in M. Kieran, ed., *Media Ethics*, London: Routledge.

Belsey, A. and Chadwick, R. eds (1992) *Ethical Issues in Journalism and the Media*, London: Routledge.

Bernstein, C. (1992) 'The Idiot Culture', *The New Republic*, 8 June, pp. 22–28.

Bird, S.E. (1992) *For Enquiring Minds: A Cultural Study of Supermarket Tabloids*, Knoxville, TN: University of Tennessee Press.

Bok, S. (1997) 'TV violence, children, and the press', in P. Norris, ed., *Politics and the Press: The News Media and Their Influences*, Boulder and London: Lynne Reiner.

Bourdieu, P. (1998) *On Television and Journalism*, Translation by P.P. Ferguson, London: Pluto.

Bromley, M. (1998) 'The "tabloiding" of Britain: "quality" newspapers in the 1900s', in H. Stephenson and M. Bromley, eds, *Sex, Lies and Democracy*, London: Longman.

Bromley, M. and O'Malley, T., eds (1997) *A Journalism Reader*, London: Routledge.

Carter, C., Branston, G. and Allan, S., eds (1998) *News, Gender and Power*, London and New York: Routledge.

Columbia Journalism Review Forum (1998) 'The erosion of values: a debate among journalists over hope to cope' (March/April), pp. 1–8.

Crispin Miller, M. (1996) 'Free the Media', *The Nation* (3 June), pp. 1– 6.

Dennis, E.E. (1996) *Media Debates: Issues in Mass Communication*, 2nd edn, Whiteplains, NY: Longman.

Engel, M. (1996) *Tickle the Public: One Hundred Years of the Popular Press*, London: Victor Gollancz.

Franklin, B. (1997) *Newszak & News Media*, London: Arnold.

Franklin, B. and Pilling, R. (1998) 'Taming the tabloids: market, moguls and media regulation', in M. Kieran, ed., *Media Ethics*, London: Routledge.

Fuller, J. (1996) *News Values: Ideas for an Information Age*, Chicago and London: University of Chicago Press.

Gordon, A.D. and Kittross, J.M. (1998) 'Manipulation by the media: truth, fairness and objectivity', in A.D. Gordon and J.M. Kittross, *Controversies in Media Ethics*, 2nd edn, New York: Longman.

Gordon, A.D. (1999) 'Infotainment programming', in A.D. Gordon and J.M. Kittross, *Controversies in Media Ethics*, 2nd edn, New York: Longman.

Graham, G. (1998) 'Sex and Violence in fact and fiction', in M. Kieran, ed., *Media Ethics*, London: Routledge.

Habermas, J. (1989) *The Structural Transformation of the Public Sphere*, (trans. by T. Burger with F. Lawrence), Cambridge, MA: MIT Press.

Hickey, N. (1995) 'The good, the bad and the "gloriously boring"', *Columbia Journalism Review* (May/June), pp. 1–7.

Hickey, N. (1998a) 'Can CBS News come back?', *Columbia Journalism Review* (January/February), pp. 1–11.

Hickey, N. (1998b) 'Money lust: how pressure for profit is perverting journalism', *Columbia Journalism Review*, (July/August), pp. 1–4.

Hoggart, S. (1995) 'Filleted fish', *New Statesman & Society* (24 March), pp. 20–21.

Hogshire, J. (1997) *Grossed-out Surgeon Vomits inside Patient!: An Insider's Look at Supermarket Tabloids*, Venice, CA: Feral House.

Hoyt, M. (1995) 'Are you now, or will you ever be, a civic journalist?: as the theory moves into practice in more and more newsrooms, the debates get sharper', *Columbia Journalism Review* (September/October), pp. 1–11.

Johnson, S. (1997) 'How low can TV news go?: A morality play in Chicago wins applause but will the news really change?', *Columbia Journalism Review* (July/August), pp. 1–10.

Jones,T. (1998) 'That old Black magic', *Columbia Journalism Review* (March/April), pp. 1–7.

Keeble, R. (1998) *The Newspapers Handbook*, London: Routledge.

Kelley, J. (1997) 'Prospects for the future', in E.E. Dennis and R.W. Snyder, eds, *Media and Public Life*, New Brunswick, NJ and London: Transaction Publishers.

Kieran, M. (1998) 'Objectivity, impartiality and good journalism', in M. Kieran, ed., *Media Ethics*, London: Routledge.

Langer, J. (1998) *Tabloid Television: Popular Journalism and the 'Other News'*, London: Routledge.

Livesey, T. (1998) *Babes, Booze, Orgies and Aliens*, London: Virgin.

Lull, J. and Hinerman, S., eds (1997) *Media Scandals*. Cambridge: Polity Press.

MacGregor, B. (1997) *Live, Direct and Biased? Making Television News in the Satellite Age*, London: Arnold.

Marliere, P. (1998) 'The Rules of the Journalistic Field', *European Journal of Communication*, **13**(2), 219–234.

Maylon, T. (1995) 'Might not main', *New Statesman & Society* (24 March), pp. 24–26.

Merrill, J.C. (1999) 'Infotainment programming', in A.D. Gordon and J.M. Kittross, *Controversies in Media Ethics*, 2nd edn, New York: Longman.

Merrill, J.C. (1998) 'Overview: foundations for media ethics', in A.D. Gordon and J.M. Kittross, eds, *Controversies in Media Ethics*, 2nd edn, New York: Longman.

Merrill, J.C (1996) *Media Debates: Issues in Mass Communication*, 2nd cdn, Whitcplains, NY: Longman.

Merritt, D. (1995) *Public Journalism and Public Life*, Hillsdale, NJ: Lawrence Erlbaum Associates.

O'Neill, J. (1992) 'Journalism in the marketplace', in A. Belsey and R. Chadwick, eds, *Ethical Issues in Journalism and the Media*, London: Routledge.

Patterson, P. and Wilkins (1998) 'Media economies: the deadline meets the bottom line', *Media Ethics: Issues & Cases*, Boston: McGraw-Hill.

Petley, J. (1997) 'Faces for spaces', in M. Bromley and T. O'Malley, eds, *A Journalism Reader*, London: Routledge.

Reuss, C. (1999) 'Infotainment programming', in A.D. Gordon and J.H. Kittross, *Controversies in Media Ethics*, 2nd edn, New York: Longman.

Shattuc, J.M. (1997) *The Talking Cure: TV Talk Shows and Women*. New York: Routledge.

Sholle, D. (1993) 'Buy our news: tabloid television and commodification', *Journal of Communication Inquiry*, **17**(1), 56–72.

Sparks, C. (1992) 'Popular journalism: theories and practice', in P. Dahlgren and C. Sparks, eds, *Journalism and Popular Culture*, London: Sage.

Stratford, T. (1992) 'Women and the press', in A. Belsey and R. Chadwick, eds, *Ethical Issues in Journalism and the Media*, London: Routledge.

Underwood, D. (1998) 'It's not just in L.A.', *Columbia Journalism Review* (January/February): pp. 1–7.

Williams, G. (1995) 'New times', *New Statesman & Society* (24 March), pp. 7–11.

8 New Labour, New Britain. Campaign politics and the ethics of spin

Stephen Hayward

INTRODUCTION: 'THE BATTLE OF SPIN'

In the opening weeks of the 1997 general election campaign the editors of *The Daily Telegraph* and *The Guardian* engaged in a frank exchange of views on the media's handling of national politics. This was a brief, but highly revealing encounter in that the perceived seriousness of the event – reporting 'the sacred moment in a democracy', no less – obliged the contributors to work up an ethical position, something which under more mundane circumstances is liable to remain unspoken and intuitive.[1] The immediate catalyst was the electoral debut of Martin Bell, a former BBC war correspondent who stood as the independent anti-corruption candidate for Tatton. His opponent Neil Hamilton was then under official investigation, thanks in large part to *The Guardian*, and the latest in a long line of Tory MPs who had been found guilty of personal misconduct or 'sleaze'. *The Daily Telegraph's* rancour centred on the idea that the election had been hijacked by the media. Quite literally in the case of Bell's candidacy, though also metaphorically in the way that the campaign appeared to consist of little more than a constant diet of photo opportunities, sound bites, and speculation. 'Real' politics and 'hard' issues had somehow got lost along the way. *The Telegraph's* solution was to reassert the authority of what might be called the 'public service' concept of communications, that is one more usually associated with the BBC, and even then in its Reithian pre-1960s heyday. According to the editor of *The Daily Telegraph* Charles Moore, the media should act as an honest broker transmitting an unimpeachable body of information in a way that 'people find interesting, honest and helpful'.[2] In reply Alan Rusbridger of *The Guardian* rejected this approach as servile and fogyish, and proceeded to uncover the hypocrisy and political bias in Moore's position using the same kind of investigative techniques that had been brought to bear on the Hamilton case. In doing so he too was appealing to another media orthodoxy, though in this case one that understood the concept of 'good journalism' in terms of freedom of speech and editorial independence in the furtherance of a liberal democracy.

What is striking about the media debate of 1997 was its certain belief in the authority of concepts whose meaning was, and is, far from unproblematic. The notion of a 'real' political agenda for example that could somehow be stripped away from the representational conventions, the idea that the 'public interest' is an undifferentiated entity, or even that a set of 'preferred' journalistic conventions developed in the context of parliamentary reporting in a broadsheet might be equally suited to the agony aunt's page in a tabloid.

In fact I am overstating the criticism here, for in other areas of *The Guardian's* 1997 electoral coverage the idea of contingency was very much to the fore. By commissioning its own focus groups, by exposing the 'mechanics' of the various party political campaigns and the performance of its rivals in the press and on TV, *The Guardian* turned the deconstruction of what it called the 'battle of the spin' into a spectator sport.[3]

Among its many media watchers Roy Greenslade made the most profound comment on the incestuous relationship between the politicians and the press. It was a product of the 'awful nature of reality'.[4] What he meant by this was that the whole jamboree – the candidates, the spin doctors, the journalists, the pollsters, the chat show hosts, even the media pundits – were locked in a kind of dance macabre responding to the irresistible power of market forces. Public interest had been replaced by what he called 'public desire', and in the present state of affairs 'information takes second place to entertainment'.[5]

In fact Greenslade's analysis was not so very different from Charles Moore's. There was the same feeling that one of the last bastions of 'proper' journalism was being drawn ever closer to an amorphous world of lesser, or alien genre, and that the broadsheet coverage of political affairs was in danger of resembling the tabloid coverage of the soap stars' love affairs. Moreover the tragedy was compounded in that the 'dumbing down' or 'Americanisation' of politics, to use expressions that are now embedded in the broadsheet consciousness, suffused the world of communications. At the time of writing the litany includes the new look Radio Four, the game show culture on commercial TV, the Brit Pop phenomenon in the arts, and anything to do with Rupert Murdoch, or the National Lottery.

Greenslade's article had opened with Tony Blair's remark that the 1997 electoral coverage was a 'conspiracy against understanding'. His conclusion reflected the difficulty of preserving, or even defending ethical standards in the face of market forces:

I would suggest that what infuriates Blair, and many politicians from all parties – yes, and many journalists – is the awful nature of reality. To build a new media culture will take even longer than two terms of a Labour government. And none of us, I am sure, is exactly sure how we can plot a 'conspiracy for understanding'.[6]

This chapter does not pretend to offer a new system of media ethics for the twenty-first century. In fact it questions the very possibility of such universal and immutable standards. Its basic objective is to contextualise the *anxiety* that surrounded the representation of politics during the general election campaign of 1997. I begin with the historical perspective, tracing the origins of what has been called the 'Americanisation' of electoral politics to the late 1950s, a time when the rhetoric and imagery of a newly recognised 'affluent society' were consciously grafted onto the political agenda for the first time. My detailed analysis of Harold Wilson's New Britain election campaign of 1964 explains how the emphasis on technological transformation resonated with what might be called a mediated 'spirit of the times'. This offers a useful contrast with Tony Blair's exposition of the 'New Britain' theme more than thirty years later. While there were similarities in the rhetorical structure of the campaigns, the media response of the 1990s was far more 'variegated'. It was as if an ideological 'commodity', i.e. politics, had been subjected to increased levels of brand differentiation. This parallels the greater use of focus groups by the party managers, and the growing spirit of competition in the media marketplace.

Underlying my historical interpretation is an effort to understand how the exercise of political rhetoric and the recent spectacle of media infighting can be brought together in a single sociological paradigm. One answer – as inspired by Pierre Bourdieu – is to regard these phenomena as different episodes in the mediation of culturally authoritative practices and beliefs. Within the metaphorical 'space' of the broadsheets the debate can be regarded as a struggle for professional hegemony, an attempt to defend, or redefine a 'proper' form of political representation that has traditionally focused on the fine print of the party manifestos.

Outside the world of the 'chattering classes' a different form of cultural manipulation has been at work. In addressing an electorate which is notoriously indifferent, the modern politician utilises the authority that resides in a less esoteric set of conventional beliefs. It is a case of activating a series of cultural levers that are as meaningful to the tabloid reader as the broadsheet constituency. Since the late 1950s successive political leaders have become increasingly adept at mobilising the 'truth' that is implicit in nationhood, prosperity, technological progress, family values, health, and social justice. This chapter focuses on two masters of the campaigning genre: Harold Wilson and Tony Blair.

THE 1959 GENERAL ELECTION CAMPAIGN AND THE EMERGENCE OF A 'FEEL GOOD' POLITICS

For each general election since 1945 a detailed review of the party campaigns and manifestos, voting patterns and contemporary press coverage has been commissioned by Nuffield College, Oxford.[7] The series as a whole illustrates the increasingly intimate relationship between politicians and the media, and provides empirical evidence for what has been seen as the 'Americanisation' or 'packaging' of modern politics (Franklin 1994; Kavanagh 1995; Negrine 1996). The paradigm is built around the emergence of a highly co-ordinated form of electioneering in which speeches, press releases, photo opportunities, TV broadcasts, and advertising work to a centralised campaign agenda. The direction of the campaign is adjusted to take advantage of any blunders that are made by the opposition, and the performance is continually evaluated by reference to representative sections of the electorate, much in the way that manufacturers develop new products in the light of focus groups.

The beginnings of this process can be seen in the late 1950s when the Conservative Party spent the unprecedented figure of almost half a million pounds in restoring its flagging fortunes in the opinion polls (Butler and Rose 1960, p. 21). In the run-up to the 1959 election it called upon the services of the advertising agency Colman, Prentis and Varley in order to re-establish its public profile and to draw in a part of the electorate that would become increasingly significant in future decades, the 'floating voter'.[8] In the late 1950s this was a relatively new and undifferentiated category embracing 'housewives, prosperous workers, and young people'; in other words those voters that the pollsters perceived to be naturally cautious, socially ambitious, politically naive, or indifferent (ibid., p. 22).

In evolving a form of easily digestible, business as usual politics, the Conservative campaign cultivated what would now be called the 'feel good factor'. In 1959 speeches, newspaper advertisements, TV broadcasts, and posters were built around the catch phrase: 'Life's better with the Conservatives. Don't let Labour ruin it'. In one of the most memorable posters – a favourite with contemporary media watchers – an archetypal suburban family is shown feverishly washing their shiny new Austin motorcar.[9] The image suggests that 1940s austerity had given way to 1950s affluence thanks to a continuing adherence to Conservative values. These included, in the words of the 1950 election manifesto: 'hard work, thrift, honesty and neighbourliness . . . Christian ethics, self respect, pride in skill and responsibility, love of home and family, devotion to country and the British Empire and Commonwealth' (Craig 1975, p. 152).

The strength of these beliefs was their suburban 'ordinariness' and familiarity. Their origins lay in the Baldwinite Conservatism of the 1920s and 1930s and the first wave of 'mass' home ownership (Schwarz 1984). In the post-war climate of full employment they suffused the expanding world of domestic consumption (Saunders 1990).

HAROLD WILSON AND THE 'NEW BRITAIN' 1964

The hegemony of Conservative values in a consumer society was something that exercised the intelligentsia of the Labour Party following yet another electoral defeat in 1959. Was its own cloth cap image an anachronistic liability? A Social Commentary report of 1960 suggested as much (Abrams and Rose 1960). It appeared that young working class voters increasingly saw themselves as ambitious, forward looking, and affluent, values they associated with the Conservatives. In contrast the Labour Party was regarded as worthy but dull. Its pioneering achievements of the 1940s in education, health care, and pensions, its nationalisation of the electricity industry – though not the railways – were all taken for granted. The generally buoyant economy of the 1950s meant that all political parties could promise new council houses, hospitals, and schools. The Labour Party had lost its distinctiveness, and its stereotypes, 'poor people, factory workers, old aged pensioners and people interested in helping the underdog', were dated and unglamorous (Abrams and Rose 1960, p. 53).

With its emphasis on image and voter recognition the 1960 Report, published by Penguin as *Must Labour Lose?*, was very much a product of its time. Like the works of Galbraith (1958), Packard (1957, 1959) and Boorstin (1962), also popularised by Penguin, it assumed a simple deterministic relationship between advertising and behaviour. In an 'affluent society', of which the United States was the paradigm, consumers were unwittingly 'persuaded', and presidents were 'manufactured'. All this was taken to heart by Mark Abrams, who after producing *Must Labour Lose?* was appointed head of the party's 'creative group' for the 1963–4 campaign (Butler and King 1965, pp. 66–71). Coming from the world of market research, with an expertise in consumer psychology, Abrams was entrusted with the 're-branding' of Labour along the modernising lines of the strategy documents *Labour in the Sixties* (1960) and *Signposts for the Sixties* (1961).

The conduct of the Labour Party's 1964 election campaign illustrates the use of techniques that are now regarded as commonplace. Abrams introduced focus groups to identify the major concerns of the 'floating voter', and to ensure that presentational style was on 'target'. When the party leader undertook a national speaking tour in January–April 1964, a campaign guide was produced in order to avoid inconsistencies in local coverage. This kept presentation 'on message', as New Labour now describe it. Finally, embarrassing party divisions relating to unilateral disarmament for example, were concealed behind a dominating media friendly personality – Harold Wilson (Rose 1967).

The message of 1960s Labour was deliberately calculated to appeal to the first generation of the post-war baby boomers: 4.5 million voters, or 17 per cent of the electorate in 1964 (Abrams and Rose 1960, p. 47). The rhetoric was constructed around the idea of scientifically driven change. Wilson's speeches were littered with references to the atomic age, the jet age, space travel, cities of the future, 'breakthroughs', and most famously of all, the 'white heat' of technology (Wilson 1964 and 1963).

As an image the scientific revolution had many advantages. At a popular level it drew upon what Christopher Booker called the 'neophilia' of the early 1960s, the naive trust in all things new that would enable the majority to ignore the warnings of CND and to see untold riches in nuclear power (Booker 1969). Indeed technology was glamorous. In 1964 the coverage of *Goldfinger*, the latest gadget-filled James Bond film, far outstripped the General Election in the popular press. Being unfamiliar, scientific change was inevitably youthful, and in its apparent efficiency could be played off against the incompetence of the existing government. Moreover in the guise of objectivity, science could be regarded as morally superior to a party tarnished by the Profumo Scandal. Being non-upper class, as C.P. Snow had explained, science was automatically populist (Snow 1959). All these themes are skilfully woven together in the 'Let's go with Labour campaign' of 1964. In a typical newspaper advertisement, a photograph of Wilson, honest, direct and plain speaking, is accompanied by the caption:

We are living in a fast-moving, exciting, challenging world. In twenty years the scientists have made more progress than in the past thousand years. Yet Britain under the Conservatives lags behind, lacking the will and the plan to bring the wealth of this scientific age within everyone's reach. We are living in the jet age but we are ruled by Edwardians. (*Daily Mirror*, 28 January 1964, p. 19).

A MESSAGE IN TOUCH WITH ITS TIMES: THE MEDIA RESPONSE TO THE 'NEW BRITAIN' OF 1964

How did the newspapers respond to Wilson's technologically driven Socialism, indeed to what extent had Fleet Street contributed to its spirit of modernity? The short answer is a great deal. For, irrespective of party affiliation, the majority of newspapers were committed to the idea of modernisation. In its pre-election day editorial the Liberal leaning *Times* demanded 'forthright and radical' change.[10] For the pro-Conservative *Daily Mail* the leading issue of the day was the 'modernising of Britain'.[11] Most telling of all was the dramatic appearance a month before the election of a new daily newspaper committed to the spirit of change. This was *The Sun*, a revamped version of *The Daily Herald* specifically intended for the rising generation of aspirational working class voters. *The Sun* offered a highly materialistic reading of Wilson's technological revolution. A vote for Labour was a vote for a social equality born of universal access to post-war luxuries. The editorial was an unabashed example of commodity fetishism:

Steaks, cars, houses, refrigerators, washing machines are no longer the prerogative of the 'upper crust', but the right of all. People believe, and The Sun *believes with them, that the division of Britain into social classes is hopelessly out of date. Public taste has been uplifted. People are interested in new houses, new inventions, new foods, modern ideas, the latest car, the newest thing. For all those millions of people with lively minds and fresh ambitions* The Sun *will stimulate the New Thinking* (15 September 1964).

Come the election it appeared that the 'new thinking' was little more than the obsession with youth, novelty, and appearance that was already a prominent feature of the advertising and leisure pages of the more established newspapers. In *The Daily Mail* consumerism slid over into electoral coverage when its traditionally female readership were offered 'A shopper's guide to the political parties'.[12]

For a more ideologically comprehensive exposition of Wilson's New Britain it was necessary to turn to *The Daily Mirror*. As in previous elections the paper was stridently partisan (Edelman 1966). That said, its presentational techniques were highly sophisticated, foreshadowing the tabloids of the present day. Pictures and personalities told the story. Wilson's attack on the aristocratic other worldliness of the Tories was neatly summarised in front page photographs of the Prime Minister; one captioned 'The patched up Premier'[13], another 'Sir Alec confesses. I forget my vote'.[14] Tory Party nepotism and the old boy network was illustrated in the feature 'Why should Britain be run by chaps mourning for George the Third?'.[15] The two nations theme continued in an election 'shock' issue, 'Is this the promised land?'.[16] Using large-scale photographs of the bleak Northern townscapes made famous by contemporary new wave cinema, the paper attacked the hypocrisy of the affluent society: 'Wash day Sampson Street, Liverpool 1964. No hot water, no bathroom. Just one of 600,000 slums in the Tories' affluent society'.[17]

The specificity of the location is important. It brought physical substance to an ideological abstraction. Elsewhere in *The Daily Mirror* this was achieved with vox pop interviews, features on what the election meant for typical readers and celebrities, and most significantly, family portraits of Harold Wilson, the personification of the New Britain.[18]

In a 'remarkable interview' with Donald Zec, Wilson is shown pouring tea in the kitchen of his Hampstead Garden suburb home. The text celebrates his heroic rise from council schoolboy to Oxford don, economist, and post-war cabinet minister. However, in spite of these achievements, Wilson remains the conscientious family man who has never lost touch with his roots. The text celebrates his popular touch:

He follows the fortunes of his home football team, Huddersfield, with the fervour if not the squeals of the average Beatles' fan'.[19]

NEW LABOUR, NEW BRITAIN 1996–7

More than thirty years after Harold Wilson had posed as the popular meritocratic advocate of technology, Tony Blair angled for a similar position in characterising New Labour as 'the shape of things to come'. The images that made up Blair's futurism were very different of course. Since the late 1960s many of the prominent icons of modernity had been discredited. Nuclear power, motorways, tower blocks, even the idea of 'progress' itself was regarded with suspicion by an increasingly environmentally conscious public. When North Sea oil became an election issue in the late 1970s, all parties balanced their enthusiasm for this economic panacea with the need for sustainability. In the late 1990s Blair needed a benign technology, in tune with the post-Fordist rhetoric that had dominated the Thatcher years (Harvey 1990; Weiner 1981). He found it in the 'information superhighway' and the personal computer, a 'positive' technology, closely associated with the transmission of knowledge, and familiar in the classroom, the workplace, and increasingly, the home. As presented in the 1997 manifesto the image of the 'national grid for learning' was non-hierarchical, individually empowering and decentralised (an important consideration in a climate of devolution).[20] At the same time it was dynamic and in Blair's phrase 'wondrous' (Blair 1996, p. 98), an example of what historians of the American experience of modernity have called the 'technological sublime' (Nye 1994).

Recast as the 'electronic workshop of the world' New Labour's vision of a twenty-first century Britain was framed in dialectical opposition to the 'old' Britain of the 1980s and early 1990s (Blair 1996, p. 106). When Blair spoke of 'breaking free of our imperial shadows' he was directly challenging the Churchillian persona developed by Margaret Thatcher (ibid., p. 268). His 'vision of the young country' – the subtitle of his collected speeches – was a direct riposte to the John Major's identification with the rural idyll dreamt up by Stanley Baldwin in the 1920s and 1930s (Samuel 1994, Schwarz 1984), and an acknowledgement of those cultural critics who had condemned the escapism of theme park Britain during the heyday of the 'heritage industry' (Hewison 1987; Wright 1985).

The symbolic turning point came in 1997, when a few months into the new parliament, the Department of National Heritage (1992) became the Department of Culture, Media and Sport. Margaret Thatcher's image of the nation 'linked by a common belief . . . in Britain's greatness' turned into Chris Smith's vision of a 'hot bed of interesting creativity and modernity.'[21]

In the General Election of 1997 the idea of democratisation via information technology and cultural participation contributed to the moral imperative of New Labour. This was the meaning of the campaign anthem 'Things can only get better' (Butler and Kavanagh 1997). It was an indictment of a carefully crafted image of the existing state of affairs. The 'yob culture' of the deregulated City, the references to trolley-bound NHS patients waiting for hospital beds, and of course, parliamentary sleaze (Blair 1996, p. 44 and p. 184). In a marvellous inversion of the Thatcherite rhetoric of the 1980s, the much trumpeted 'Victorian values': self help, free enterprise and family morality, were recast as Dickensian values: selfishness, public squalor and hypocrisy (Hall and Jacques 1983).

Having colonised the moral high ground Blair's Labour Party was free to appropriate the hegemonic values of post-war conservatism; the idea of 'one nation', the commitment to Christian ethics, the idea of the 'home owning democracy', and the 1997 election mantra 'tough on crime, tough on the cause of crime'.[22] The process was made simpler by the constitutional changes of 1994–1995. By jettisoning the block union vote at the party conference, by abandoning the commitment to the public ownership of the means of production (Clause IV of the party's 1918 constitution), New Labour purged itself of its most controversial policies, leaving a left of centre 'communitarianism' that could be interpreted as something as unthreatening as good neighbourliness.[23] Committing himself to the 'Third Way' Blair could dismiss the 'student Marxism' of the 1970s, and express a public admiration for Margaret Thatcher's brand of conviction politics, as more 'radical than Tory'.[24] In the course of the campaign he could advocate private–public partnerships, 'welfare to work', and rights as well as responsibilities, safe in the knowledge that all vestiges of ideological factionalism would be obscured behind a media friendly persona.

THE 'PACKAGING' OF NEW LABOUR 1997

When, in the early 1960s, Harold Wilson had played a similar game, it was quite possible to cultivate an accessible, and thus trustworthy persona on the basis of a raincoat, a reputation for comic repartee, and a few TV interviews. Far more was expected of Tony Blair. In the intervening years the boundary that separated public from private life had become increasingly blurred as the lifestyle feature spread from the colour supplement to all areas of the media, and the tabloids in particular made a speciality of delving ever deeper into the personal lives of the rich and famous.[25]

The 'packaging' of political issues in terms of personality was most apparent in *The Sun's* treatment of New Labour (Franklin 1994). The coverage was entirely dominated by the Blairs, revealing an indebtedness to President Clinton's 1992 election campaign (Butler and Kavanagh 1997, p. 56). 'Tony' was featured with sporting stars, the family was seen at home and going to church, and even holiday snaps and wedding photographs were included to add to the sense of authenticity. Old Labour renegades were skilfully marginalised (Butler and Kavanagh 1997, pp. 56–57). *The Sun* headline 'Blair kicks out Lefties' was a reminder that in the 1980s and early 1990s most of Fleet Street had supported the Tory Party.[26] At times the effort to relocate traditional Conservative values in the New Labour's 'first family' verge on the sentimental and mawkish. An eve of election *Sun* exclusive was devoted to the leader's personal credo, the 'Blair necessities': 'My wife and kids are the rock of my life – politics is important but they come first'.[27]

The Sun's presentation of Blair was not entirely a question of political partisanship, though the Prime Minister in waiting did contribute regular articles to the newspaper. The presentation of politics in terms of human interest was one way of making a notoriously dull subject palatable. The apathy factor was long recognised. In a Gallup poll conducted a few months before the 1959 election 38 per cent felt that 'it mattered little, or not at all which party was in power'.[28] In a 1964 pre-election poll only 44 per cent expressed a strong commitment to one of the two main parties. By 1974 this had fallen to 27 per cent. Moreover in spite of *The Sun's* best efforts, the turnout for the 1997 election registered at an all time post-war low of 71.2 per cent.[30]

Across the media the scenes of everyday life in NW3; the interviews with the Blair's neighbours, the speculation on the value of the family house and the cost of Cherie's wardrobe, the personal confessions of her reprobate father, the actor Tony Booth, brought elements of the unreconstructed Womens' Page to the month-long proceedings.[31]

The basic popularising strategy may once again be traced back to the early 1960s. In cultivating the common touch Wilson had peppered his speeches with references to 'Coronation Street slums', and 'Stop-go and Son' economics (i.e. *Steptoe and Son*), and most famously of all had awarded the Beatles an MBE in 1965.[32] That said the quantity and degree of popularisation was of a different order in 1997. To just take one example, *The Mirror* presented the New Labour manifesto in terms of its impact on 'Britain's favourite TV soap characters'. Among these hypothetical consequences were a 'decent education' for *Eastenders'* Billy Jackson, and a 'stable economy' for *Coronation Street* entrepreneur Mike Baldwin.[33]

THE CONTROVERSY OF 1997

This was one of the more amusing examples of the elision between hard news and 'fantasy', popular culture and 'real' life that so exercised the media watchers when reviewing the 1997 election. In other instances of 'irregular' practice, *The Daily Mail* set up a phone line in order that MPs could register their opposition to a single European currency and thus direct the election towards what it considered to be the real issue 'The Battle for Britain'.[34] Meanwhile *The Mirror* introduced its own hot line inviting readers to 'tell us your NHS horror story'.[35] The following day its agenda was dominated by the 'Death of the NHS' and the front page revelations of a sobbing nurse.

Naturally there was a good deal of old fashioned political partisanship at work here. *The Daily Mail* – a right of centre newspaper from its inception (1896) – was stirring up the Eurosceptic wing of the Conservative Party, while the *Mirror* – an outpost of Socialist thinking even in the 1980s – was reinforcing New Labour's promise to rescue the Welfare State. However, the way that these newspapers seemed to be 'manufacturing', or at least precipitating events was seen as controversial. For the broad sheet pundits the tabloids were ignoring the manifestos and writing their own agendas. They were misleading the electorate at a 'sacred moment in a democracy' to quote Charles Moore of *The Telegraph*.[36]

The broad sheet debate of 1997 took as its starting point the idea that the media could be divided up into two opposing factions. The first allied to the notion of 'real news', ethical standards, and professional accountability (or mutual recrimination as in *The Telegraph* versus *Guardian* debate); the second bound by the logic of the marketplace, with a news agenda that was determined by the readers' desire for novelty, sensation, and human interest. The sense of anxiety within the 'quality' press operated along two fronts: the historical and the cultural. On the one hand there was a sense that a traditional style of journalism was being usurped by the new techniques of the tabloids, a feeling summed up in the expression 'tabloidisation'. On the other that superior cultural standards were being undermined by a lower form of cultural discourse, that is, the press was being 'dumbed down'.

OLD VERSUS NEW : TABLOIDISATION

Looking back over the past twenty or thirty years, the broadsheet conception of the press was still in the ascendant in the late 1970s. At the time of the last major Royal Commission on the Press (1974–77) the moral and social responsibilities of the media were paramount. This is how the Final Report defined the 'Functions and Freedom of the Press'.

Newspapers and periodicals serve society in diverse ways. They inform their readers about the world and interpret it to them. They act as both watchdogs for citizens, by scrutinising concentrations of power, and as a means of communication among groups within the community, thus promoting social cohesion and social change. Of course, the press seeks to entertain as well as to instruct and we do not dismiss this aim as trivial, but it is the performance of serious functions which justifies the high importance which democracies attach to a free press (Royal Commission 1977, p. 8).

This was the media in the role of the 'Fourth Estate', monitoring and facilitating the democratic process on behalf of the 'people' (Curran and Seaton 1991). Clearly the definition alludes to a dominant news agenda – something which was confirmed by an empirical review of the press content of the day – and an idea of hierarchy, with instruction taking precedence over entertainment. The idea the news trickled downwards from the great and the good was reflected elsewhere in the Report. The readership survey was based on the responses of two groupings: the 'general public' and 'influential citizens', while the criteria that were used to gauge the performance of the media – completeness, accuracy, bias, etc. – were derived from the practices of the 'quality' as opposed to the 'popular' press (ibid., pp. 81–84).

The Commission had been triggered by a feeling that the increasing number of newspaper amalgamations and closures was jeopardising the true democratic mission of the press. Under this rubric the public interest was best served by editorial independence and political diversity. A decade or so later the official line would be very different. During the 1980s the ownership of the press had become still more concentrated with the Murdoch group in particular advancing a new kind of populism. Its more notorious aspects – cheque-book journalism, long range unsolicited photographs, invasive royal reporting, etc. – called into question the traditional rights and responsibilities of the media. This at least was how the Home Secretary saw it when he appointed the Calcutt Committee on Privacy (Calcutt Report 1990). Calcutt questioned the sanctity of the 'public interest' concept, suggesting that the term had been devalued by the antics of the tabloid editors. Public interest was not to be confused with what was 'interesting to the public' (ibid., p. 8).

In fact the hegemony of the public interest idea had already come under attack in the mid-1980s. Margaret Thatcher was particularly suspicious, if not downright hostile to the term, regarding it as an ethical smokescreen put up by the various public sector elites in order to protect their own interests (Thatcher 1993, p. 634). The Prime Minister's attack on the professional integrity of teaching, medicine, the law, and the BBC was all part of an effort to reign in the public sector, and to precipitate a deregulated 'entrepreneurial' culture (Hall and Jacques 1983). These ideological objectives were aided and abetted by technological factors. In the face of cable and satellite television and the rise of the pay-as-you-view principle, was it still appropriate to cling to the idea of a national broadcasting service funded from a uniform licence fee? Was the paternalistic identity of the BBC, as built up under the directorship of Sir John Reith (1927–1938) still appropriate in an increasingly pluralistic society? (Scannell and Cardiff 1991). These were some of the issues considered by the Peacock Committee when it met to consider the future funding of the BBC in 1985.

From a historical angle the contrast between the Peacock Report's understanding of the public interest and that of the 1977 Royal Commission on the Press is striking. The stereotypical audience no longer consisted of passive recipients of information, but rather fickle and individualistic 'consumers' of entertainment. The Peacock Report opened by characterising the viewpoint of what might be called the new 'consumer citizenry':

Judging from the many letters that we received from individuals from all over the country most people want to be able to choose programmes that interest them most and not those which talk down to them or treat them simply as fodder for advertisements, though limited advertising seems to many of them a reasonable price to pay for not having to fork out for a licence to finance programmes that they may not want to watch (Peacock 1986, p. 2).

Clearly there has been a shift of emphasis – and power – here, from what the broadsheet editors of 1997 might have understood as a top-down public service model of communications to one that was bottom-up, or in Roy Greenslade's phrase, the 'public desire' paradigm. In terms of news delivery the new regime favoured accessibility, informality, variety of choice, and entertainment values. In other words many of the characteristics that we have already seen in the context of the tabloid coverage of the Blair campaign.

HIGH VERSUS LOW: 'DUMBING DOWN'

The Peacock enquiry also raised the spectre of advertising on the BBC and fanned the flames of a controversy that would continue to exercise the media pundits at the time of the 1997 election – the threat of 'dumbing down'. This was how Paul Johnson viewed the impending catastrophe. The piece first appeared in *The Daily Telegraph* just after the announcement that Martin Bell would be standing as a candidate for Tatton:

The voters must realise that if they vote for Mr Bell they will be voting not just for a reporter with a famous face, but for the media as a whole, at the expense of the political process. They will be voting for the Sun *and for the* News of the World, *for their hidden cameras and their wired-up character assassinations. They will be voting for Rupert Murdoch and all he stands for. They will be voting for television – with its endless sex and violence – and for Channel 4 – and its boss Michael Grade – Britain's pornographer in chief'* (*The Guardian*, 14 April 1997 Media Supplement, p. 3).

When *The Guardian* reprinted this passage it was presented as the ravings of a right wing lunatic. In fact when it is reduced to its basic elements it is only the latest version of a cultural panic that has exercised a broad spectrum of the British intelligentsia for more than a century (Carey 1992). The classic expression of the dumbing down thesis was probably the work of the Cambridge literary don F.R. Leavis. *Mass Civilisation and Minority Culture* (1930) not only set out the fundamental opposition between the depersonalising tendency of modern consumerism and the idea of an authentic cultural heritage – or in the 1997 case, the amorality of tabloid culture and the ethical certainty of *The Daily Telegraph* – it also contained many of the key words that continue to articulate this debate. For example the idea that the national culture was being 'Americanised', the concept of a 'high brow' tradition, and the fear of 'levelling down' (Leavis 1930, p. 7, 10, 24).

Since the 1930s the thesis has served guardians of an indigenous national culture on the right (Eliot 1948), and critics of Americanisation on the left (Hoggart 1957). One difficulty for the latter faction has been the historical association between cultural excellence and social elitism. It was after all Leavis's original contention that the treasures of the past must be nurtured by an intellectual priesthood. In advocating the democratisation of this heritage, or the 'long tradition' as he called it, Raymond Williams recognised that it would be necessary to uncouple the concept of excellence from elitism. This was as much the case in the context of broadcasting or tabloid journalism, as in the areas of art appreciation or literature. As he explained in his study of the media world of the early 1960s *Communications* (1962, 1976):

We must always be careful to distinguish the great works of the past from the social minority which at a particular place and time identifies itself with them (ibid., p. 110).

Clearly this distinction was not being recognised in the context of the media debate of 1997. *The Daily Telegraph's* understanding of good journalistic practice was intimately bound up with a whole range of socially exclusive attitudes. Quality was more important than quantity, the written word took precedence over the television image, morality and the authentic exercise of political judgement resided in a relatively small and discerning readership, whilst the tabloid mass market was driven by an uncritical voyeurism.

NEWS AND HABITUS

At the heart of this argument was the unspoken assumption that 'top people read the *Daily Telegraph*', that the broadsheet way of seeing the world derived a special status from its proximity to a social and economic elite. This is a thesis that has been applied to a whole raft of cultural indicators by the French sociologist Pierre Bourdieu. *Distinction: A social critique of the judgement of taste* (1986) sees preferences in diet, clothing, and leisure pursuits, even religious and political affiliations as an interrelated field of significant attitudes and dispositions – a 'habitus'. According to the social snapshots on which Bourdieu's work is based, the various habitus groups or taste cultures are hierarchically arranged, reflecting their differential access to economic, social and intellectual capital. Very broadly his findings are as one would imagine with a popular press, characterised by human interest stories and sport, gravitating towards those lifestyles in which intellectual capital, or education is at a premium. This means of course that the reading of a tabloid does not necessarily imply economic poverty or social disadvantage. As one moves upwards through Bourdieu's spatial diagram the opportunities for choice and self-invention become far more pronounced. Bourdieu is particularly concerned with the cultural identities of the bourgeoisie. The faction fighting that takes place within the bourgeoisie, the attempt of the 'left bank' to outdistance the 'right bank', of the avant garde to distinguish itself from the conservative, provides an engine for cultural change (Bourdieu 1986, pp. 244–256). On a day-to-day level the symbolic struggle determines what is fashionable. On a more profound intellectual level it determines what is progressive and true.

Bourdieu's idea of rival sections of the bourgeoisie struggling for cultural hegemony offers an intriguing perspective on the media debate of 1997. If we consider a newspaper as a kind of habitus in microcosm the conflict between the Reithian public service ethic and a more heroic form of campaigning journalism looks very like right bank versus left bank faction fighting. From this point of view the response of the different broadsheets to tabloidisation and dumbing down resembles an attempt to assert their market positions. For the relatively high circulation *Telegraph* it was a question of reinforcing a reputation for evolutionary change within the parameters of the dominant culture. For *The Guardian*, a title with around half the readership, it was a matter of asserting a distinctiveness founded on 'radical' or alternative forms of cultural capital. During the election this could include the media punditry that I have been referring to, or more generally, new and emerging forms of knowledge relating to ethnicity, new technology, or sport and popular culture considered with the same degree of 'seriousness' as high culture.[37]

CONCLUSION

This chapter set out with the modest aim of contextualising the sense of anxiety that overtook the broadsheets in the course of the 1997 election campaign. To a certain extent I have simply fleshed out the impression that there has been a qualitative change in political communications over the past thirty or forty years. Taking the present day preoccupation with image and presentation as my starting point I looked back at the rhetoric that characterised Harold Wilson's New Britain campaign of 1964. In doing so I have not attempted to give an exhaustive survey of Labour's economic policies, or to enquire whether the technological vision was in any sense practicable. In fact the pseudo-scientific jargon had almost entirely disappeared from the party agenda by the time of the 1966 election, suggesting that the potency of political rhetoric can wax and wane. When Blair incorporated similar themes in his programme of 1996–7 it was only *The Telegraph* that took up the bait, and even then as an opportunity to pour scorn on the candidate it daubed 'Period Sixties Man Exemplified'.[38]

The absence of a coherent response to New Labour, the sense in which there was no longer a totalising 'spirit of the age', leads on to my second chronological finding: the substitution of an overtly top-down 'public service' model of official communications, by one that is based on a new sense of 'consumer citizenship' and the rhetoric of choice. My empirical survey of post-war elections situated the origins of this trend in the 'affluent society' of the late 1950s and a discourse addressed to the everyday desires of the 'floating voter'. New technology and the Thatcherite assault on public sector institutions precipitated the development in the 1980s. This had obvious implications for a traditional understanding of journalistic practice, as evident in the current debate on 'dumbing down' and tabloidisation'.

Mapping out these historical tendencies goes some way towards explaining the broadsheets' own understanding of the crisis facing the media in 1997. However, it does not explain how electoral imagery works, or why the sense of anxiety should have turned into a debate about ethics. In this chapter I have suggested that a common answer lies in the symbolic power that is associated with dominant systems of practice and belief. In the context of elections a portmanteau of hegemonic values have been used to authenticate or normalise a variety of social and economic projects. I have concentrated on the pseudo-scientific trappings that were applied to different generations of Labour party policy – old and new, Keynesian and Keynesian – Neo Liberal, or 'Third Way'. The chameleon-like adaptability of such myths is quite typical. A study of the use of heritage or patriotism in the 1980s would have to include both Margaret Thatcher's identification with Churchill and the Labour Party's penchant for Elgar; as seen most famously perhaps in the 1987 election broadcast, since daubed 'Kinnock – The Movie' (Franklin 1994, p. 138).

I have suggested that such representations suffuse the world of the media and in the context of the quality or tabloid press take on a local colour. The more basic question of course is how these discourses acquire their cultural authority? Why are new technology, progress, or home ownership deemed to be significant? In this chapter I have drawn on Bourdieu's sociological answer; namely that dominant kinds of knowledge and attitudes originate from an ongoing dialectical struggle for 'distinction' that takes place between different sections of the bourgeoisie. It is a thesis which is clearly pertinent to the idea of intellectual 'fashions' and helps not only to explain the emergence of 'New Labour', or what has been disparagingly termed 'designer Socialism', but the vociferous tone and moral posturing that accompanied the 1997 'Battle of the Spin'.

ACKNOWLEDGEMENT

I am grateful to David Berry for his help in the preparation of this chapter.

ENDNOTES

1. The *Guardian* Media Supplement, April 1997, pp. 2–3.
2. Ibid., p. 2.
3. The *Guardian*, 14 April 1997.
4. Ibid. 23 April 1997, p. 18.
5. Ibid.
6. Ibid.
7. McCallum and Readman (1947); Nicholas (1951). Subsequent titles have been written or co-written by David Butler.

8. The term 'floating voter' is cited in academic discourse from at least 1955. (Rose 1967, p.74) The term was popularised by Cummings in his election cartoons for the *Daily Express* (Butler and King 1965, p.187)
9. Butler and Rose (1960, between pp. 152 and 153); Rose (1967, p. 121).
10. *The Times*, 14 October 1964.
11. The *Daily Mail*, 19 September 1964, p. 2.
12. The *Daily Mail*, 25 September 1964, p. 2.
13. The *Daily Mirror*, 22 May 1964.
14. Idem. 26 September 1964.
15. Idem. 12 October 1964.
16. Idem. 14 October 1964.
17. Ibid. On new wave cinema see Hill (1986).
18. The *Daily Mirror*, 14 October 1964, p. 15; 8 October 1964, pp. 16–17.
19. The *Daily Mirror*, 25 September 1964, p. 16.
20. Seldon (1997, pp. 368–371, 401–407).
21. *The Times*, (1983, p. 288). Smith (1997, p. 9).
22. *The Times*, (1997, pp. 307–331).
23. Butler and Kavanagh (1997, pp. 46–67), Blair (1996, p. 209).
24. Blair (1996, pp. 30 and 206).
25. *The Sunday Times* Magazine first appeared on 4 February 1962.
26. The *Sun*, 28 April 1997.
27. Idem. 29 April 1997, pp. 8–9.
28. Butler and Rose (1960, p. 19).
29. Butler and Kavanagh (1980, p. 2).
30. Butler and Kavanagh (1997, Appendix I).
31. See especially The *Daily Mail*, 10 April 1997, p. 29, The *Express*, 5 and 7 April and 1997, *The Times*, 4 April 1997, p. 18.
32. Butler and King (1965, p. 114).
33. The *Mirror*, 4 April 1997, pp. 6–7.
34. The *Mail*, 15 April 1997.
35. The *Mirror*, 17 April 1997, p. 7.
36. *The Guardian* Media Supplement 14 April 1997, p. 2.
37. *Daily Telegraph*, 1997 monthly circulation: 1,126,000. 1996 average readership: 2,542,000. *The Guardian*, circulation: 402,000. Readership: 1,270,000. Butler and Kavanagh (1997, p. 157).
38. The *Daily Telegraph*, 24 April 1997, p. 5.

REFERENCES

Abrams, M. and Rose, R. (1960) *Must Labour Lose?* Harmondsworth: Penguin.

Alloway, L. (1959) 'The long front of culture', reprinted in Russell and Gablik 1969.

Barthes, R. (1957) *Mythologies*, London: Jonathan Cape 1972.

Baudrillard, J. (1981) *For a Critique of the Political Economy of the Sign*, St. Louis: Telos.

Belsey, A. and Chadwick, R., eds (1992) *Ethical Issues in Journalism and the Media*, London: Routledge.

Bennett, T. *et al.* (1984) *Formations of Nation and People*, London: Routledge.

Blair, T. (1996) *New Britain. My Vision of a Young Country*, London: Fourth Estate.

Booker, C. (1969) *The Neophiliacs: A study of the revolution in English life in the fifties and sixties*, London: Collins.

Boorstin, D.J. (1962) *The Image, or What Happened to the American Dream*, Harmondsworth: Penguin.

Bourdieu, P. (1986) *Distinction: A Social Critique of the Judgement of Taste*, London: Routledge and Kegan Paul.

Butler, D. (1952) *The British General Election of 1951*, London: Macmillan.

Butler, D. (1955) *The British General Election of 1955*, London: Macmillan.

Butler, D. and Kavanagh, D. (1997) *The British General Election of 1997*, London: Macmillan.

Butler, D. and Kavanagh, D. (1980) *The British General Election of 1979*, London: Macmillan.

Butler, D.E. and King, A. (1965) *The British General Election of 1964*, London: Macmillan & Co.

Butler D.E. and Rose, R. (1960) *The British General Election of 1959*, London: Macmillan & Co.

Calcutt (1990) *Report of the Committee on Privacy*, Cmnd 1102. HMSO.

Carey, J. (1992) *The Intellectuals and the Masses. Pride and Prejudice among the Literary Intelligentsia 1880–1939*, London: Faber.

Craig, F.W.S. (1975) *British General Election Manifestos 1900–1974*, London: Macmillan.

Curran, J., Smith, A and Wingate, P. (1987) *Impacts and Influences. Essays on media power in the twentieth century*, London: Methuen.

Curran, J. and Seaton, J. (1991) *Power without Responsibility*, London: Routledge.

Edelman, M. (1966) *The Mirror – A political history*, London: Hamish Hamilton.

Eliot, T.S. (1948) *Notes towards a definition of culture*, London: Faber.

Ferguson, M., ed. (1990) *Public Communication. The new imperatives. Further directions for media research*, London: Sage.

Franklin, B. (1994) *Packaging Politics. Political Communications in Britain's Media Democracy*, London: Edward Arnold.

Frow, J. (1987) 'Accounting for tastes. Some problems with Bourdieu's Sociology of Culture', *Cultural Studies*, **1**(1), January, 59–73.

Galbraith, J.K. (1958) *The Affluent Society*, London: Penguin.

Hall, S. and Jacques, M. (1983) *The Politics of Thatcherism*, London: Lawrence and Wishardt.

Harvey, D. (1990) *The Condition of Postmodernity*, Oxford: Blackwell.

Hewison, R. (1987) *The Heritage Industry: Britain in a climate of decline*, London: Methuen.

Hill, J. (1986) *Sex, Class and Realism. British cinema 1956–1963*, London: BFI.

Hoggart, R. (1957) *The Uses of Literacy*, London: Chatto and Windus.

Howard, A. and West, R. (1965) *The Making of the Prime Minister*, London: Cape.

Kavanagh, D. (1995) *Election Campaigning The new marketing of politics*, Oxford: Blackwell.

Labour Party (1960) *Labour in the Sixties*, London: Transport House.

Labour Party (1961) *Signposts for the Sixties. A statement of Labour party home policy*, London: Transport House.

Leavis, F.R. (1930) *Mass civilisation and minority culture*, Cambridge: Minority Press.

McCallum, R.B. and Readman, A. (1947) *The British General Election of 1945*, Oxford University Press.

McQuail, D. (1992) *Media Performance. Mass communications and the public interest*, London: Sage.

Moore-Gilbert, B. and Seed, J. (1992) *Cultural Revolution? The challenge of the arts in the 1960s*, London: Routledge.

Negrine, R. (1996) *The Communication of Politics*, London: Sage.

Nicholas, H.G. (1951) *The British General Election of 1950*, London: Macmillan.

Noel, G.E. (1964) *Harold Wilson and the New Britain*, London: Victor Gollanz.

Nye, D.E. (1994) *American Technological Sublime*, M.L.T. Press.

Packard, V. (1957) *The Hidden Persuaders*, Harmondsworth: Penguin.

Packard, V. (1959) *The Status Seekers*, Harmondsworth: Penguin.

Peacock (1986) *Report of the Committee on Financing the BBC*, Cmnd 9824. HMSO.

Rose, R. (1967) *Influencing Voters. A study of campaign rationally*, London: Faber.

Royal Commission (1977) *Royal Commission on the Press*, Cmnd 6810. HMSO

Russell, J. and Gablik, S. (1969) *Pop Art Redefined*, London: Thames and Hudson.

Samuel, R. (1994) *Theatres of memory: Vol. 1 Past and present in contemporary culture*, London: Verso.

Saunders (1990) A Nation of Home Owners, London: Unwin.

Scannell, P. and Cardiff, D. (1991) *A social history of British Broadcasting Volume One 1922–1939*, Oxford: Blackwell.

Schwarz, B. (1984) 'The Language of Constitutionalism: Baldwinite Conservatism' in *Formations of Nation and People*, T. Bennett, *et al.*, eds. London: Routledge.

Seldon, A. (1997) *Major – a Political Life*, London: Weidenfeld and Nicolson.

Seymour-Ure, C. (1974) *The political impact of the mass media*, London: Constable.

Smith, C. (1998) *Creative Britain*, London: Faber.

Snow, C.P. (1959) *The Two Cultures and the Scientific Revolution*, Cambridge University Press.

Thatcher, M. (1993) *The Downing Street Years*, London: Harper Collins.

The Times (1983) *Guide to the House of Commons June 1983*, London: Times Books.

The Times (1997) *Guide to the House of Commons May 1997*, London: Times Books.

Weiner, M. (1981) *English Culture and the Decline of the Industrial Spirit, 1850–1980*, Cambridge University Press.

White, T. (1961) *The Making of the President 1960*, London: Jonathan Cape.

Williams, R. (1962, 1976) *Communications*, Harmondsworth; Penguin.

Wilson, H. (1963) '*Labour and the Scientific Revolution*', Annual Conference, Scarborough, 1 October 1962, reprinted in Noel 1964.

Wilson, H. (1964) The New Britain: Labour's Plan outlined by Harold Wilson, *Selected Speeches*, Harmondsworth: Penguin.

Wright, P. (1985) *On living in an old country: The national past in contemporary Britain*, London: Verso.

9 Parody, pastiche or purloining?

The uses and abuses of artistic imagery in media representations

Sanda Miller

Ever since Marcel Duchamp appropriated Leonardo da Vinci's famous portrait of *Mona Lisa* readapting it to his own mischievous ends, by endowing it with moustache, goattee and scabrous inscription and put it to good use as a magazine cover, art lost its hitherto unchallenged status of 'sacred cow' of all humanistic endeavours.

This essay investigates the implications, legal, ethical and otherwise of the way such 'borrowings' could be justified through a simple category shift we call 'parody', 'pastiche', 'virtual', 'hyperreality' and much more besides, but never – for the obvious reasons – purloining.

The two case-studies selected by way of examples, provide an uncomfortable testimony to the contrary; namely that in spite of the multifarious linguistic games we employ, more often than not, we are dealing with instances of plain and brazen purloining.

CASE STUDY NO. 1

Bridget Riley's seminal contribution to the 1960s artistic movement known as 'Op. (optic) Art' cannot be overemphasised; '. . . no one could deal with the international phenomenon of Op Art without giving Bridget Riley pride of place; for her immaculate, finely honed visual achievement far transcends the now nostalgic period look at most 1960s optical vibration'(Rosenblum 1987, p. 97).

'Op Art' is intrinsically linked to 'Kinetic Art' to the extent of being
used interchangeably, which explains why Riley's work has been
labelled both. Its origins can be traced back to Hungarian born Victor
Vasarely, who lived and worked in Paris and became one of the prime
movers of the seminal exhibition held in 1955 at galerie Denise René,
which included the likes of Marcel Duchamp, Alexander Calder, side
by side with Vasarely himself. The manifesto he wrote for the occasion
is curiously prophetic of one of the central tenets of Post-Modernism,
which proclaims the end of the division between 'high' and 'low' art
in favour of an all embracing production of cultural artefacts,
eliminating all categorical distinctions in the process:

*L'ensemble des activités plastiques s'inscrit donc dans une vaste
perspective en dégradé: arts decoratifs – mode-publicité et propagande
par l'image-décors des grandes manifestations de l'industrie, des Fêtes,
des Sports – décors des spectacles – usines modèles polychromes –
signalisations et urbanisme – film d'art documentaire – musée
recréateur – édition d'art – synthèse des Arts plastiques – enfin,
recherche de l'avant-garde authentique. Les traditions dégénèrent, les
formes usuelles de la peinture périssent sur des voies condannées ...
Il est douloureux, mais indispensable d'abandonner d'anciennes valeurs
pour s'aurer la possession de nouvelles* (Ceysson et al. 1986, p. 42).

Bridget Riley's status right from the beginning of her career was
unchallengeable. She was seen as:

*Probably the most brilliant of all kinetic artists who have worked in
two dimensions ... Her work is often intricately programmed: the
forms and their relationship to one another conform to
predetermined mathematical series, but the progressions are arrived
at instinctively ... Miss Riley once worked entirely in black and
white but now, having moved through a phase where muted colours
were used, she has embarked on a series of dazzlingly colourful
pictures which explore the way in which one colour can be made,
by optical means, to blend into another; or the way in which the
whole picture surface can be made to move from warm to cool
through the progression of hues. In contrast to the work of the
colour painters, the surface does not remain inert, but ripples with
musuclar energy'.* Thus wrote the distinguished English critic
Edward Lucie-Smith (1969, pp. 169–170).

Bridget Riley justified her bold experiments both with black and white and colour through an interest in contemporary optical and scientific developments:

When she began to invent pictures like Arrest IV *it was not with the intention simply of creating a physiological disturbance in the brain. She wanted the viewer to savour the perceptions which she sets in motion by the precisely formulated notations on the canvas. The term 'Op Art' was invented to describe the paintings and Riley's work stimulated an extraordinary acclaim in the 1960s. Indeed, the commercial imitations carried out on fabric flooded the clothes market for a short time. On one level this can be seen as an unusual conjunction of the tempo of art and life. On another it was the ultimate misunderstanding of her art form, which in its fullest implications is intended to be metaphysical* (Compton 1987, p. 357).

It must be obvious by now that short of falling into the trap of the 'Intentional fallacy', we are in no position to solve the dilemma over and above the realm of speculation. Abstract art is of necessity self-referential, however heavily backed by theory, and for that reason our putative 'ordinary man in the street' is entitled to wonder, puzzle or even be angered by seemingly meaningless patterns and colours purporting to be 'art' instead of decorative wall-paper or lamp-shades or patterns for frocks. Why not use them interchangeably – one may be as 'pretty' or 'ugly' as the other. This is crudely put, the case for the defence, against the apologia for abstract art famously inaugurated by Wassily Kandinsky's little book *Concerning the Spiritual in Art* published in 1912 in which he warns against the artist who:

Seeks material rewards for his facility, inventiveness and sensitivity. His purpose becomes the satisfaction of ambition and greediness. In place of an intensive cooperation among artists, there is a battle for goods. There is excessive competition, over-production. Hatred, partisanship, cliques, jealousy, intrigues are the natural consequences of an aimless, materialist art ... The spiritual life to which art belongs, and of which it is one of the mightiest agents, is a complex but definite movement above and beyond, which can be translated into simplicity. This movement is that of cognition (1992).

That Bridget Riley is a serious and committed artist is beyond dispute; unfortunately, however metaphysical in content, the visual seductiveness of her work has backfired to the extent that in 1965 when she exhibited her black and white paintings at the MOMA in New York in the show entitled *The Responsive Eye*, fame came tinged with a degree of thoroughly unwanted popularity evident in the frocks the visitors to the exhibition were – no doubt proudly – sporting. Later in 1989, Lawrence Marks was commenting on the event in an article in *The Observer*:[1]

In 1965, her (Bridget Riley's) black and white paintings were the focus of the MOMA's exhibition The Responsive Eye, *which toured America. She got stuck with the label 'Op Art' coined by John Borgzinner of* Time *which seemed to her to debase her experiments with paintings on the effects of light to the level of optical trick and she had to threaten legal action to deter the first of a succession of business men who hijacked her designs for fabrics, advertisements and window displays, crassly treating her as a commercial trend-setter.*

It marked also the beginning of a succession of conflicts between the artist and the commercial world which did not go unnoticed and in 1989, *Evening Standard's*[2] Brian Sewell had this to say:

Bridget Riley is an abstract painter of hard-edged bands of colour that, though they verge on optical confusion and induce migraines would as fabrics make charming cotton frocks and pretty deck chairs. She is a painter of whose work such things as '. . . In the very act of questioning, the process of interrogation is conducted with such authority that it provides its own answer' are written, when the question and answer are a stripe of ice cream pink.

The first serious confrontation between the artist and the world of commerce happened during that very year, 1989: an advertisement produced by Young and Rubicam for Yorkshire Television used dazzling patterns similar to Bridget Riley's, with the caption: 'some people will have a fit when they see this'. The advertisement was designed to address people with problems and by implication present to the world the 'caring' face of Yorkshire Television. What is astonishing, certainly with hindsight, is the seeming lack of awareness of the real implications with regard to Bridget Riley's work. Not surprisingly, they caused the artist a great deal of upset and she decided to sue, unless both the television company and advertising agency publicly apologised to her both for appropriating her work as well as insinuating the disagreeable side-effects it purported to have on the viewers. The media were quick to capitalise on the situation and we find *The Sunday Times'* media correspondent writing:[3]

Bridget Riley, one of Britain's leading artists, is threatening to sue an advertising agency which used wavy lines similar to those in her famous 'op art' paintings. The advertisement produced by Young and Rubicam from Yorkshire T.V. has been banned after complaints to the Advertising Standards Authority that it caused people to pass out . . . but Riley who has several of her works hanging in the Tate Gallery is claiming the advertisement has breached her copyright. She is threatening to sue for libel and damage to her 'moral standing' . . . She maintains the Yorkshire TV advertisement is a rearrangement of part of a painting called Crest *which she did in 1964. She says it could lead people to believe that her paintings can provoke epileptic fits.*

The brief of the advertising agency Young and Rubicam who received £3 million from Yorkshire Television was to improve their allegedly stale image. Their creative director was quoted by the *Sunday Times* as saying:

We haven't just picked up one of her paintings and bunged it on paper. We created our own wavy lines. I can't see what the problem is unless you can get copyright on wavy lines.

Nor was this the last of Bridget Riley's confrontations with the world of commerce. In 1994, another 'borrowing' occurred when 'Sun Pat Stripey Peanut Butter', took their 'inspiration' from her painting entitled *Fall* in the collection of the Tate Gallery for one of their advertisements for the product. As a consequence, the advertising agency responsible for the offensive advertisement, Ogilvy and Mather publicly apologized – or rather were coerced to – after having lost in a lawsuit brought against them – in the *Evening Standard*[4] to Bridget Riley:

The artist (and those who know and respect her work) and who might have suffered distress and concern by any impression created that we based our recent advertisement for 'Sun Pat Stripey Peanut Butter' on Bridget Riley's painting Fall.

As an act of good faith, Ogilvy and Mather had made a generous donation in support of the fine arts to the 'Elephant Trust' at the request of Miss Riley. The whole story was detailed by Susannah Herbert in the *Daily Telegraph*:[5]

Bridget Riley, the abstract painter whose passion for bold stripes has spawned innumerable imitations, yesterday won a year-long legal battle over an advertisement for Peanut Butter. Miss Riley won redress from the food giant Nestlé and the advertising agency Ogilvy and Mather after complaining about an advertisement showing a jar of Sun Pat Stripey Peanut Butter against a black-and-white stripey background which reminded her of one of her more celebrated paintings Fall, *a 1963 work currently owned by the Tate Gallery. Although Ogilvy and Mather and Nestlé – which owns the Sun Pat Brand – have denied all charges of passing off or of copyright infringement, they agreed yesterday to publish a fulsome apology in an advertisement in the* Evening Standard.

The reason for the artist's objection given was that:

She was distressed because she has never allowed her paintings to be exploited in any commercial way and she was upset that people thought she'd made an exception for Sun Pat'. She hadn't and for that reason the courts decided that she ought to receive compensation by way of a public apology and monies, which she generously donated to a charity, well known for its support of art and artists.

CASE STUDY NO. 2

My second, very recent case study concerns the now famous artist Gillian Wearing, recipient of the 1998 prestigious Turner Prize, who collided nastily with Volkswagen as she herself stated in no uncertain terms: '... VW advertisement firm stole my ideas claims artist', ran the headline of an article written by Paul McCann, media editor of *The Independent*, in June of 1998. Gillian Wearing was planning legal action against Volkswagen's advertising agency, who plagiarised her work entitled: *Signs that say what you want them to say* in an advertisement for VW Golf made by advertising agency BMP DDB. The reason?

Both feature people holding paper signs that express how they really feel in contrast to their appearance. Ms Wearing is particularly unhappy about the adverts which include a night club bouncer holding a sign that says 'Sensitive' and its similarity to an image in her work of a policeman holding a sign saying 'Help'. Her work also includes someone saying, 'I'd rather be in the countryside' and the advert has a man on a mountain who'd rather be in the city. Both also feature a surprising business man. VW's businessman's sign says: 'At weekends my name is Mandy'. Wearing's work pictures a businessman holding a sign saying 'Desperate'.[6]

Unlike Ogilvy and Mather however, BMP DDB were unrepentant, by claiming that their 'inspiration' did not even come from Wearing but from altogether different sources, they were quite happy to reveal. One was a campaign for Levi's for its Dockers brand and the other from Bob Dylan's video 'Subterranean Home Sick Blues' where the singer holds up cards as he sings.

Gillian Wearing resented the implication that she was working for an advertising agency: '. . . After the Levi's adverts I went out on the streets again and people knew what to expect. If I describe my work to someone they say "oh, like the advert"'. Her main objection was not so much against the notion that she might have offered her services to the commercial world but the consequences of this unauthorised use of her ideas which stripped her at the same time of the right to decide which product she might decide to endorse by allowing her work to be put to good use has been taken away from her:

Everybody, or at least lots of people know the Dylan video. A parody of that would be more in the order of homage. But if you are relatively unknown like me it feels more like being exploited behind your back.

The 'work' entitled *Signs* was the result of photographing several hundreds of randomly chosen people in the street who she approached and invited to write whatever they chose on a blank piece of cardboard she provided. *The Times*[7] media correspondent, Carol Midgley reported the event using stronger language, 'VW ad rips off my work, says Turner Winner', runs the bold title:

The winner of this year's Turner Prize is taking legal action over a new Volkswagen Golf commercial which, she says, plagiarizes her art. Gillian Wearing claims that the television advertisement, which shows characters holding up cards bearing descriptions that contrast with their actual appearance, is a copy of her own award-winning series Signs. *For her collection, Wearing invited people in the street to write down what they were really thinking. The result was a set of acclaimed pictures which included a policeman holding up a card saying 'Help'. A slick businessman standing behind a card saying 'I'm desperate'.*

Another ordinary looking person's board reads, 'I have been certified as mildly insane.' In the £8 million VW Golf Campaign similar images are used. A macho-looking bouncer holds up a card saying 'Sensitive' while a conventional suburban male commuter's sign says, 'At weekends my name is Mandy'.

The slogan at the end of the commercial reads, 'Sometimes what you see isn't what you get' ... Yesterday Wearing, 34, who won the £20,000 Turner Prize for her video *Sixty Minutes' Silence* showing 26 police officers struggling to stay silent and still for an hour, said that the similarities between the commercial and her series were obvious.

Naturally, the artist was not pleased, especially since a lot of people believed that she actually devised the Golf advert. Unlike the case of Bridget Riley, however, the advertising agency BMP DDB remained unrepentant; moreover – unlike Bridget Riley who, in spite of how she chooses to apply her paint on canvas, remains a traditional painter – Gillian Wearing's work is anything but, to the extent that what she produces is difficult to classify for lack of accommodating artistic categories. Thus, in one instance she is described as a 'documentarist artist',[8] working with videos and photographs: 'The art of making a £10,000 video', runs the title of an article by Roz Laws written for Birmingham's *Sunday Mercury*. 'The "failure" from Birmingham who made it to the top'. Patriotically, Laws goes on to comment that Wearing is:

Considered to be one of the most gifted artists of her generation. The Brummie who left school with no qualifications and was sacked by McDonalds for being inept has been short-listed for the prestigious Turner Prize which could bring her £20,000.

In fact it was the work entitled *Signs* which brought her first sale when an American paid £200 for the photo of the 'desperate' businessman. Currently her photographs sell for up to £10,000 apiece. Wearing did however go on to train, first on a B.Tech course and then on to Goldsmith College.

Even more than Bridget Riley, Wearing attracted the wrath of some critics, notably the *Evening Standard's* Brian Sewell[9] who referred to one of her videos entitled *Sacha and Mum*, shown at the Tate and introduced as showing the 'intimacies' between a mother and a daughter at home whereas what we get is more like a fight. Sewell does not mince his words in describing the video as a: '. . . thoroughly nasty evidence of two real people in a tussle that has the ring of truth about it, vicious, spiteful and self-justifying'. The article ends by categorizing the piece as a:

. . . squalid domestic episode technically inept, intellectually pretentious, supported by the extravagant machinery of state and praised as art – that's the real obscenity, that's the one to ban.

In contrast *The Times* critic, Richard Cork presents us with a complimentary piece plus allegedly witty pun by way of title: 'Wearing her art on her sleeve',[10] whereby we are told that the artist, '. . . has explored other people's experiences with compassion, humour, patience, courage and irony.' The subsequently notorious *Signs* is here explained in the following terms:

Collaboration is her aim, and in an extended early project called Signs *she invited people in the street to write down their thoughts on paper. The directness of the resulting photographs where each individual holds up the written message, is remarkable.*

Meanwhile *Sacha and Mum* acquires a Brechtian dimension:

Marked by a Brechtian willingness to emphasize artifice at every turn. Sacha and Mum *is a harrowing dramatisation of an ambivalent yet destructive relationship clearly performed by actors. And Wearing removes them even further from cine-verité by running the video backwards, heightening the disastrous choreography of alternating affection and violence.*

The conclusion in both these instances is straightforward enough: we witness an unfriendly conflict between two reputable artists and the world of commerce which led to litigation. Why? The accusing fingers of both Bridget Riley and Gillian Wearing were clearly pointing to the world of commerce perceived as appropriating, stealing, purloining, ripping off their work for commercial gain. Whether in the case of the former we deal with wavy lines or a less clearly definable 'conceit', in the latter case, is perhaps less important than what is here described as 'factual' evidence. Whilst 'purloining' is both illegal as well as ethically wrong, 'pastiching' is considered elegantly post-modernism; 'borrowing' acceptable and 'being inspired' a flattering homage.

What we are really faced with is a number of concepts which function by degree, from a mere hint of 'inspiration' to blatant lifting. In literature we have a legal term, 'plagiarizing,' but in the visual arts, we don't have a term of equal authority. Artists have always been inspired by their predecessors and peers and it is also in many ways an indirect homage to greatness. But how do you establish precise criteria in order to draw the line between inspiration from one artistic source to another which is acceptable, desirable even, and at what point does that 'inspiration' begin to metamorphosise into something which warrants another word, such as 'borrowing' then on to 'pastiching' and finally to 'purloining' is difficult to gauge.

Dictionary definitions are always helpful as a starting point in any debate; thus 'inspiration' is 'breathing in,' or a 'stimulation by a divinity, a genius, an idea or a passion'. Wonderful. 'Borrowing' is 'adopting from a foreign source'. Acceptable but with caution. 'Pastiche' is defined as 'a jumble; a pot-pourri a composition (in literature, music or painting) made up of bits of other works or imitations of another's style'. Etymologically this curious word is derived from the Italian 'pasticcio' (pasta) figuratively used to mean: mess, muddle, humbug, botch. Quite.

The word has been rendered fashionable by Fredric Jameson in his seminal essay: *Postmodernism and consumer society* (1988, pp. 194–195). 'Pastiche,' here carefully distinguished from 'parody' with which people tend to: '. . . confuse with or assimilate to'. Both 'parody' and 'pastiche', Jameson argues: '. . . involve the imitation or, better still, the mimicry of other styles and particularly of the mannerisms and stylistic twitches of other styles'. There are also differences, as outlined in his much quoted definition of 'pastiche' defined as:

The imitation of a peculiar or unique style, the wearing of a stylistic mask, speech in a dead language: but it is a neutral practice of such mimicry, without parody's ulterior motive, without the satirical impulse, without laughter, without that still latent feeling that there exists something normal *compared to which what is being imitated is rather comic. Pastiche is blank parody, parody that has lost its sense of humour; pastiche is to parody what that curious thing, the modern practice of a kind of blank irony, is to what Wayne Booth calls the stable and comic ironies of, say, the eighteenth century'* (ibid.).

The definition of 'purloining' is plain filching, stealing, practising theft. No appeal here.

What conclusion can we draw from the two case studies presented here? It must be by now obvious that what we are dealing with is a more complicated process which could not – in my opinion – be justified even via post-modernist discourses, such as the often reiterated breakdown of all hitherto established barriers not only between 'high' and 'low' art, between economic, political and cultural manifestations, etc . . . allegedly caused by the shift from a society based on production to one based on consumption whereby the art object is replaced by some other values, residing in process, fragmentation and/or spatio-temporal manifestations replace the physical object as pointed out by Fredrick Jameson:

For one thing commodity production and in particular our clothing, furniture, buildings and other artifacts are now intimately tied in with styling changes which derive from artistic experimentation; our advertising for example, is fed by postmodernism in all the arts and inconceivable without it. For another, the classics of high modernism are now part of the so-called canon and are taught in schools and universities, which at once empties them of any of their older subversive power (ibid., p. 205).

There is little doubt that if modernism is defined in terms of avant-guardism and avant-guardism has lost its power as already argued in the 1960s by the likes of Clement Greenberg and Hilton Kramer, then we have been witnessing its demise and subsequent replacement by post-modernism. More problematic remains the issue of commodity production and its 'intimate ties' with artistic experimentation, as Jameson so elegantly put it. Are the two case studies under discussion the exception to an already existing happy collaboration? Difficult to assess but one thing remains certain: neither Bridget Riley nor Gillian Wearing were pleased with the process of 'friendly' osmosis between their work and that of the advertisers; in fact the opposite is the case.

We could perhaps conclude with the most celebrated and undoubtedly misunderstood quote of all times, from Niccolo Machiavelli's masterpiece *The Prince*, written in 1513: '. . . where there is no impartial arbiter, one must consider the final result' 1979, p. 135).

ENDNOTES

1. See Laurence Marks in *The Observer*, 2 July 1989.
2. See Brian Sewell in *The Evening Standard*, 20 July 1989.
3. See Geordie Greig and Rufus Olins, *The Sunday Times*, November 1989.
4. *The Evening Standard*, 4 April 1994.
5. See Susannah Herbert in *The Daily Telegraph*, 8 April 1994.
6. See Paul McCann in *The Independent*, 12 June 1998.
7. See Carol Midgley in *The Times*, 12 June 1998.
8. See Roz Laws in *The Sunday Mercury*, Birmingham, 13 July 1997.
9. See Brian Sewell in *The Evening Standard*, 18 December 1997.
10. See Richard Cork in *The Times*, 13 January 1998.

REFERENCES

Ceysson, B. *et al.*, cds (1986) 'Manifeste jaune', published on occasion of the exhibition entitled, 'Le Mouvement' at galerie Denise Rene, Paris: 6–30 April, 1955 in *Vingt-cinq ans d'art en France 1960–85*, Paris: Larousse.

Compton, S. (1987) *British Art in the Twentieth Century* (the Modern Movement). Exhibition catalogue of the show held at the Royal Academy, London: June 15–April 5, 1987.

Jameson, F. (1988) 'Postmodernism and Consumer Society', in Kaplan, E.A., ed., *Postmodernism and Its Discontents*, London: Verso.

Kandinsky, W. (1992) 'Concerning the Spiritual in Art', in Alperson, P., ed., *The Philosophy of Visual Arts*, Oxford University Press.

Machiavelli, N. (1979) 'The Prince' in Bondanella, P. and Musa, M., eds, *The Portable Machiavelli*, Harmondsworth: Penguin Books.

Rosenblum, R. (1987) 'British Twentieth-Century Art: Transatlantic View,' in Compton, S., ed., *British Art in the Twentieth Century.*

Lucie-Smith, E. (1969) *Movements in Art Since 1945*, London: Thames and Hudson.

10 'Shock': the value of emotion

Jason Barker

Figure 10.1 'The real face of war'

INTRODUCTION

The aura of the photographic image is a complex one which also encompasses numerous ethical and moral questions. The modern invention of photography in the 19th century signifies a revolution in the arts comparable to the discovery of perspective in the Renaissance. Yet what accompanies that artistic revolution and has threatened to efface its aura ever since is, as Walter Benjamin recognises, the mechanism of reproduction. Something happens to the image alongside photography's subsumption by the mass media. A change occurs between portraiture and the altogether different agenda of the news event.

In an age in which media images can be relayed around the globe in less time than it takes an eye witness to respond to the event itself, it seems pointless to still adhere to ideas that the media has an 'ideological effect' on reality, or else offers us some sort of emotional release from everyday life. If the media does have an effect then allow me to suggest that it is more akin to a 'black hole effect' than an ideological effect, whereby our emotional responses cannot emerge beyond this universal machine. In this chapter I will be exploring the presumed relationship between the viewer and the media image (a relationship which, at the risk of invalidation, I have occasionally been obliged to use different terms to define).[1] Working from the basic premise that the media no longer simply represents or mediates viewers' interests, but instead has become synonymous with the very concept of public opinion, I will be arguing that one cannot so easily distinguish between 'viewers' rights' on the one hand, and 'media responsibilities' on the other.

In its analysis of media output, media effects research has been predicated on the idea that the media image affects the audience in ways which can be measured in positive or negative terms.[2] According to such theories the image enacts a *transfer* of information. Typically, this process may be understood in one of two ways: *Either* the image stimulates – or 'shocks' – the viewer's emotional sensibilities (or informs a body of opinion); *or* it exploits them. In this sense one might say that the image has 'value' in its ability to induce a certain type of attitude in the viewer, thereby alerting him (her) to life's circumstances. However, it will be my ultimate aim to dismiss such common sense notions. Undoubtedly the image possesses value, just as the media produces effects. But if the media no longer governs the perceptions of its audience, then its values and effects cannot so easily be ascribed to the specialist interests of 'media actors' (media practitioners versus viewers). Finally, with the latter in mind, I will conclude my study by considering the concept of media ethics, arguing that any ethical framework is inseparable from the media's overall power in society.

'RESPONDING' TO SHOCK

In examining this hypothesis I want to present, first of all, the following case study which relates to *The Observer*'s publication of the photograph of a dead Iraqi soldier in the aftermath of the Gulf War. The whole nature of the encounter between moral objectors and moral champions of the paper's decision to publish appeared to be emblematic of the ethical decisions facing newspaper editors on a daily basis: the responsibility to inform, balanced against the duty to respect the wider values of their audience. The image – which depicted the soldier's charred remains clutching the windscreen of his lorry on the road to Basra, and appeared under the headline 'The real face of war' – was undoubtedly provocative despite being situated mid-section (*The Observer*, 3 March 1991 – Fig. 1). The following week's letters to the paper confirmed its profound effect in impassioned terms. The resulting opinions, presented as objective testimony and carefully drawn from either side of the political spectrum, fell discretely into two categories. Yet it was also apparent that what emerged with the publication of that image was no less than the makings of a discourse on the ethics of journalism – not to mention the paper's own interpretation of how such a discourse should be read.

The first strand of opinion – which represented *The Observer's* own editorial line – I will call the 'liberal-humanist response', which is often encountered in ethical defences of press freedoms. Whilst sensitive to issues of invasion of privacy and the inevitable personal tragedy involved, liberal-humanist reactions saw the image's significance as more symbolic than referential. In these accounts the tragedy stands as no less than a *document* of the '100,000 Iraqi soldiers . . . killed or maimed' in the war. As 'horrific' as such images are in themselves, their horror is nevertheless more instrumental in 'stripp[ing] away the glamour found in comics and films.' According to such negative reasoning it is almost as if, by being confronted by what we don't really want to see, the truth is brought ever more starkly into focus. In this sense the image is not so much reflexive of a real life event as it is symbolic of the bigger picture, that with every bomb that was fired, not just one man died, but had family, a mother, father, brother and sister . . . (*The Observer*, 10 March 1991).

In a manner of speaking one might say that the power of this image is its effect of shocking us out of our emotional complacency, thereby forcing us to see what might otherwise remain hidden behind the photograph.

As Benjamin recognises in his famous study, 'The Work of Art in the Age of Mechanical Reproduction', photography is fundamentally altered from the moment it ceases to capture the unique – that moment of 'fleeting expression' – and becomes 'standard evidence for historical occurrences' (Benjamin 1968, pp. 219–20). Today there is a very real sense in which our relationship with photography represents an important social discipline. It's not as if 'free-floating contemplation' is now impossible, just somehow irrelevant to our modern ways of thinking about, viewing and practising photography. Today, photography – both in its private and public realms – functions as documentary, its main purpose being to prove that we were there, or at least that something really happened. The photograph has become that indispensable record of events, a kind of badge of existence: the proof that life exists.

The situation is somewhat ironic however. For as Benjamin insists, the invention of the reproduction techniques of photography and film *transforms* our sense perceptions in new ways. With photography the moment of existence – the image's presence in time and space – is alluded to, but never emerges as such (ibid., pp. 216–7). Photographic images differ from those seen by the naked eye in that the former capture nothing of the *real* social circumstances of the image's existence, nothing of its specific historical or emotional context. The structures of news production certainly don't allow such revelations, lest we should become alerted to some unsavoury social contradiction (war, poverty, social inequality). The media's ability to frame its subject, to not so much deceive as to reorientate the viewer's perceptions in the preferred way, is often considered by liberal opinion as a common sense, unwritten rule of editorial practice. Despite the fact that the camera never lies, most of us would accept that photography is far more revealing when employed as an *anti*-rhetorical device. This is especially important in moments of social crisis, when official rhetoric like 'collateral damage' replaces 'civilian casualties', or 'friendly fire' becomes inoffensive shorthand for 'wrongly killed by US missiles'. For the liberal-humanist, it seems, the value of this image is that it manages to deglamorize (i.e. to strip away the facade of) media-reality. In its unique shockingness the image restores a sense of authenticity, and puts us back in touch – however fleetingly – with real events.

The opposite strand of opinion, which I shall refer to as 'neo-conservative', was not so liberated. Here the emotional impact of the image was outweighed by its moral effects. Inevitably this articulated itself as a defence of family values. As one indignant reader put it,

In thousands of homes on Sunday morning the first ones to look at the paper are children – and consider that some of them might just have learnt that their father or brother was killed in action and might look just the same (The Observer, 10 March 1991).

Another reader similarly regarded the publication of the image as a purely moral rather than a practico-ethical question, inviting the paper's editorial staff to imagine how *they* would feel if the soldier was their son, 'displayed for all and sundry to gawp at'. For the neo-conservative the sense of fascination which accompanies the shocking can serve no emotional – let alone political – imperative, but merely alerts sensible opinion to a moral transgression. Whereas liberal-humanist opinion can conceive of circumstances in which public interest in the image takes precedence over the subject's right to privacy and, furthermore, to what end such a responsibility must be directed (the upholding of liberal democratic principles), the neo-conservative would prefer to ban such intrusions outright.

Despite being virtually impossible to maintain in journalistic practice, the idea of there being exclusive realms of public and private interest cannot be underestimated in ideological terms. The neo-conservative position is in some ways reminiscent of Habermas's depiction of a feudal society in which public spectacle or 'publicity' was reserved for exalted status. Representation was not, as we consider it in its contemporary, liberal sense, that:

In which the members of a national assembly represent a nation or a lawyer represents his clients [one might add, 'or a photo-journalist represents his subject'] (Habermas 1989, p. 7).

Feudal representation did not uncover what might be hidden from view, instead it 'pretended to make something invisible visible . . .'. Furthermore in this context:

Something that has no life, that is inferior, worthless, or mean, is not representable. It lacks the exalted sort of being suitable to be elevated into public status, that is, into existence (ibid.).

For the neo-conservative this 'inferior' image represents nothing real in respect of its referent since its referent is non-representable. After all, how can an image which is too shocking for the children on a Sunday morning convey anything except the unmentionable? The neo-conservative position therefore defers judgement away from the image itself. Whereas the liberal-humanist views the image as the sign and opportunity for understanding a unique social contradiction, the neo-conservative instead sees it as a *symptom* of a more general moral malaise of which the media is the prime embodiment.

The idea that the media is the natural sign of the moral decline of Western civilization can be traced back to the rise of the mass circulation press, particularly of the mid-19th century, when critics such as Matthew Arnold would regularly lament the effect it was having on literary culture. In an age of sprawling industrialism, the newspaper was simply one further example – if one were needed – of the levelling of civilization and the ennoblement of 'the best which has been thought and said in the world', by the anarchy of mass opinion (Arnold 1971). According to Arnold's interpretation there could be no sense in which emotion, or general intelligence, could possibly emerge from the newspapers – or, indeed, from the mouths of politicians! which he decried in the same breath. For Arnold, both were intemperate. Throughout the intervening period of modernity the press in particular has retained a powerful and inherent association with 'shock' and 'sensationalism': what amount to the gratuitous exploitation of cultural values, purely for the sake of boosting circulation.

To recap, we have identified two types of values as characterised by two opposing strands of opinion. On the one hand, the liberal-humanist side, the image is of *instrumental significance* in restoring the viewer's sense of social awareness through its sheer emotional power. In this case the image possesses a truth value which emerges via an anti-rhetorical operation of 'deglamorization', i.e. opposing the routine image (what we've come to expect) with the unique (what we don't). On the other hand, the neo-conservative side, the image is *a-signifying* in alienating the viewer's moral status, or his own understanding of his place in the natural order. In this case the image can be regarded as exploitative, its value measurable as a pure commodity.

And yet, despite their respective differences what underlies these moral positions is fundamental common ground. For whether or not one chooses to accept the legitimacy of this image what remains irrespectively taken for granted is (1) its emotiveness, and/or (2) what sometimes – though not always – amounts to the same thing, its significance. We can object on the grounds that the image is *too* emotive, or we can dispute its significance – we can even question the validity of photographic evidence as sometimes happens with tabloid journalism. But what we cannot deny is the image's ability to *confront us* with a snapshot of social reality. The structure of the image media and its relationship to 'us', the audience, is not only immanent to any ethical consideration of the media's effects, it is also and increasingly a concept of human cognition. Sit a child in front of a television screen for long enough and its consciousness of itself and the world around it will gradually become articulated on the media's terms (the objective 'I' of news, the subjective 'me' of drama . . .).[3] Indeed, the fact that the structure of the media today provides the foundation for civil society and not the reverse inevitably challenges the presumed relationship of image to viewer, and puts into question the idea that the image can convey a meaningful 'picture' of our social environment. The degree of intervention of media structures and processes in our daily lives therefore raises the question of the extent and conditions under which such images can effectively stimulate public sentiment at all, especially in ways which do not simply reproduce and assimilate the diverse expressions of individual viewers to the media's universal logic of production.

THE REALM OF EMOTION

The status of photography as an expressive art form capable of uncovering profound emotional truths has an established heritage which originates alongside the birth of the medium. The reason for the aestheticisation of such an overtly mechanical technique in representation can be attributed to the great many painters who, sensing the revolutionary consequences of paper-print photography for their profession in the 1850s, sought to reinfuse their artistic production with a degree of autonomy by appropriating the new medium on their own terms. That the new technology required no specialist training or creative insight to operate posed early photographic artists such as Henry Peach Robinson immense challenges, which the latter took up in typically defiant defences of the new artistic craft. The following extract sums up rather neatly the romantic designs Robinson and his contemporaries held for photography.

It is only the unthinking who will accuse impressionism, thus understood, of being an easy slap-dash kind of painting. To appreciate the exactly right force of definition for the parts in relation to the whole is a task that employs the rarest faculties of vision, since to a sensitive eye a single false accent will destroy a whole picture. If it be argued that all this is a matter of mechanical and realistic rendering of facts, the assertion is manifestly untrue. Attention is governed by feeling, every change in the definition of an object means a change in our emotion about it . . . (Robinson 1980, p. 95).

In this highly nostalgic account no attempt is made to recognise the mechanical or technical demands of the new medium on the artist's work. The fact that impressionist painting is used as a template and standard for photographic practice can be read as a deliberate act of exclusion on the part of the academy (Robinson was elected as vice-president of the Royal Photographic Society in 1888). The photographer-as-artist is endowed with that rare faculty of vision which he employs in *harnessing* the image. It is nothing so incidental as the technical restrictions of his craft, less the subject before the camera, than it is the *impression of feeling* which governs the 'new' artistic vision, and which it is the photographer's moral duty rather than social responsibility to communicate. Needless to say it is even less the photographer's position in the production process which determined the value of his work, for the photographer-artist does not deal in products, but emotions (which transcend all social circumstances).

Writing on the same subject, Victor Burgin argues that the romanticist sensibility is linked to photography in a further sense, for it is with romanticism that the image becomes a 'relay', a means of projecting living presence 'either between one human subject and another, or between a human subject and reality' (Burgin 1982, p. 10). Within the structure of this relationship the empathy of the image affords the viewer the privilege of an *encounter*. Few could deny the expressive power of actually experiencing the reality of war for oneself. In its allusion to the terms of such an encounter the photographic medium channels the viewer's diffuse, everyday experience into direct correspondence with the outside world. Moments such as these, it seems, offer the viewer a way out of the routine flow of media(ted) events, even if such exits are invariably blocked by processes beyond the viewer's control.

Of course, to suggest that emotion can function within the realm of the viewer's experience is to underestimate the extent to which 'emotion' has itself become part of the routine of journalistic practice. Nowadays the primacy of the image's 'emotional content' is a practical consideration, both in the production and editorial selection of news photographs. The viewer's emotional investment, or 'valorization interest' as Negt and Kluge refer to it in their study of the mass media, is closely regulated by short- and long-term capital interests, interests which are normally far removed from the viewer's own. On the one hand Negt and Kluge describe short-term capital interest as a 'valorization [of] use-values that can also have long-term significance (for instance, experiential content, the crystallisation and expression of resistance, as in the protest song movement).'

On the other hand:

Similarly, long-term capital interest, which expresses itself in varying degrees through notions such as the 'common good' and the 'public interest', has immediate, short-term, restrictive consequences, such as programming guidelines or censorship (Negt and Kluge 1993, p. 104).

In Negt and Kluge's scheme of things 'shock' and 'violent contrasts' are classified as short-term interests, along with 'the ability to generate high audience ratings'. Such interests are much more likely to lead the viewer *into* the general circuit of exchange-value (which governs the selection of media images), than offer him or her an effective way out of the routine encounter. The commodification of the viewing experience does not make it illusory or ineffective for the viewer, simply incredibly difficult to engage with, in any radically alternative way, at the level of consumption. Despite their 'oppositional value', shocking images can always find a receptive market. After all, is it not the universal function of capital to covert not just human misery but also *the struggle against it* into an object of consumption? (cf. Benjamin 1982, p. 25ff.).[4]

Walter Benjamin was among the first to recognise how the mass media irrevocably alters the nature of spectatorship in modern society. Such alteration was not to the detriment of any presumed correspondence of the image to truth or the 'real world'. The image, whether manifest in the depiction of the religious icon, or in the form of photography or moving pictures, is nevertheless always a product of the prevailing social and economic relations of production – and reproduction – of a particular society. The aura of the work of art is attributable to its exhibition potential, which is in turn a question of social *praxis*. Likewise film is shocking, Benjamin informs us, not due to some ethereal quality that The Image has on the screen, but because the cinematic techniques of film production make mere contemplation redundant, if not physically impossible, for a viewing audience unaccustomed to such revolutionary techniques (Benjamin 1968, pp. 230–2).[5]

For Benjamin the media's alienation of the masses was a materialist question, rather than a cause for moral indignation, which harboured democratic potential. The answer lay partly in the refinement of techniques in film and photography which could then more effectively challenge prevailing moral expectations. However, such refinements could not bring about the desired effect without an accompanying reorganisation of the audience's relationship to the means of production itself. 'Shock', although emotionally stimulating, is only truly 'shocking' if there exist the material conditions – i.e. accessible production and distribution networks – which allow the consumer of images to upset the normal rules of identity in becoming their producer. Moral reflection on images is all well and good, but ultimately impotent, if the social conditions of their production are not practically criticised with a view to being altered (Benjamin 1982).

One might observe at this point, perhaps with good reason, that our conception of the viewing experience thus far presumes a definition and degree of activity on behalf of viewers who overwhelmingly do not understand, let alone subscribe to, such definitions of 'democratic' participation. Far more significantly, it also overlooks the fact that neither examples of nor discourses on media ethics are transcendental, but are *themselves* products of any prevailing set of social and economic forces. The market *is* the universal mode of expression. And as Marx understood all too well the difficulty in expressing one's resistance to capitalism's excesses is precisely the same difficulty by degrees of offering any alternative ethical framework, especially if such frameworks are based on an idea of man's basic emotional needs and moral duties.

There is no easy way out of such metaphysical dilemmas. As Louis Althusser informs us in his famous essay on state apparatuses and elsewhere, the communications media, as an ideological apparatus, functions in accordance with an 'ideology *in general*' which presents the very structure of representation. Furthermore, communications media, as specific ideological apparatuses amongst a set of 'overdetermined' social practices, present us with no particularly privileged sites for gauging the significance of the viewer's experience, at least no more so than other analogous structures in the social formation (e.g. 'family' or 'legal ISAs' etc.) (Althusser 1969, 1971). Without wanting to revisit the full implications of Althusser's essays *in toto*, suffice to say that we can no more practically divorce the expressions or interests of viewers from the images, structures and processes which give vent to them than we could imagine a world in which the media did not exist.

SUMMARY

We began by examining two types of opinion which emerged from *Observer* readers' responses to the publication of the photograph of a dead Iraqi soldier. We then moved on to examine whether the viewer's emotional investment in the photographic image can oppose the media's mechanism of reproduction. We have discovered that, despite liberal-humanist and neo-conservative opinions to the contrary, the image cannot simply be used either to expose, or to exploit, any prevailing moral agenda presided over by the media at large. In this regard the idea that the image can, under certain conditions and at certain moments ('shock'), penetrate the facade of journalistic routine can be largely attributed to a romanticist legacy which sees reality behind appearances. This might lead some to conclude, somewhat hastily, that the reification of the viewing experience requires a reorganisation of existing media structures in ways which better facilitate the viewer's direct involvement in the production process along 'democratic' lines. However, it is arguable that any such reorganisation is both subject to constraints (e.g. widespread public access to technology; capital reproduction) and nevertheless presumes a degree of human behaviour and emotional needs on the part of the viewer which are 'not sensually demonstrable'.

I want to suggest that the idea of a media ethics as a framework against which photographic images can be judged is based on the structure of a relationship between viewer on the one hand, and image on the other which is difficult to maintain given the power of the media in contemporary society. In its publication of the image the newspaper doesn't challenge a set of moral expectations held by the viewer – it doesn't confront us with life's circumstances – *it subsumes us in them*. The viewer does not stand in *contradiction* to the media – rather he or she is one among its many modes of existence.

All this is not, however, to preside over any lapse into moral relativism. I am not suggesting in light of the above that all value judgements on photographic images and their publication are epistemologically flawed. As Christians *et al.* rightly point out in the introduction to their own book on media ethics, the 'rough and tumble of social realities' 'does not permit the luxury of merely playing mental games' with ethical principles (Christians *et al.*, 1998, p. 5). Having said that it does seem fair to point out that in order to arrive at *any* valid framework of media ethics we must be clear about the nature of the 'social realities' in which 'the media' is not only presently situated, but also is being constantly reproduced. Such considerations, it seems fair to say, have not played a huge role in discourses on media ethics thus far, although it is toward such considerations that I now want to turn, albeit briefly, in conclusion.

CONCLUSION: TOWARDS A MEDIA ETHICS

To accuse the media of 'shock tactics' is arguably to risk underestimating the extent to which such practices in fact comprise the media's essence. As was noted earlier, the idea of sensationalism and the 'shocking' subject matter which arouses intense emotional responses is one which characterises the historical emergence of the mass circulation press. Furthermore 'mass opinion', as opposed to 'informed opinion', still retains traces of the sort of philistinism that thrives on such public spectacle. Today, therefore, to accuse the media of excess, of breaching the bounds of 'sensible opinion' for gratuitous ends is simply to express one's ignorance of the media's history, its power, and the scope of its potential influence over society. At the risk of simplifying a complex sociological question of how to define 'the media', it would at least seem reasonable to dispense with the idea that the media, in any one or all of its parts, today simply equals a set of localised institutions or concrete apparatuses. The media is a highly adaptable mode of signification, forever modifying its effects and adapting the modes of its intervention into everyday life. These media interventions do not simply affect the lives of individuals in the determinate sense; they also help to *constitute* the very concepts of 'individual' and 'society'; 'viewer' and 'image'; 'ethics', 'morality' and 'shock'; concepts which, in their reflexivity, ground and situate our social experiences.

This way of theorising the question of the media poses a challenge to would-be proponents of a media ethics. For the idea that the media is relatively constitutive of such apparently universal ideals not only makes media practitioners subject to the media's ethical framework, but *viewers too* become enmeshed in this arrangement. In this context it is no longer appropriate to distinguish between the 'moral responsibilities' of practitioners on the one hand, and the 'rights' of viewers on the other as if their respective identities were each grounded in some sort of written constitution. 'The viewer' and 'the journalist' are both mutable parts of a greater sum of capital arrangements grouped around the ownership, control and circulation of media products. Now, this does not mean that ethical considerations should, or indeed will, always come second to economic ones. Nor does it mean that ethical criteria are invalidated by the hard-nosed reality of the media as an industry. In this case it is simply to suggest that every photographic image, in its material existence, is a product of complex social forces which include not only the practices of those directly employed in its production (photographers, journalists, editors, etc.), but also the reactions and opinions of those who are not (informed and uninformed viewers alike).

Turning our attention back to our case study the implications are far reaching. For if there can be no image, no representation, independent of the social forces which combine to create it, then shock resides not with the image in itself, but alongside the set of often complex social arrangements which constitute the public's so-called 'response'. As media consumers we tend to accept our responsibilities without a second thought. 'We' have a moral duty to view and listen, while the media has a moral duty to respect the boundary between pure information and intrusive intervention. Yet this boundary is an infinitely multiple relation, and certainly one which no empirical study can hope to retrieve. The media does not 'measure' public opinion; instead, national events have become practically unthinkable – nonsensical – outside the terms of media discourse. 'Public opinion' now assumes a gravity and importance simply by virtue of being newsworthy. For example, the possibility of there being a truly representative debate on a major constitutional issue is highly problematic, as such issues are nowadays framed and articulated in the manner of tabloid opinion polls. Public opinion, in reality of course, is a question of the *presentation* of numerous and conflicting social identities which constantly threaten to efface the status quo. Therefore there can be no axiomatic distinction made between the media and its addressee; and, what is more, the suggestion that effective codes of conduct or consumer rights should be drawn up to police such a boundary is a highly abstract one which ignores the metaphysical transformation which the media is bringing about in modern society.

We have been investigating the conditions in which a media ethics might be conceivable. In light of what has been said it must be clear by now that there can be no behaviour, no set of values, normative or otherwise, which can be applied to the media while at the same time remaining independent of the media's power. Allow me to conclude, therefore, by suggesting that any media ethics worthy of the name cannot be one which seeks to set a limit or condition on a type of behaviour or practice in a specific context, but instead one which does no more than seek to understand the *true* realm of the media's power: the *true* extent of its involvement and influence in the outside world.

ENDNOTES

1. I have sometimes used terms such as 'audience', 'public' and 'spectator' synonymously, on the whole where context demanded it, instead of 'viewer'. Where I have substituted 'media image' for 'photograph' I have done so in order to convey the sense in which a photograph is nowadays *necessarily* an object of reproduction.
2. For a comprehensive analysis of media effects research, including some important methodological considerations, see Blumer and Gurevitch, 'The Political Effects of Mass Communication' in Gurevitch *et al.* (1995).

3. On how subjectivity can be made 'productive and compatible to social conditions', see Guattari (1995, pp. 19–20).

4. In his essay, 'The Author as Producer', Walter Benjamin considers that the problem of photography and photographic production is that, like other forms of authorship under capitalism, they lack a proper 'organising function' which could effectively involve the spectators in their works. Although I touch on this question, the pressure of space has meant that I have been unable to do little more than reiterate the gist of Benjamin's argument.

5. We must remember that Benjamin was writing in the 1930s at a time when the revolution of cinematic spectatorship and the spread of photography as a mass medium were still in their infancies.

REFERENCES

Althusser, L. (1969) 'Contradiction and Overdetermination', in *For Marx*, trans. Ben Brewster, London: New Left Books.

Althusser, L. (1971) 'Ideology and Ideological State Apparatuses', in *Lenin and Philosophy and Other Essays*, trans. Ben Brewster, London: Monthly Review Press.

Arnold, M. (1971) *Culture and Anarchy*, Cambridge: Cambridge University Press.

Benjamin, W. (1968) 'The Work of Art in the Age of Mechanical Reproduction', in Hannah Arendt, ed., *Illuminations*, trans. Harry Zohn, London: Fontana, 1992.

Benjamin, W. (1982) 'The Author as Producer', in Victor Burgin, ed., *Thinking Photography*, Basingstoke: Macmillan Press.

Berman, M. (1983) *All That Is Solid Melts Into Air*, London: Verso.

Burgin, V. ed. (1982) *Thinking Photography*, London: Verso.

Christians, C.G. *et al.* (1998) *Media Ethics: Cases and Moral Reasoning*, 5th edition. New York: Longman.

Deleuze, G. (1988) *Spinoza: Practical Philosophy*, trans. Robert Hurley, San Francisco: City Lights.

Guattari, F. (1995) *Chaosophy*, Sylvere Lotringer, ed., New York: Semiotext(e).

Gurevitch, M. *et al.*, eds. (1995) *Culture, Society and the Media*, London: Routledge.

Habermas, J. (1989) *The Structural Transformation of the Public Sphere*, trans. Thomas Burger, with the assistance of Frederick Lawrence, Cambridge, MA: MIT.

Negt, O. and Kluge, A. (1993) *Public Sphere and Experience*, trans. Peter Labanyi, Jamie Owen Daniel and Assenka Oksiloff, Minneapolis: University of Minnesota Press.

Robinson, H.P. (1980) 'Idealism, Realism, Expressionism', in Alan Trachtenberg, ed., *Classic Essays on Photography*, Stony Creek: Leete's Island Books.

Sartre, J-P. (1996) *Sketch for a Theory of the Emotions*, London: Routledge.

The Observer, Sunday 3 March and Sunday 10 March 1991.

11 Cyber-ethics: regulation and privatisation

Paul Walton

It is important to remember as we examine the history and nature of the digital dilemmas that exist as stop signs and short cuts on the information superhighway, that there are complex ethical issues involved in the so-called information revolution. As David Brown, in his philosophically informed *Cybertrends*, observes, the so-called information superhighway is often mistakenly equated with the Internet. The highway is a metaphor for the expanding digital information society and the paths across it, whilst the Net is in fact a factual description of a decentralised constellation of computers linked together that can draw upon vast stores of digital information and is now at least thirty years of age (Brown 1998, p. 4). The World Wide Web is a graphical front end for the Net which if one can afford it is becoming increasingly user friendly and multimedia rich in content and form.

These digital technologies and the access to them come with their own history, their own determination and at an economic, social and cultural price. Some overly utopian and optimistic members of the digerati insist that the best way to understand this digital transformation is to grasp it as the difference between bits and atoms. Nicholas Negroponte (1995) argues that:

The information superhighway is about the global movement of weightless bits at the speed of light. As one industry after another looks at itself in the mirror and asks about its future in a digital world, that future is driven almost one hundred per cent by the ability of that company's product or services to be rendered in digital form (ibid., p. 12).

Whilst even Negroponte pulls back from the ultimately absurd metaphysical logic of such a position he shares with many of the hyper-enthusiasts of cyber culture, a boundless ahistorical sci-fi like celebration. This view conveniently forgets the infrastructure costs and end user equipment needed to hook in, boot up and be digital. As a playwright friend, who recently returned from Africa, replying to the suggestion that he could have remained in contact via e-mail, that in spite of living in the fourth biggest town in the country there were only four computers. This seems to demonstrate restrictions on public access to new technology and therefore has consequences for limiting democratic citizenship and rights to information technology.

Not since Eden, some would have you believe, has humankind been in such a state of grace as is now enjoyed by users of the Internet. In the new dimension of Cyberspace, real freedom is at last possible. A virtual world of true democracy where no speaker is more powerful than any other has been created, unplanned and unsanctioned by the potentates of telecommunications and computing. A world, moreover, that appears to be, to all intents and purposes, free and unregulated. As the authoritative *Economist* magazine put it:

The growth of the Net is not a fluke or a fad, but the consequence of unleashing the power of individual creativity. If it were an economy, it would be the triumph of the free market over central planning. In music, jazz over Bach. Democracy over dictatorship (February 1994).

This hyperbole suggests that the World Wide Web is virtually free (or at least only the price of a local phone call) and also supposedly offers us the first step along the road to virtual democracy. This type of media representation of current developments in the digital arena is essentially wedded to an immaculate conception approach to technologies and so obscures and indeed prevents reasoned discussion about the nature and historical determinants of technological change and the accompanying need to have a developed social, ethical, and legal policy.

SOME HISTORY AND THEORY

The Web, far from emerging from Eden as a democratic infrastructure available to all, has in fact been closely controlled and limited in access since its inception. Indeed, one could argue that this is true in general of all communications technologies. No new technology is taken up by society until the need and demand for it is heavily shaped and determined by existing market, government and other forces. Moreover, communications technology is a special instance of such a rule, in that in all known instances where that technology could have been used for extending democratic access, such access has only occurred after its democratic potential has been constrained and limited by legislation and control.

The history of the press since the Gutenberg revolution indicates just this. That the production of books and then newspapers have always been surrounded by licences, censorship, copyright and national, moral and market constraints. The same restraint occurred in the development of both radio and television and to this day it is illegal to simply open a radio or TV station without the agreement of government. So why should any of us believe that the Internet was or is different? Brian Winston (1998) argues that:

Beyond the hype the Internet was just another network. This is to say its social effects could (and would) be as profound as, for example, those of that far more ubiquitous network, the telephone (ibid., p. 336).

David Brown observes in his book *Cybertrends: Chaos, Power and Accountability in the Information Age*, that:

With any true revolution, there is an initial period of chaos in which established relativities explode and it seems as if almost any wondrous possibility can take shape. This helps to explain the optimism about (digital) democracy, global enlightenment, and the empowerment of common men and women . . . (1998, p. 13).

What Winston and Brown are criticising is the dominant optimistic view of the democratic potential of the digital revolution and the WWW. They both insist that like any other communications medium the computer and digital technologies do deliver advances, yet these advances occur within the limits of present stratified structure of society. Brown observes:

Interestingly, the computational language in which 'efficiency' is now expressed seems to share a great deal with that of deregulatory, free market 'liberalism'. Both carefully exclude any serious consideration of the important long term costs of their agendas, which include the widening inequalities of wealth and opportunity and the resulting social and ecological ferment (1998, p. 7).

Even Bill Gates is given to flights of utopianism. In the chapter on education in his book, *The Road Ahead*, Gates rhapsodises:

The highway will allow new methods of teaching and much more choice. Quality curriculums can be created with government funding and made available for free. Private vendors will compete to enhance the free material (1995, p. 198).

Yet this advice is offered in a traditional, randomly accessible, portable, energy free, re-readable device – a book. Its cultural form has been around for over five hundred years. This public utopianism of Gates with regard to digital choice in education increases one's techno-scepticism. Gates addresses one of the central issues for interactive technology users, namely community standards and educational policy and observes that:

Having students connected directly to limitless information and to each other will raise policy questions for schools and for society at large . . . how much freedom should they have? Should they have access to information that their parents find objectionable on moral social, or political grounds? . . . Should the teacher be able to monitor what is on every student's screen or to record it for later spot-checking? (1995, p. 204).

These questions and ethical issues are not trivial because digital interactivity implies in one sense at least a greater degree of freedom than previous technologies allowed. Non-linear and non-narrative searches and sites allow massive increases in access to previously private, adult, or secure information. Moreover, the possibilities for plagiarism, forgery, data manipulation, rapidly multiply as the interactive elements grow in volume, traffic, size and complexity. Meanwhile the cultural consequences of a privatised information superhighway, with no free space is unthinkable.

If public education and public libraries were the crowning achievement of the 19th and 20th century cultural reformers, where are the equivalent publicly funded sites and institutions in the digital age of expanding interactive choice?

Furthermore whilst community standards, local content requirements, copyright and permissions, balanced political and news output, watershed viewing hours, and broad classification systems, and now home encryption systems, can with occasional controversy work for film, broadcast television and to a lesser extent video, what happens to such constraints in the narrowest individual environment of digital cyberworld. As Diffie and Landau (1998) point out in their book, *Privacy on the line*, the US government has practically banned private usage of digital encryption as it would render monitoring by government and others virtually impossible, they suggest that, fortunately and unlike credit data bases, the struggle for cryptographic freedom is a fight in which privacy and commerce are on the same side.

The continual legal and political struggles over community standards on the Internet are now public knowledge, but whilst criminal prosecutions can and have occurred and are expanding, they occur long after the event if at all. One of the largest providers of Internet services, the aptly named Demon, argues that it is not technically possible to filter content, action can only be taken retrospectively. The Internet providers association argue that government threats to prosecute groups threatens the free speech ethos of the net, but in any case the technical problems of monitoring the estimated 200,000 photos and articles put on the net every day are probably impractical.

William Mitchell, dean of architecture at MIT, in his book, *City of Bits: Space, Place, and the Infobahn*, argues that, 'the task of the twenty-first century will be to build the bitsphere – a worldwide, electronically mediated environment in which networks are everywhere . . .' (1995, p. 167).

All this may come to pass, we may and are developing on-line museums, virtual galleries, and digital libraries, these are not however perfect substitutes for the real thing. Reading a book on a train or plane is easier and more enjoyable than reading from a lap-top. The materiality of visual and sculptural form is not easily displaced by virtual imagery.

In any case, when considering the digital revolution it is wiser to ask David Brown not, 'what can the electronics do? but rather, who will control the keys? Who (or what) will capture the all-important role of trusted intermediary in the digital domain' (1998, p. 14). As he observes, 'The values of cybernetics – that towering paradigm of governance by informational means – will determine which segments of society are most empowered in the cybernetic domains' (ibid.).

In short whilst the cybercultural movement appears to offer a more direct link with the public, this access itself is now increasingly subject to control. In contradiction to the view that the Internet is friction free at the centre of the current debate over usage there exists the contradictions and moral politics that arise between the need for security and the need for freedom, there is a large gap between commerce and community. Which politics will prevail is uncertain but what is clear is that the intensity of cyberpolitics will increase in parallel with digital information's rising centrality and price as a commodity.

Both Brown and Winston share an important position regarding the difference between the concept of *communication* and the concept of *cybernetics*. Raymond Williams (1988), defined communications as follows, 'To make common to many. To share. To impart'. To 'transmit', as Williams notes, communications always had a double meaning. On the one hand to share and on the other transmit a one-way process. This conflict has never really been resolved and it is rewritten in the history of most communication technologies that they can be used to share, i.e. many to many or they can be used to transmit, i.e. one to many.

The difference in the social dialogic relations between these forms of different social structures is of course immense, for one implies free communication and the other controlled communication. It is therefore one of the undoubted attractions of the Web in that it appears to allow communication in the better moral sense, i.e. to share information in common from many to many. However, as I believe, and Winston and Brown concur, this is not a realistic view of the history of computing and the Web.

The invention of computing and the digital revolution draws its rationale and philosophy in part from information theory, which in turn owes much to a formal paradigm developed by C. E. Shannon and W. Weaver in their work, *The Mathematical History of Communications* (1949). Cybernetics, developed by Norbert Wiener in 1948, is commonly understood as founding the science of communications and control theory along with Shannon and Weaver's information theory, both rest upon the notion of feedback in a controlled system. The simplest application is a thermostat in which the automatic controls are set so that if the external feedback tells the system it is too cold then the system turns on more heat and vice versa if it is too hot. As Brown and others have pointed out, this approach restricts the feedback to desired ends which are pre-set. Indeed, the term Cybernetics is derived from the Greek 'Kybernetes' which can be translated as 'pilot' or 'governor', 'steering' or 'management'.

In fact the advance of the digital and cyber revolution has been built around a philosophy, mathematics *and* engineering which has as its centre, notions of tightly controlled feedback. Indeed in information and communications theory unwanted feedback which may interfere with other signals between the transmitter and receiver is called noise and the engineer's job is to improve the signal to noise ratio.

The detailed history of the Web and the debates around its democratic and other potentials oscillate between this larger definition of communication, i.e. to share or make common to many, and the notion of tightly managed information and control.

THE ORIGINS OF THE NETWORK

Most communication technologies require some sort of network of relationships, wired or unwired, connecting audiences, readers, users, writers, producers and disseminators, e.g. a radio or TV network are obvious cases. The Internet is little more than a computer-based hybrid between a telephone exchange and a broadcasting system. Originally the Internet was conceived as a post-apocalyptic command grid. Data was transmitted between the mainframes at the heart of the military–industrial complex and was about the necessity to diffuse government and military information across as many cities as possible in case any one of them became a target for nuclear attack.

Winston (1998) argues that this work, begun by computer and defence scientists in the 1960s was driven by the need for a literally atomic-bomb-proof communication system. The enabling agency for the Internet was the Advanced Research Projects Agency (ARPA) created by the American government in response to the technological achievements of the Russians who, via Sputnik and the rest of their space programme, shocked the Americans into action.

In 1973, a meeting at the University of Sussex (UK) established the first International Network Working Group at which the first international e-mails made their appearance. This group was also presented with what eventually became the Transmission Control Protocol (TCP) which allows the computers to talk to each other, probably the most essential component of the Internet. The basic protocols for e-mail appeared in 1972 and within a year 75 per cent of Internet traffic was in the form of e-mail. The 1970s also saw the first steep rise in usage of the Internet largely through use in universities.

CompuServe, the first major Internet Service Provider (ISP) appeared in 1979, reflecting the increased access and usage patterns that were emerging outside the military complex. The development of corporate and commercial usage was completed by the handing over to the private sector by the American government of the backbone of the system in 1995. In the space of less than twenty years these services had become a huge growth industry and with the development of the Web, the graphical/multimedia front end of the Internet, the cheapening of memory and the development of digital phone systems, they began to converge with some of the multimedia characteristics of the entertainment giants who had begun to invest heavily in them.

Their contents are now beginning to take on the form of home entertainment systems with the emphasis firmly on multimedia approaches. From the early 1990s onwards, the buzzword in the telecommunications, information and entertainment industries became 'convergence', the notion that each of these technologies was converging and becoming part of the same technological roller coaster. In part this account ignores the fight over potential monopolies and which set-top box and/or TV companies are to survive the onslaught of digital? Who and what is to be controlled has become an issue led in part by the emergence of the US Justice Department's determination to lay down some protocols and standards for major giants such as Intel and Microsoft.

In a world where half of humanity are more than a two-hour walk away from a telephone we need to remember, that we are talking about the 'Haves', whilst ignoring the 'Have-nots'. Even the 'Information-Haves' are not that blessed with this technology either. The commonly cited figure of hundreds of millions of Internet users seems exaggerated. Internet demographers from Austin, Texas estimated the number of hosts at a maximum of 50 million in 1998 and also suggested less regular usage time than one may suppose. In the end how many more hours per week, or is it minutes, can people actually increase their usage by?

Internet-connected computers in the UK probably numbered no more than three million. Who are these users? They are predominantly, white, university-educated, middle-class professional males.

In Internet mythology, the non-military Net was created in an unplanned, unstructured fashion by individual computer enthusiasts linking up their modems. But, on the contrary, it is a by-product of the growth of the world economy, a handmaiden of the transnational corporation. Far from being unplanned its main trunkline (the backbone) was operated by the National Science Foundation of the United States government and the Net's history is no different from other communication technologies whose real democratic potential has still not been realised, e.g. TV. Weren't we all going to get an electronic vote at some point?

When closely examined the case for what can be termed 'digital exceptionalism', rests primarily on the *myth* that the Internet was supposedly an 'unauthorised' and 'democratic' application of computing and telephonic technologies.

Cyberspace appears to be free but this is more apparent than real and is changing rapidly. When in 1995, the National Science Foundation handed the Net's backbone over to the private sector they became the gatekeepers, or principal access points. Before this development, many Internet utopians were in the grip of the strange delusion that they and their communications system stood outside of capitalism. Nevertheless, they all have to buy or have access to bought computers, modems, software, subscriptions to on-line services, telephones and satellites.

Their illusion of getting something for nothing was primarily based on fast data transmission times being significantly reduced. But, however fast and however efficient the routing, this is still not 'free'. Like the much vaunted paperless office that would arise from computing, the free or democratic Net is an urban myth.

The telephonic infrastructure is being paid for by users, these costs become largely invisible because the Net itself is a very efficient user of the infrastructure. To believe that the Internet is, in fact, free is exactly the same as believing that commercial television is 'free to air'.

PRIVACY AND PROTECTION

The use of cookies, small programs that are delivered to the home computer upon entering a site, add another dimension to this economic imperative of the Web. Cookies are set by the builders of the Web to access the user's system and return information to the company's system. Most people are unaware of the existence of cookies as browsers by default are set to accept them without warning the user. It is a simple procedure to set the browser to warn of a cookie arriving but most users still do not refuse them. This information gleaned can range from the banal issues of where a user is accessing from, to performing a search to determine details about the user's profile. This information is invaluable in building user profiles for marketing purposes. Probably the first thing that happens to this information is that it is sold on to marketing and advertising providers who then resell to manufacturers, who then target the consumer, based on specific information and not merely as one component of a socio-economic group.

The very nature of digital information on the Net can tell the corporations and/or governments who you are, what you buy, where you travel, etc. This information can be sold on, as a very profitable sideline, to other firms. The decline of posted junk mail is replaced by electronic equivalents that are tailored exactly to fit our exact buying patterns.

It is clear that anyone buying products over the net allows firms to work out their income and spending power by simple deduction. Their likely political affiliations may be deduced in a similar fashion by examining what sites they view or buy access to. These factors can lead to a very subtle form of control being exercised which is similar to the notion of regulation in terms of broadcasting licences. Its dissimilarity lies in its extreme subtlety which is hidden behind the glossy technological front.

The ethical concerns over digital information has become such that the eighth Georgia Institute WWW survey of 1997, undertook a special survey of the surveyed Web users and found the following results: 25 per cent of users did not know what cookies were, 22 per cent felt cookies were acceptable, 23 per cent have set their machine to warn them before accepting a cookie so that they can make a case-by-case decision whilst 14 per cent have no cookie policy. Male response from Europe tends to be more knowledgeable about cookies. Females who know about cookies tend to be more cautious, 48 per cent want warnings compared to only 38 per cent of knowledgeable males. 33 per cent of women accept cookies compared with 41 per cent of males.

Moreover, with regard to Internet privacy laws most respondents agree either strongly, 39 per cent, or somewhat, 33 per cent, that there should be new laws to protect privacy on the net. Again women feel slightly more strongly than men about this issue. This is not surprising in light of the recent cases of the women murdered or stalked by someone contacted through the Net. Netiquette, has become a major political battlefield.

Companies also know that nearly all active consumers of the Web have credit cards and are therefore most transactions are conducted via credit and not cheque or cash. The so-called digital economy or e-commerce is growing. In the case of direct payment by credit card, only nominal warnings are given that information could be used by third parties, and indeed it may not actually be secure from fraudulent usage. There are serious issues emerging from Internet banking and other digital financial transactions.

The cyber utopians argue that the Internet is now too complex to be controlled and priced because of the intrinsic nature of the technology. But how true can this be in the long term? It is surely illogical on the one hand to claim this while at the same time suggesting that the same computing power can track what is happening for e-commerce and adult filtering. Handing the backbone over to commercial firms is only one of a number of reasons for supposing that the current invisible level of control and price will not long continue. Infrastructure pricing systems will be adjusted to take cognizance of the fact that data streams can be valuable marketing resources to bulk commercial users. Where does all this leave the Net's potential for democratic speech? Many people have now been charged by the police for abuses on the Internet mostly relating to pornography, fraud or pederasty. Pressure from the state on Internet Service Providers has led to Internet connections to users being cut in both the US and Europe.

By mid-June 1995 America On-line – the largest single commercial provider for message senders on the mailing lists which were examined – was reportedly cutting off half a dozen users a day for 'net abuse'. In June 1998, Netscape announced that Communicator 4.5 will have encoding in it allowing adult filtering of access to violent and sexually explicit sites, and Disney and other large corporations are pouring resources into developing safe sites for children. Internet Explorer has had this since version 3 and although this is enforced and used by the concerned parent, the question arises, how long will it be before these filters are controlled by the Internet Service Providers (ISP). This is being tried but is not yet 100 per cent effective as evidenced by the no doubt apocryphal story of net users in the town of Scunthorpe, England, being unable to even log on due to an ISP's automatic filtering of embedded sexual vernacular.

There is then increasing evidence that despite the vision and myth of the Internet as a technology which is democratic and ethically progressive, it is going the way of previous communication technologies, i.e. it is becoming increasingly subject to economic, private and state control and governmentality.

This is not to say that the Net is simply conservative in its communication practices. There are networks such as the global 'Association for Progressive Communications' (the APC), which have been providing low cost net access to over 100 communities both in the developed and developing world. There exist reports that during the Soviet coup of 1991 the Russian staff of the Moscow-based GlasNet opposed to the coup provided the most direct and immediate reports of what was happening.

Despite such positive findings, since the early 1990s a whole range of American groups including the Electronic Frontier Foundation, The

American Civil Liberties Union (ACLU), and other First Amendment supporters have had to struggle against tendencies pushing control and privatisation. It is clear that the ISPs and the state authorities can and do monitor exchanges, and not just the state. For instance, various newspapers reported that in the UK private security forces had joined GreenNet for the express purpose of monitoring the behaviour of activists working on anti-road campaigns. China went on-line in 1998 with a company entitled China Internet Corps. The Chinese Internet will not be an open and democratic Web, it will carry commercial information funded by large US firms.

ACCESS AND CONTROL

The techno-optimists, unfailing enthusiasm for all new technology is coming to be challenged. A Harvard conference on the Internet and Society, reported in On-line in *The Guardian* that Ernest Wilson, suggested that the Internet is doing nothing to address dystopian issues such as inequality. Wilson argues, that:

'Information technology may be widening this gap.' He asks that, 'If land was the source of wealth during the agricultural revolution, and company shares in the industrial period, what will it be in the information age, access to information and the capacity to filter, manipulate, use and apply that information' (28 October 1997)

Businesses are already using filtering and manipulating information. The Economic League in the UK provides a commercial database set up to monitor the status and whereabouts of people who were considered to be involved in activities that were potentially detrimental to the successful operation of an employer.

The old notions of state control that people have railed against historically may well be on the verge of disappearing in the triumph of economic control by oligarchic corporations. The insult in this injurious state, is that the very people who are controlled most will be paying for the privilege of using the system, which appears to offer a service to the consumer.

A recent survey of Internet usage by MORI, published in *The Guardian* revealed that, whilst 11 per cent of the UK population use it regularly that breaks down to 15 per cent of men but only 6 per cent of women and is obviously a long way from becoming a popular tool. The percentage of people who had heard about the net or the Web but were not interested in using it actually went up over the year from 25 per cent to 29 per cent. The largest reason for not using it, 40 per cent, was because they do not have access to a computer (28 October 1997). The research indicates that whilst the personal computer industry is still growing, it is being mainly driven by repeat buyers. In short the spread of technology may yet hit a digital ceiling.

The Guardian, in its leader comment, suggests that whilst the entry point for the information revolution is unquestionably the Internet, the set-up costs are still a major entry bar for a majority of the population. They suggest that the government must give priority to a national grid, linking schools, libraries, etc., to the information superhighway. They suggest that this current situation, 'sadly but inevitably, makes it the prerogative of the "Haves" unless access is provided . . .', and they ask, 'How long will this unfair situation last?'

Whilst all communication technologies from the printing press onwards have democratic potential, history reveals that these potentials are normally suppressed. The danger with the current debates over the Internet is that because they simply look at technological possibilities, they direct attention away from what is actually happening. Freedom on the Internet is not inevitable. It is rather, as ever, a question of cultural and political vigilance.

In June 1998, *Wired* magazine reported that the US government is being criticised for its planned policy on cyber copyright and its revamping of the domain name system. Lawrence Lessig, a Harvard Law Professor who is special advisor in the Microsoft anti-trust case, in a public session sponsored by the New York Media Association entitled *Internet and Public Policy*, criticised President Clinton's policy on new domain names and technology laws, suggesting that they were implemented in order to pacify strong special interest groups before thoroughly examining the effect of these laws on the average net user's freedom. He denounced the plan to form a private non-profit organisation to establish Internet addressing policy, as it raised serious legal and constitutional issues. He rhetorically asked, 'A non-profit organisation devoted to the public interest – isn't that what government is supposed to be? And we would add, outside of any direct public accountability' (June 1998).

In Europe, the European Data Protection Directive (1998) is an attempt to set and enforce strict regulations concerning the use, collection and exchange of personal information but it is questionable just how effective these will prove to be as 'leaked' information is very easy to produce and distribute in electronic form. It is much easier to copy and distribute information digitally than to copy paper documents stored in filing cabinets. Digital technologies have the added dilemma of it being possible to do this remotely from the other side of the world. The benefits of digital storage, retrieval and transfer systems to anyone wishing to exchange information are a two-way street.

At this juncture the problems of private organizations taking over the information superhighway is revealed as the central dilemma. Until now application has been relatively socially benign and have clearly been democratic in impulse which has caused concerns for governments, individuals and corporations. As soon as a clear financial imperative appeared, the corporations began to march in:

Now, with the advent of the Net, we are privatising government in a new way – not only in the traditional sense of selling things off to the private sector, but by allowing organisations independent of traditional governments to take on certain 'government' regulatory roles. These new international regulatory agencies will perform former government functions in counterpoint to increasingly global large companies and also t/ individuals and smaller private organisations who can operate globally over the Net too (Dyson 1997, p. 104).

Esther Dyson is regarded as one of the leading gurus of the digerati and one of the more profound thinkers regarding the ethical and policy implications of digital communications. She focuses her most recent book, *Release 2.0; A Design for Living in the Digital Age*, around the joint issues of responsibility and governance that go along with the decentralised self-regulation and disclosure which is occurring on the Net. Her approach stands in marked contrast to the much quoted view of Bill Gates that, 'The Internet is friction free'. She has a narrative that examines the contradictions and frictions that arise between the need for security and the need for freedom or between commerce and community.

Yet strangely enough at this moment when we may need government, it is abandoning its role and is attempting to persuade private bodies to enforce and control. The Cyber-ethical dilemma of the transnational corporate digital age is how and who can call into account a collection of undemocratically rich information providers? Like all previous communication technologies the central struggle is between public access and private ownership.

ENDNOTES

This essay partly draws upon collaborative work with Brian Winston and Richard Adams. See the following:

Winston, B. and Walton, P. (1996) Netscape: Virtually Free, *Index on Censorship*, **25**, issue 168, Jan/Feb.
Walton, P. and Adams, R. (Forthcoming) *Digital Dilemmas*, London: Macmillan.

REFERENCES

Brown, D. (1998) *Cybertrends: Chaos, Power and Accountability in the Information Age*, London: Penguin.
Diffie, W. and Landau, S. (1998) *Privacy on the line*, London: MIT Press.
Dyson, E. (1997) *Release 2.0; A Design for Living in the Digital Age*, London: Penguin.
Gates, B. (1995) *The Road Ahead*, London: Viking.
GVU's Eighth WWW User Survey.
Mitchell, W.J. (1995) *City of Bits: Space, Place and the Infobahn*, USA: MIT Press.
Negroponte, N. (1995) *Being Digital*, Great Britain: Coronet Books, Hodder and Stoughton.

Shannon, C.E. and Weaver, W. (1949) *The Mathematical History of Communications*, USA: University of Illinois Press.

The Guardian, 22 October 1997.

The Guardian, 'Casting the Net Wide', 28 October 1997.

Wiener, N. (1961) *Cybernetics*, 2nd edn, New York: Wiley & Co.

Williams, R. (1988) *Keywords*, New York: Fontana.

Wilson, E. Director of the Centre for International Development and Conflict Management at the University of Maryland, printed in *The Guardian*, 20 May 1998.

Winston, B. (1998) *Media Technology and Society*, London: Routledge.

12 'Sweet sell of sexcess': the production of young women's magazines and readerships in the 1990s

Anna Gough-Yates

Magazines produced for women have provoked vigorous debate in recent years. Politicians, journalists, religious groups, traditional moralists, educationalists, parents, youth workers, and health workers, are among the many groups who have commented on the commercial femininities represented in the pages of women's and of young women's magazines. 'Teen' magazines such as *19, J-17*, and *Sugar*, as well as magazines aimed at older groups of young women in their twenties and thirties including *Cosmopolitan, Company*, and *Marie Claire*, are frequently criticized for their emphasis on sexual content, and for the sexual explicitness of cover lines, which are thought to be 'smutty', 'lewd' and 'in poor taste'. The debates on women's magazines, and on young women's magazines in particular, have converged around their possible effects on their readers, with magazine producers frequently being considered morally irresponsible and corrupting of the women who read their products.

One of the key issues in the debates has been the threat to traditional forms of femininity which women's magazines are seen to pose. Cover lines such as 'Men Unzipped! The Secret of Male Sex Appeal' (*19*, August 1998), and 'Come Again? 29 Truly Astonishing Sex Tips for try-anything-once women' (*Cosmopolitan*, March 1998) have been thought to actively promote 'deviant' and 'masculinized' sexual identities which challenge conventional gender norms. The magazine industry's desire for profit, it is argued, results in the representation of non-traditional feminine identities in the pages of magazines which pander to the base instincts of women readers.

Magazine producers, however, maintain that they are entirely responsible, and argue that the sexual content in their magazines is not merely a sensationalist tool for boosting circulation. They point to the role of women's magazines as a provider of good quality information about sexual matters which help women to make informed, responsible decisions about their behaviour. Their magazines, they argue, are a reflection of the lives of women in the 1990s, and provide women with the information they require to enable them to make sensible life decisions. What is certain, is that women continue to buy successful titles, such as the 'teen' title *Sugar* and young women's magazine *Cosmopolitan*, which regularly achieve monthly circulation figures above 450,000.[1]

In commercial operations, the ethics of cultural producers, of which magazine production is but one example, are inexorably linked to the inter-related processes of production, distribution and consumption.[2] The ethics of young women's magazines have frequently been understood as having a moral dimension which can 'improve', or possibly 'corrupt', young people who have not yet established a permanent world-view and style of living. Only certain styles of living are 'approved', and these assume that heterosexuality, marriage, and family are inherently unchallengeable within human relationships. Those who express concern about the effects of young women's magazines on their readers, who usually fail to support their claims with substantive research, do not examine them in relation to an empirically constructed world of young people. Instead, they hark back to a set of imagined and unquestionable values which are thought to be enduring. Magazine production, on the other hand, concerns itself less with what should be than with what is.

'NOTHING BUT SEX, CLOTHES AND BOYFRIENDS'

The use of sexual content in print media and the adverse effects of it on the morality of women readers is not a new concern, and is to be found in contemporary debates in the nineteenth century. In her study of women's magazines, Margaret Beetham notes, in particular, the anxieties associated with the effects of cheap print and 'sensational' reporting on the women readers of Sunday papers and cheap serialised fiction from the 1840s onwards (Beetham 1996, pp. 115–130).

Beetham highlights the way in which commentators adopted the term 'sensation' to describe the increasingly sexualised content of particular forms of nineteenth century print media (ibid., p. 125). She observes that 'sex' had long been staple subject matter for popular journalism, but argues that it became increasingly acceptable as a social/political issue in 'respectable' journalism, aimed at the middle-classes during the 1880s and 1890s (ibid.).[3] Many critics argued, however, that the increased inclusion of sexual content in print media was an unacceptable and 'sensationalist' tactic for boosting circulation, and suggested that this form of reporting was potentially dangerous for the moral well-being of both working-class and/or women readers who were thought to lack 'the objectivity and cool rationality of the middle-class male reader' (ibid.). Anxieties over the print media consumed by women have re-emerged form time to time. Jennifer Craik's work, for example, has noted pre-occupations and concerns over the sexual content of women's magazines in the 1920s, and the appearance of similar debates with the publication of titles such as *Honey, Nova* and *Cosmopolitan* in the 1960s and 1970s (Craik 1994, pp. 44–69).

Similarly, such fears have re-emerged in the 1990s, and the producers of magazines have been perceived as lacking ethical behaviour and moral responsibility. Brian Braithwaite's (1995) review of 300 years of women's magazine publishing in Britain observes that magazine publishers in the 1990s have taken sex:

To their bosoms with an over-abundance of enthusiasm. They analyse it, proselytize it, describe it, dissect it, romanticize it and generally wallow in it. No sexual holds have been barred, no byway unexplored (ibid., p. 157).

Although sex in magazines is frequently used as 'a cynical camouflage for building circulation', it is a subject that he recognizes as 'here to stay' (ibid.). Whilst the sexual content of magazines may enable titles to maintain and improve circulation figures, the concern among many commentators remains that such material is 'harmful' to the minds, and will have undesirable effects on the actions of women readers.

Numerous articles in newspapers have suggested that it is the novelty of sexually explicit content in young women's magazines, as opposed to a sophisticated understanding of the lives and aspirations of women readers, that builds magazine circulations in the 1990s. Interviewed in *The Guardian* in 1992, David Durman, editor of *Woman* magazine, 'where a picture of a penis would lose him his job overnight' (Cook 1992) censured women's magazine editors for using sex as an irresponsible form of marketing tool. Durman was unconvinced that women's magazines were satisfying a pre-existent demand for explicit sexual material, and argued that:

[i]t's rather like going topless the first time on holiday. You may not really want to but everyone else does it and when you do it doesn't seem so bad (ibid.).

The same piece in *The Guardian* called a number of magazine editors to account for the sexual content of their magazines. Editors Marcelle d'Argy Smith (*Cosmopolitan*), Mandi Norwood (*Company*) and Glenda Bailey (*Marie Claire*) all argued that their titles gave their young women readers what they wanted. They covered all aspects of women's lives, and took both an entertaining and moral approach to sexual matters. Mandi Norwood, in particular, justified the sexual content in *Company* by arguing that it had a duty to meet the needs of women in the 1990s:

[T]he magazine has become far more straight talking for a very good reason – the increasing need for awareness of Aids [sic], HIV infection and sexually transmitted diseases. The majority of women turn to magazines for information on those subjects. Some might see it as titillation but I regard it as an essential transfer of information (Cook 1992).

Justifications such as Norwood's have not convinced the commentators in the press who have written condemnatory articles on the content of women's magazines. In 1995, for example, Catherine Bennett in *The Guardian* traced the recent history of sex related themes in women's magazines, noting a transition from 'vaguely worded articles about exotic techniques' to 'top tips' which are 'anatomically correct' (Bennett 1995). Bennett concluded that, whilst coverage of sex in magazines might ensure that women were more educated about sexual activity, she was not convinced that '30 years of magazine sex [had] made readers any happier', or that they really understood that much more about sex than women of a previous generation (Bennett 1995). The following year, Caroline Sullivan bemoaned the 'overall lowering of standards' of women's magazines, and the devaluation of 'privacy in sexual matters' in their pages (Sullivan 1996). Blaming the impact of what she called 'yob' culture' on the magazine industry, Sullivan called for a 'vestige of restraint' among magazine publishers, who were, she claimed, pursuing an immoral course (ibid.).

In November 1997, the independent think tank, the Social Affairs Unit (SAU), published its controversial report, *The British Woman Today*, which criticized the sexual content of women's titles and led to a spate of newspaper articles which summarized its findings (Anderson and Mosbacher 1997a).[4] *The British Woman Today* offered qualitative analyses of eleven leading women's magazines (including *Company*, *Cosmopolitan*, and *Marie Claire*) by twelve leading academics and journalists; Professor Kenneth Minogue (formerly of the London School of Economics), Dr Robert Grant (University of Glasgow), and Dr Athena S. Leoussi (University of Reading) among them (Anderson and Mosbacher 1997a). All who commented on the publications were unanimous that the content of women's magazines was highly irresponsible, and offered their readers 'a depressing portrait of the modern British woman' (ibid., p. 18).

From their analyses, the SAU drew up a composite picture of 'Magazine Woman', the typical magazine reader; she had 'no children, no cares, and no responsibilities' and lived a life of 'indulgences of a distinctly tawdry kind' (ibid., p. 9). The report pointed to the extensive coverage in many of the magazines which suggested that 'Magazine Woman' viewed sex from a traditionally 'masculine' perspective. She was 'predatory and aggressive' (ibid., p. 13), and her language displayed 'coarseness, savagery and voyeurism' in its sexual crudity (Burrows 1997, p. 57). *Company* magazine, in particular, was singled out by the writer and broadcaster Lynette Burrows, for displaying a 'Magazine Woman' who was:

Just so nasty, so designed to create contempt and loathing for fellow human beings, that it reminds one chillingly of the well-documented fact that women can be, once corrupted, both more disgusting and degraded than men. As Shakespeare said, 'Lilies that fester smell far worse than weeds' (ibid.).

She firmly reprimanded the producers who, she argued, displayed a 'barbaric lack of feeling' in the pages of the magazines (ibid.). In particular, it was feared that by portraying brutality, the producers were actually encouraging it in their readers. The writers for magazines, Burrows argued, needed to recognize their moral responsibilities towards their readers, particularly when, she assumed, they consisted of 'poorly-educated girls' (ibid.).

The sheer volume of press criticism aimed towards women's magazine titles in the 1990s could be read as an indication that magazine producers have indeed over-stepped the mark. The argument that the pressures of the market have compelled magazine producers to throw caution to the wind and offer their adult and teenage readers explicit sexual content is now common currency where women's magazines are discussed. Yet such criticisms have failed to contextualize the issue of sexual content in women's magazines within shifts in the moral cultures of contemporary Britain, and in relation to broader debates about morality, femininity, youth and media regulation. In so doing, such arguments may have failed to appreciate the nature of the appeal, and more importantly, the user reading pleasures of women's magazines in the 1990s.

MORALITY, 'THE FAMILY' AND MEDIA REGULATION

Robert Bocock observes the marked level of attentiveness paid to sexual morality in general by the British Conservative Governments of the 1980s and 1990s (Bocock 1997, p. 78). He refers, in particular, to the attention given to the morality of sexual behaviour that manifested itself in the call for a return to 'Victorian values' which was prevalent amongst Conservative politicians during the Thatcher years of 1979–90. These re-appeared, Bocock notes, in the form of John Major's 'Back to Basics' campaign which harked back to a time when 'self-reliance, respect for the law and the supremacy of the nuclear family could be taken for granted' (Ibid., p. 79). This trend continues under Tony Blair's 'New Labour' and its revitalist calls for a 'New Britain' which, in part, suggests a Britain where the institution of 'the family' is reinstated to a position of central importance in everyday life.

The wider debates about morality in British society have also touched on areas of media consumption. Bocock argues that British governments have tended to pursue general policies relating to the media which favour a free-market and neo-liberal approach but, in contradiction, have attempted state regulation of sexual moralities. He gives the example of the effective ban on the broadcasting by satellite of programmes with erotic content by the British Government in 1995. The British supply of 'smartcards' which would have unscrambled signals for television stations such as *Red Hot Dutch, TV Erotica* and *XXX TV* was prohibited. If this ran contrary to policies of privatisation and de-regulation which were the dominant approach in the broadcasting field, no contradiction was admitted (ibid.).

This period also saw debates about the potential for corruption by new technologies which were 'capable of portraying people in sexually "meaningful" ways', such as videos, satellite channels, cable TV and the Internet (ibid.). 'Traditional moralists' foregrounded these ideas, and issues of 'Victorian' and 'family' values were integrated with the debates on media de-regulation (ibid.). The capacity of parents to monitor and control the corrupting effects of the media on their families was central to these issues. John Murray notes how 'the family' emerged as a broader signification of the national 'US' (sic), which was perceived as being threatened by a range of sinister 'forces' from outside (Murray 1991, pp. 30–31). 'The Family', Murray argues, was consistently deployed by public figures, the media and major institutions as a rationale for their actions, where it had:

star billing in an historical romance of post-war national decline (the result of promiscuity, permissiveness and loss of school and parental authority) in the 60s and 70s; and renewal, the gradual restoration (though always vulnerable) of 'family values', 'standards' and 'national pride' (ibid., p. 31).

The signifier of 'the family' became a powerful and popular way of discussing a range of subjects. Murray observes that the rhetorical device of 'the family' was deployed to articulate a range of New Right positions on gender, and to pronounce the 'threat' to traditional masculinities that the decline of 'the family' posed (ibid.). As in earlier generations, these anxieties about threats to masculinity were mirrored in concerns about the erosion of traditional forms of femininity, which manifested themselves in debates about, for example, the moral recklessness of young single mothers, about the contribution of women and feminism to the decline in family values, and in questions about the perceived shift towards aggressive behaviour by young women.[5]

The media was conveniently foregrounded as a prime target in these debates, and the perceived effects of media content on audiences were frequently offered as explanations for shifting moralities. The world of the media was often represented as distinct from the world of reality; many guardians of morality and their representatives in the media argued that, as a result, it prioritised marginal, as opposed to mainstream views. Not only was the media seen to be exploring behaviour and sexualities of a marginal and 'non-traditional' kind, in programmes for gay audiences like *Out on Tuesday, Out, Dyke TV*, and *Gaytime TV*, for example, the perceived potential of the media to undesirably influence the behaviour of its audiences meant that it was frequently represented as a 'menace' which threatened the very fabric of British society (ibid.).

Concerns about the influence of the media, and in particular its impact on its young consumers, found their most grotesque expression in 1993 in the moral panics that followed the murder cases of sixteen-year-old Suzanne Capper and of two-year-old James Bulger. In both cases, the youth of the convicted killers raised suggestions that violent videos watched in the home had influenced their behaviour. There was not sufficient evidence in either case to demonstrate these claims, but the cases led to the increased regulation of violent video recordings with The Criminal Justice and Public Order Act of 1994, which tightened legislation on the classification of video recordings by the British Board of Film Classification (BBFC).[6]

'Teen' magazines for young women, and magazines aimed at young people, also met with calls for stricter controls over their content. In February 1996, the Conservative MP for Worcestershire Mid, Peter Luff, proposed the Periodicals (Protection of Children) Bill which would require the publishers of young women's magazines to display an age suitability warning on the covers of their magazines, analogous to the classification of videos by the BBFC. Although Luff's anxieties can be contextualized in relation to the broader concerns about the content of young women's magazines outlined above, Luff also had more specific anxieties about the possible effects of these magazines on his own eleven-year-old daughter whom he had found reading one of them. His concern was, in the main, that explicit sexual content within the magazines would have detrimental effects on the behaviour of young women, encouraging them to think that sexual activity below the age of consent was 'normal' (Wellings 1996).

Luff's aim was to ensure that the contents of magazines aimed at young men and women were appropriate for the age group and factually accurate, but he was also concerned with guaranteeing a standard of common decency in magazines generally. Parliamentary support for the Bill was widespread in February 1996, but the Bill was opposed in March. Opponents of the Bill tended to concur with the opinions of Simon Hughes, Liberal Democrat MP for Southwark and Bermondsey, who argued that it would prove to be both counter-productive and unworkable.

Hughes forcefully argued that age ratings on young women's magazines would increase the aspirational appeal of the magazines for women below the target age. More importantly, Hughes suggested, the recommendations of the Bill would be unworkable, as age ratings would be impossible to enforce and monitor from month to month and week to week. Luff eventually withdrew the Bill in July 1996 (ibid.).

In the same year the magazine *TV Hits* (which had a significant readership of ten- to thirteen-year-olds) sparked a row by publishing a reader's letter titled 'My boyfriend wants us to have oral sex. What does he mean?' Parents complained that the answer left 'nothing to the imagination', and leading supermarkets and W. H. Smiths pulled the title from their shelves (Locks 1996). The *TV Hits* case sparked a substantial amount of television, radio and national newspaper coverage, with the *Daily Mail*, frequently at the centre of debates around film and video censorship, characteristically campaigning for the censorship of sex in 'teen' magazines.

Publishers and the Periodical Publishers Association (PPA) attempted to restrict the damage to the reputations of magazines by accepting the need to take action with regard to young women's magazines. After consultation with the Home Office, both publishers and the PPA agreed to an immediate 'toning down' of content, as well as to offering clearer guidance to newsagents about the appropriate places to display titles. It was believed that magazines such as *More!*, which contained features such as 'Position of the Month' deemed appropriate for older audiences of women, were mistakenly being displayed alongside younger titles like *It's Bliss* on newsagents' shelves. A voluntary Code of Conduct for magazine publishers, which would both guarantee the quality and sources of information and provide some moral limits to the information provided by 'teen' magazines was established, and an arbitration panel (TMAP) which would independently deal with any complaints about the 'teen' titles was established (ibid.).

Despite the sometimes contentious discussion on the relationship between women's magazines and the behaviour of their readers, there is little or no evidence to substantiate claims that women's magazines incite women to challenge the accepted norms and values of society by behaving in morally irresponsible ways. Nevertheless, the wave of moral panics around the links between women's magazines and a decline in the morality of young women has placed publishers under considerable pressure to self-regulate their activities.

FEMINIST MAGAZINE SCHOLARSHIP AND WOMEN'S MAGAZINES

Feminist magazine scholarship has, since the 1970s, attempted to understand the relationships between women's magazines and their readers, yet although the arguments have been more complex than those of traditional moralists and their representatives in the media, much of it has also taken an un-optimistic and moralistic approach towards women's consumption of magazines.

Janice Winship (1987), Ros Ballaster *et al.* (1991), and Ellen McCracken's (1993) work on magazines, for example, argue that the commercial nature of women's magazines means that their texts can be viewed as little more than agents in the reproduction of what they see as patriarchal and capitalist relations of exploitation.[7] Although they agree that women readers can resist the narrative interpellations of women's magazines, and they combine analyses of texts and their reception in varying degrees, resistance to the texts are described as only ever partial or temporary, and in the last instance, it is the interests of capitalism and patriarchy which are served. Women's magazines then, in their current form, are seen to be barriers to women's liberation, offering undesirable representations of commercialised femininities to their readers that systematically erase the realities of women's oppression.

As in the popular debates on women's magazines, the approach of many feminist scholars has emphasised the textual moment of magazine reading. The effects of magazines on women readers are presumed to be fairly predictable, and the contents of the magazines are thought to be detrimental to the well-being of their women readers in that they conceal the 'reality' of women's existence under a cloak of impenetrable ideology. The overall assumption is that on the whole, women are rendered passive in their consumption of magazine texts, and that magazines have politically undesirable effects on the everyday lives and behaviour of their readers. More recent orientations in academic magazine scholarship have argued that studies which focus on textual analysis of women's magazines have not placed adequate emphasis on the active nature of reading practices. Myra Macdonald (1995) and Linda Steiner (1991) have both argued that magazine texts can facilitate oppositional reading strategies, whilst Elizabeth Frazer (1987), Angela McRobbie (1991) and Mary Jane Kehily (1999) have conducted research on specific groups of readers of teen magazines. Ulla Outtrup and Birgitte Ramsø Thomsen (1994) have also produced a valuable unpublished study of women reading *Cosmopolitan*.

The most important and substantial study of readers of women's magazines and everyday media use is by Joke Hermes, who criticises feminist scholarship on women's magazines for refusing to let go of their 'older feminist position of concern' (Hermes 1995, p. 3). Hermes questions the assertion that women's magazines can 'harm' readers, and also their implicit suggestion that the constructions of femininity within women's magazines are any more 'harmful' than those in other media. Hermes proposes that cultural criticism of women's magazines needs to be both self-reflexive on the part of the researcher, and that it should be combined with research methods 'that let readers speak for themselves' (ibid., p. 5).

Negotiating a pathway between studies of media which privilege genre and text, and studies which privilege the 'situatedness' and 'everydayness' of media use, Hermes attempts to address the ways in which women's magazines 'become meaningful exclusively through the perception of their readers' (ibid., p. 6). At the same time she maintains a postmodern feminist awareness that it is her own 'interpretation of how readers interpret women's magazines' (ibid.).

Hermes draws on seventy-five interviews with readers of women's magazines, but notes her initial disappointment with her interview material: '[t]he emancipated audience didn't strike me as all that active and celebrating. Nor did the interviews, at first sight, make any clearer how women's magazines or other media are made meaningful' (ibid., p. 495). It was the interview process itself, however, which helped her to realise the impossibility of distinguishing between the magazine text and the context of reading.

Hermes asserts that her interviewees did not differentiate between their explanations of reading women's magazines and their explanations of their everyday lives. In fact, her interviewees often seemed to have very little to say at all about the magazines themselves, whilst they talked more about how the magazines they read fitted into the routines of their daily lives. Readers gave meanings to women's magazines which Hermes found to be quite independent of the magazine text, employing them at particular moments as tools in the formation of fantasy and imagined 'new selves' (ibid., p. 146). She concludes that women's magazines are not meaningful when analysed outside of the contexts of everyday life. The texts themselves are not significant, as there is 'no essential meaning that can be actualized nor is there an essential viewing mode or practice of media use' (Hermes 1993, p. 504).

Hermes's work on the reading of women's magazines has shifted feminist magazine scholarship away from a moral concern with the supposed role of women's magazines in the maintenance of female oppression, towards more empirically grounded research. Hermes recognises the complexity of the consumption process, and her methods allow her to see the relationship between women's magazines and readers as complicated and dynamic.

The methods and motivations of the magazine producers which have obsessed commentators in the press are, however, strikingly absent in all of these academic studies, and the media world of the producer is perceived as far from the 'real' world of the reader. Angela McRobbie's analysis of the young women's magazines of the 1990s such as *Elle, Marie Claire*, and *More!* has recently acknowledged this inadequacy, and has called for work which reconceptualises what she calls the 'interdiscursive space' of production (McRobbie 1996). In her investigation of the 'new' women's magazines of the 1990s, McRobbie argues that the project for cultural studies must be 'to generate a more rigorous account of the complex and multilayered relation between the production of meaning in the magazine and the diverse ways in which these meanings are consumed by readers' (ibid., p. 178).

McRobbie proposes the re-introduction of a 'more sociological approach' to magazine scholarship, which would employ a combination of ethnographic methods, hard data, and textual analysis, informed by a postmodern feminist understanding of gender and subjectivity (ibid., p. 193). These methods, she claims, have enabled her to understand the complex ways in which 'the reader' operates as a discursive category within the magazine industry, and as a space of 'projection' for the magazine editor, entrepreneur and journalist. Her findings indicate that within the context of magazine production, 'the reader' is understood in an emotional and intimate way, and is often described by practitioners as one of their 'own circle of friends and acquaintances' (ibid., p. 180). Market researchers are industry intermediaries, shaping this 'ideal' reader into a concrete consumer profile that can be offered to prospective and existing advertisers, and ensuring that the magazine keeps its finger on the pulse of the cultures of young women. Recruitment policies at the magazines also contribute to this process, ensuring that, as much as possible, the employees embody the qualities of this 'ideal' reader, and that they see themselves as the appropriate '*Just Seventeen*' or '*Cosmo*' girls.

The social purpose of women's magazines, according to McRobbie, is a normative one, which attempts to ensure that readers share a 'commitment to dominant femininity' (ibid., p. 182). The responses of readers to this normativity, however, are uncertain, and magazine producers know that they have to work hard at both evoking, and entertaining their readers in their pages. Readers, as fluctuating economic and statistical data testifies, are unpredictable and frequently disloyal in their purchasing habits.

In order to trace the shifting discursive constructions of 'the reader' over time, McRobbie returns to textual analysis, investigating commercial constructions of feminine identities through the pages of various young women's magazines. She finds that, since the 1970s, there have been substantial changes in the ways in which these identities are drawn, which reveals that the grip of normative femininity has loosened. The currency of feminist discourses within contemporary society has meant that sexuality has replaced romance as the ideological focus of magazines, and the result has been an increase in 'strong, frank, and explicitly sexual representations' (ibid., p. 192). In addition, the employees of the magazines are well versed in these languages of sexual politics, are magazine readers themselves, and are frequently graduates of university degree courses which would have encouraged them to adopt a critical view of media texts. Some of them, therefore, understand and agree with feminist criticisms of the magazine form, and retain an interest in cultural studies and magazine research – some even identify themselves as 'feminists'. Their readers, they assert, have similar world-views. The new magazines thus speak to readers about sexuality, McRobbie observes, in languages which are 'mocking and ironic', which provides a counter-hegemonic space for 'critical reflection', turning the tables on men and boys who have traditionally scrutinised women within magazines (ibid., p. 183).

The importance of McRobbie's work is that it has moved feminist magazine scholarship towards an account of women's magazines which is attentive to the complex nature of the production–consumption nexus. This theoretical shift in thinking about women's magazines indicates the different ways in which the practices of cultural production take place in relation to the activities of consumption. The emphasis on macro-structures and corporate control within early research on women's magazines, and within more recent studies of political economy, have characterised the culture industries as destroyers of creativity, cultural diversity, and real consumer choice. McRobbie's research argues, however, that cultural industries cannot be represented as stable entities, and that they are reliant on specific systems of micro-relations to function. One set of micro-relations that they need to get to grips with is the complexity of identity. The understanding, and articulation of identities is crucial, as cultural producers seek both to represent themselves, and to offer projections of their consumers, in order to compete in the increasingly competitive commercial sphere.

My own interviews with magazine professionals have supported McRobbie's claims that the worlds of the magazine producer and the world of the reader are, of necessity, not mutually exclusive. Magazine producers believe that far from imposing alien, and possibly morally reprehensible representations of women's culture onto women readers, they represent pre-existent cultures of women, albeit in a commercial form. They argue that they employ both formal and informal methods of reader research which assist them in remaining 'in touch' with the changing cultures of their readers, a necessary process in the successful marketing of magazines.

Mandi Norwood (whom I interviewed in January 1997) is now editor of the UK edition of *Cosmopolitan*. She summarized both the informal and formal methods that she uses to keep in touch with the dynamic cultures of the *Cosmo* readership. These methods are, she argues, particularly important to her work on *Cosmopolitan* as she is in her thirties and therefore older than the typical 'Cosmo girl'. Informal methods of research include 'my own guts and my own instinct', reading readers' letters, and being 'receptive to the mood of the country and the mood of young women'. Her methods also embrace listening to her staff and involving their contributions, and she describes them as 'mid-twenties and still very much in touch'. Norwood combines these informal methods with more formal techniques of reader research, although 'we don't do heaps of market research [and] I certainly won't let it dictate'.

Norwood was powerfully conscious as to what could be represented within the pages of *Cosmopolitan*, and it is evident that her efforts to acquire knowledge about the cultures of young women accounts for her phenomenal success as a magazine editor. She describes her position as 'autonomous'; she, and she alone, polices the content of the magazine, answerable to the National Magazine Company only if there is a problem with content after publication or if sales were to fall. In her time at *Cosmopolitan*, she claimed, no such issues had arisen. Norwood argued that a magazine which attempted to shape the values of readers, as opposed to reflecting them, would offer a cautionary tale for those who believe that women's magazines are agents in the formation of the sexual behaviour of young women. On the subject of the sexual content in women's magazines, she was adamant that this content was not only present in *Cosmopolitan* to improve its sales. She argued that critics who took a dim view of sexual content were failing to understand the lives of young women, and suggested that they 'Wake up to the real world!'

SHIFTING CULTURES OF FEMININITY IN THE 1990s

Any understanding of the experiences of young women in the 1990s must be situated in relation to broader shifts in the social formations of late twentieth century Britain. 'Society' can no longer be understood as the crowd, a homogeneous mass; greater understanding comes from an appreciation of fragmentation and diversity in social formations. 'Society' is increasingly made up of numerous groups that hold many disparate views on issues as diverse as music and travel, as well as on sexual morality. In the 1990s, the idea that there is a single 'code' for sexual behaviour that should be held by all people in a society is frequently contested, and even dismissed. The internationalisation of the media, as well as the emergence of social movements in Britain after the Second World War, such as gay liberation and feminism, have in part contributed to an increased awareness of the presence of a 'plurality' of moral perspectives in British society, and to increased debate about moral issues including the choice and regulation of sexual activity (Bocock 1997, p. 102).

It is difficult to make generalisations about changes in women's lives during this period, but Angela McRobbie has observed that recent years have witnessed a climate of change and a new ' "semi-structure of feeling" ' which indicates 'some deep and apparently irreversible shift across the whole social domain' (McRobbie 1997a, p. 159). Young women's lives, and particularly their position in relation to the family, are qualitatively different from those of their mothers. Part of the reason for these shifts in the world view of young women is due to the growing perception that work and careers are central to the lives of women, who are no longer compelled to see men and marriage as the only routes to success.

McRobbie argues that these shifts in the cultures of femininity find their symbolic forms most visibly in consumer culture, on television programmes such as *The Girlie Show*, in commercial Hollywood films such as *Clueless*, and especially in the pages of magazines which show 'girls "behaving badly" ' (ibid.). Bill Osgerby has also noted the presence of more assertive and rebellious forms of feminine identity in consumer culture, arguing that they have been especially visible in the field of mainstream British pop (Osgerby 1998, p. 61). In particular, the recent popularity of the Spice Girls, with their 'Girl Power' slogan, and 'blend of brazen cheek, fun-seeking energy and confident sexuality' suggests a culturally visible form of femininity which, although largely 'manufactured' by the music industry, can be read as partially transgressing traditional norms and conventions (ibid.).

Given that magazine producers are necessarily concerned with remaining close to the cultures of their readers, it is unsurprising that new representations of female sexualities have appeared in the pages of successful women's magazines. Yet the sexual content of the magazines, as I have argued, is popularly discussed in terms of the horrors of declining morality by media commentators, who see 'sex' as a sales gimmick which will appeal to the more prurient natures of vulnerable readers.

It is interesting, however, that the concerns of moral commentators about the coverage of sex-related issues in women's magazines have centred upon the explicitness of the information, and have tended not to involve accusations of misinformation. It is extremely rare that women's magazines are accused of actually misleading their readers in such matters, and the quality of journalism is widely recognised to be high. *Marie Claire*, for example, has won prestigious awards for the quality of its coverage of issues relating to women's health and human rights, whilst *Cosmopolitan* has run effective campaigns which aim to highlight women's health issues where official routes have failed, such as its recent campaign to promote the safer screening of cervical cancer.

A review of the role of magazines for young teenage women in the sexual health education of young people, which was conducted by Kaye Wellings (London School of Hygiene and Tropical Medicine) for TMAP, also found the quality of the information to be commendable, particularly in the features designed to help young people to adopt routine safer sex behaviour (Wellings 1996). Wellings noted that, unlike sex education from school and official health education leaflets, young women's magazines had a unique capacity to 'discuss sex frankly and openly, to raise issues relating to sexual desire and pleasure and to provide role models with whom young women can identify' (ibid.). She concluded, in fact, that the information on sexual behaviour, might actually 'empower women', and enable them to 'make effective choices and exercise control over their own lives'. They can also help provide a language with which sex can be discussed and offer guidance on a 'script' for use in sexual encounters (ibid.).

Some reservations were expressed in the report about the uniformity and lack of diversity in the role models which the magazines offered young people (for example, heterosexual relationships are accepted as the norm in the popular women's press), and this is probably because women's magazines are ultimately capitalist enterprises, which offer readers representations of femininity which are highly commercial. They must appeal to advertisers who increasingly use heterosexual love to sexualise products, such as cosmetics and clothes, in their campaigns.[8]

Although moral commentators have argued that women's magazines are commercial products, and therefore have greater potential for irresponsibility and exploitation in their content, their publishers and journalists are, in fact, restricted by a number of formal and informal regulatory factors which are closely related to the processes of magazine production. Magazine professionals, as they attempt to juggle the conflicting definitions from readers, advertisers and publishers of a 'successful' women's magazine, have to consider these factors on a day to day basis. Although they are frequently represented as having a 'free rein', magazine producers are, in reality, highly constrained by the requirements of the marketplace, advertisers and readers. For magazine producers the bottom line when assessing whether or not a magazine is successful is a combination of prestige and profit. Advertisers seek magazines which will penetrate appropriate markets for their products. For readers, a 'successful' magazine needs to simultaneously entertain and correspond to the realities of their daily lives.

All of these definitions regulate the content and representations of women's magazines in some way. Magazine producers face ethical dilemmas in relation to the conflict of the interests of the reader with commercial interests on a day to day basis. Out of deference to particular advertisers and/or companies, magazine producers may, for example, have to consider backing away from covering particular stories (such as, for instance, the testing of cosmetics on animals, or the low pay of those working in fashion manufacturing). They may also be faced with particular moral dilemmas in choosing to cover controversial topics such as abortion, homosexuality, child abuse, and pornography. They negotiate a path that must be attractive for advertisers, inoffensive for distributors, profitable and prestigious for their employers, and appealing and informative for readers. In this sense, the issues they face are no different in kind to the issues facing other commercial media producers such as those in television and radio.

Women's magazines in the 1990s are part of the broader debates about sexual morality and social change. Their efforts to appeal to readers, marketers and advertisers have compelled them to represent an increasingly diverse set of life choices for women. But as recent scholarship on women's magazines has shown, the acknowledgement of new sexual moralities within magazines does not mean that the reader has been forcibly persuaded to adopt the life style and world views on offer. Magazines perform a wide range of functions in the lives of women, and at the most it can be argued that magazines for women inform their readers about a broad range of lifestyle choices, which they can integrate into their knowledge and their pre-existent moralities.

It can be argued, that the objection of traditional moralists to the content of young women's magazines is less a moral objection, than an expression of deep rooted anxieties towards profound shifts in gender relationships that are fundamentally altering the lives of women, and ultimately the shape of British society in the 1990s. The styles of life represented in women's magazines should be considered as no less 'moral' than those offered to women of previous generations. The producers of magazines for young women are no less ethical. Young women's demands for equality of gender relations in all facets of their lives indicate that instead of rejecting moral standards, women are consciously dealing with moral issues on an everyday basis. The calls among young women for women's magazines which offer a wide range of high quality information on aspects of their lives, including sexual matters, is one way of ensuring that they have access to knowledge which will assist them to confront the moral issues of discrimination and prejudice which they frequently encounter. The concerns as to the effects they are having are, perhaps, best understood in a historical context, for the knowledge and awareness that such magazines provide may ultimately help young women to gain greater assurance and genuine equality in their relationships with men. The ethical framework within which women's magazines function enables producers to provide information and respond, within commercial parameters, to the demands of young women in contemporary society.

I would like to express a debt of gratitude to Mandi Norwood for granting me an interview, to Ulla Outtrup and Birgitte Ramsø Thomsen for sharing the findings of their research with me, and to Kevin Gough-Yates for his thorough and helpful comments on several drafts of this paper.

ENDNOTES

1. In the period 1 January 1998 to 30 June 1998 *Sugar* achieved average total sales of 459 984 and *Cosmopolitan* sales of 472 263 (source: Audit Bureau of Circulation).
2. The link between commercial operations and processes of production, distribution and consumption were foregrounded in early cultural studies work which offered programmatic agendas for British Cultural Studies, the most influential being Stuart Hall's (1980) 'Encoding/Decoding' paradigm and Richard Johnson's (1986/87) 'cultural circuit' model. More recently, Douglas Kellner (1997) and Angela McRobbie (1997b) have lamented the absence of studies which fully realise the implications of the 'cultural circuit', arguing for a return to examinations of the culture industries which considers each moment of the cultural circuit in relation to others.
3. Here Beetham cites the notorious campaign of journalist W.T. Stead in the *Pall Mall Gazette*, which dramatically personalised the story of a girl who had been bought at the age of thirteen and taken to a brothel, which resulted in the passing of the Criminal Law Amendment Act as a measure to protect working-class women against 'the predatory upper-class male' (Beetham 1996, p. 125).
4. See, for example, Gaudoin (1997), Anderson and Mosbacher (1997b) and Grant (1997).
5. Angela McRobbie explores these issues further in McRobbie (1994, 1997a).
6. Bill Osgerby (1998) discusses the relationship of this to broaden concerns about media, youth and crime.
7. Other studies of women's magazines which adopt similar approaches, include Joy Leman (1980), Nona Glazer (1980), Sandra Hebron (1983) and Jacqueline Blix (1992).
8. See Stevi Jackson (1996) for a further discussion of the endorsement of heterosexuality in the pages of young women's magazines.

REFERENCES

Ahmed, K. (1997) 'Sex, sex, and a bit of fashion on the side', *The Guardian*, 24 November.

Anderson, D. and Mosbacher, M., eds (1997a) *The British Woman Today: A qualitative survey of the images in women's magazines*, London: The Social Affairs Unit.

Anderson, D. and Mosbacher, M. (1997b) 'Sex mad, silly and selfish,' *The Guardian*, 24 November.

Ballaster, R., Beetham, M., Frazer, E. and Hebron, S. (1991) *Women's Worlds: Ideology, Femininity and the Woman's Magazine*, Basingstoke: Macmillan.

Beetham, M. (1996) *A Magazine of Her Own? Domesticity and Desire in the Woman's Magazine, 1800–1914*, London and New York: Routledge.

Bennett, C. (1995) 'Sex! Sex! Sex! How dull can it possibly get?', *The Guardian*, 16 September.

Blix, J. (1992) 'A Place to Resist: Re-evaluating Women's Magazines', *Journal of Communication Inquiry*, **16**(1).

Bocock, R. (1997) 'Choice and Regulation: Sexual Moralities,' in *Media and Cultural Regulation*, Kenneth Thompson, ed., London: Sage.

Braithwaite, B. (1995) *Women's Magazines: The First 300 Years*, London: Peter Owen.

Burrows, L. (1997) 'The divergent character of women's magazines: uneventful gentility, undue reverence and unabashed crudity', in *The British Woman Today: A qualitative survey of the images in women's magazines*, Digby Anderson and Michael Mosbacher, eds. London: The Social Affairs Unit.

Cook, S. (1992) 'Sweet sell of sexcess', *The Guardian*, 27 July.

Craik, J. (1994) *The Face of Fashion: Cultural Studies in Fashion*, London and New York: Routledge.

Ferguson, M. and Golding, P. (1997) *Cultural Studies in Question*, London: Sage.

Ferguson, M. (1983) *Forever Feminine: Women's Magazines and the Cult of Femininity*, London: Heinemann.

Frazer, E. (1987) 'Teenage Girls Reading Jackie', in *Media Culture and Society*, **9**.

Gaudoin, T. (1997) 'Nothing but sex, clothes and boyfriends?' *The Times*, 24 November.

Glazer, N. (1980) 'Overworking the Working Woman: The Double Day in a Mass Magazine', *Women's Studies International Quarterly*, **3**(1).

Grant, L. (1997) 'Meanwhile, back in the real world', *The Guardian*, 25 November.

Hall, S. (1980) 'Encoding/Decoding' in *Culture, Media and Language*, Stuart Hall *et al.*, eds., London: Hutchinson.

Hebron, S. (1983) '*Jackie* and *Woman's Own:* Ideological Work and the Social Construction of Gender Identity'. Unpublished BA (Hons) dissertation, Department of Communications Studies, Sheffield City Polytechnic.

Hermes, J. (1993) 'Media, Meaning and Everyday Life,' *Cultural Studies*, **7**(3).

Hermes, J. (1995) *Reading Women's Magazines: An Analysis of Everyday Media Use*, Cambridge: Polity.

Jackson, S. (1996) 'Ignorance is Bliss, when you're Just Seventeen', *Trouble and Strife*, **33**.

Johnson, R. (1986/87) 'What is cultural studies anyway?', Social Text 16 reprinted in *What is Cultural Studies? A Reader*, John Storey, ed., London: Arnold, 1997.

Kehily, M.J. (1999) 'More Sugar? Teenage magazines, gender displays and sexual learning', *European Journal of Cultural Studies*, **2**(1).

Kellner, D. (1997) 'Overcoming the Divide: Cultural Studies and Political Economy', in *Cultural Studies in Question*, Marjorie Ferguson and Peter Golding eds. London: Sage.

Leman, J. (1980) 'The Advice of a Real Friend': Codes of Intimacy and Oppression in Women's Magazines 1937–1955,' *Women's Studies International Quarterly*, **3**(1).

Locks, I. (1996) Teenage Magazines – The British Experience, Periodical Publishers Association, London, 15 May.

McCracken, H. (1993) *Decoding Women's Magazines: From Mademoiselle to Ms*, Basingstoke: Macmillan.

Mcdonald, M. (1995) *Representing Women: Myths of Femininity in the Popular Media*, London: Arnold.

McRobbie, A. (1996) 'More! New Sexualities in Girls' and Womens's Magazines', in *Cultural Studies and Communications*, James Curran, David Morley and Valerie Walkerdine, eds., London: Edward Arnold.

McRobbie, A. (1997a) 'Pecs and penises: the meaning of girlie culture', *Soundings: A Journal of Politics and Culture*, **5**.

McRobbie, A. (1997b) 'The Es and the Anti-Es: New Questions for Feminism and Cultural Studies', in *Cultural Studies in Question*, Marjorie Ferguson and Peter Golding, eds., London: Sage.

McRobbie, A. (1994) 'The moral panic in the age of the postmodern mass media', in *Postmodernism and Popular Culture*, London and New York: Routledge.

McRobbie, A. (1991) *Feminism and Youth Culture*, Basingstoke: Macmillan.

Murray, J. (1991) 'Bad Press: Representations of AIDS in the Media', *Cultural Studies from Birmingham*, **1**.

Osgerby, B. (1998) *Youth in Britain since 1945*, Oxford: Blackwell.

Outtrup, U. and Ramsø Thomsen, B. (1994) Mixed Messages – Mixed Feelings: Women Reading *Cosmopolitan*. Unpublished MA dissertation, Denmark: Department of Languages and Culture, Roskilde Universitetscenter).

Steiner, L. (1991) 'Oppositional Decoding as an Act of Resistance' in *Critical Perspectives on Media and Society*, R. K. Avery and D. Eason eds. New York: Guilford Press.

Sullivan, C. (1996) 'Sex!', *The Guardian*, 18 June.

Wellings, K. (1996) '*The Role of Teenage Magazines in the Sexual Health of Young People: A Briefing Document.*' TMAP Research for the Periodical Publishers Association: November 1996.

Winship, J. (1987) *Inside Women's Magazines*, London: Pandora.

13 A social drama: media violence controversies and anti-violence campaign groups

Annette Hill

INTRODUCTION

The role of anti-violence campaign groups in relation to media violence controversies has received little attention in the discipline of media ethics. It is my intention in this chapter to outline the problematic ethical situation that emerges when we look at the way in which British anti-violence campaign groups target media violence as a moral and environmental hazard. Media violence is perceived to be both hazardous to vulnerable victims, such as children, and to the cultural environment as a whole. Films such as *Child's Play 3* (Jack Bender 1993) or *Natural Born Killers* (Oliver Stone 1994) are labelled as evil and depraved; it is alleged that such films are the cause of real violence and symbolic of a lack of morality in society. Media violence is presented as a moral risk, and specific controversies such as the murder of James Bulger, or the Dunblane massacre spark a moral panic that can be seen to be part of the 'social drama of risk' (Palmlund 1992), a theory that will be outlined in order to help us understand more about anti-violence campaign groups and the ethical position they take with regard to media violence. These campaign groups adopt a public ethical standard with regard to the protection of children and moral values that is somewhat different from their private ethical position as organisations who believe in a way of life based on the teachings of the bible. The social drama of media violence controversies in many ways masks the intentions of anti-violence campaign groups who would like to see a mass media that is committed to religious morality, not moral plurality.

A BRIEF OVERVIEW OF BRITISH ANTI-VIOLENCE CAMPAIGN GROUPS

The most vocal British anti-violence campaign groups are The National Viewers and Listeners' Association (NVALA), Christian Action Research and Education (CARE) and the Movement for Christian Democracy (MCD).[1] What the NVALA, CARE and the MCD have in common is a shared belief that contemporary society has lost touch with religious morality. These associations do not only campaign to reduce levels of media violence. As Barratt (1997, p. 1) points out:

These groups are engaged in a political struggle over the lifestyle choices of society: attacks on television, cinema and video form only one front in the battle against 'permissive society' which stands opposed to the fundamentalist Christian ideal. Both CARE and MCD actively campaign against homosexuality, abortion, euthanasia, genetic engineering, and single-parenthood in their support of 'traditional' family life underpinned by Christian morality.

Media violence is only one factor in the struggle to maintain religious morality, however, before focusing on why media violence has been chosen to be one of the most visible campaign agendas in the 1990s, it is necessary to take a brief look at the background history to these organisations.

In 1964, Mary Whitehouse and Norah Buckland began 'The Clean-up TV Campaign' which targeted the 'permissive society' and what was perceived to be a sharp, moral decline in standards of taste and decency on British television, in particular the BBC. The first meeting was attended by 2000 people, and after this the NVALA was established in 1965. The NVALA campaign through private lobbying and court cases. They campaign against a diverse range of media texts. For example, in the 1970s the NVALA campaigned against the BBC television programme *Till Death Us Do Part, Oz* magazine, and *Gay News* (see Newburn 1992).

In many ways Mrs Whitehouse was responding to what she perceived as 'the new morality' (ibid., p. 39), which involved a decline in the church's authority regarding moral standards. This decline was symbolised by John Robinson's book *Honest to God*, published in 1963:

[Robinson argued] that nothing of itself could be labelled as wrong, an argument which became associated with a school of thought known as 'situational ethics' and which, described more fully, suggested that 'our moral decisions must be guided by the actual relationships between the persons concerned at a particular time in a particular situation, and compassion for persons overrides all law. The only intrinsic evil is lack of love' (ibid., p. 175).

Robinson's ethical position is in many ways a forerunner for Joseph Fletcher's *Situation Ethics* (1966) which argued that a particular type of love, one inspired by God, can be applied to any ethical situation. This type of ethical theory builds upon moral relativism, where universal ethical principles cannot be applied to every moral dilemma; instead, each ethical situation must be considered on its own merits (Gordon *et al.*, 1996, p. 21).

The NVALA was a direct response to this type of situational ethics which Whitehouse saw as undermining the principles of the church. Film and television were one prominent example of this 'new morality', a morality which was not based on the teachings of the bible. The NVALA campaigns for a 'a set of firm traditional (essentially Christian) moral principles that outline those forms of behaviour that are condemned and those that are not' (Newburn 1992, p. 175). The NVALA state:

The Association campaigns for: higher standards in the media; the eradication of pornography and violence; bad language and blasphemy to be cleaned up; . . . wholesome family viewing helping to strengthen marriage and family life; . . . the portrayal of good moral behaviour and standards.[2]

The NVALA clearly state that standards of taste and decency and family values should be upheld in television programmes.[3] However, because the NVALA is a religious organisation, their position is also one of religious morality, or divine command theory, whereby belief and faith in the bible is thought to be sufficient ethical guidance for society (Gordon *et al.*, 1996, p. 15).

The same ethical positions are also adopted by CARE and MCD. CARE is a Christian charity that specializes in issues affecting family life, in particular children. It began as the Nationwide Festival of Light (NFOL) in 1971, but quickly re-organized itself to become a more effective lobbying organisation. It now has a membership of 80 000, and a head office only five minutes away from the Houses of Parliament (see Barratt 1995, p. 22). Thompson (1992) describes the background to this organisation:

CARE provides educational material relating fundamentalist beliefs to politics; co-ordinates a nation-wide network of Christian welfare programmes for the casualties of the 'permissive society' – single parents, pregnant girls and drug addicts; provides the resources and expertise for Christians to be involved in politics; lobbies local and national government through its core-groups in each constituency and representation at national level; and also helps to co-ordinate the political activities of fundamentalists who have employment in the medical, teaching and social welfare professions (ibid., p. 77).

Unlike the NVALA, CARE do not campaign through private lobbying or court cases, but rather concentrate on encouraging political activism and direct involvement in the political process. CARE (1994, pp. 27, 28, 33) states:

It has been involved in assessing the impact of the media on society for over twenty years. Through its separate non-charitable lobbying arm, CARE Campaigns, CARE has sought changes to legislation affecting broadcasting and other media. In particular, we have been involved with the Protection of Children Act 1978, the Indecent Displays (Control) Act 1981, the Local Government (Miscellaneous Provisions) Act 1982, the Video Recordings Act 1984, the Broadcasting Act 1990 and several Parliamentary attempts to reform the 1959 Obscene Publications Act ... CARE believes that violent and sexually explicit videos, television and other media can have a very damaging effect on children, especially if they have repeated exposure to such media . . . We recommend a review of the law to assess the differences in arrangements for controlling the content of different media.

As can be seen from this extract taken from the Home Affairs Committee on Video Violence and Young Offenders (1994), CARE is a campaign group of some power. It has set up a non-charitable lobby group, CARE Campaigns, in order to campaign successfully against, among other things, media violence.

The MCD is a relatively recent organisation, whose most prominent member, the former Liberal Democrat MP, David Alton, has conducted high profile campaigns against abortion and media violence. It has a membership of over 10 000, and a monthly newsletter, *The Christian Democrat* (Barratt 1997, p. 1). Alton and the MCD campaign to reduce the corrupting effects of the media on audiences, in particular children; they campaign to alter legislation regarding cinema, television and video in order that universal principles (based on Christian values) are adopted in relation to media content in Britain. This fact ensures that this organisation also adopts the ethical position of religious morality, but this is something that Alton and the MCD are at pains to suppress. At the time of the James Bulger case and the debate about media violence, Alton wrote: 'the MCD should be very careful with the media. We could find ourselves being caricatured as a worthy but eccentric God-squad and that would damage us in the future. We have to go way beyond the Christian constituency in order to win some of these arguments.'[4] Thus we can see that MCD are sensitive to the unpopularity of an ethical position such as religious morality, and adopt a more secular approach when discussing such controversies as media violence.

MEDIA VIOLENCE CONTROVERSIES AND THE SOCIAL DRAMA OF RISK

In the previous section, we began to touch on the role that MCD and CARE played in the media violence controversy surrounding the murder of James Bulger. A fuller account will be given in this section, in order that we can understand why media violence has been chosen by these organisations as a high profile campaign. The controversy surrounding 'video nasties' and the James Bulger case shall be used as a case study in relation to the social drama of risk, a theory developed by Ingmar Palmlund (1992) which examines the role of emotional drama in risk controversies, specifically environmental risks.

There has been a great deal of literature which has examined the relationship between moral panics and media violence, in particular see Pearson (1983), Barker (1984) and Barker and Petley (1997), amongst others, for a detailed discussion of the way in which media violence has been a subject of ethical concern for some time. There is not time here to engage in a discussion about media effects, but this is a topic that certainly dominates ethical discussions of media violence and pornography (see Day 1991; Gordon *et al.* 1996). We can see from the way in which NVALA, or the MCD campaign to reduce levels of media violence in society that these organisations are critical of current regulatory bodies such as the British Board of Film Classification (BBFC), the Broadcasting Standards Commission (BSC), and the Independent Television Commission (ITC), and their approach to the issue of media violence. The BBFC, BSC, and ITC seek a moderate solution to this ethical problem, considering each case in context before they reach decisions about whether a film or TV programme may be harmful or not to viewers.[5] The BBFC and the BSC take into account the alleged negative effects of media violence (which include the copycat effect, where someone may be triggered into committing an act of violence after watching a film or TV programme which contains violence) but they consider each case in point before reaching a decision. This is the opposite approach to anti-violence campaign groups who would like to see a substantial reduction in current levels of media violence because of the alleged harm it may cause to innocent people, especially children.

The murder of James Bulger is an example of how the alleged risks of media violence can become caught up in a wider discussion about family values and ethical standards in society. In 1993, two-year-old James Bulger was murdered by two ten-year-old boys. Buckingham (1996, p. 21) writes:

In the weeks following their arrest, the Prime Minister and the Home Secretary both made high profile speeches about the need to curb television violence. Television executives were called to account, and new guidelines on TV violence were promised ... the NVALA also used the Bulger case as fuel for its attacks on television violence, eventually culminating in a 'research report' sensitively titled 'Did he die in vain?'

The judge involved in this case suggested that the two boys may have been influenced by violent video films, and despite any evidence to suggest that either boy had watched this film, the video *Child's Play 3* became linked with this crime. It was suggested that there were similarities with this film and the death of James Bulger, and the national press campaigned to have this video withdrawn from circulation, the *Sun* newspaper even printing a front page depicting copies of this film on fire with the headline 'For the sake of ALL our kids, BURN YOUR VIDEO NASTY' (cited in Buckingham 1996, p. 23). Both Barker (1997) and Buckingham (1996) have shown that the film bears no resemblance to the way in which James Bulger was murdered, but this is not the point. The point is that this horrific murder enabled campaign groups such as the NVALA, CARE and MCD to mobilise their campaign against media violence so that they were seen to respond directly to popular press and public concerns about youth and violence in society.

The MCD asked Elizabeth Newson to produce a report on the 'risks' of media violence to children, and her report 'Video Violence and the Protection of Children' claimed that there was undeniable evidence that a causal link exists between media violence and real violence. The Newson Report claimed that the 'liberal ideals of freedom of expression' are no longer appropriate to the 'sadistic cruelty' that is now available on our television screens; 'by restricting such material from home viewing, society must take on a necessary responsibility in protecting children from this as from other forms of child abuse' (Newson 1994, p. 7). This claim that the 'permissive society' and the right to freedom of expression are the root of the problem concerning media violence is one that we encountered when we looked at the growth of the NVALA in the 1960s. Newson undertakes no scientific research of her own, but rather draws upon the guiding principles of the MCD and similar campaign groups, to attack current regulation of film and television and video.

This report was distributed to the national press, with the support of 33 professionals working with children, ten days before David Alton was to table an amendment to the Criminal Justice and Public Order Bill. This Bill would require that the BBFC should pay particular attention to the harm or potential harm that children may be subject to as a result of watching violent scenes in video films, including 18 certificate films intended for an adult audience. The Newson Report was a great victory for the MCD. It was hailed by the national press as evidence that academics were no longer sceptical of media effects. This was a successful campaign plan. As Barratt (1997, p. 1) notes:

Public attention was captured not because the majority of people want to see the re-instatement of fundamentalist Christian doctrine at the heart of the nation, but because a trusted commentator was offering proof (or what was taken as proof) that the media can have a deleterious effect on children. But by uncritically supporting this position, the wider aims and objectives of the evangelicals are being served by the public; and this without any members of the public even being aware of the existence of these groups.

The result of the Newson Report and a sustained attack on media violence in the national press can be seen in the amendment to the Criminal Justice and Public Order Act (1994) and the Video Recordings Act (1994) which requires that the BBFC must pay specific attention to scenes of violence, drug-use and sexual behaviour in any video recording.

Ingmar Palmlund's concept of the social drama of risk is a concept that is useful to apply to media violence controversies. Palmlund believes that 'When society deals with risks . . . it is engaged in a political process' (1992, p. 198).The social drama of risk is when society becomes caught up in the emotional drama of a risk conflict, a conflict that takes centre stage. This risk conflict, and here Palmlund is talking about environmental hazards, must have emotional appeal, where 'loss, grief and moral responsibility' can become part of the tragedy (ibid., p. 201).

Palmlund lists five criteria which must be met if a specific technological risk will become a social controversy:

1 The risk should be tied to effects that appear familiar and close to people;
2 The effects should stir up emotions of fright and fear;
3 The risk should concern a large or important enough group of people for politicians and senior administrators to worry about their support;

4 Raising the issue of risk in national politics should not obviously threaten fundamental national interests of major importance;

5 The issue should ideally be such that the mass media can grasp it and assist politicians in placing it and keeping it on the agenda in national politics so as to satisfy the public's need of spectacular drama (ibid., p. 210).

If we substitute technological risk for moral risk, and if we use the James Bulger case as an example of the 'risks' of media violence, there are striking similarities between Palmlund's criteria for a risk controversy and a media violence controversy.

First, the death of James Bulger appeared familiar and close to people; there appeared to be no explanation for such a violent death, it was a random act of violence which could have happened to anyone, in any part of the country. The death of a child, in particular, increased public concern for the welfare of children in society as a whole, and parents voiced an anxiety that children were growing up in an amoral world. Second, the discussion about the alleged negative effects of violent video films, in particular *Child's Play 3* and the Newson Report, stirred up feelings of fright and fear in the general public as it now appeared that everyone's children could be vulnerable to the 'risks' of media violence. *The Sun*'s headline 'For the sake of ALL our kids, BURN YOUR VIDEO NASTY' is evidence of this widespread panic that 'video nasties' are hazardous to all children. Third, the then Prime Minister, John Major, and the then Home Secretary, Michael Howard, had both spoken out about the need to reduce media violence in society directly after the death of James Bulger. This is in part because the Conservative party wished to appear tough on crime and disorder, and one way for them to be seen to address the problem of juvenile crime was to attack the entertainment industry for corrupting the young. This supports the beliefs of politicians such as David Alton and campaign groups like MCD and CARE, who also know that there is public support for this approach to the problem of how to deal with real violence in society, a problem that a large proportion of the public wish to see resolved. Fourth, by suggesting that media violence is a primary cause of violence in society, amendments to the Criminal Justice and Public Order Bill can be seen to be quick-fix solutions that do not really address the long-term problem of the causes of real violence in society, such as unemployment or poor living conditions. Fifth, the way in which the mass media assisted campaign groups and politicians to keep media violence on the national agenda in 1994 certainly satisfied the public's need for spectacular drama: talk shows, radio programmes, news editorials, letters pages all discussed the reasons why such a violent act could have happened to someone so young. The day after the Alton amendment had been discussed in parliament, the *Daily Mirror* ran this dramatic headline: 'BANNED – Thanks to your *Daily Mirror*' (cited in Buckingham 1996, p. 31).

Anti-violence campaign groups like MCD, NVALA or CARE know that media violence is a political issue, and they choose to campaign to reduce the 'risks' of media violence because this allows them to campaign for the return of family values, clear moral guidelines and a society that acknowledges the authority of the church, above other secular organisations, such as the BBFC, or the BSC. These campaign groups adopt specific roles in the social drama of the risks of media violence. For example, the 'risk bearer' in Palmlund's view, must have an advocate, and it must have a clear enemy (1992, p. 204). Thus, innocent children are defended by these campaign groups in order to defeat the evil monster 'video nasties'. 'Risk researchers' must gather information to help the 'risk bearer's advocate' (see Elizabeth Newson), and a 'risk arbiter' must seek to resolve the conflict (see the government's amendment to the Criminal Justice Act). Throughout all of this, the 'risk informers in the mass media are engaged in placing the issues on the public agenda and scrutinising the action' (ibid.). The information distributed to the press by groups like MCD (for example, the Newson Report) act as an important means of placing issues such as media violence on the public agenda. The media's function, according to Palmlund, 'is analogous to that of the chorus in classical dramas – portioning out praise and blame' (ibid.). Palmlund has in mind roles in classical tragedy, and the case study of the James Bulger case shows there are dramatic roles to be played by specific groups in relation to media violence controversies, and anti-violence campaign groups ensure that they are perceived to be the heroes in this social drama.

ETHICS AND MEDIA VIOLENCE

The discussion about the role of anti-violence campaign groups in relation to media violence controversies has served to show how complex this situation is in relation to theories concerning ethics. On the one hand, anti-violence campaign groups demand that current levels of media violence should be substantially reduced, and in some cases banned altogether from our film or television screens. This is because, in theory, media violence is hazardous and dangerous to certain 'vulnerable' members of the public. These campaign groups believe they represent the general public when they argue that films such as *Child's Play 3*, or *Natural Born Killers* should not be part of our society, because it is not worth the risk to endanger the lives of innocent people, especially children. Those who oppose such campaign groups defend the right to freedom of expression (see French 1996). Children should be protected from media violence, but this does not mean to say that all artists should eliminate any reference to violence. These defenders of freedom of expression are generally seen to adopt a liberal approach, and in relation to campaign groups, are often presented as defenders of a 'permissive society', everything that organisations such as CARE or the NVALA wish to campaign against.

Article 10 of the European Convention of Human Rights has two parts which neatly sum up these opposing ethical positions. Part 1 states that: 'Everyone has the right to freedom of expression. This right shall include freedom to hold opinions and receive and impart information and ideas without interference by public authority...' However, part 2 states: 'The exercise of these freedoms, since it carries with it duties and responsibilities, may be subject to such formalities, conditions, restrictions or penalties as prescribed by law ...' The prevention of disorder or crime, and the protection of health or morals come under the conditions as prescribed by law, and it is in the second part of Article 10 that organisations such as MCD, or CARE concentrate their campaigns against media violence. Despite the fact that everyone has the right to freedom of expression, such expression should not threaten the health or morals of the general public.

Regulatory bodies such as the Broadcasting Standards Commission, the Independent Television Commission or the British Board of Film Classification adopt a moderate solution to this ethical problem. On the one hand, these regulatory bodies enforce codes of conduct, and undertake to control existing levels of media violence. For example, the BSC and ITC demand that television companies adhere to the 9 o'clock watershed, and only show programmes of a more adult nature after 9 o'clock in the evening. The BBFC views all movies and videos before they are made available to the general public, and will cut or ban certain scenes or films if they believe that such material may be harmful to viewers, in particular children. At the same time, these organisations also acknowledge that not all media violence should be banned from our screens, and television programmes such as *Cracker*, or films such as *Natural Born Killers* can be seen by British audiences, despite the fact that they are perceived to be controversial in nature. Thus, *Cracker* is transmitted after the watershed on our television screens and *Natural Born Killers* was edited to reduce the violent content, before it was given an 18 certificate for its cinematic release in 1994.

However, what this chapter has shown is that the issue of media violence is more complicated than this. In relation to ethics, for example, the distinctions between right and wrong are far from clear in discussions of media violence. For anti-violence campaign groups, what is right and wrong is based on the divine command theory. The bible dictates what is right and wrong. This is quite different to discussions in the national press about the legitimacy of media violence, where right and wrong is discussed in relation to secular beliefs, such as scientific proof that media violence can cause harm to children. These contesting claims about what is right and what is wrong are not openly discussed in the public domain. Thus, fictional violence is presented by anti-violence campaign groups as a moral risk, as a form of entertainment that is unethical for a secular society, when what is really being discussed are the principles of a 'permissive society' that values freedom of expression and moral plurality.

Campaign groups such as NVALA, CARE and the MCD, who campaign against abortion, homosexuality, single parenthood as well as media violence, adopt an ethical position that is one of religious morality. Indeed, the NVALA specifically responded to situational ethics in the 1960s by asserting that religious morality and the divine command theory are viable (if not the only) options for contemporary society. These organisations, in particular the MCD, mislead the general public, misrepresenting information in order to achieve the end result of reducing the moral risks of mass media, a media that is seen to 'actively promote humanistic and amoral lifestyle choices' (Barratt 1997, p. 2).

There is no simple way to resolve this complex ethical issue. One solution would be for these organisations to be more open about the ideological basis to their arguments against media violence. This would not solve the problem of how to balance freedom of expression with the need to control and regulate media violence, and it would not stop pro-censorship campaigners from dramatising the 'risks' of media violence, but it would at least ensure that the public and regulatory bodies could make an informed decision based on all the evidence, rather than a partial presentation of the alleged risks of media violence.

ENDNOTES

1. Other organisations include the Community Standards Association (CSA). The CSA was initiated by Ms Whitacker and contained organisations across the country who campaigned against pornography, amongst other things. See Thompson (1992) for more details. The Voice of the Listener and Viewer (VLV), is an independent association which focuses on maintaining 'quality, diversity and independence in British Broadcasting'. The VLV is not to be confused with the NVALA, which is quite a different organisation altogether.
2. This quotation about the VLV is taken from a personal letter, 21/7/98.
3. This is essentially a de-ontological ethical position. For further discussion of this see Day (1991) and Gordon, Kittross and Reuss (1996).
4. Cited in Barratt, (1997, p. 1) taken from *The Christian Democrat*, June 1994.
5. This position can be examined in relation to Aristotle's Golden Mean (Day 1991; Gordon *et al.* 1996).

REFERENCES

Barker, M., ed. (1984) *The Video Nasties: Freedom and Censorship in the Media*, London: Pluto Press.

Barker, M. (1997) 'The Newson Report' in Barker, M. and Petley, J. eds, *Ill Effects: the Media/Violence Debate*. London: Routledge, pp. 12–31.

Barker, M. and Petley, J., eds (1997) *Ill Effects: the Media/Violence Debate*, London: Routledge.

Barratt, J.A.B. (1995) Moral Minorities in Sight and Sound, *Forbidden Cinema Supplement*, **22**(6) pp. 22–23.

Barratt, J.A.B. (1997) '*Faith over Reason*', (unpublished) available on Web Site http://www.users.dircon.co.uk/~ajbb/response.html

Buckingham, D. (1996) *Moving Images: Understanding Children's Emotional Responses to Television*, Manchester: Manchester University Press.

CARE (Christian Action Research and Education: (1994) 'Evidence to the Home Affairs Committee', London: HMSO, pp. 27–33.

Day, L.A. (1991) *Ethics in Media Communications and Controversies*, 2nd edn, Belmont, CA: Wadsworth.

French, K., ed. (1996) *Screen Violence*, London: Bloomsbury.

Gordon, A.D., Kittross, J.M. and Reuss, C. (1996) *Controversies in Media Ethics*, New York: Longman.

Newburn, T. (1992) *Permission and Regulation: Law and Morals in Post-war Britain*, London: Routledge.

Newson, E. (1994) 'Video Violence and the Protection of Children', mimeo, Child Development Research Unit, University of Nottingham.

Palmlund, I. (1992) 'Social Drama and Risk Evaluation' in Krimsky, S, and Golding, D., eds, *Social Theories of Risk*, Westport: Praeger, pp. 197–214.

Pearson, G. (1983) *Hooligan: A History of Respectable Fears*, London: Macmillan.

Thompson, W. (1992) 'Britain's Moral Majority', in *Religion: Contemporary Issue. The Canterbury Paper V*, Wilson, B., ed., London: Bellew.

14 Consuming interests in a culture of secrecy

Miranda Basner

INTRODUCTION

When journalists mount a 'public interest' defence for their conduct, they are essentially engaged in a conflict over secrecy. They are, in other words, staking a claim to the moral high ground for disclosing or investigating matters which others would prefer to keep concealed.

At present, I suggest, the British press frequently loses its moral compass because it is party to a code of practice which sidesteps secrecy as an ethical issue. Instead, journalists are obliged to defend their position on the basis of how effectively their activities 'protect' the public. What this emphasis tends to produce is considerable confusion about the particularistic meaning of public interest to journalists and a press which not only routinely underestimates news audiences' informational needs but which ultimately colludes with institutional policies of concealment.

Case-by-case, pleas to withhold information may certainly carry weight, but these ought to be viewed against the broad backcloth that Britain has one of the 'most centralised and unaccountable' systems of government in the industrialised world (Sampson 1992, p. 154). Where institutional secrecy flourishes, it is crucial that a proper balance is struck in adjudicating journalistic arguments for disclosure; otherwise very little real progress is likely to be made towards breaking a destructively vicious circle of excessive news control and prurient, obsessive prying.

Print journalists in the UK are currently enjoined to view the public interest along lines laid down by the Press Complaints Commission's Code of Practice, which offers a definition by listing three outcomes of journalistic activity that would support claims to be 'serving' the public in the face of opposition:

(i)   detecting or exposing crime or a serious misdemeanour;
(ii) protecting health and safety;
(iii) preventing the public from being misled by some statement or action of an individual or organisation.

The Commission acknowledges the incompleteness of this list by stating that 'any cases raising issues beyond these three definitions . . . will require a full explanation'; but what still emerges is that the news-receiving public should principally be regarded as a vulnerable entity in a potentially dishonest, dangerous and duplicitous world. Its most legitimate 'interest', therefore, is to be alerted to such perils. This does not, of course, mean that members of the public are viewed as *solely* interested in matters which might endanger or disadvantage them; only that where issues of 'lesser' importance than the ones listed are concerned, their needs are not overriding.

What is implicit here is that a considerable burden of proof lies on those pleading the case for disclosure. Secrecy is acknowledged to be of fundamental value, with those arguing for concealment by no means always doing so for sinister or self-interested reasons. Indeed, a good deal of the confusion which arises in ethical debate comes when opposing sides use precisely the same 'public interest' parlance to justify themselves. A newspaper reporter, for example, might claim to be 'serving the public interest' by publishing a paedophile's name and address, while a police officer argues that it is he who is 'serving the public interest' by trying to stop the reporter. The journalist contends that publication will usefully alert the community to a menace in its midst; the policeman says his primary concern is to avoid an outbreak of lynch law.

Debates of this sort are conducted very much in the consequentialist frame, which in its simplest utilitarian form aims to produce the best outcome for the greatest number of people. Where journalism is concerned, such reasoning is clearly brought to bear when arguing the case for publishing an account which may harm an individual or small section of the community while bringing benefits to a wider public. The main difficulty which arises here – as the paedophile scenario perhaps illustrates – is that it is seldom possible to predict the outcome of our actions with absolute certainty. A great deal of guesswork is inevitably brought into play, and much depends on how compellingly the arguments are presented: how far the sympathies of those sitting in judgement are engaged, and how far the adjudicators' own beliefs and experiences converge with the parties involved.

My concern is that the PCC's code reflects a predisposition by the adjudicators to view the public interest not from any neutral perspective, nor from a journalistic one, but rather too squarely from a perspective which holds that members of the public are often best served (or at least not unduly harmed) by being kept in the dark.

THE POWER OF SECRECY

Let us first consider secrecy's moral foundation in general terms. Sissela Bok points out that to have no capacity for concealment is to be out of control over how others see us, leaving us open to coercion (1989, p. 19); furthermore, without the ability to choose when to reveal our secrets we would lose our 'sense of identity and every shred of autonomy' (ibid., p. 282). As far as individuals are concerned, a strong resonance may be detected here between the benefits of secrecy and privacy, but a distinction does need to be drawn. Bok defines secrecy as being the deliberate concealment of information (or evidence of that information) by one party from another (ibid., p. 6). It is, in other words, very much a *capacity* for control in which concealment is the defining trait. Privacy on the other hand need not involve concealment at all, and is, rather, a self-protective *condition* – a condition very commonly asserted as a 'right' – of needing to limit unwanted access by others (ibid., pp. 10–11). A film star, for example, might stroll topless on a public beach and not find the stares of other bathers uncomfortable in the least; but having her photograph placed before the gaze of fully-clad newspaper readers during their office tea break may extend the zone of observation to a point she finds very uncomfortable indeed.

Where those claiming needs for privacy and secrecy often do overlap is in challenging what the public is entitled to have access to at their personal 'expense', and it must be said that the consequences can be devastating for those who lose the capacity to control what is said and known about them through the media. A former ombudsman of the *Washington Post*, Richard Harwood, made this observation of journalism:

The 'media' in their long history have shattered countless reputations and destroyed countless careers. We have driven people to suicide. We have caused immeasurable emotional pain, suffering and humiliation, not only to individuals but to families . . . and to entire communities (Goodwin and Smith 1994, p. 280).

This catalogue of damage is not, of course, wholly attributable to penetrations of secrecy or privacy; complaints of *untruthful* reporting in fact consistently occupy the bulk of the PCC's workload.[1] But it does illustrate a potential level of destructive power in serving the news imperative which cannot be ignored when pleading its case consequentially. Indeed, Bok maintains, conflicts over secrecy – whether between parents and children, government and citizens, or journalists and institutions – are essentially conflicts over power: 'the power that comes through controlling the flow of information' (1989, p. 19).

As well as producing broad autonomy, informational control by way of concealment can obviously be a vital factor in achieving pragmatic goals. The success of military strategy, for example, often heavily depends on concealing troop movements; commercial success may hinge on the development of a secret formula; wage negotiations will more easily be won by a management whose workforce is kept in the dark about how much the firm really can afford. It is also fair to say that pragmatic secrecy of this sort is not always exercised in the interests of the secret's holders, but with the benefit of others at heart. As we saw earlier, for instance, the policeman arguing the case against publication of a paedophile's name and address was not (*prima facie*, at least) doing so to maintain his own operational power, but to produce a level of order which he believed was beneficial to the local community.

In assessing the informational power balance, however, the attainment of pragmatic goals and autonomy are by no means the only advantages secrecy can bring. One important facet of its exercise is that secrets are almost always shared. And the act of sharing a secret essentially requires trust.

Secrecy is used as part of the socialisation process through which we develop loyalty to our peers, with the measure of our loyalty very largely being judged according to how faithfully we keep promises 'not to tell'. The secret may, or may not, be a significant one in itself; what is important is that someone has taken us into their 'confidence' and expects us to repay this trust by being trustworthy in return. Confidential relationships are secured in three primary ways. The first involves express promises which amount to 'contracts' between the people involved, whether they are written, verbal, or take the form of an oath. The second relies on a broad sense of good faith in which there is an expectation that secrets will be kept out of affection, perhaps, or friendship. The third binds the parties because their confidential relationship is recognised by law (Day 1991, pp. 130–131).

In Britain, where institutionalised secrecy is 'as much a part of the . . . landscape as the Cotswolds' (Hennessy 1989, p. 347), the value placed on confidentiality is immense. It is also frequently misplaced and misused; for while confidential relationships can produce undoubted benefits, these have to be evaluated against secrecy's potential for dishonesty and destructiveness.

A MULTITUDE OF SINS

Bok points out that the exercise of secrecy can be damaging both to those engaged in it and those who are excluded: 'When the freedom of choice that secrecy gives one person limits or destroys that of others, it affects not only his own claims to respect for identity, plans, action, and property, but theirs' (1989, p. 26). Secrecy can impair judgement by erecting shields against criticism and feedback, bogging people down in beliefs and patterns of thinking which, because they are not open to scrutiny, may often be harmful or erroneous; and it can affect character in similar ways. People who use secrecy to disguise weak, immoral, or unhealthy traits are not only in a position to mislead or damage others by the facade, but also put themselves beyond any help that scrutiny or criticism could bring. While not all secrecy is designed to deceive, Bok stresses, all deceit does rely on secrecy; and the same may be said for most other forms of wrongdoing. Secrecy can, in summary, 'hamper the exercise of rational choice at every step' (ibid., pp. 25–26).

One of secrecy's most pernicious qualities is its tendency to spread, and this is of particular relevance when weighing up the informational power balance in Britain. The researcher Judith Cook observes that there is now 'no aspect of our everyday lives, from the food we eat to the way we travel or how our children are recorded at school, that is not contaminated with excessive secrecy' (1985, p. 4). And the evidence is compelling.

As good a guide as any to the range of institutions currently hedged to some degree by capricious secrecy can be obtained by looking at what a Freedom of Information Act might cover. A 1998 White Paper includes:

- Government departments and agencies.
- Local councils; quangos, nationalised industries, and public corporations.
- The National Health Service.
- Courts and tribunals.
- The police and armed forces.
- Schools and colleges.
- Public service broadcasters.
- Private sector organisations working on behalf of the government.
- Privatised utilities.

It is, however, in the White Paper's recommended 'exceptions' that we finally discover what an extraordinary scope of subject matter is routinely and unyieldingly withheld from public view:

- National security.
- Defence.
- International relations.
- Internal discussion of government policy.
- Law enforcement.
- Business activities which could 'unfairly damage' a company's business standing.

While some of these areas of information may from time to time legitimately be kept under wraps, this is by no means always the case. Richard Norton-Taylor points out that the commercial exemption, for instance, can cover a multitude of sins, while 'international relations' effectively covers any dealings with the EC.[2] Indeed, it is not just the range but the sheer arbitrariness of secrecy in British institutional and administrative life which can be staggering. A highly illuminating list of subjects which have been 'banned' as Questions to the House of Commons[3] includes agricultural workers' wages; the day-to-day business of the British Sugar Corporation and White Fish Authority; the existence of the Nuclear Police Force; arms sales; the number of near-misses in civil aviation; the whereabouts of regional seats of government to be used in the event of nuclear war; and the scale of telephone tapping (Cook 1985, p. 14).

What the seemingly random diversity of such a list rather invites is a suspicion of *ritual* concealment – a profound value placed on secrecy as an end in itelf – rather than as a pragmatic protective mechanism. Indeed, a ritual of secrecy lies at the very heart of British government, with all new cabinet ministers obliged to kneel, kiss the hand of the Queen, and swear the Privy Council's 13th century oath that they will ' "keep secret all matters committed and revealed to you" ' (Paxman 1990, p. 58).

This ceremony may appear to be no more than mildly absurd, but it is nonetheless significant; for it is undoubtedly in the political sphere that policies of concealment are most comprehensively executed. The development of the Official Secrets Act is particularly instructive here, not only in demonstrating secrecy's tentacular quality but also because it ultimately sheds a good deal of light on 'official' perceptions of the public and its interests.

The Act began as a body of law passed with unseemly haste in 1911 'one hot August day when most Members of Parliament were more pleasurably engaged' (O'Higgins 1972, p. 36), and was essentially designed to help the authorities to catch spies. Its wording, however, was vague in the extreme, and this meant it actually covered both an enormous breadth of information and range of people bound by it. Section 1 of the Act, for example, made it a serious criminal offence 'for any purpose prejudicial to the interests or safety of the State' to obtain, make, or communicate 'any sketch, plan, model or note which is calculated *or might be* or is intended to be directly *or indirectly* useful to an enemy' (ibid., p. 37) (my italics). Section 2, meanwhile, which is of most imminent relevance to journalists and others seeking intelligence about the workings of government, first makes it a criminal offence for anyone in the following categories to communicate unauthorised information: those given information 'in confidence' by Crown office-holders such as ministers, civil servants, judges, and the police; people themselves holding Crown office; holders of Crown contracts – for example, stationery suppliers; employees of those holding Crown office; and people employed by those having a contract with a government department (ibid.). Secondly, this section makes it a criminal offence to receive information if one knows – *or ought to have known* – that its communication involved a violation of the Act.

Since 1911, the legislation has been progressively revised, with 'little inclination on the part of the executive to limit the range of alleged secrets' (Williams 1965, p. 207). Today, it is an offence for civil servants to disclose *any* information acquired through their official duties to an 'unauthorised' person unless they have received official permission to do so; and this stricture applies not only during their employment but after they have left the Civil Service. It is also illegal (under Section 7) to do anything 'preparatory to the commission of an offence', which means that a journalist would, for example, be breaking the law by topping up the glass of a civil servant in the hope of encouraging a morsel of unauthorised gossip. As Peter Hennessy observes, the Act 'has a completeness of which any totalitarian would be proud' (1989, p. 253).

According to one calculation, over 2000 differently worded charges can be brought [under Section 2]. The leading characteristic is its catch-all quality . . . It makes no distinctions of kind, and no distinctions of degree. All information which a Crown servant learns in the course of his duty is 'official' for the purposes of Section 2, whatever its nature, whatever its importance, whatever its original source (ibid., p. 343).

The Act's expansion can be explained by two crucial dynamics of institutional secrecy. The first is that once the power of secrecy is experienced, ever-increasing possibilities of advantage can be envisaged. The second is that secrecy contains an inherent weakness: it invites prying – 'attracting attention by its obvious anxiety' (Sampson 1982, p. 242). Those who are denied information naturally become suspicious or envious of those withholding it and attempt to loosen the grip. This will largely be done by trying to undermine the bonds of trust which secure the secret, and – particularly if the sabotage is successful – the more contractual and far-reaching such bonds will then become. In such an atmosphere, any negative or corruptive qualities of secrecy will tend to be magnified, producing yet more 'disloyalty' among insiders disturbed by it, and concomitantly by those prepared to exploit it. Loyalty eventually becomes almost the whole rationale of the secrecy rather than the secrets themselves, with 'Us' who are informationally empowered valiantly standing our ground against 'Them' . . . the troublesome, untrustworthy public outside.

Haughty as such a perspective might be, it remains to be seen whether the public is actually *harmed* by the prevailing culture of secrecy. Journalists are, after all, mandated to act as public watchdogs on three fairly broad fronts where concealment can be damaging. What other real 'need' does the public have for news beyond being alerted to misleading statements, threats to health and safety, and criminal activity?

EVALUATING NEWS

The historical researcher Mitchell Stephens (1988) maintains that the importance of news transcends the importance of the items on which it focuses:

More than specific information about specific events, the great gift news bestows on us is the confidence that we will learn about any particularly important or interesting events. The news is more than a category of information or a form of entertainment; it provides a kind of security (ibid., p. 18).

Clearly events which are likely to endanger us would be high on a priority list of what is 'important' or 'interesting'; and so, too, would events which impacted directly – for better or worse – on the general quality of our everyday lives. Political events are widely emphasised as being of crucial significance to the public in democratic life because western values of autonomy and freedom are viewed as being ultimately secured by an ability to make choices based on informed decisions about who should govern, what policies they should pursue,

and what levels of service they should provide. A 1949 Royal
Commission on the Press declared:

The democratic form of society . . . assumes that [its members] are
sufficiently well informed . . . to be able to form the broad judgements
required by an election, and to maintain between elections the
vigilance necessary in those whose governors are their servants and
not their masters . . . Democratic society, therefore, needs a clear and
truthful account of events, of their background and their causes
(Williams 1965, p. 93).

Members of the public are not, however, just actors in a political
arena. They also belong to families, friendships, towns and cities,
unions and professional associations, and a good deal more: football
fans belong to the sports public, chess players are part of the chess
world, and those who frequent the theatre are part of the theatre
community (Cohen 1992, p. 19). Much of our autonomy may lie in
being able to make political choices and having an alertness to danger,
but our overall sense of communal security would seem to require a
good deal more from journalists than their watchdog qualities.

We simultaneously expect them to provide us with pragmatic
information about our hobbies, the weather, technological
developments, and the mystical conjunction of the planets; amuse and
uplift us with accounts of comedy, tragedy, and heroism; and give us
all the latest gossip about celebrities we have come to 'know' through
the media. Such is our hunger for news of all kinds, it would seem,
that it is frequently described in terms of a physical or pathological
'need': 'Western civilisation needs good flows of information like it
needs good flows of air' (Wilson 1996, pp. 28–29); it is 'an addictive
drug' (Browne 1996, p. 135). Stephens postulates that one way to
understand the attraction of news is to see how people respond to its
absence, and he cites research in which respondents have described
feelings of 'anxiety', 'starvation' and 'pain', of being 'lost', 'like being
in jail', and 'suffering' (1988, p. 17). Perhaps what we hear ultimately
is an 'echo of some ancient fear [of being] left in the dark' (ibid.,
p. 231).

In this frame, journalism patently has a moral mandate which goes
somewhat beyond protective injunctions; for if it is possible that
members of the public can be so harmed by news deprivation, there is

a rather greater burden of proof on those arguing the case for concealment to demonstrate either disproportionate harm to themselves, or some compelling compensating benefit to the people deprived. In saying so, however, we need to tread cautiously. After all, members of the public are hardly being *starved* of news in contemporary Britain; some might even say there is too much on their plates. The sense of deprivation only comes when we begin to suspect that the menu on offer is a worryingly incomplete, imbalanced, and inaccurate one. At the end of the day, the public has to take it on trust that journalists are making efforts to be as roundedly aware as possible of what is happening in the world and from this vantage point reaching considered decisions about which information from the plethora we would most like, or need, to know – gathering information as well as they can and then telling the truth as they find it (Goodwin and Smith 1994, p. 6). If choices are made too largely on the basis of what is easiest to gather in the face of massive obstruction and manipulation, the danger is that a perfectly understandable taste for informational junk food will be served, or even cynically exploited, at the expense of a properly balanced and healthy diet.

British journalism's ethical track record in this respect has certainly not been good. Much criticism has been levelled, particularly at the red-top tabloids, for making news priorities of events which engage the public only on a prurient or voyeuristic level and for focusing their reporters' investigative talents on 'soft' targets who are not in a position to bite the watchdog back. Arguing that this is the sort of news the public 'wants' (as evidenced by large circulations) does not hold water if the quality of harm remains disproportionate to the benefits; and even if the desire should be so great as to constitute a 'need', a correct balance still has to be struck. On a case-by-case basis, there are undoubtedly many victims of media intrusion who require protection, and it is right that an ethical code of practice should seek to provide it. Where the PCC's code does a disservice both to genuine victims and to the news-receiving public is not in the detail, but in the round.

SQUARING THE CIRCLE

A flourishing culture of institutional secrecy can substantially shape the public's overall view of the world. Those in a position to control the flow of information are able to influence not only whether the public feel safe or unsafe, led or misled, but also place limits on public expectations of what is possible, what is legitimate, and what is desirable. A process of self-fulfilling prophecy can then too easily follow. Members of a public whose parameters of knowledge and expectation are entirely reduced to trivia will naturally value news about trivial events; it then becomes the position of those withholding information that this particular public is too frivolous to be trusted with 'important' information. A public which is given only sanitised accounts of war is too 'easily shocked' to be told the truth; people who only ever hear two sides of an argument are 'not interested' in a third. No public is, of course, wholly vulnerable to this process. Personal experience of events, for example, will always override or replace conflicting accounts and omissions, and the aspirations and beliefs of some people will always go against the official grain. It remains the case, however, that considerable blame for an unethical press must lie at the door of those whose empowerment lies in controlling information through concealment. If journalists pry it is because a culture of secrecy invites it, and it is not surprising that a good deal of the snooping is directed at those who do not deserve it: secrecy in *every* shape and form is newsworthy in a culture of secrecy; and it is only unfortunate that paltry secrets are rather easier to unearth than pernicious ones.

The ethical quagmire does not end there, however. As we have seen, the spread of secrecy largely comes about through the dynamics of its weakness. The more successfully it is exercised, the more it is likely to be challenged, and the more rigorously and broadly it then has to be secured. During this cycle reporters are placed in the invidious position of perpetuating systems of concealment whether they rise to the challenge or not. Those who fail to resist effectively become the conveyors of propaganda rather than the carriers of news which accurately and roundedly informs the public and this is certainly the most comfortable option. Authorised information, after all, comes safely packaged, and is also expertly selected and presented by spin doctors, lobbyists and press officers who know exactly 'what journalists want'. Anything concealed will then remain concealed because it is unsearched-for; and any information that ultimately misleads or even endangers the public will go undetected because it is unquestioned.

Propagandists who succeed in getting journalists 'on side' do so by cultivating their trust. Reporters tend, however, to be sceptical by nature and training, and their trust is not all that easily won. The most successfully secretive organisations are those which are able to harness journalists as securely as their own members through bonds of confidentiality; for the more journalists can be made to feel 'one of Us', the more likely they will be to serve the interests of the institution in relation to 'Them' out there.

The PCC's Code of Practice states quite unequivocally: 'Journalists have a moral obligation to confidential sources of information'. This is not, as it happens, a misguided injunction, but it is highly problematic in this context. On the one hand it offers vital protection to those who wish to expose corrupt practices, since only by being absolutely confident that a reporter will not disclose their identity can many whistleblowers take the risk of speaking out. On the other hand it offers a shield to unscrupulous or manipulative sources of information. Journalists who challenge systems of concealment are no less vulnerable to exploitative and malicious leakers and whistleblowers than those who succumb to the temptations of propaganda. Indeed, they are perhaps more so; for the more doggedly a challenge is mounted, the more necessary it becomes for the reporter to trust – and be trusted by – those whose loyalty is cast in doubt. Such journalists are not only in danger of becoming so embroiled in contracts of confidentiality that they become part of the very culture they seek to undermine, but also unwittingly help to consolidate that culture by obliging the 'loyalists' to further tighten their grip.

Against this background, a Code of Practice is presented to journalists which essentially takes its lead from the distorted and distorting perspective of institutional secret-holders: that it is journalists, and not they, whose powers are too great and whose moral conduct is too murky; journalists, and not they, who are unreasonable in wanting to secure information which has uses beyond ensuring the most basic levels of social wellbeing; that it is journalists – and not they – who must ultimately be held to account for the harm which is done to hapless victims caught in the crossfire.

The balance needs to be tipped dramatically, and this is perhaps quite easily achieved. Let us consider what would happen, for example, if the code's public interest clause were reworded in this way: 'It is against the public interest to exercise secrecy unless the detection or publication of that secret would result in:

(i)   Crime or serious misdemeanor;
(ii) Risks to health and safety;
(iii) Misleading statements'.

There would doubtless be howls of outrage! Since those exercising secrecy plainly believe their own needs and vulnerabilities to be much wider-ranging, they would almost certainly want to add – and on tablets of stone – the following (and perhaps more) 'undesirable' results of publication:

(iv)   Operational inefficiency;
(v)   Unfair commercial, financial or political disadvantage;
(vi)   Loss of jobs;
(vii) An undermining of morale;
(viii) Injustice;
(ix)   Intrusions into privacy.

What we now have in fact is a far better acknowledgement of the real diversity of the *public's* interests; for it is just as reasonable to suppose that members of the public, too, are likely to feel harmed if institutional secrecy renders them inefficient (or hides inefficiency at their expense), places them at a financial or political disadvantage, causes them to be unjustly treated, leads to job losses, undermines their morale, and threatens their privacy. The public might, however, similarly want to add a few further items to the list – for example, environmental damage and developments which would rob them of social amenities – which in turn would find favour with many keepers of institutional secrets.

If we now consider this consensus from a slightly different angle, there is very little disparity between what the conflicting parties want out of life; only a divergence on how best and how widely to secure these benefits. A consequentially-based ethical code should perhaps reflect (and in as much detail as possible) what are universally-regarded *beneficial* social outcomes and then let the contenders argue their corners on a fair footing about whether these are best achieved through disclosure or through concealment. The PCC's code could much more usefully and forcefully guide journalists by setting out a declaration of human rights in place of its somewhat limited catalogue of human wrongs:

It is in the public interest that its members should be law-abiding, healthy and safe, told the truth . . . able to make fully-informed political choices . . . secure in their work . . . justly served . . . afforded privacy . . . and so on.

Reporters would then, for example, be obliged to regard privacy as a consensually valued condition and have to defend its intrusion from a much higher standard of proof; and at the same time their attention would be urgently drawn to a much wider world in which the public has a legitimate interest. The code could also productively go further in one other respect. If journalists are to be encouraged to extricate themselves as far as possible from the corruptive tendencies of institutional secrecy, a cautionary rider needs to be attached to the clause covering confidential sources of information. It might simply borrow from injunctions which appear in other clauses by adding:

Promises of confidentiality should not be made except where the material concerned ought to be published in the public interest, where there is an overriding need to make such a promise, and where that material cannot be obtained by any other means.

It is highly unlikely that such shifts of emphasis would be considered, however, for they considerably challenge the cultural status quo. The PCC was founded in the belief that it had a much greater chance of success in regulating the misdeeds of the press if its rules and codes were drawn up by the newspaper industry itself – an industry which has as much vested interest in preserving the climate of secrecy as any other commercial institution. What most of today's proprietors require of news is that it produces wealth not only through its own commodity value, but also by allowing them to exercise power and influence in global empires which have little or nothing to do with newspapers at all: spheres as diverse as oil fields and plastics, entertainment and travel, property and finance; and to this end, many are actively interventionist on the political front. No less than politicians, therefore, and certainly no less than other industrial giants, limiting the flow of information is vital to maintaining and increasing the media conglomerates' competitive edge. 'The players [are] not interested in checking the abuses of power, but in joining the power-game' (Sampson 1992, p. 126). Journalists are drawn into the game, sometimes willingly, sometimes naively, and sometimes with painful reluctance. It does little to help that they are regulated by a body whose ethos is that of newspaper employers, and whose members, moreover, are unelected . . . and appointed in secret.

ENDNOTES

1. In its 1996 Annual Report, the Press Complaints Commission notes that almost seven out of ten complaints related to inaccurate reporting, which was a 'similar proportion to previous years'.
2. The Labour Party's Progress magazine (Issue 7) Winter 1998 gives a summary of the White Paper and commentary on it by Richard Norton-Taylor, pp. 26 and 27.
3. List publicised in the *Sunday Times*, 12.12.71.

REFERENCES

Bok, S. (1989) *Secrets: On the Ethics of Concealment and Revelation*, New York: Vintage Books.

Browne, C. (1996) *The Prying Game*, Robson Books.

Cohen, E.D. (1992) *Philosophical Issues in Journalism*, Oxford: Oxford University Press.

Cook, J. (1985) *The Price of Freedom*, London: New English Library.

Day, L.A. (1991) *Ethics in Media Communications: Cases and Controversies*, California: Wadsworth.

Goodwin, G. and Smith, R.F. (1994) *Groping for Ethics in Journalism*, Iowa State University Press.

Hennessy, P. (1989) *Whitehall*, London: Secker & Warburg.

O'Higgins, P. (1972) *Censorship in Britain*, London: Nelson.

Paxman, J. (1990) *Friends in High Places: Who Runs Britain?* London: Michael Joseph.

Sampson, A. (1982) *The Changing Anatomy of Britain*, London: Hodder & Stoughton.

Sampson, A. (1992) *The Essential Anatomy of Britain*, London: Hodder & Stoughton.

Stephens, M. (1988) *A History of News*, New York: Penguin.

Williams, D. (1965) *Not in the Public Interest*, London: Hutchinson.

Wilson, J. (1996) *Understanding Journalism*, London: Routledge.

15 And the consequence was...

Dealing with the human impact of unethical journalism

Mike Jempson

INTRODUCTION

This chapter concentrates largely upon the human impact of inaccurate and intrusive newspaper stories and PressWise who assists the public with complaints about print and broadcast journalism. I begin with a look at what PressWise does, set in the historical and political context of debate about whether journalistic ethics exist and provide examples of the damage that can be caused by 'bad' journalism.

Pseudonyms have been used to protect the identity of some 'victims of media abuse'. Simply retelling stories can reopen wounds, and some sections of the media feel no compunction about returning to the attack when former victims articulate their concerns. One of our clients was warned by lawyers acting for a national daily that if she went ahead with plans to criticise the paper on TV more damaging stories about her might be published. She did not appear on the programme.

This imbalance of power between the public and the mass media is at the heart of the issues dealt with here, and my final section includes observations about more effective and accountable systems of media regulation.

PRESSWISE – THE MEDIA ETHICS BODY

Like most journalists I spend much of my time listening to people with stories to tell of injustice, tragedy and despair. But in my case the villains of the peace are often other journalists.

At PressWise we assist people to pick their way through the minefield of complications that arise when anyone tries to set the record straight or obtain redress after print or broadcast journalists have got things wrong. Although founded by 'victims of media abuse' who might be expected to take an antagonistic view of the trade, the core objective of PressWise is to promote high standards of journalism.

While some journalists scoff at the very idea of 'a media ethics body', those who suffer at the hands of sloppy or irresponsible journalism are delighted to discover that within the trade there are people willing to listen to their side of the story and to acknowledge that even top writers, editors and programme-makers have feet of clay.

The majority of our clients are 'ordinary people', confused, angry, and shocked to find themselves in the public eye. Many express an anxiety extending almost to the point of paranoia that everyone 'knows about them' and that their every move is being observed. It is not a state of mind conducive to preparing coherent complaints, which may explain why the press find it easy to dodge criticism by dismissing so many out of hand.

The journalist in me is vaguely reassured by the outrage that our clients express. They cannot believe what is happening to them, because they cannot believe it could happen to anyone. In other words, at least until their story appeared, they had retained some faith in the role of the journalist as public watchdog. We may all claim to be sceptical about what we read in the papers, but most of us retain a sneaking suspicion that if it's in the newspaper it must be true.

People who find themselves in the media spotlight quickly learn that all is not what it seems, but being wise after the event is no compensation for the instant distress and longer-term damage that can flow from simple errors and sloppy journalism.

Our primary aim is to overcome their overwhelming sense of powerlessness and isolation by letting them know about others who have had similar experiences and by explaining the journalistic process and the pressures that can lead to mistakes.

Many are shaken to the core by the cynicism of the reporters and researchers who come knocking on their door. Few understand that these people are rarely responsible for what eventually appears in print or on screen. Their 'ownership' of copy ends as soon as it enters the production process. Our clients certainly do not appreciate, in any sense of that term, that people with whom they have had no contact – sub-editors and programme editors – may literally reconstruct events by adding their own creative spin and seldom refer back to the original sources.

We also warn clients that trying to put things right can be as traumatic as the damage done by the offending article. Assembling the evidence to satisfy an editor or regulator that a complainant has a valid case takes far longer than it did to construct the original story. Small wonder that about fifty per cent of our callers decide to go no further.

ARE JOURNALISTS SUPPOSED TO BE ETHICAL?

First and foremost journalists are communicators, assembling information and recasting it in a way that will successfully connect with their target audience. A thorough grounding in ethics is neither an essential nor even, in some employers' eyes, a desirable prerequisite for entry into the trade. Nonetheless, journalists are expected to operate in a more or less ethical way.

Many harbour a cavalier attitude towards 'ethics' and remain in denial about their power to mess up innocent people's lives. David Randall, a former assistant editor of *The Observer*, sums it up in his book *The Universal Journalist*:

The high-minded in the business attempting to teach their morals to the fast and loose at the popular end . . . stand as much chance of having an impact as someone trying to advocate celibacy to a group of sailors arriving home in port after six months at sea.[1]

There will always be amoral hacks willing to concoct anything for cash, but most journalists try to seek out 'the truth' (or more accurately verifiable facts). They want, indeed expect, people to believe what they write. This value system, tempered by recognition that the production process inevitably takes liberties with their copy, offers a starting point for discussion of 'journalistic ethics'.

A gulf of unknowing exists between those who construct mass communication products and those who 'consume' or even contribute to them. The producers often forget that the 'consumers' are unaware of the pressures which typify the phenomenon of journalism. However, while TV producers and presenters are happy to persuade guileless 'ordinary people' to let cameras into their homes, not one of the leading media professionals I breakfasted with before a session on ethics at the 1997 Sheffield International Documentary Festival, would allow their domestic lives to be filmed.

This mismatch of experience and expectations is why we need formal and accessible codes of conduct, and independent systems of adjudication and redress in which the public can have confidence.

In the UK broadcast journalists work within fairly stringent guidelines backed by statutory powers of the Independent TV Commission, the Radio Authority, and the Broadcasting Standards Commission. Each broadcasting company adds its own gloss to the rules laid down by the regulators. A complaint can set an investigation in motion, even within the BBC with its unique Royal Charter and comprehensive Producer Guidelines with which all staff and contractors must comply.

Less formally, journalists owe allegiance to codes drawn up by their trade union or professional association. The vast majority of journalists in the UK and the Republic of Ireland are members of the National Union of Journalists (NUJ) which has had a Code of Conduct since 1936.

At one time complaints from members of the public result in internal disciplinary proceedings with fines or even expulsion from the union for those found to have breached the Code. Ironically, the Code was never accepted by employers and resistance from members in the national press and the large-scale de-recognition of the NUJ has undermined this unique system of self-regulation. The NUJ still has an Ethics Council which promotes the Code and offers guidance to members.

After the Second World War the NUJ wanted a more comprehensive system of ethical self-regulation for newspapers and magazines and called for a Royal Commission on the Press. The industry dragged its feet when the Royal Commission proposed the creation of a General Council of the Press (GCP), and as a result the draconian Defamation Act 1952 reached the statute book.

It was only after parliamentary moves to force the issue that the GCP was set up in 1953. The effectiveness of the Press Council, as it was to become, gradually deteriorated.[2] It was severely criticised by two subsequent Royal Commissions (1962 and 1977), and the Younger Committee on Privacy (1973); editors sometimes ignored its adjudications which took a long time to prepare.

In the late 1980s, under the reforming chairmanship of Louis Blom Cooper QC, the Press Council at last adopted a formal code against which erring editors and journalists might be judged. It derived from the NUJ's Code, and the union, which had lost patience and left the Council in 1981, rejoined – only to learn that the industry was withdrawing its funding.

The Thatcher government had appointed Sir David Calcutt in 1989 to investigate intrusive press coverage of private lives[3] and the threat of statutory controls was in the wind. The industry's strong sense of self-preservation led to the creation of the Press Complaints Commission (PCC) in which the NUJ had no role to play. Since 1991 the PCC, entirely funded by the industry, has provided a system of self-regulation for newspapers and magazines by policing a Code of Practice devised by editors.

The PCC sets great store by the employers' commitment to the Code, which has had to be updated with each new public crisis of confidence in the credibility of self-regulation. It is supposed to be incorporated into editors' contracts, and both staff and freelances are expected to abide by its exhortations.

It is reasonable to infer from all this that standards of accuracy and human decency are expected of the journalistic product, if not the journalists themselves. With some 10,000 complaints a year[4] being made to regulatory bodies by those members of the public tenacious enough to discover how the system works, it would appear that those with whom journalists are supposed to communicate also expect standards of veracity and integrity from the trade.

STRAINING CREDIBILITY

The consistently poor standing of journalists in opinion polls seems to suggest that the public has little confidence in their ability to deliver. Yet journalists and the publications and programmes they work for depend for their authority and market position upon the public's willingness to trust them. Often editors and journalists fail to see what all the fuss is about. Why should they worry about getting the odd name or date wrong when so many far more important things are happening out in the big bad world?

While seeking evidence to support his proposal for an Independent Press Authority to defend press freedom and adjudicate on complaints, Clive Soley MP circulated a letter for publication in local papers during 1992 asking for examples of inaccurate reporting. The *Brighton Evening Argus* added a footnote to his letter stating that; 'The *Argus* strives to be fair, balanced and accurate. Occasionally mistakes slip through and it is our policy in such cases to correct them quickly'.

An *Argus* reader wrote to Soley about the paper's refusal to correct inaccuracies in the figures published of votes cast for unsuccessful candidates in a local election. The *Argus* acknowledged the errors in correspondence, but prevaricated about putting them right in the paper. The matter was referred to the PCC which ruled that the complaint had been made 'out of time' (more than one month after the original publication).

'I know of no time limit on the truth,' responded the complainant, annoyed that the electorate's main newspaper of local record had left voters with a false impression about the electoral support of rival political parties, a key issue in an open democracy.[5]

Editors often cause extra agony by the length of time they take to reply to complainants. Neil Bennett, former Deputy Managing editor of the *Daily Mirror*, told a parliamentary enquiry:

I'm an old hand at this game. When a newspaper gets a complaint you can tell in 30 seconds flat whether it is any good. If it is going to stick it goes on a long circuitous route. It is called 'kick it about until you lose it'.[6]

When editors do reply they can display breathtaking arrogance. In correspondence with a distraught father who wanted to correct false information published about his son's murder, including the spelling of his name, the editor of one South London newspaper persisted in mis-spelling the complainant's name for months.

Some editors try to shrug off errors by suggesting that a complaint is not worth pursuing, or even challenging people to sue – a technique favoured by brash *Mirror* editor Piers Morgan, and backed by the PCC on at least one occasion, even after the London *Evening Standard* had published an apology and paid damages for repeating the offending *Mirror* story.

A woman who went on TV to criticise the now defunct *Today* newspaper for unethical behaviour found herself and the programme being threatened with writs by one of the journalists involved.

Such attitudes – and the apparent immunity of those who adopt them – upsets members of the public when they get caught in the media's net. It makes them doubt themselves and many are fearful about complaining. Even without a solicitor it can take months and cost a great deal trying to put the record straight. People who may not even have access to a typewriter are expected to meet tight deadlines and produce watertight cases if they want to be taken seriously.

If their complaint is upheld, there is no compensation for any damage caused to their lives. Under the terms of a convenient compact between the highly competitive commercial industry and the system of self-regulation it pays for, newspapers merely agree to publish PCC adjudications. And that can only happen if a member of the public is aware that a mistake has been made and systematically pursues a complaint.

More often than not the public does not know it is being misled. Reminiscing about his years in Africa, *The Daily Telegraph*'s Chris Munnion explains how in difficult circumstances the press 'pack' confers to agree on the same basic story, even if it means relying on dubious sources or making things up.[7] Nik Gowing, former diplomatic editor of Channel 4 News, argues that one consequence of journalists presenting a distorted picture of the 1966–97 'refugee crisis' in Burundi, Rwanda and Uganda was that genocide in Rwanda went 'unseen and virtually unreported'.[8]

Set against such massive disasters the damaging consequences of simple errors closer to home may seem petty to editors, but they are no less tragic.

While working on the *East London Advertiser* I was approached by the Citizens' Advice Bureau worker who wanted to put right an error which had caused a single parent to lose her benefits. An inquest report in the paper stated that a male friend who suffered a fatal collapse while visiting her, had *lived* rather than simply *died* at her address. Social Security staff had seen the story and accused her of benefit fraud for cohabiting.

My editor refused to correct the error. His instant response was that the report had come from a reputable agency and the woman was probably 'having it off' with the man anyway. Most journalists will recognise the attitude. Finding out where the error had crept in was too much effort, and might cause problems with a news agency that supplied juicy stories from the coroner's court on the cheap.

A personal tragedy had been compounded by a silly mistake, and the cynicism or cowardice of an editor. One word had made all the difference to that woman's life, but she couldn't do anything about it.

A simple apology might have saved the life of Barry Melarickas. In a front-page splash and a leader column the *Bristol Evening Post*[9] claimed that he was betraying those in real need by continuing to sell *The Big Issue*, the magazine produced for sale by homeless people, because he had a flat and a P-registration car.

The *Post* reported that Barry had 'no trouble running away' when a photographer tried to take his picture. But Barry was physically incapable of running anywhere – he had lost both kneecaps in an accident. He had also lost his job and his family, following a nervous breakdown. With the help of *The Big Issue*, which he was still eligible to sell, he was now putting his life back together. He invited reporters into his housing association flat, which had been burgled and where he had recently been robbed at knifepoint, and volunteered information about his specially adapted car obtained quite properly under the government's mobility scheme.

Errors in the published story were 'not considered significant' by the PCC, who claimed the reference to his ability to run would be 'taken figuratively'. But Barry had been identified and vilified on the front page of his local paper. His children had seen him presented as a fraudulent scrounger. He felt he had let down his family, his homeless friends and *The Big Issue*, so he killed himself. The *Post*'s investigation won the reporter the Daily News Journalist of the Year Award from BT.

Teenage actor David Scarboro (star of *Grange Hill* and *East Enders*) threw himself from Beachy Head in April 1988 after several national papers had published inaccurate and damaging stories about his private life and then pursued him and his family as his mental health deteriorated.[10] His libel action died with him and his parents subsequently left the country, appalled by the apparent impunity with which the press are able 'to get away with' the destruction of their son.

The parents of Alan Watson also fail to see anything ethical about a system which left their teenage son dead, clutching the press cuttings which besmirched the name of his murdered sister, Diane. A columnist in the *Glasgow Herald* had cast inappropriate and inaccurate aspersions about Diane following the conviction of another teenage girl for her murder during breaktime in the schoolyard. There is no remedy for the expression of hurtful opinions however, unless they are libellous or can be shown to incite race hatred or otherwise damage public order.

Later another journalist fuelled the family's despair by presenting the murderer's discredited version of events in a campaigning article for *Marie Claire* about children detained at Her Majesty's Pleasure. Again the Watsons sought to put the record straight. Alan killed himself in December 1992 when it became clear that his parents' efforts to obtain redress had failed.

The utter hopelessness of such people is not uncommon. In one bad week during 1997 I found myself dissuading three different clients from seeking solace in suicide. Their lives had been turned upside-down by inaccurate newspaper coverage, but their despair had been brought on by the way they had been treated by the PCC.

'Martha' had been wrongly categorised as male at birth and spent a distressing nine months undergoing medical examinations and gathering evidence to support a complaint against *The People*, which had published a prurient story about her alongside a snatched photograph. As so often happens, the PCC rejected Martha's claim that unethical methods had been used to obtain personal information about her. Curiously, the PCC also decided the story had not breached the Code of Practice, despite legal and medical evidence that demonstrated its inaccuracy, and offered a 'public interest' defence for the intrusion into her privacy although the newspaper had not called for this 'get out' clause.

The uncorrected story remains in the cuttings files with the ever-present threat of repetition. It had reduced her employment prospects, held her up to ridicule, and contained errors that might even put her entitlement to benefit at risk. Had it done so she saw suicide as her only option. Martha later agreed to talk about her experience to journalism students, under copyright conditions, and then had to endure further intrusion when a member of the audience wrote up the story for her local paper.

'Doreen' was accused by a Scottish newspaper of having a criminal record, in damaging stories about her relationships with convicted criminals. The only way she could correct the errors was to reveal confidential personal information which no reporter had discovered or had any right to know. She became scared that the newspaper might publish it, and was driven to despair.

The newspaper had claimed justification by referring to an equally erroneous story published years earlier. Doreen had not then known how to obtain redress, although she had told the reporter his facts were wrong. However, just because she had not sought and obtained a formal correction, the original lies continue to haunt her.

Suicide seemed to be one way out for 'Anne-Marie' when the PCC rejected her complaints about the way local papers in the Home Counties covered the trial of a violent adulterer who had seduced her daughter. After he was convicted of a horrifying attack on their home, their assailant spoke to reporters and the papers gave prominence to his version of events. As a result the women, who had tried to avoid publicity, suffered abuse locally and felt obliged to abandon the college courses they had embarked upon in the year since the crime, and put the family home on the market.

Strict rules govern the reporting of court cases, but quite often the selection and presentation of evidence raises ethical issues especially about the media's treatment of victims and their relatives.[11]

TIME IS NOT THE GREAT HEALER

Journalists often claim that in times of distress grieving relatives are pleased to talk to reporters, yet most know that there are aspects of their own private lives which they would not wish to be publicised.

They give little thought to the consequences of turning the confidences they receive from distraught 'lay people' into public spectacles.

'Hilary' opened her heart to a *Sun* reporter who broke the news to her of her celebrity husband's adultery. Her emotional outburst at a time of great vulnerability became a two-page feature, blighting her life and that of her children. She was branded a 'bitter woman' and her attempts to seek redress failed. She had to live with the knowledge that the contents of the offending article could now be repeated with impunity. She spent much of the time indoors, convinced that her home was under observation. One of her children had to abandon a degree course after fellow students were offered money by journalists to supply information about the family.

It can take years to mend bridges with friends and family when false stories appear, and those who cannot afford lawyers may live with the consequences for generations. Some change their identities to avoid being scalded again, and even those strong enough to go on the offensive sometimes wish they hadn't.

One respected Irish journalist was forced into hiding with his family for several years after a UK broadsheet wrongly accused him of IRA membership,[12] and it took a similar period for campaigners in the UK and Europe to clear their names after a newspaper published uncorroborated claims in a Foreign and Commonwealth Office Briefing that they were part of an international network of IRA sympathisers.[13]

Children make good copy, and the more extreme the circumstances the better it would seem.[14] The mother of a child whose medical condition had caused very disruptive behaviour patterns quit the country after *The Sun* branded her son 'The Worst Brat in Britain' and 'Terror Tot'.[15] Such sensational stories invite sequels, especially when neighbours realise that they may be able to cash in by selling 'information' about people in the media spotlight.

In 1984 a surrogate birth gave the 'Smiths' the child they thought they could never have. The 'rat pack' were soon on their doorstep bidding for an exclusive and the Smiths were persuaded to accept an offer from one newspaper to keep the others at bay. They did not realise they would lose control of their lives for years to come.[16]

The PCC has since ruled that they cannot stop continuous newspaper identification of their son because they had placed him in the public domain by accepting money for the story of his birth. They could do nothing to protect their son from the taunts of his peers as he entered puberty and a new school because, 14 years ago, they had been taken in by unscrupulous journalists in search of a 'good story'.[17]

The 'Johnstons' went into hiding with their new born baby after the *News of the World* ran a sensational story about their surrogacy arrangement, based on information it had paid for. The couple had committed no crime and, if anything, were victims of another's duplicity. PressWise helped them to submit a complaint to the PCC, and eventually they returned home and began to reconstruct their lives. Then the *Sunday Mirror* found a new angle and repeated many of the disputed 'facts' from the original story before the complaint had been resolved. Their family business suffered and the Johnstons were so frightened they left the country. They no longer knew whom they could trust. When they returned they abandoned all efforts to put the record straight for fear it might excite the curiosity of yet another newspaper keen to boost sales with a follow-up.

It is even more difficult to obtain redress on behalf of groups of people. Ethnic minorities, refugees, asylum seekers and 'travellers' in the UK frequently suffer the consequences of negative or prejudicial coverage yet not one of some 600 complaints to the PCC about allegedly racist or xenophobic coverage have been upheld since 1991.[18]

The boycott of *The Sun* by Liverpudlians following its insensitive and inaccurate coverage of the Hillsborough disaster is a rare example of a sustained protest by a community hitting the press where it hurts.[19]

OPEN TO INTERPRETATION

Journalists have a responsibility to those who contribute to or merely consume the finished product, precisely because all forms of mass communication are constructions. Journalistic 'quotes' for instance offer an honest approximation of what has been said, to fit the space available, yet people expect to be quoted *verbatim* forgetting that few of us utter coherent or even complete sentences when under pressure.

Often it is the implicit 'message' of newspaper stories that drives people to distraction. We constantly have to alert potential complainants to the fact that the words on the page don't actually say what they *think* they do. Yet the impression they have formed is exactly what other readers are likely to derive from the published words and images. Journalists may see this as the *apogee* of their craft, but it causes dismay to those who expect newspapers to mean what they say and say what they mean.

When *The Daily Mirror* accused a businessman of malpractice and alleged that his office was 'being besieged by customers demanding refunds and threatening to take him to court', the man complained. He conceded that 'three clients had expressed dissatisfaction over the phone in the previous nine months', but that hardly justified the paper's claims. According to the editor this was 'a trivial complaint about interpretation'; the term 'besieged' had been used in 'the metaphorical sense'. 'How', asked the complainant 'were the readers supposed to know that?'

The PCC found the editor's explanation acceptable since 'other descriptions were clearly figurative and unlikely to mislead in the context of the article'. Yet the PCC's ruling inaccurately described the man as a Company Secretary, laying him open to charges under the Companies Acts if the newspaper account was to be believed. He was far from impressed with the ethical standards of both the newspaper and those who are supposed to safeguard the public from abuse of media power.

Some 'red tops' now regard public shaming, often about trivial matters, as their legitimate business, as if commercial enterprises have some special right to act as the conscience of individual citizens.

When 'Tom', an unemployed young father, short of funds at Christmas, answered an advert from a strip-o-gram agency, he did not regard it as something shameful. He was not to know that his first job would be part of an elaborate *News of the World* scam to trap a solicitor alleged to be running an escort agency from the offices of a law firm.

Tom was persuaded to bring his wife along for what was supposed to be a surprise birthday strip for a visiting Arab dignitary. They were whisked off to a top London hotel in a chauffeur-driven limo. Before going to the man's room they were plied with drinks and given amyl nitrate capsules to deliver to him. They were completely unaware that everyone else, apart from the man who had booked them, was working for the newspaper. The story that appeared identified them, with pictures. They were immediately ostracised by friends and family and prevented from visiting Tom's mother-in-law who was seriously ill in hospital. They were fearful of leaving the house or sending their children to school. The local paper was sympathetic but unwilling to run the couple's side of the story because of its family readership.

However, the *News of the World* had wrongly identified the law firm their target was supposed to work for. A week later the paper published a substantial apology of the sort that usually accompanies a handsome cheque in compensation, but refused to make good the harm caused to the couple, who had done nothing illegal and never received their fee. The paper saw nothing wrong with the tactics it had employed and regarded them as guilty by association with the man it had set out to expose.

THE BOTTOM LINE

As we have seen the printed word can be as fatal as the scalpel, and the media are quick to point out that a refusal by hospital doctors and health administrators to admit to mistakes can lead to unnecessary injury and death in the operating theatre.

Editors are notoriously reluctant to admit mistakes. Indeed media lawyers advise that staff should not even acknowledge errors over the phone to minimise the risk of awards for damages. This may be sound business practice but it is no comfort to those who are simply seeking a swift correction of an already published error.

Getting things right should be a matter of pride for the individual journalist and their editors. Yet in recent years national newspaper editors have been promoted or head-hunted after publishing stories that breached the industry's Code of Practice. Sensational and salacious stories are valued marketing devices to enhance profits by enticing new readers and advertisers. The bottom line after all is the bottom line.

The notion of press freedom seems to have been hijacked to defend the market forces argument that proprietors must not be restricted in the exercise of their right to publish anything that will make a profit.

Hence the frequently repeated refrain: 'If people don't like what we publish they can always buy someone else's paper.'

PressWise, like many of Britain's trades unions, takes the view that freedom of the press comes with a responsibility to those who rely upon the mass media for accurate information. The media unions in particular have campaigned for the statutory right of reply enjoyed by citizens of other European countries, including the emerging democracies of the former Soviet Union, but their power has been whittled away by legislation and de-recognition over the last twenty years.

During that period media professionals have had to operate in an increasingly hostile employment environment with short-term personal contracts, no formal career structure, and fierce competition for jobs. There is no universally respected 'conscience clause' which allows them to refuse an assignment. Like everyone else most journalists would prefer an easy life, and many feel their best interests are served by satisfying the demands of editors whose own security rests upon improving the commercial prospects of their titles.

WHERE NEXT?

Most national and local newspapers and magazines in the UK are now part of vertically integrated conglomerates with interests in a wide range of sectors[20] which have become more complex, profitable and powerful as communication technologies converge. We all rely upon these institutions to keep us informed, accurately and promptly, about what is happening in the world; our decisions about how to vote and how to interpret the world depend upon their presentation of such matters. It is a mighty responsibility.

Yet the nearest we have to ethical supervision of one of the most influential forces in society is a system designed primarily to protect the industry from statutory regulation. On the rare occasions when an editor is found to have breached the industry's code – the PCC has found in favour of no more than 1 per cent of all complaints made since 1991 – all that is required is publication of the PCC's ruling. There are no fines and no compensation for the victims – unless of course they can afford to mount a successful legal action.

At the moment the people see only a body which claims unique privileges to itself without any of the concomitant responsibilities . . . prepared to change . . . but only when it suits them. They see a body scornful of whether or not its proceedings command public confidence. It cannot go on like this'. That was how a Guardian *leader in November 1996 challenged parliamentary self-regulation at Westminster.*

It applies equally well to the PCC. The same leader quoted Lord Nolan's comment that, 'the public needs to see that breaches of rules are investigated as fairly, and dealt with as firmly by Parliament, as would be the case with others through the legal process'. Change 'Parliament' to 'the Press' and you have, in a nutshell, the case for a more independent and effective system of press regulation.

However, it is doubtful whether confidence in the print media's efforts to improve ethical standards will increase until real sanctions can be imposed against those who breach its Code. Offending editors, and the newspapers they manage, must be prepared to accept more than the passing opprobrium of their peers.

If each breach resulted in a dent in profits, through automatic fines and/or compensation for victims, they would quickly learn the value the public place upon the integrity of information they publish. After all, commercial broadcasters risk fines and loss of their licences for breaches of their contracts, and the convergence of communications technology makes it increasingly difficult to continue to justify treating the print media as a breed apart.

PressWise has long advocated the incorporation of the European Convention of Human Rights into UK law, in the belief that editors would become more circumspect about the presentation of 'human interest' stories once the right to privacy and the right to freedom of expression are on a legal par.

Now, under the Human Rights Act 1998 we all have rights as citizens which the courts must protect. Once the Act is fully operational the PCC, like the other regulators, will be obliged to take them into account when adjudicating on complaints.

Until then individual journalists must look to their personal integrity if they are to win the confidence that the citizenry should have in their function as watchdogs of the public good. They may have little time to consider what *might happen* when their proper preoccupation is recording what *has happened* already.

Their inquisitiveness (*'Why is this bastard lying to me?'*) should extend to a questioning of everyone's motives including their own and their employers. Journalists should be sceptical about whether the ends ever justify the means, and have sufficient self-confidence to be able to say 'No' when asked to undertake assignments they find repugnant. But they cannot be expected to become beacons of ethical behaviour while editors' do not risk the sack for breaches of the Industry Code.

In the meantime *The Guardian's* reassuring daily Corrections & Comments Column offers a model that other publications would do well to emulate, acknowledging that mistakes can be made and having the decency to say you're sorry.

ENDNOTES

1. *The Universal Journalist* by David Randall, Pluto Press, 1996.
2. *The People Against the Press: An Enquiry into the Press Council* by Geoffrey Robertson, Quartet Books, 1983, ISBN 0 7043 2384 2.
3. *Report of the Committee on Privacy and Related Matters*, Chaired by David Calcutt QC, June 1990, Cmnd 1102, HMSO, ISBN 0 10 111022 7.
4. Aggregate figures drawn from latest annual reports of statutory and voluntary regulators.
5. Quoted in *The Genesis of the Freedom and Responsibility of the Press Bill* by Clive Soley MP, Appendix 2, *Report of Special Parliamentary Hearings on Freedom and Responsibility of the Press*, edited by Mike Jempson, Crantock Communications 1993 (available from PressWise).
6. Quoted from his verbatim evidence in *Report of Special Parliamentary Hearings on Freedom and Responsibility of the Press*, edited by Mike Jempson, Crantock Communications 1993 (available from PressWise).
7. See in particular *'Why You Unshot?'*, Chapter 6 of *Banana Sunday: Datelines from Africa*, by Chris Munnion, William Waterman Publications, 1993, ISN 0 9583751 7 8.

8. See *'New Challenges and Problems for Information Management in Complex Emergencies: Ominous lessons learnt from the Great Lakes and Eastern Zaire in late 1996 and early 1996,'* by Nik Gowing, and *'The Zaire Rebellion and the British Media: an analysis of the reporting of the Zaire crisis in Nov 1996 and 1997 by the Glasgow Media Group'*, edited by Greg Philo. Background papers for the Dispatches from Disaster Zones Conference, London, 28 May 1998.

9. 'Taking the P', front page lead *Bristol Evening Post*, 6 Dec 1996.

10. *My Brother David*, Produced by Roger Tonge for BBC TV.

11. Colin Caffell has written movingly of the distress caused by the media frenzy that erupted when his former wife died in a multiple killing for which her brother Jeremy Bamber was convicted (*In Search of the Rainbow's End: the inside story of the Bamber murders*, Hodder & Stoughton 1994, ISBN 0 340 61745 4) and Vicky Harper recounted the agony caused when the press highlighted the disputed defence case of three men facing charges over the death of her twin daughters in a mysterious fire (*Double Take*, Young Woodchester 1996, ISBN 0 9524796 4 8).

12. See 'Evidence of Witness "A" ', Appendix 3, *Report of Special Parliamentary Hearings on Freedom and Responsibility of the Press*, edited by Mike Jempson, Crantock Communications 1993 (available from PressWise).

13. See *'A shameful Anniversary'*, by Mike Jempson in *Interference on the Airwaves: Ireland, the Media and the Broadcasting Ban* by Liz Curtis and Mike Jempson CPBF, 1993, ISBN 1 898240 01 9.

14. PressWise has taken a particular interest in the ethical dilemmas faced by children who suffer physical, sexual or commercial exploitation, their carers and the journalists who seek to expose such abuse. See *Child Exploitation and the Media Forum Report and Recommendations*, edited by Mike Jempson, ACHE/PressWise/ Smallwood Publishing, 1997. See also *Children in the Picture: media, ethics and the reporting of child labour*, Mike Jempson, IFJ, 1997, and *Information and Child Rights: The Challenge of Media Engagement. An international survey of journalistic standards*, Mike Jempson & Bill Norris, IFJ/UNICEF, May 1998 (all available from PressWise).

15. Quoted in *'The Genesis of the Freedom and Responsibility of the Press Bill'* by Clive Soley MP, Appendix 2, *Report of Special Parliamentary Hearings on Freedom and Responsibility of the*

Press, edited by Mike Jempson, Crantock Communications 1993 (available from PressWise).

16. Chequebook journalism raises many ethical questions. PressWise regards the practice as the antithesis of press freedom and cautions against entering into exclusive contracts. See PressWise leaflet *'What's the cost of selling your story to the papers'* (available from PressWise). PressWise evidence to the National Heritage Select Committee quoted in *Press Activity Affecting Court Cases* (HMSO Jan 1997 ISBN 0 20 207097 0) and PressWise Briefing Paper *'Cheque-book Journalism'*.

17. *'Leave my son alone!'*, contribution to *Child Exploitation and the Media Forum Report and Recommendations*, edited by Mike Jempson, ACHE/PressWise/Smallwood Publishing (available from PressWise).

18. See also *Telling it like it is: Report of the Ethnic Minorities and the Media Forum*, edited by Mike Jempson, PressWise/CRA, May 1998.

19. *No Last Rights: The denial of justice and the promotion of myth in the aftermath of the Hillsborough disaster*, Phil Scraton, Ann Jemphrey & Sheila Coleman, Liverpool City Council, 1995, ISBN 0 904517 30 6.

20. See for instance *Britain's Media – how they are related: media ownership and democracy*, Granville Williams CPBF, 1996, ISBN 1 898240 04 3.

16 A degree of uncertainty: aspects of the debate over the regulation of the Press in the UK since 1945

Tom O'Malley

All that makes existence valuable to anyone, depends on the enforcement of restraints upon the actions of other people. Some rules of conduct, therefore, must be imposed, by law in the first place, and by opinion on many things which are not fit subjects of the operation of law. What these rules should be is the principal question in human affairs; but if we except a few of the most obvious cases, it is one of those which least progress has been made in resolving
(Mill 1973, p. 130).

In the United Kingdom self-regulation of the newspaper press dates from 1953. In that year the Press Council was established. Funded largely by the owners of newspapers, the Council was established, in part, to:

Show up and condemn any practices which could only bring the Press into disrepute, investigate complaints, and, where these are justified, to seek redress and to answer criticisms which are unfair or ill founded (Press Council 1954, p. 3).

Self-regulation of the press on matters of ethical standards continued thereafter into the 1990s under the Press Council's successor, the Press Complaints Commission. Superficially then, the continuation of self-regulation for over forty-five years implies the existence of a consensus between governments, politicians and other interested parties, in favour of self-regulation. This continuity, however, masks a

297

much more turbulent history involving disagreements between government sponsored inquiries, and between government, MPs and pressure groups about whether, to use Mill, 'rules of conduct' in the press, should 'be imposed by law'. This chapter explores aspects of these disagreements.

The purpose of this chapter then, is not to weigh up whether there should, or should not be statutory regulation of ethical standards in the press, nor is it to decide on whether it is possible to have statutory regulation and still promote press freedom. It does not, in addition, seek to determine the implications of particular proposals for statutory reform. These are complex issues which have been rehearsed extensively in the 1990s (Jempson 1993; Cram 1998). The purpose is to draw attention to the uncertainty that has existed in the post-war period over whether there should be statutory regulation, and, by implication, to argue that the question of statutory versus voluntary regulation has remained unresolved in principle even though the latter remained both the status quo and the favoured option of governments.

THE REMOVAL OF STATE CONTROLS

Pre-publication censorship of the press ended in 1695 when the Licensing Acts, measures which had formed a cornerstone of press control, were not renewed by Parliament. From 1712 until the 1860s successive governments used taxes in order to exercise some control over the industry. Newspaper publishers had to pay taxes on paper and on advertisements (stamp and advertisement duties), as well as, at different times, having to deposit bonds or sureties on pain of forfeit if the law was breached. In addition government ministers secretly funded publishers and journalists to put their case, and also instigated prosecutions for criminal libel against troublesome publishers. The object of these measures was to provide some tools for control, of one sort or another, over the press (Harris 1996). In the nineteenth century political opinion amongst the governing elites changed and successive governments saw fit to dismantle the panoply of stamp and advertisement duties, most of which had gone by the late 1860s (Koss 1990; Curran and Seaton 1997).

From the late nineteenth century onwards the newspaper press in the UK expanded. After the 1890s the daily readership of cheap newspapers extended to all classes, with a rapid expansion taking place in papers appealing to the lower middle and working classes, including the *Daily Mail* and the *Daily Mirror* (Lee 1978; Murdock and Golding 1978). This expansion took place in a context in which proprietors, journalists and politicians proclaimed their support for the idea of a Free Press. In practice, this meant that no politician wanted to be seen to be passing laws, like the Licensing Acts or the Stamp Acts, which could be interpreted as interfering with Press Freedom. The battle against overt state control of the press had been hard fought and was a genuine achievement that few wished to see reversed. Equally, as the twentieth century progressed, the examples of Nazi Germany and Fascist Italy provided plenty of support for the argument that State control of the press was profoundly undesirable (Wickham Steed 1938, pp. 161–176).

THE PROBLEM OF STANDARDS

But there was a problem. As the press grew after 1900 and competition intensified, so a number of developments troubled people within and without the industry. Newspapers engaged in questionable practices to build circulation, including invasions of privacy, sensationalism, inaccuracy and exaggeration. One price of Press Freedom in the twentieth century seemed to be a decline in ethical standards. For example, public distaste for the antics of the press led to juries awarding, as owners saw it, increasingly large sums to plaintiffs. In 1936 one proprietor commented that:

The struggle for sensation, to go one better than one's competitors, the intrusion into private grief, the utter lack of good taste which are the principal characteristics of a large and widely read section of the press are a cause of much lack of sympathy in the very real difficulties we face today (O'Malley, P. 1975, pp. 245–250).

By the end of the Second World War (1939–45), these pressures, plus concerns about monopoly, led to the establishment by the Labour government of a Royal Commission on the Press in 1947 (O'Malley, T. 1997). Amongst its terms of reference was 'the object of furthering the free expression of opinion through the Press and the greatest practicable accuracy'. Whilst overwhelmingly supportive of the Press, the Commission pointed to problems of accuracy, distortion and sensationalism:

In assessing the standard of accuracy of the Press we have found some evidence of willingness to be satisfied with what at best corresponds only roughly to the truth and of readiness to make statements on inadequate evidence.

News values, with their stress on the new and on human interest angles led to distortion and in more extreme instances resulted not only in 'a debasement of standards of taste, but also in a further weakening of the foundations of intelligent judgement in public affairs.' The Commission also noted the existence of triviality and sensationalism, which they attributed 'mainly to the competition for mass circulation' (RCP 1949, iii, paras, 553, 559, 563).

In determining how best to deal with these problems, the Commission considered that 'Free enterprise is a pre-requisite of a free Press' and argued that 'State control o& the Press' would be no solution:

We prefer to seek the means of maintaining the free expression of opinion and the greatest possible accuracy in the presentation of news, and, generally, a proper relationship between the Press and society, primarily in the Press itself.

Accordingly the Commission recommended a solution favoured by many contemporaries (O'Malley, T. 1997), that the industry establish a General Council of the Press, of twenty-five members, with 80 per cent coming from the industry and the rest from the public:

The objects of the General Council should be to safeguard the freedom of the Press; to encourage the growth of the sense of public responsibility and public service amongst all engaged in the profession of journalism – that is, in the editorial production of newspapers – whether as directors, editors, or other journalists; and to further the efficiency of the profession and the well-being of those who practise it (RCP 1949, paras 683, 684).

The Commission ruled out legislation to protect privacy, not on grounds of principle, but because it would 'be extremely difficult to devise legislation which would deal with the mischief effectively and be capable of enforcement'. The Commissioners ruled out the idea that newspapers should be made to carry a column in which an 'outside critic or expert authority' commented on 'incorrect and misleading statements' and expressed a view different to the editorial opinion of the paper. In principle they objected to 'compelling a newspaper to publish controversial material over which it has no control' (RCP 1949, paras 643–645). Its solution was that the General Council of the Press, as well as monitoring ownership and control in the industry and promoting training, would:

By censuring undesirable types of journalistic conduct, and by all other possible means . . . build up a code in accordance with the highest professional standards. In this connection, it should have the right to consider any complaints which it may receive about the conduct of the Press or of any persons towards the Press, to deal with these complaints in whatever manner may seem to it practicable and appropriate, and to include in its annual report any action under this heading (RCP, 1949: para 684).

Two of the Commissioners, Sir George Waters and R.K. Ensor, registered formal reservations against having lay people, other than the Chair, on the Council. Waters felt that the General Council would get off to a better start if staffed by members of the press alone. Ensor argued against lay people on the grounds that they were 'not usual in analogous bodies, and I am aware of no peculiar disability among Pressmen calling for such an innovation' (RCP 1949, pp. 179–180).

When it ruled out state control and statutory compulsion in the area of inaccuracy, the Commission was reflecting the orthodox view that the State should not interfere in the press. But it was not consistent. It did not rule out a privacy law on grounds of principle, but for reasons of practical difficulty. It recommended vigorous voluntary reform, involving the public, monitoring economic developments in the industry and establishing and enforcing a professional code. Ensor and Waters' reservations were pointers to the future, in that the industry proved reluctant to draw the public into the process, and, more importantly, engaged in a long drawn-out process of foot dragging over the implementation of the Commission's recommendations.

SELF-REGULATION AND THE SECOND ROYAL COMMISSION

The Labour government supported the recommendation for a General Council of the Press, but reserved its position on whether or not to legislate. Thus, the deputy Prime Minister and Lord President of the Council, Herbert Morrison said, on 28 July 1949:

If it should turn out – though I hope it will not be the case – that the Press should not be willing to take steps for the appointment of such a General Council, the Government and Parliament would have to consider the situation (House of Commons Debates, 1949).

In fact the industry delayed in setting up the General Council, to the point of creating exasperation amongst informed observers. In 1952 the issue was revived through the publication of a series of letters to *The Times* by, amongst others, the Chair of the Commission, Sir David Ross, which queried the delay in setting up a Council. This, combined with a debate over a Private Members' Bill, proposing statutory intervention to establish a Press Council, forced the proprietors' hand. The owners set up a Press Council in July 1953 (Levy 1967, pp. 8–9).

Thus the question of statutory versus voluntary control was resolved, after a fashion, only after substantial political pressure was brought to bear on owners. The activities of the Press Council in the 1950s did not, however, stem criticism of the industry. When, in 1962 the second Royal Commission on the Press reported it adopted a much stronger position on the question of statutory measures than did its predecessor. The second Commission was not directly concerned with how the Press Council regulated standards, but it considered that the Council's overall record was so bad that statutory intervention might be needed. The Press had failed to appoint a lay Chair, 'indeed there was no lay element at all', and the Council had failed to properly monitor economic developments in the industry, in part because proprietors had not funded the organisation well enough for it to conduct this work. The Commission urged the industry to revise the Press Council's constitution so as to comply more closely with the recommendations of the first Royal Commission on questions of objectives and membership, and, amongst other things, to enlarge its functions so that journalists could complain to it about examples of undue influence being exercised by advertisers on the content of newspapers. But, unlike its predecessor, the second Commission made no bones of the fact that statutory intervention was, in principle, a distinct option:

If however the Press is not willing to invest the Council with the necessary authority and to contribute the necessary finance the case for a statutory body with definite powers and the right to levy the industry is a clear one . . . We think that the press should be given another opportunity itself voluntarily to establish an authoritative General Council with a lay element as recommended by the 1949 Commission. We recommend, however, that the Government should specify a time limit after which legislation would be introduced for the establishment of such a body, if in the meantime it had not been set up voluntarily (RCP 1962, paras 320–326).

So, the failure of the industry to adhere to the terms of the 1949 Commission's recommendations was sufficient evidence for the 1962 Commission to argue that statutory regulation should be considered.

The Press Council was, as a result, reconstituted. Lay membership was increased, its funding rose and, under its new lay Chair, it took a more high profile role on questions of Press Freedom (Levy 1967, pp. 21–22; Robertson 1983, p. 12). But a deep-seated concern about the efficacy of voluntary regulation remained. In 1961 Lord Mancroft introduced a Bill to deal with Privacy, as did Alex Lyon MP in 1967 and Brian Walden MP in 1969. All three failed to become law (Wacks 1995, p. 3. n. 4). This concern about privacy led to a further inquiry, the Younger Committee on Privacy, which sat in the early 1970s. In the Younger Report, published in 1972, it was recommended that there be an increase in lay membership of the Press Council, and that lay members should be appointed, not by sitting members of the Commission, but by an independent appointments committee. It also recommended that the Council insist that its adjudications be published with equal prominence to the offending article, and that it codify its adjudications on privacy. In the event, lay membership was increased to ten out of thirty members, but little progress was made on the other recommendations (Robertson 1983, p. 12; Whale 1977, p. 130; RCP 1977, paras 20.40, 20.58).

This period then saw the inadequacy of voluntary regulation exposed by the action of MPs and government enquiries, and the industry responding to threats of statutory regulation by making long overdue alterations to the constitution and practices of the Press Council. From 1962 until the mid-1970s then, there was, in a sense, a stand-off between the industry and its critics.

THE THIRD ROYAL COMMISSION AND AFTER

The period between 1974 and 1993 saw pressures intensify. During the post-war period evidence emerged that questions of media accountability became of increasing interest to wider sections of the public. An awareness of the rights of viewers, listeners and readers emerged in public forums, which ran parallel with more traditional concerns about Press Freedom from State control (O'Malley, T. 1998). Some of the tensions this led to were expressed in the report of the third post-war Royal Commission on the Press which was published in 1977. The Commissioners devoted a chapter to the Press Council, largely because:

It is unhappily certain that the Council has so far failed to persuade the knowledgeable public that it deals satisfactorily with complaints against newspapers, not withstanding, that this has come to be seen as its main purpose (RCP 1977, para 20.12).

The Commission made twelve recommendations designed to bolster self-regulation. These included having equal numbers of lay and industry members; inviting nominations for membership from any source; appointing a conciliator to deal with complaints; that the Council should uphold the idea that a newspaper should make space 'available to those it has criticised inaccurately'; and that the Council should draw up a code of behaviour which 'should set out in some detail the spirit which should govern the conduct of editors and journalists' (RCP 1977, pp. 235–236).

Unlike the 1962 Commission, this one did not recommend legislation in the event of the failure of reform, but it did strongly suggest that the price of failure might be legislation:

We reject as potentially authoritarian suggestions for a standing commission for broadcasting and the press, representative of all major sections of the community and responsible to a Minister for monitoring the performance of the press. The Press Council must also show a determination to be independent of the press . . . willingness on the part of the press to accept and conform to the rulings of the Council is the only alternative to the introduction of a legal right of privacy, and perhaps of a statutory Press Council (RCP 1977, para 20.1).

The balance had shifted back to the position of the 1949 Commission. Just as the first Commission had justified rejecting statutory intervention for fear of the spectre of State Control, so the 1977 Report allied questions of statutory intervention – in this case a proposal for a standing commission on broadcasting and the press – with the notion of authoritarianism. But the Report was ambiguous, for like Morrison in his speech from 1949, quoted above, it hinted that other measures might follow, in this case legislation, if self-regulation failed. The Report did not then mount a sustained defence of the principle of self-regulation, more a half-hearted assertion of a preference for the status quo, and it also left the door open to statutory intervention.

In 1979 the Campaign for Press Freedom was established. Backed by the media trade unions, other unions and a wide range of individuals, it set out 'to encourage debate about how press freedom can be extended'. One of its aims was 'To campaign for a reformed reconstituted Press Council to promote basic standards of fairness and access to the press on behalf of the public'. It cast a sceptical eye over the success of voluntary reform:

It would be better if these Press Council reforms were introduced voluntarily. But when one examines the history of the Press Council it becomes clear how irrelevant its 'voluntary' nature has been in extending press freedom or giving the public any adequate means of redress (Campaign 1979, pp. 13–14).

The Campaign supported and wrote a series of Private Members' Bills in the 1980s and early 1990s, put forward by Frank Allaun MP, Ann Clwyd MP, Tony Worthington MP and Clive Soley MP. All tried to establish some form of Right of Reply. The last three bills gained substantial cross-party support, but were all defeated because the government was unprepared to give them support. In the 1980s there was also a further flurry of activity around privacy, with MPs seeking again to legislate on the matter. This pressure led to the establishment in 1989 of a Committee on Privacy and Related Matters, chaired by David Calcutt. As its Report suggested the reason for the Committee's existence was because of the continued existence of concern about press regulation:

The immediate background to our appointment was the extent of parliamentary support during the 1988/9 session for two Private Members' Bills on Protection of Privacy and Right of Reply. These were introduced by John Browne MP and Tony Worthington MP respectively. . . . Neither proposal was new. Similar Bills had been introduced in the previous parliamentary session by William Cash MP and Ann Clwyd MP respectively. These in turn were based on earlier Bills (Report 1990, para 1.3).

The issue, then, in spite of the continuance of self-regulation, remained unresolved. In one sense, the Calcutt Report of 1990, re-echoed the theme of the 1962 Royal Commission. It recommended that the Press Council be disbanded and replaced by a Press Complaints Commission, funded by the industry, which 'should concentrate on providing an effective means of redress for complaints against the Press'. Unlike the 1949 and 1977 Commissions' Reports, it had no inhibitions about using statutory means to achieve effective regulation of standards. It rejected a statutory Right of Reply because it had doubts about how practical it was to legislate for a speedy correction of inaccuracy; like the 1949 Commission's rejection of Privacy laws, Calcutt stressed practical, not in principal, objections to Right of Reply. Calcutt also thought that a revised Code of Practice, the law of defamation and a new Press Complaints Commission could deal with the issues raised by the need for a Right of Reply (Report 1990, p. x; paras 11.15, 11.16). The Report recommended that:

If maverick publications persistently declined to respect the authority of the Press Complaints Commission, the Commission should be placed on a statutory footing. It should be given sufficient statutory powers to enable it to require any newspaper, periodical or magazine to respond to its enquiries about complaints and to publish its adjudications as directed. It should be able to recommend the payment of compensation (Report 1990, p. xi).

The Press Council was replaced by the Press Complaints Commission. But this did not stop a further attempt by Clive Soley MP, to introduce a statutory Right of Reply to factual inaccuracies in 1992 (Jempson 1993). In 1992 David Calcutt was asked to review the state of press regulation, again, and this time, considering the response of the industry to the 1990 Report inadequate, his second Report (1993) recommended an end to voluntary self-regulation. The government of the day rejected this recommendation (Cram 1998, pp. 102–105).

AN UNRESOLVED ISSUE

A number of points stand out about the development of public discussion about press regulation since 1945. The first is the recurrence of concerns amongst, to paraphrase the 1977 Commission, knowledgeable people about the ethical performance of the press, concerns which have not been allayed by either the Press Council or its successor, the Press Complaints Commission. The second point has been that proprietors have only acted to significantly improve the practice of self-regulation when either threatened by legislation or when placed under scrutiny by high profile inquiries. Had proprietors been more proactive over the period surveyed, it is possible that the concerns which prompted the continual criticisms of self-regulation, would have been allayed.

In addition there has been no consensus amongst the government sponsored Commissions and Reports on the press as to whether or not it would be wrong, in principle, to substitute statutory for voluntary regulation. The 1947–49 Commission was against State control of the press, and the use of compulsion to make editors print columns of corrections. But its objections to privacy laws were objections based on grounds of practicality, not of principle. Like its predecessor the 1961–62 Commission preferred voluntary action, but was less ambiguous about its attitude to statutory reform, seeing no principle objection to placing the Press Council on a statutory footing. The 1974–77 Commission, somewhat ambiguously, held out the prospect of legislation as an alternative to self-regulation, whilst avowing its opposition to other forms of statutory regulation. In the end, after another almost twenty years of public discussion, the second Calcutt report, published in 1993, finally lost patience with the industry and recommended statutory regulation.

Whilst governments have studiously avoided taking measures to put regulation on a statutory footing, they have acted within a context in which the case for allowing the status quo post-1953 to continue was never adequately resolved in favour of the principle of self-regulation by the range of inquiries that have been set up. Reluctance to use statute to impose effective regulation had its roots in the well-established fear of state intervention in the press. But the implications of the positions adopted by all the inquiries surveyed here, is that this fear did not constitute sufficient grounds for opposing, in principle, and at all times, all forms of statutory regulation of standards. Equally, this fear did not stop critics from demanding some form of statutory regulation.

This chapter has drawn a4tention to the uncertainty that existed in the post-war period over whether there should be statutory or voluntary regulation of the press and to argue that the question has remained unresolved in principle. In fact, if the post-war history of these discussions tells us anything, it is that the press, politicians, governments, inquiries, and critics have failed to arrive at a workable consensus on the question of press regulation. It also suggests that until such a consensus is reached the cycle or public criticism, inquiry, threat of legislation, burst of reform, and return to public criticism will continue. To adapt Mill's words from the opening quotation, in the post-war period, the question of whether the law should or should not impose 'rules of conduct' on the press has been one of those about 'which least progress has been made'.

ACKNOWLEDGEMENT

I would like to thank Tim White for comments on an earlier draft of this chapter.

REFERENCES

Campaign For Press Freedom (1979) *Towards Press Freedom*, London: Campaign For Press Freedom.

Cram, I. (1998) 'Beyond Calcutt: the legal and extra legal protection of privacy interests in England and Wales', in M. Kieran, ed., *Media Ethics*, London, Routledge, pp. 97–110.

Curran, J. and Seaton, J. (1997) *Power Without Responsibility*, 5th edition, London: Routledge.

Harris, B. (1996) *Politics and the Rise of the Press. Britain and France, 1620–1800*, London: Routledge.

House of Commons Debates (1949) 5th series, Volume 467, col. 2696, 28 July 1949.

Jempson, M. ed. (1993) *Report of Special Parliamentary Hearings on Freedom and Responsibility of the Press December 1992*, Bristol: Crantock Communications.

Koss, S. (1990) *The Rise and Fall of the Political Press in Britain*, London: Fontana.

Lee, A. (1978) 'The Structure, Ownership and Control of the Press, 1855–1914', in Boyce, G., Curran, J., and Wingate, P., eds, *Newspaper History: From the 17th Century to the Present Day*, London: Sage/Constable, pp. 117–129.

Levy, H. (1967) *The Press Council. History Procedure and Cases*, London: Macmillan.

Mill, J.S. (1973) 'On Liberty' (1859), in Warnock, M., ed., *Utilitarianism*, London: Fontana.

Murdock, G. and Golding, P. (1978) 'The Structure, Ownership and Control of the Press, 1914–76', in Boyce, G. Curran, J. and Wingate, P., eds., *Newspaper History: From the 17th Century to the Present Day*, London: Sage/Constable, pp. 130–148.

O'Malley, P.T. (1975) *The Politics of Defamation: The State, Press Interests and the English Libel Laws*, Phd thesis, University of London.

O'Malley, T. (1997) 'Labour and the 1947–9 Royal Commission on the Press', in M. Bromley and T. O'Malley, eds, *A Journalism Reader*, London, Routledge, pp. 126–158.

O'Malley, T. (1998) 'Demanding Accountability. The Press, the Royal Commissions and the Pressure for Reform 1945–77', in M. Bromley and H. Stephenson, eds, *Sex, Lies and Democracy*, London, Longman, pp. 84–96.

Press Council (1954) *The Press and the People: The First Annual Report of the General Council of the Press*, London, Press Council.

Report of the Committee on Privacy and Related Matters (1990) Cmnd 1102, London: HMSO.

Robertson, G. (1983) *People Against The Press. An Enquiry into the Press Council*, London: Quartet.

Royal Commission on the Press 1947–1949 Report (1949), Cmnd 7700, London: HMSO.

Royal Commission on the Press 1961–62 Report (1962) Cmnd 1811, London: HMSO.

Royal Commission on the Press Final Report (1977) Cmnd 6810, London: HMSO.

Wacks, R. (1995) *Privacy and Press Freedom*, London: Blackstone Press.

Whale, J. (1977) *The Politics of the Media*, London: Fontana.

Wickham Steed, H. (1938) *The Press*, London: Penguin.

17 Codes and cultures

Philip Dring

The debate about journalism ethics has centred, in the UK, on the feeling that there has been in recent years a decline in the standing and status of the press. There have been various responses to this that have looked at the situation in other countries to consider whether the adoption of alternative standards could improve the situation in Britain. This chapter seeks to draw attention to potential problems with this approach and argues that the development of the ethical framework is often deeply rooted in the journalistic environment of the country concerned and that this might not, necessarily, translate easily to other contexts.

The preface to Andrew Belsey and Ruth Chadwick's *Ethical issues in Journalism and the Media* (1992) opens with the statement that, 'The practice of journalism as a profession raises many ethical issues'. The chapter 'New Ethics' in David Randall's *The Universal Journalist* (1996) begins with the view that 'There is more nonsense written and spoken about ethics than any other issue in journalism'.

Belsey and Chadwick are both philosophers whose work on journalistic ethics has been informed by developments in the area of ethics applied to medical practice. Randall is a journalist, a former assistant editor of the London *Observer*, and a media consultant. On a first reading there would appear to be a considerable gulf between these two positions. In the UK there is a long tradition of mutual mistrust between journalists and academics undertaking the study of journalism.

There are obvious historical reasons for this – there is no history of journalism education, as distinct from craft related training, in the UK. This demonstrates a distinctly different pattern to the development of journalism education in the USA where journalism schools were established in colleges of higher education from the early 1900s. Similarly, much of Europe has seen a different pattern of development in the relationship between journalism practice and journalism education. In several instances this interaction has roots in political expediency, including the rise of Fascism. In some cases this has led to a strange legacy in terms of journalism education which has, in its extreme form, left the Italian system of journalism training, the Albo dei Giornalisti, as a rigorous examination based primarily on an appreciation of politics and government.

These differing patterns of development have, in turn, led to alternative views of the relationship between journalism and ethics. In the USA there has been a reasonably consistent line connecting the practise of journalism and ethical perspectives derived from moral philosophy and, indeed, there appears to be a limitless production line of textbooks which argue the case either for journalism ethics by a historical, philosophical survey or others which present ethical issues in journalism on a case study basis which encourages students to explore the issues around principles of moral philosophy.[1] Mention should also be made here of the approach suggested by Mathew Kieran (1997) which reinforces the use of philosophy in the understanding of issues in the media on the basis that it assists the individual in learning to think about and to examine critically issues which will, thus, inform their practice.

It is easy to see why this approach may alarm journalists schooled in the British tradition whose views could be summarised by Randall's (1996) dismissive comment that ethics:

are either the codification of prevailing behaviour and culture, or an irrelevant exhortation to standards of behaviour which are doomed to be unmet. Either way there is not much point to them (ibid., p. 92).

Randall then goes on to list a series of highly generalised pointers towards the creation of an ethical approach to journalism. These comprise a list of guidelines relating to professional practice such as

'Every story should be an honest search for the truth' and 'No inducements to publish should be accepted'.

This somewhat mechanistic approach might be seen as typical of a European pattern of development which has placed a greater faith in the ability of laws and issues of professional practice to protect the freedom of the press and to force the media to serve the public.[2] In the USA the approach is much more one of the individual journalist being able to make moral and ethical decisions. At its extreme form John C. Merrill's comment that 'Journalists must seek ethical guidance from within themselves, not from the codes of organisations, commissions or councils'[3] might stand, and it is worth noting that Merrill believed that social responsibilities placed on journalists posed a real threat to expressive freedom.

The emphasis in the USA is very much on the individual journalist being enabled to wrestle with ethical problems. The strategy might be summarised as the need for the journalist to construct a pattern of ethical deliberation that can be explicitly outlined in which the relevant considerations can be isolated and given appropriate weight.[4] The recommended approach is frequently through the application of a formulation such as the Potter Box of Moral Reasoning, the use of which leads to defensible ethical decisions.[5]

In the case that I am taking as being emblematic of the position in the UK, Randall concludes his chapter with a section described as 'grey areas'. The considered view is that the journalist needs 'considerable experience' in dealing with these problem areas. However, it is worth noting that there is a greater concern with the journalist's working context than is allowed for in the examples drawn from the US textbooks.

The historical background to the sense that the responsibility for the maintenance of journalistic ethics falls on the individual journalist in the USA is, of course, in part because of the constitutional protection afforded to freedom of the press. This, and a greater perceived sense of freedom of information than in the UK, leads to a different journalistic environment. There is something of an irony here in the way that the British journalistic environment has separated from the US experience, and has come to be seen as somewhat more European in its nature. This has seen the adoption of European modes of broadcasting, the acceptance of European regulatory codes, the provision of shared

European news programming and so on. However, as Jean L. Chalaby (1996) has indicated there is a case for saying that the nature of journalism, as we currently understand it, was very much an Anglo-American concept. Although Chalaby does not refer directly to ethical concerns several of the distinctions that he draws between French journalism, as it developed in the mid-nineteenth century, and those developments in Britain and the USA were very much related to concerns which we now identify as ethical. British and US newspapers contained more information and news than their French counterparts and this information was more factually accurate, 'more complete, more objective and more neutral'. Information in Anglo-American newspapers was 'more factual' and 'more reliable' and French journalism (he is dealing here with the period of the Third Republic, 1870s–1940) suffered from 'endemic corruption'. The French tradition was altogether more literary and interpretive in its approach to news gathering and the presentation of that news. Indeed, Chalaby claims that techniques such as interviewing and reporting were invented by American journalists.

Whilst there is room for argument about this interpretation (Chalaby, perhaps, diminishes the literary influences on early British journalism reducing this important developmental strand to a passing mention of Dickens as a rather misguided attempt to become a literary-journalist), and Chalaby does indicate alternative readings, it does serve to highlight widespread historical differences between British journalism and what might be termed mainstream European journalism. All of this would be unimportant were it not for the widespread notion that all is not well in the world of British journalistic ethics. Numerous British commentators have drawn attention to this apparent crisis. Government ministers have described, somewhat ironically, the British press as being at the last chance saloon and commentators have stressed the need for the debate to be opened up by journalists and journalism educators to 'undertake a critical examination of the enterprise before others do it for them'.[6]

The difficulty for British journalism is seen as being that it is somehow caught in a range of factors which affect in various degrees the issue of ethics. The traditional craft professionalism has already been noted, but to this must be added codes of ethics, the various notions of professionalism, including the traditional, the network of media law that has developed in Britain, the marketplace, access and ownership. Interestingly, given the concerns highlighted by Chalaby, Richards relates the emergence of these problems to the New Journalism which developed in Britain in the late 1890s and which could be seen as having its antecedents in American journalism from the mid-nineteenth century.

The response to these concerns has seen a series of attempts to relocate British journalism within good practice in other countries. There has been something of the nature of the grass always being greener to much of this debate and it is clear that there has been very little serious evaluative work done in this area. In the most wide ranging survey of journalistic codes of practice, Tiina Laitila (1995) has conducted a survey of 31 European codes of ethics covering 29 countries to establish whether there is sufficient ground to consider the development of a common, shared code of practice. Her methodology is to identify six key functions which might be considered as essential to any code. These are, under the general heading of Accountability – to the public, to sources and referents, to the state and to the employers and under the heading Professional Identity – protection of the integrity of journalists and protection of the unity of the profession. These headings are then divided into 13 categories which are central themes represented in the majority of the codes. Beyond this Laitila identified no less than 61 specific principles of journalistic ethics.

The sheer complexity of this undertaking highlights some of the problems inherent in this approach. Laitila's conclusions are that of her 13 main categories all but two (respect for state institutions and protection of the solidarity within the profession) find support in over two-thirds of the codes. Moreover, there are 24 common principles which are shared by more than half of the codes studied. Laitila postulates that there is here at least the common basis to begin the consideration of a common European journalist code of ethics.

This project, by the nature of its approach, inevitably collapses a number of issues in a rather simplistic way. First, there are codes of behaviour which seek to inform individual journalists, in a manner related to the individualistic approach reviewed earlier (the National Union of Journalists' Code of Conduct may be seen as falling into this framework). Secondly, there are the codes which seek to create regulatory frameworks which apply to the broader journalistic environment. The Press Complaints Commissions Code of Practice, for example, makes reference to editorial responsibilities and the role and function of newspapers within certain contexts as well as issues relating to the position of the individual journalist.

However, Laitila's classification is an interesting and original one and may pay further consideration. Perhaps significantly, the primary response to the apparent crisis afflicting British journalism has been to show considerable interest in evaluating whether there is anything that could be gained by examining the situation in individual countries which are seen as having established a framework of regulation which functions effectively.

Much attention here has focused on the situation in Sweden. Drawing attention to the position in the UK around the Press Complaints Commission, James Curran and Jean Seaton comment that:

An alternative beefed-up version of this approach is provided by the system of self-regulation in Sweden, where a code of conduct is negotiated between the publishers' organization and journalists' union.[7]

Peter J. Humphreys (1996) has said that:

Sweden offers the best example of a self regulatory system that actually does regulate . . . the Swedish version of self-regulation, it has been suggested, has a certain model character. It would appear to have safeguarded generally high journalistic standards and a very open system of access to information (ibid., p. 64).

This then is becoming a central issue for the debate concerning the nature of regulation and ethics in Britain. However, these rather bland assertions about the superiority of the Swedish system do disguise the fact that it has a somewhat complex history rooted in Swedish culture which needs to be considered further if it is, indeed, to be considered a role model for the UK and the rest of Europe.

Sweden has, arguably, the oldest and most liberal legal framework around the press anywhere in the world. The system embraces both freedom of the press and freedom of speech. The first Swedish Press Law goes back as far as 1766. This law guaranteed freedom from censorship, but with certain limitations, such as criticism of the royal house, the government, fundamentals of the legal system and the church. The 1766 law encouraged greater freedom of political debate, but did not introduce public freedom of speech and Swedish commentators have noted that the debate on newspaper freedom in Britain at this time was clearly more 'free' than that taking place in Sweden (Hadenius and Webull 1997). However what is, perhaps, the 1766 law's most important aspect is that it contained an element of freedom of information in that it granted public access to official records and appears to have been formulated to counter the possibility of an authoritative state control of media systems. The press had been seen as an important element of state propaganda and Sweden's first newspapers, from *Ordinari Post Tijdender* in 1645, clearly demonstrate this tendency.

In this form the law lasted only until 1772 when, with the succession of King Gustav III, a series of restrictions were imposed and the notion of a comprehensive press law disappeared. However, the concept was revived in 1810 when issues of press freedom were included within a new constitutional framework. There were subsequent adaptations to this, notably in 1812. Further major change took place in 1949 with the introduction of new legislation. Importantly this went back to the original 1766 law for its fundamentals, providing continuity across two centuries. The law only dealt with the press. Radio was incorporated in legislation in 1967 and in 1992 a new law was introduced covering radio, television, film and video. The essential aspect of this legislation covering the electronic media was that it embraced the basic principles of the law applying to the press.

The key, common aspects of this legislative framework can be summarised as follows:

(i) freedom to establish – every citizen has the right to publish newspapers without restriction from the state or other public bodies. Each publication must have a publisher who has responsibility for the content;

(ii) a ban on censorship – any censorship by a public body prior to publication is forbidden as is the attempt to take action to attempt to stop publication or the circulation of printed material;

(iii) the protection of anonymity of sources and of communication – all sources are protected and those working in the media have a right to anonymity. Moreover, all state bodies are prohibited from trying to find out who is supplying the media with information;

(iv) rules of responsibility – there must be a responsible publisher for all published material and broadcast programmes (radio and television). The publisher has to be appointed by the proprietor. It is the publisher who is responsible for the content not the journalist or writer or the makers of the programme.

This comprehensive legal framework is supported by measures assuring openness in government. All documents, including databases, which are kept by public authorities should be made publicly available with exemptions for documentation in preparation and those which are confidential for reasons of national security. In Sweden the freedom of speech and the press laws are regarded as taking priority over other legislation. However, there is some growing sense that the Swedish system provides less protection for the individual than it should and that other countries that have broadly followed the Swedish model, such as Finland and Norway, have built in greater legal protection in this area. There is, in Sweden, some feeling that the Press law was established so early that issues such as defamation were not considered as being as important as they now appear (Thorsten 1992).

The underlying principle to this legal framework is the liberal, libertarian one of enabling publishing to take place with as few restrictions as possible. However, the media industries have also established a series of codes of conduct which, in the main, are concerned with establishing an ethical framework around the editorial aspects of publishing. Codes have been formulated by interests with a wide range of concerns in the publishing field. These include Publicistklubben (PK) and Svenska Tidningsutgivareforeningen (TU), both publishers' organisations, Swedish Radio and TV (SR and STV), the journalists' trade union (Svenska Journalistforbundet, SJF) and the association governing radio broadcasting (Radiotgivareforeningen).

Indeed, the involvement of these professional bodies in ethical concerns goes back to the early decades of the twentieth century. The reasons behind this relationship are instructive. There was, historically, in Sweden a tension between the drive to establish and publish the truth and the need for discretion on the part of the publisher. This led to a famous instance where a judge, an advocate of the truth principle, was asked how an honourable man should defend himself against accusations of adultery. His answer was 'by not committing adultery' (Axenberger 1994). The legislation was, however, framed within the context of discretion and this has remained an aspect of the legal framework ever since as well as being an informing principle of the various ethical codes. Essentially the litmus test is whether something is likely to place a person in a negative light even if it is true. Publication of material in this contentious area can fall foul of libel laws. Naturally enough there are clauses which qualify this to some extent and provide a justification for publication on 'reasonable grounds'. These are generally seen to be related to issues and concerns which are deemed to be of use to society.

However, there was some recognition that this had led to a somewhat weak protection of the individual – there are only about ten cases brought to court each year and of these, on average, only three are found in favour of the plaintiff. As a response to the perceived view that the law was weak in respect to its treatment of the individual the publishers' organisation, which had been formed in 1875 and brought together both publishers and editors and had a concern with the development of good standards in journalism, began to consider the issue. In 1900 they published principles concerning the reporting of court cases and as early as 1916 introduced a court of honour, in effect a press council (the first of its kind in the world), and in 1923 extended this by introducing an ethical code. There is a system of right to correction with anyone considering that they have been badly treated in a newspaper having the right to request that a correction be published.

This system of self-regulation has been reinforced on a number of occasions, notably in 1969, with the introduction of an ombudsman and in 1980 with the addition of a deputy ombudsman. This was, in part the outcome of criticism about the trend towards sensational journalism from the mid-1960s which led to the problem reaching parliament. The case against further restriction of the press, in particular, centred on the issue of press freedom, but even so the perception was that the press was going through a probationary period (Thorsten 1992).

Redress for the individual through the present system means that anyone who feels that they have been misrepresented can go direct to the newspaper and demand that a correction be published. Alternatively the individual has recourse to the ombudsman who can assist the individual with the previous procedure or can refer the case to the press council.

The twelve strong council is constituted in two parts. Each part has six members – one representative from each of the PK, SJF and TU and two members of the public (nominated by the Swedish Lawyers' Association and by the justice ombudsman), plus a chair drawn from someone of the standing of a judge. There are requirements for the result to be published and a sliding scale of fines based on readership figures applies.[8]

In radio and television a similar system applies with a review board considering the cases. All broadcasting organisations have an obligation to refer all complaints to the board. The board, like the press council, has the right to follow up cases which it feels merit such treatment without the intervention of a complainant.

The Swedish system is, therefore, characterised by a mixture of libertarian theory embracing issues such as freedom of information, wedded to a strong influence derived from notions of social responsibility. The emphasis for responsibility falls across a broad spectrum including publishers, editors and journalists, although the ultimate responsibility is on the nominated publisher rather than the individual journalist and this distinguishes it from the American position, where the responsibility right through the system from education and training to practice emphasises the responsibilities of the writer in ethical judgements and, to a lesser extent, the situation in Britain. It is worth noting that in Randall's (1996) interpretation of journalistic ethics the publisher/employer and editorial functions are seen as being analogous with the issues of competition and market forces within the industry.

Does this mean that the Swedish system is too idiosyncratic to translate into other cultures? It must be noted here that the basic principles of the Swedish model have been adopted by the neighbouring states of Finland and Norway. However, the complexity of the structure of the system in Sweden, with its series of checks and balances from a complex of legislation, a range of self-regulatory codes and a formal press council referral system suggests that there would be a great deal of work to be done if it was to be adopted by Britain or, even, across Europe. Some aspects of the Swedish model, especially the proactive activities of the press council, appear to meet the requirements of critics of the British Press Complaints Commission, such as the Chairman of the Parliamentary Labour Party, Clive Soley.[9]

However, there is another aspect of the debate over journalistic ethics which gets very little attention – that of readership and audience expectations. In his speech to the Guild of Editors in Cambridge, November 1998, Soley, whilst emphasising that he felt there was a need for strengthening the protection of individual privacy from an intrusive press, notes that the public do not see this as a priority (which lays with the accuracy of news reporting). There are here, I think, echoes of the Swedish debate over the principle of truth and the principle of discretion, but the whole issue does bring into question what kind of press the public expect.

This is an under-researched area and the evidence that is available is ambivalent. Research undertaken by Paul S. Voakes (1996) in the US Midwest suggests that journalists and the public have very different views of the importance of ethical considerations to journalistic practice. Using criteria derived from Shoemaker and Reese, Voakes, in line perhaps with our view of the US situation, defines 'professional ethics' as a common system of norms and values in the practise of journalism. Working from the viewpoint that ethics has to be seen as fundamentally a social phenomenon Voakes' findings suggest that the public attribute the ethical position of journalists to 'a generalized occupational disposition'. That is, they believe that journalists' ethical decision making stems from legal, competitive and occupational influences.

On the other hand, journalists believe that their ethical cues are derived from organisational directives, the relevant law and their individual moral reasoning with 'the newsroom environment being the strongest predictor of a journalists' ethical orientation'. Voakes then uses this to suggest that the line of argument indicated by his research might go some way to assist in the resolution of 'differences over ethics' and that an understanding of the expectations of readerships can help avoid public outrage over ethical issues in the first place.

There is clearly great need for further work in this area. However, it is worth considering what impact Voakes' findings might have in our concern with the possibility of a common European code of ethics. To do this we need to examine the three elements which Voakes has indicated are central concerns to journalists – organisational, legal, and moral.

In the case of the organisational there appear to be two extreme ways that this impacts on the journalist. In the Anglo-American model the organisational influences are often placed in a negative light. Randall provides one example of this but Polly Toynbee has frequently weighed in on the subject against the British tabloids, recently discussing them as a 'fount of crude cultural barbarity'.[10] In contrast with this the discussion of organisational influences in the Swedish press centres more on the shared responsibilities between media organisations and journalists and, importantly, this has deeply seated historical roots.

The legal is, I think, less controversial. However, it should be noted that the system in Sweden which is frequently cited as an example is predicated on a legal framework designed to protect press freedom whereas the debate in Britain is increasingly being centred on the need to frame legislation to protect individual privacy and restrict media intrusion.

I have already considered the debate relating to moral reasoning and its importance to the US model and the possible impact that this has had on the British system. However, it is clear that this represents another area of distinction between the Anglo-American approach and the Swedish. Once again the difference centres around the question of corporate responsibility and the responsibility of the individual journalist.

In one other respect there seems a need to question Voakes' findings in that he considers that there is some frequency of public outrage over ethical issues. There is, I believe, considerable scope for misreading public responses here. Whilst there was apparent public concern over media coverage over the death of the Princess of Wales the fact is that *Private Eye*, the only publication to have action taken against it over the coverage was also the only publication which did not profit from her death as its editor Ian Hislop made clear. This suggests a confusion of values at best.

Where does this leave us over the issue of whether or not a common code of ethics is possible in Europe? The examples of Britain, France and Sweden all demonstrate that there are very different historical and cultural backgrounds to the journalistic environments and that, replicated across Europe, even with the similarities identified by Laitila, there must be doubts about this enterprise. However, it could also be noted that the 'ideal' model that has developed in Sweden, has been adopted in other countries which have a similar historical and cultural background.

There is also evidence to suggest that the current debates over the nature of the ethics and the British press are being discussed in the wrong reference frames. This does, I believe, become a problem both in the educational context and in the way that the debate is related to rather unspecific references to public wishes. This is partly to do with the fact that there is no common agreement over what is meant by ethics in a journalistic context. The debate has undoubtedly been confused by long traditions of journalism training in the UK and the ideological baggage that has been carried with it. There is clearly a great deal to be done, but as I have indicated this work is unlikely to be meaningful unless the ground is cleared in advance.

ACKNOWLEDGEMENT

I would like to thank Jenny Johansson for the work on translation and for many stimulating discussions which have contributed to this work.

ENDNOTES

1. See, for example, Louis Day, *Ethics in Media Communications*, London, Wadsworth, 1997, S.R. Knowlton, *Moral Reasoning for Journalists*, London, Praeger, 1997 and S.R. Knowlton and P.R. Parsons, *The Journalists Moral Compass*, London, Praeger, 1995.
2. C.J. Bertrand, 'Media quality control in the USA and Europe', in H. Stephenson and M. Bromley eds, *Sex, Lies and Democracy: the Press and the Public*, Harlow, Addison Wesley, 1998, p. 114.
3. Quoted in R. Knowlton and P.R. Parsons, *The Journalists Moral Compass*, London, Praeger, 1995, p. 223.

4. See, for example, P. Patterson and L. Wilkins, *Media Ethics*, McGraw Hill, 1998, pp. 98–102.
5. The Potter Box, is of course, only one such example. For another see the use of SAD Formula in L. Day op. cit. pp. 61–65.
6. M. Richards, 'Obtrusive, unscrupulous, irresponsible invaders of privacy . . .', in *Journalists and Journalism education revisited: Media Arts Working Paper*, 4, Southampton Institute.
7. J. Curran and J. Seaton, *Power Without Responsibility*, London, Routledge, 4th edition, Curran and Seaton have currently refined this position – see the 5th edition, 1997, pp. 368–370.
8. *Spelregler for press, radio, television*, Stockholm Pressens Samarbetsnamnd, 1997, pp. 5–6.
9. *The Independent*, 10 November 1998.
10. *The Guardian*, 11 November 1998.

REFERENCES

Axenberger, H-G. (1994) Pressetik: Stockholm.

Belsey, A. and Chadwick, R. eds. (1992) *Ethical Issues in Journalism and the Media*, London: Routledge.

Chalaby, J. (1996) 'Journalism as an Anglo-American Invention: a comparison of the Development of French and Anglo-American Journalism, 1830's–1920's,' *European Journal of Communication*, **11**(3).

Hadenius, S. and Webull, L. (1997) *Massmedier*, Falkengurg: Bonner Alba.

Humphreys, P.J. (1996) *Mass Media and Media Policy in Western Europe*, Manchester: MUP, p. 64.

Kieran, M. (1997) *Media Ethics*, London: Praeger.

Laitila, T. (1995) 'Journalistic Codes of Ethics in Europe', *European Journal of Communication*, **10**(4).

Randall, D. (1996) *The Universal Journalist*, London: Pluto.

Thorsten, C. (1992) *Pressentiken i praktiken*, Stockholm.

Voakes, P. (1996) 'Public Perception of Journalists' Ethical Motivations' *Journal of Mass Communication*, **74**(1).

18 Media ethics at the sharp end

Bill Norris

The world is awash with Codes of Journalistic Ethics. The PressWise collection, still incomplete, runs to seventy-four. They range from the succinct homilies of the British National Union of Journalists (NUJ) and the International Federation of Journalists (IFJ), to the ponderous German code. The proscriptions on journalistic behaviour are many and various, but they all have one thing in common: they are not worth the paper they are written on.

This is not because so few of these codes contain any provision for sanctions against offenders. There are laws of libel and other legal restrictions in most countries – some would say too many restrictions – which cope with the grosser journalistic transgressions without any need of further help. Rather, it is because the nature of the job is not amenable to regulations set in stone. Every story is different, and every reporter is driven by the compulsion to get the story and get it first. To imagine that he or she is going to consult the union's code of ethics while struggling to meet a deadline is to live in cloud-cuckoo land.

This is not to say that all journalists set out consciously to trample on the lives of others. Some, thankfully a small minority, do so because they are blind and deaf to the feelings of their victims. Others are so driven by their employers' commercial interests and fear for their own jobs that they have little choice. The current British tabloid press provides obnoxious examples every day. But most reporters do try to avoid harming the innocent. Most also try, not always successfully, to get it right. The problem is that even with the best of intentions, a reporter cannot always foresee the consequences of his or her actions. Let me tell you a story.

THE NIGERIAN CIVIL WAR

The year was 1967, and the Nigerian civil war was at its height. On one side was the Federal Government, led by General Gowon and supported by the British. On the other, the breakaway province of Eastern Nigeria, known as Biafra and headed by a bearded rascal named Colonel Ojukwu. Biafra had the fortune, or misfortune, to possess the bulk of Nigeria's oil reserves, which were being developed in the main by Shell-BP. Nobody supported the secession of Biafra; officially, that is. *Unofficially* there was clandestine help from the Portuguese, and a lot of murky activity from other countries interested in getting their hands on the oil.

So much for history. As Africa Correspondent of *The Times*, I was assigned to cover the war and found myself one day accompanying a Federal patrol near the Biafran border. My presence was unofficial – the Federal Government kept reporters as far away from the action as possible – but a few of us got there just the same. As we trampled through the jungle there was suddenly a shout and a group of soldiers dashed into the undergrowth. They returned holding a youth in civilian clothes, actually rags, and began an intense interrogation. As far as I could tell, the lieutenant in charge of the patrol suspected the man of being a Biafran soldier in disguise. Whether or not this was true, I have no idea.

From my position outside the ring of soldiers I could see little of what was going on. I held my camera over my head and snapped a couple of pictures, more in hope than expectation of actually getting anything worthwhile. Moments later the lieutenant shouted an order, two soldiers led the man behind a tree, and two shots rang out. The soldiers returned alone, and I realised that I had just witnessed a prisoner being murdered in cold blood.

Such things happen in war, but they are not supposed to happen in front of reporters. I said nothing. The important thing was to get the story and pictures back to London, and I had an uneasy feeling that any protest on my part would lead to a second body in the jungle.

The picture, as it turned out, exceeded all expectations. There was the terrified youth being harangued by the lieutenant, clearly knowing what was about to happen. *The Times* devoted half the back page to it, along with my explanatory story. I was delighted: I had achieved a scoop.

The Federal Government, however, were less pleased. Their carefully-cultivated image of being the good guys in this conflict had suffered a severe blow, and they acted quickly to restore it. The unfortunate lieutenant was arrested, swiftly court-martialled, and condemned to death by a firing squad. In a final twist, every foreign reporter and cameraman in Nigeria was ordered to attend the public execution. We were to be left in no doubt that it was we, the media, who were responsible for this man's death. But it wasn't 'the media' – it was me.

I learned a lesson that day about the possible consequences of reporting. The story was true; it was important. Perhaps it prevented the summary execution of other prisoners. I don't know. All I could think of that day, as I surveyed the sagging corpse tied to a crude post, was that by clicking a shutter at the right (or wrong) moment, I had killed a fellow human being.

War reporters come in two basic flavours: there are those who make a genuine effort to find the action, and those who establish a comfortable base, attend official briefings (where they are invariably lied to), and try to milk the brains of their more adventurous colleagues when the latter return from the front line. *If* they return – this can be a dangerous business.

For the second group there are few ethical problems, unless you count it a sin to pass on propaganda to your readers or to profit from the initiative of your competitors. Life is more complicated for those who want to get to the actual war, for the simple reason that those who are waging it rarely want reporters to see what is really going on. The rigid control of press and television activity during the Falklands conflict and the Gulf War are good examples of media management.

To do his or her job conscientiously, the war correspondent must therefore defy authority, often tell lies, and frequently resort to subterfuge in order to get the story and avoid censorship. All this is probably highly unethical. Take a personal example:

In the early days of the Nigerian war, frustrated by the refusal of the authorities to allow journalists to travel outside Lagos (which was 350 miles from the front line), I abstracted a piece of headed notepaper from an office in Defence Headquarters and placed on it the most official-looking rubber stamp I could find. Back at the hotel I typed the following message: 'This is to introduce William Norris of *The Times*, who has a right to be where he is'. I then scrawled an illegible signature across the rubber stamp, and made plans to set out for the front with my friend John Parker (now deceased) who was representing ITN.

The fake pass worked like a charm. At the time Nigeria was infested with road-blocks, manned either by the regular army or armed militias. You could always tell the militiamen because they read the letter upside-down, but they were still impressed by the rubber stamp. We always told them that we were only going as far as the next town or village. One by one the men at the road-blocks waved us through, until at last we came to the real war.

Once there we were briefly arrested and taken to the local commanding officer – an imposing figure in a scarlet silk dressing gown, who was drinking whisky-and-soda outside a mud hut. I forget his name, but he was ex-Sandhurst and delighted to see a gentleman from *The Times*. This was no surprise. Unlike the military bureaucrats back at headquarters, it has always been my experience that the men doing the actual fighting are pleased to meet reporters. He showed us all his campaign maps, explained the disposition of his own and the enemy forces, then took us on a tour of the front line. To my intense satisfaction, I had beaten the rest of the press corps and obtained the first first-hand account of the Nigerian Civil War. But, of course, I had only done so by dint of petty theft and a good deal of lying.

I confess that this has never troubled my conscience particularly, but when I told this story to a group of American journalists attending an ethics seminar in Florida some years ago they were truly shocked. How could I do such an unethical thing? Well, I said, it was the only way to get the story, and the story was in the public interest. Not good enough, they said. We would never do a thing like that.

They probably would not. American reporters lack the anarchic spirit of the British. They tend to obey the voice of authority in such situations. What is more, they have a habit of believing what they are told, especially if the source is their own embassy. This is almost always a great mistake.

When covering wars, perhaps more than in any other form of journalism, we all have to live by our personal code of ethics. For myself, I will not wear a uniform, carry a gun, or act as a spy for my own government or any other. Yet I have known reporters who will do any or all of these things and regard them as perfectly ethical.

It is not often realised that reporters frequently know more about what is going on than officialdom. They travel more widely, and they are trained to observe. This makes them potentially valuable as intelligence agents – a fact brought to my attention when the Military Attaché at the British High Commission in Lagos asked for a word in my ear. He had heard that I was about to make a trip up north. Would I mind counting the number of battalions up there, and give him some idea of their armament, combat-readiness, state of morale, etc. My views on the quality of officers and NCOs would also be of interest. There would, of course, be a modest fee for my services.

When I refused, with some indignation, the colonel was genuinely puzzled. I was British, damn it, and I worked for *The Times*. How could I refuse this chance to serve my country? Quite easily, I said rather pompously. It was against my code of ethics. I later learned that his offer had been taken up by one of my colleagues on a rival paper, whom I will not name because the poor chap is in enough trouble already. He got caught, and there was a major scandal. I felt a little smug.

Once upon a time, the aspiring young journalist learned objectivity and ethics at his news editor's knee. This was in the days before academia got in on the act, and degree courses in journalism began to provide steady employment for a lot of would-be reporters and sub-editors who might not otherwise have made the grade. I am talking of the 1950s and 60s, when the entry route to the profession (to dignify the trade) was to join a local newspaper as a cub reporter and learn on the job. Applicants with degrees were actively frowned on; largely because they were older and therefore, under union rules, had to be paid more.

There was something to be said for this system. You worked incredibly long hours for insultingly little money, but you also learned useful skills like shorthand and typing, and gained a basic knowledge of newspaper law and the structure of local government. Literary pretensions were knocked out of you by brutal sub-editors, and you became at ease in talking to all manner of people at grass-roots level. Since these people you wrote about lived in the same town, there was a powerful incentive to get your facts right, spell their names correctly, and report both sides of an argument. If not, you were liable to find your subjects on the editor's doorstep in the morning. None of this knowledge could be gained by entry at the Fleet Street level, where most of us hoped to end up. But if you came up through the hard grind of a local weekly, local daily and national news agency, a lot of the habits stuck.

Among them were the essential fly-on-the-wall nature of good reporting; non-judgemental observation, a passion for accuracy, a sense of fairness and, when necessary, compassion. You learned a sense of detachment and strove at all costs to keep yourself out of the story.

All these things are second nature to a good reporter, and pretty easy to maintain when you are reporting politics, crime, a parish council or a train disaster. But there are times out in the field when detachment becomes impossible and personal involvement inevitable. It happened to me in the spring of 1968.

Up to that time, no journalists had been allowed on the Biafran side of the Nigerian conflict. I was back in London, writing leading articles as part of my duties as Africa Correspondent of *The Times*, when I received an invitation from MarkPress, the Biafran public relations agency in Geneva, to visit the beleaguered province. It was a difficult journey. I flew to Lisbon where an ancient and unmarked Constellation airliner, painted in flat grey, sat on the far side of the tarmac. Apart from a few seats in front, the aircraft had been stripped to make way for a cargo of arms and powdered milk. The pilot was a mercenary – a jovial Texan who took great pleasure in telling his passengers about the improvised runway we would be landing on, and the number of wrecked aircraft we would find there. 'Last time I landed', he said, 'we flipped on our back and went all the way down the runway upside-down. Nobody got hurt'. This was very encouraging.

Since we had no permission to over-fly any country, the flight involved a long grind around the bulge of Africa, stopping only in the Ivory Coast for refuelling. This was paid for by a whip-round among the passengers. Totally blacked-out to avoid attracting Nigerian anti-aircraft fire, we finally reached Biafra in the middle of a thunderstorm and landed safely on what had once been a main road through the bush. As the pilot had forecast, the wreckage of those who had failed to make it lay everywhere.

Our accommodation, thoughtfully provided by the rebel regime, was in the remains of a luxury hotel in Port Harcourt. The air-conditioning in my room consisted of a shell-hole through the outside wall. Next morning I set off in an army jeep to see if the MarkPress reports of the dire conditions in Biafra were really true. My destination was Aba, a small market town in the middle of nowhere. As we drove down the arrow-straight road between tall jungle trees, my driver suddenly pulled into the side and pointed skywards. I saw a twin-engined jet, which looked very much like an RAF Canberra bomber, flying parallel to the road. As I watched, five bombs fell from it, and I heard the explosions as they landed. We drove on. It was high noon. Aba, which was nothing more than a collection of ramshackle houses set in a clearing beside the road, had been crowded with the local population from miles around enjoying market day. I say 'had been'. Now it was a scene of carnage such as I had never seen, and hope never to see again. Bodies and parts of bodies lay everywhere. Young girls, some of them pregnant, had been eviscerated; babies were headless; old men and women had been blown apart. Five 200-kilogram fragmentation bombs dropped in a crowded market-place are the equivalent of Armageddon. I saw no young men, and certainly no soldiers among the bodies.

Rightly or wrongly, there was no question of remaining a neutral observer. I did what I could to help the survivors, which was not much, and then the driver and I joined in the awful task of carrying the dead to a makeshift mortuary about a mile down the road. There I found that the small building inside a high chain-link fence had already overflowed, and the remains were being piled, higgledy-piggledy, on a small mountain of human flesh which already stood six feet high. We added our load to the pile, and then I remembered my job. I began photographing the awfulness of the scene.

At this point it is important to know that the British government had given solemn assurances to the House of Commons that no bombing of the civilian population in Biafra was taking place. I now had dramatic first-hand evidence to the contrary. The Biafrans, for their part, believed that the bombers themselves, the pilots and the bombs, were British. In fact it was an Ilyushin, flown by an Egyptian mercenary, and the bombs were of Russian manufacture. The inhabitants of Aba, however, were not to know this. As the long procession of grieving relatives reached the mortuary, the first thing they saw was a hated Englishman taking pictures of the remains of their loved-ones.

There was a high keening noise as they came at me through the gates of the compound. I had never encountered a lynch mob before, but I knew one when I saw it. There was no place to run, and I didn't even try. I just stood there. In an odd way, I didn't blame them for what they were about to do. And then, in the nick of time, a young Biafran lieutenant led a flying wedge of his men through the crowd, grabbed me violently and dragged me out through the fence. I owe him my life.

Back in London the pictures proved too gory for *The Times* to print, but I could not let it rest there. I took them to Arnold Smith, the Commonwealth Secretary General, who up to that time had believed the British government's denials of civilian bombing. Now he was a very angry man. He picked up the telephone and demanded an immediate interview with Michael Stewart, the Foreign Secretary, and within minutes we were in Carlton House.

Stewart, whom I had known during my previous incarnation as Parliamentary Correspondent of *The Times*, looked at the pictures coldly. 'Biafran propaganda', he said. 'But I took these pictures myself', I protested, and recounted the full story. 'It's just Biafran propaganda,' Stewart repeated, and tossed the photos back across his desk. I should have known better: a reporter should never get involved in his own story. I was also guilty of subjective reporting (aka 'biased'), but the incident illustrates the problem faced by many reporters in the modern world. Good and evil co-exist, and for the journalist to stand on a detached pinnacle and pretend that there is no difference between them is neither practical nor, I would suggest, moral. What he or she must do is to make every effort, collect every fact, examine every motive, to ensure that the truth is told. For today's reporter, faced with the speed of modern communications leading to ever-tighter deadlines, this is a monumental task. It is not made easier by spin-doctors, public relations specialists, and other promoters of self-interest, who are well aware of the pressures upon journalists to produce rapid copy, and whose agendas may not coincide with the truth. Their lies can travel around the world so fast that the truth never gets a chance to catch up. A healthy dose of scepticism is therefore an essential weapon in every reporter's armoury. Believe what you see, mistrust what you hear, is not a bad rule of thumb.

In an ideal situation, which rarely occurs, the investigative reporter will have the time and the financial backing to travel far and dig deep. Even then those troublesome ethics are lying in wait; mantraps set to snare the journalistic conscience.

THE HUDSON REPORT

Take the case of the Hudson Report. I was writing a book[1] when I heard about it; a book about ninety-seven people who died in a Pan American airliner when it crashed on Pago Pago in the South Pacific in 1974. It was the latest in a series of disasters suffered by the same airline, and the FAA had commissioned a distinguished airman by the name of Jack W. Hudson to report on Pan American's safety practices. My informant told me that the report was a damning indictment of Pan Am, yet it had never appeared in the trial which found the airline guilty of wilful misconduct in causing the crash, nor had it ever been made public. Why not? I asked. Because, said my lawyer friend, the judge in the case, a certain Judge Matthew Byrne, had placed it under judicial seal. He knew where there was a copy: in the depository of the US District Court in Los Angeles, where it was literally under lock and key. I had to see it, I said. He wished me luck.

Ethical questions aside, there was a legal barrier to be overcome. A judge had ruled that the Hudson Report was to remain forever secret. If I had managed to obtain a copy of such a document in Britain, I would rapidly find myself behind bars for contempt of court. But the American system is different. Under the First Amendment to the Constitution, which guarantees freedom of speech, if you can get it, you can print it. Curiously enough, it had been the same Judge Matthew Byrne who had ruled, some years previously, that Daniel Ellsberg had been legally entitled to publish the purloined Pentagon Papers. I was about to try to hoist him with his own petard.

The clerk in charge of the exhibits section of the district court was a pleasant and efficient young man named Lee Torbin Jr. Mr Torbin

333

received my request to look at the relics of the Pago Pago trial with polite disbelief. It was clearly beyond his experience that anyone, even a crazy British author, should want to see such things. I had the distinct impression that he had no idea where the stuff was kept, but luckily my total ignorance of the report's file number, which had to be provided before the request could be granted, saved him from having to admit the fact.

The response was discouraging, but I had all day. Having travelled a long way and spent a lot of money to stand in that office, I was not going to give up without a struggle. Mr Torbin stayed on one side of his high wire grille. I stayed on the other, and for an hour or two we swapped polite suggestions and refusals while the more orthodox business of the record office went on about us.

At length he seemed intrigued by my persistence. It was becoming plain that I had no intention of going away and leaving him in peace. 'Hey Charlie', he called to one of the other clerks, 'didn't they put all that Pago Pago stuff in a cellar someplace'? Charlie thought they had. Someplace. Perhaps Room 64G. All at once Lee Torbin Jr reached a decision, probably born of desperation. Come on', he said to me. 'Let's go look'.

For a journalist there is a very special thrill in being where he ought not to be, seeing what authority wishes him not to see, or reading what he is not supposed to read. I felt it strongly that day.

Past a sign forbidding public entry and down a steep flight of steps, Room 64G lay behind a padlocked green door in a catacomb of roughcast concrete and dusty pipes. The contents were a shock. Where I had expected neat rows of filing cabinets and boxes of exhibits in duly labelled sequence, I saw instead a mountainous jumble of paper. The cellar, perhaps thirty feet square, was filled on every side to a height of about six feet with a great amorphous hotchpotch of boxes and files. Here and there the top of a filing cabinet poked through the surface like an iceberg in an angry sea.

The relics of Pan Am Flight 806 had not been laid to rest by a tidy mind. Where the hell did I start? I looked at Mr Torbin, and Mr Torbin looked at me. I cleared the front of one filing cabinet and began to open the drawers. It became rapidly apparent that there was no more order inside the cabinets than out. Sheaves of paper, some in folders, some not, and none with any discernible label, tumbled out as I dug deeper. The damn things must have been breeding in the dark. A quick glance seemed to show that none was of any interest, though it was difficult to tell. I had the horrid feeling that the story of the century could be lurking in this Augean cellar, and I would be none the wiser.

Three filing cabinets were stripped and discarded. Time passed. The sharp regular sound behind me was Lee Torbin Jr, tapping his foot. And then I had it. In a plain brown envelope, unsealed, was a report addressed to the Assistant Administrator, AEU (whoever he might have been) from a certain Jack W. Hudson. A quick glance showed that it was, indeed, dynamite.

'I'll take that', said Mr Torbin, stretching out his hand. We returned to his wire-caged office. 'I don't think I can let you have this', he said. Oh shit, I thought. There it is, so close. I could just grab it and run. I had visions of being pursued from the courthouse by a screaming mob of legal bureaucrats led by Lee Torbin Jr. But the thought came and went. Anyway, the wire cage was locked. 'Why not?' I asked. As though it hardly mattered. 'I have a vague feeling', Torbin said, 'that some of these exhibits were put under judicial seal by Judge Byrne. I think this might be among them'. My heart landed in the region of my toecaps. I knew damned well that the Hudson Report was under seal. I had hoped against hope that he would not. 'I'll have to check', he said.

The next fifteen minutes lasted a long time. First Torbin telephoned the judge's clerk, Lori Sherif. She was new to the job and did not know the answer. He rang the court reporter, who could not remember. He rang, and rang, and rang, until my nerves were in shreds and there seemed to be no one left in the whole court building who had not been asked the question. But none of them knew the answer.

'Surely', I ventured, 'that must mean that the report is clear. If it had been under seal, one of these people would be bound to know.' But the ultra-cautious Mr Torbin was having none of it. He had to have a positive answer before he would let me see those papers. I could not blame him. It was his neck.

Finally he had an idea. 'I know who can tell us', he said. 'Judge Byrne had a clerk at the time of the trial who retired not long ago. I'll call her'. He found the number and explained the problem. His next words were ominous. 'Is all the Pago evidence under seal?'

Four-letter words passed silently in coarse procession through my mind. The envelope on the desk before me seemed to blur and recede. So near, and yet . . . I stood there like a dummy while the conversation continued. I could make little sense of what was being said, and by now was paying scant attention. It was just a question of gritting my teeth, thanking Mr Torbin for his help with as much sincerity as I could muster, and writing off the whole episode to experience. Perhaps there would be another way to get hold of the Hudson Report. I doubted it.

At length Lee Torbin Jr put the receiver down and smiled. 'Do you want copies?' he asked. 'They'll cost you fifty cents a page.' And so I got the Hudson Report and I published it, much to the chagrin of Pan American Airways. (I subsequently discovered that Judge Byrne's former clerk had hated her boss, and had denied the existence of the judicial seal out of pure revenge.)

The question is: were my actions ethical? I had not exactly stolen the report, but I had certainly engaged in deceit to get it. And I had acted without any thought of the consequences to a humble clerk – I hope Lee Torbin Jr kept his job, but I frankly do not know.

Over the years I have laid the facts before quite a few undergraduate classes and asked for their opinion. The answers have been confused, as answers to ethical questions in the field of journalism frequently are. My own view is that the public interest was clear and paramount. For whatever legal reason, people were being kept in ignorance about the misdeeds of an airline which could, not to put too fine a point on it, kill them. I ripped away that cloak of secrecy, and I am glad I did it.

At the start of this chapter I made the outrageous suggestion – coming from one supposedly dedicated to upholding ethical standards – that current codes of conduct are not worth the paper they are written on. If that is true, and I believe it is, why do these things proliferate like rabbits? Are they genuine attempts by the right-minded to keep their colleagues under control, or are they professional fig leafs designed to conceal the awful truth? A little bit of both, perhaps. The fact remains that things are done in the name of journalism which should not be done, and that by and large the miscreants get away with it.

But if codes of conduct are not the answer, what is? I would suggest a two-fold approach. In the first place, given that journalists – for better or worse – now learn the rudiments of their trade in the classroom, there is an excellent opportunity to indoctrinate them with ethical habits. Ethical behaviour should become a key part of every journalism course, and students should be exposed to real situations and real people who have become victims of the media. They should be made to appreciate the very real human consequences of ethical mistakes and taught to think before they write.

My second recommendation may be even more far-reaching. It is that all contracts of employment for journalists should contain a 'conscience clause'. This would specify that he or she should be able, without suffering any penalty, to refuse any assignment that conflicts with their union's code of conduct or even (in the UK) with the Press Complaints Commission Code of Practice. Some journalists, notably those in Sweden, already enjoy this privilege. As a single measure, it would probably do more than any other to improve the situation. It would curb the power of editors and proprietors to ride rough-shod over the ethical principles of those at the sharp end, and it would give some meaning, at last, to all those codes of conduct.

ENDNOTES

1. Norris, W. (1984) *Willful Misconduct*, W.W. Norton & Co.

Index

339

www.focalpress.com

Visit our web site for:

- the latest information on new and forthcoming Focal Press titles
- special offers
- our email news service

Join our Focal Press Bookbuyers' Club

As a member, you will enjoy the following benefits:

- special discounts on new and best-selling titles
- advance information on forthcoming Focal Press books
- a quarterly newsletter highlighting special offers
- a 30-day guarantee on purchased titles

Membership is FREE. To join, supply your name, company, address, telephone/fax numbers and email address to:

Elaine Hill
Email: elaine.hill@repp.co.uk
Fax: +44(0) 1865314423
Address: Focal Press, Linacre House, Jordan Hill, Oxford, OX2 8DP

Catalogue

For information on all Focal Press titles, we will be happy to send you a free copy of the Focal Press Catalogue.

Tel: 01865 314693
Email: carol.burgess@repp.co.uk

Potential authors

If you have an idea for a book, please get in touch:

Europe

Beth Howard, Editorial Assistant
Email: beth.howard@repp.co.uk
Tel: +44(0) 1865 314365
Fax: +44(0) 1865 314572

USA

Marie Lee, Publisher
Email: marie.lee@bhusa.com
Tel: 781 9042500
Fax: 781 9042620